SPANISH-
AMERICAN
LITERATURE

SPANISH-AMERICAN LITERATURE
A History

VOLUME TWO

by *Enrique Anderson-Imbert*
HARVARD UNIVERSITY

second edition (1969)
revised and updated
by Elaine Malley

first edition (1963)
translated from the Spanish
by John V. Falconieri

Wayne State University Press

Detroit / 1969

Second edition, revised, enlarged and updated.

*Copyright © 1969 by Wayne State University Press,
Detroit, Michigan 48202, USA. All rights reserved.*

*The first edition, 1963, was translated from the third Spanish
edition by John Falconieri.*

*...nd edition were translated
...e Malley.*

*...y the Copp Clark Publish-
...est, Toronto 2B, Canada.*

...mber 70–75087

*Standard Book Numbers 8143–1387–6 (cloth)
and 8143–1388–4 (paperback)*

Waynebook Number 29

CONTENTS

VOLUME ONE

Echeverría and Others / Sarmiento / HISTORICAL NOVEL IN ARGENTINA: Parenthetical Remarks on the Theme of the Pirate / Other Argentinian Romantics: Ascasubi, Mármol / Uruguay and Chile / Bolivia / Mexico and Cuba: Avellaneda and Others / Venezuela and Colombia: José Eusebio Caro / THE SECOND ROMANTIC GENERATION / A. MAINLY POETRY: Gutiérrez González, G. Blest Gana, Guido y Spano and Others / B. MAINLY PROSE: Riva Palacio, Mera, A. Blest Gana, Mansilla and Others / C. THEATER

IX. 1860-1880

Authors born between 1835 and 1855 / p. 258

Historical framework: Organization.
Cultural tendencies: Second Romantic generation. Early indications of the Parnassians and naturalists.

INTRODUCTION / A. MAINLY POETRY / (i) Mexico: Acuna, Flores / (ii) Central America / (iii) Antilles / (iv) Venezuela: Pérez Bonalde / (v) Colombia: Pombo / (vi) Ecuador / (vii) Bolivia / (viii) Chile / (ix) Argentina: Del Campo, José Hernández, Andrade, Obligado, Almafuerte / B. MAINLY PROSE / 1. NOVEL AND SHORT STORY / (i) Mexico: Altamirano, López Portillo y Rojas / (ii) Antilles / (iii) Venezuela /(iv) Colombia: Jorge Isaacs / (v) Peru: Ricardo Palma / (vi) Bolivia / (vii) Chile / (viii) Uruguay: Acevedo Díaz / (ix) Argentina: The Generation of '80: Wilde, Groussac, Cambacérès and Others / 2. ESSAY / Sierra, Varona, Hostos, Montalvo, González Prada / C. THEATER

X. 1880-1895

Authors born between 1855 and 1870 / p. 301

Historical framework: Prosperity.
Cultural tendencies: Parnassianism. Naturalism. The first generation of Modernists.

INTRODUCTION / A. MAINLY POETRY / 1. THE LAST ACADEMICIANS, ROMANTICS, AND TRADITIONALISTS / (i) Central America / (ii) Antilles / (iii) Venezuela / (iv) Colombia / (v) Ecuador / (vi) Chile / (vii) Uruguay / (viii) Argentina / Othón, Zorrilla de San Martín / 2. THE FIRST MODERNISTS: Díaz Mirón, Martí / 3. THE OTHER MODERNISTS: Gutiérrez Nájera, Silva, Del Casal, and Others, from North to South / (i) Mexico / (ii) Antilles / (iii) Venezuela /

XI. 1895-1910

Historical framework: Industrialization. Growth of international capitalism.
Cultural tendencies: Height of modernism.

BIBLIOGRAPHY / *p. 421*

INDEX OF AUTHORS / *p. i*

VOLUME TWO

Prolog / *p. 441*

Translator's Foreword / *p. 448*

PART THREE: CONTEMPORARY PERIOD

XII. 1910-1925

Authors born between 1885 and 1900 / *p. 453*

Historical framework: Social Revolution in Mexico and the effects of World War I.
Cultural tendencies: Modernist artifice set aside in favor of a simpler expression of American reality. Experimentation in new "isms."

INTRODUCTION / A. MAINLY POETRY / 1. NORMALITY / 2. ABNORMALITY / 3. SCANDAL / (i) Mexico: López Velarde / (ii) Central America: Salomón de la Selva, Cardona, Miró / (iii) Antilles: Brull, Moreno Jiménes, Ribera Chevremont / (iv) Venezuela: Andrés Eloy Blanco / (v) Colombia: Barba Jacob, De Greiff / (vi) Ecuador: Medardo Ángel Silva / (vii) Peru: César Vallejo / (viii) Bolivia / (ix) Chile: Gabriela Mistral, Rokha, Huidobro / (x) Paraguay: Fariña Núñez / (xi) Uruguay: Agustini, Ibarbourou, Sabat Ercasty / (xii) Argentina: Banchs, Fernández Moreno, Storni, Capdevila, Girondo / B. MAINLY PROSE / 1. NOVEL AND SHORT STORY / (a) Narrators More Subjective than Objective / (b) Narrators More Objective than Subjective / (i) Mexico: Martín Luis Guzmán / (ii) Central America: Arévalo Martínez / (iii) Antilles: Hernández Catá / (iv) Venezuela: Rómulo Gallegos, Teresa de la Parra / (v) Colombia: José Eustasio Rivera / (vi) Ecuador: Gonzalo Zaldumbide / (vii) Peru: Ventura García Calderón, Valdelomar / (viii) Bolivia: Armando Chirveches / (ix) Chile: Eduardo Barrios, Pedro Prado, Jenaro Prieto, Mariano Latorre, Manuel Rojas / (x) Paraguay / (xi) Uru-

guay: Ballesteros / (xii) Argentina: Ricardo Güiraldes /
2. ESSAY / Alfonso Reyes / Pedro Henríquez Ureña / Martínez Estrada / C. THEATER / From Mexico to Argentina
/ Ramos, Herrera, Eichelbaum

XIII. 1925-1940

Authors born between 1900 and 1915 / p. 565

> *Historical framework: The outbreak of World War II. The
> Depression. Greater participation by the masses in gov-
> ernment leadership.*
> *Cultural tendencies: Vanguardist literature. Pure poetry and
> surrealism.*

INTRODUCTION / A. MAINLY POETRY / PURE POETRY
AND SURREALISM / (i) Mexico: Pellicer, Villaurrutia, Go-
rostiza / (ii) Céntral America: Cardoza y Aragón, Coronel
Urtecho / (iii) Antilles: Florit, Guillén, Ballagas, Cabral,
Palés Matos / (iv) Venezuela: Queremel, Gerbasi / (v)
Colombia: Pardo García, Maya, Carranza, Rojas, Aurelio
Arturo / (vi) Ecuador: Carrera Andrade, Gonzalo Escu-
dero / (vii) Peru: Adán, Westphalen / (viii) Bolivia / (ix)
Chile: Pablo Neruda / (x) Paraguay / (xi) Uruguay: Sara
de Ibáñez / (xii) Argentina: Molinari, González Lanuza,
Bernárdez / B. MAINLY PROSE / 1. NOVEL AND SHORT
STORY / (a) Narrators More Subjective than Objective /
(b) Narrators More Objective than Subjective / (i) Mexico:
Agustín Yáñez / (ii) Central America: Miguel Ángel
Asturias, Salarrué, Carlos Luis Fallas / (iii) Antilles: Alejo
Carpentier, Novás Calvo, Dulce María Loynaz, Laguerre,
Bosch / (iv) Venezuela: Uslar Pietri, Díaz Sánchez / (v)
Colombia: Osorio Lizarazo / Caballero Calderón / (vi)
Ecuador: José de la Cuadra / (vii) Peru: Ciro Alegría, José
María Arguedas / (viii) Bolivia / (ix) Chile: Bombal,
Brunet / (x) Paraguay: Casaccia / (xi) Uruguay: Onetti,
Amorim / (xii) Argentina: Jorge Luis Borges, Eduardo
Mallea, Roberto Arlt / 2. ESSAY: Picón-Salas, Germán Ar-
ciniegas / C. THEATER / (i) Mexico: Usigli / (ii) Cen-
tral America / (iii) Antilles / (iv) Venezuela / (v) Colom-
bia / (vi) Peru / (vii) Bolivia / (viii) Chile / (ix)
Uruguay / (x) Argentina: Nalé Roxlo

XIV. 1940-1955

Authors born between 1915 and 1930 / p. 688

> *Historical framework: World War II ends. The "cold war."
> Evolution toward planned economies.*

Cultural tendencies: Surrealism. Existentialism. Neonaturalism.

GENERAL CHARACTERIZATION / A. MAINLY POETRY / INTRODUCTION / (i) Mexico: Octavio Paz, Alí Chumacero / (ii) Central America: Cardona Peña / (iii) Antilles: Cintio Vitier / (iv) Venezuela: Ida Gramcko / (v) Colombia: Cote Lamus / (vi) Ecuador: Alejandro Carrión / (vii) Peru / (viii) Bolivia / (ix) Chile: Arenas, Parra, Arteche / (x) Paraguay: Elvio Romero / (xi) Uruguay: Idea Vilariño, Sarandy Cabrera / (xii) Argentina: Etchebarne, Devoto, Wilcock, Girri / B. MAINLY PROSE / 1. NOVEL AND SHORT STORY / (i) Mexico: Arreola, Rulfo, Fuentes / (ii) Central America: Monterroso, Joaquín Beleño, Ramón H. Jurado / (iii) Antilles: Virgilio Piñera, René Marqués / (iv) Venezuela / (v) Colombia: García Márquez / (vi) Ecuador: Adalberto Ortiz / (vii) Peru: Zavaleta, Ribeyro / (viii) Bolivia: Botelho Gosálvez / (ix) Chile: Fernando Alegría, José Donoso / (x) Paraguay: Roa Bastos / (xi) Uruguay: Martínez Moreno, Benedetti / (xii) Argentina: Murena, Cortázar, Denevi / 2. ESSAY / From Mexico to Argentina / C. THEATER / (i) Mexico: Magaña, Garro / (ii) Central America / (iii) Antilles / (iv) Venezuela / (v) Colombia / (vi) Peru: Salazar Bondy / (vii) Chile: Heiremans / (viii) Paraguay / (ix) Uruguay: Antonio Larreta / (x) Argentina: Del Carlo, Dragún

XV. 1955-1966

Authors born since 1930 / p. 746

Historical framework: The First Communist Regime in Hispanic America.
Cultural tendencies: Awareness of the literary profession. Change in values.

GENERAL CHARACTERIZATION / A. MAINLY POETRY (i) Mexico: Montes de Oca / (ii) Central America: Chávez Velasco / (iii) Antilles: Fernández Retamar / (iv) Venezuela: Calzadilla / (v) Colombia: Arango / (vi) Ecuador / (vii) Peru / (viii) Bolivia / (ix) Chile: Efraín Barquero, Jorge Teillier / (x) Paraguay / (xi) Uruguay: Ibargoyen Islas, Washington Benavides / (xii) Argentina: María Elena Walsh / B. MAINLY PROSE / 1. NOVEL AND SHORT STORY / (i) Mexico: Mojarro / (ii) Central America / (iii) Antilles: Marcio Veloz Maggiolo / (iv) Venezuela: Salvador Garmendia / (v) Colombia / (vi) Ecuador / (vii) Peru: Vargas Llosa, Congrains Martín, Castro Arenas, Oviedo / (viii) Chile / (ix)

BIBLIOGRAPHY / *p. 757*

INDEX OF AUTHORS / *p. i*

PROLOG

Of the many dangers an historian of literature risks, two are quite serious: that of specializing in the study of isolated great books, and that of specializing in the study of the circumstances under which those books were written. If the historian elects the first, he produces a collection of unconnected critical essays, that is, a history of literature containing very little history. If he chooses the second, the result will be a series of external references to the process of civilization, that is, a history of literature containing very little literature. Is it possible to achieve a history of literature that fulfills both the true historical and the true literary function? At least, it is possible to attempt one. It would be a history that gave meaning to the expressive moments of certain men who, through the passing of the centuries, set themselves to write. Instead of isolating the literature produced, on one hand, and the circumstances under which it was produced, on the other, this history would integrate the two within the concrete existence of the writers. Each writer asserts those esthetic values that he has formed while contemplating the possibilities of his historical environment, and these are the values that should constitute the real subject matter of any history of literature.

This is all well and good, as theory. But if we were mindful only of esthetic expression, to what thin line would this history which we are about to offer reduce itself? The effective contributions of Spanish-American literature to international literature are minimal. Yet we Spanish-Americans have done a great deal if one were to consider the many obstacles with which our literary creation has had to contend and is still contending. The Inca Garcilaso, Sor Juana Inés de la Cruz, Andrés Bello, Domingo Sarmiento, Juan Montalvo, Ricardo Palma, José Martí, Rubén Darío, José Enrique Rodó, Alfonso Reyes, Jorge Luis Borges, Pablo Neruda, and a dozen more, are figures who would do honor to any literature. But, in general, we are afflicted by improvisation, disorder, fragmentation, and impurity. Necessarily, many unaccomplished writers will have to be included here.

We cannot prevent a certain amount of farrago from slipping into this history. But to be sure, what does interest us here is the reality which has been transmuted into literature. Although we witness, respectfully and patiently, a long procession of writers and try to understand their contribution, the fact is that we anxiously look for the few who have expressed esthetic values. Our subject is Literature, that is to say, those writings that can be assigned to the category of beauty.

Of course, in the first chapters we had to admit many men of action or thought who wrote chronicles and treatises without any artistic intentions; yet, even in these cases, it was the literary portion of their writings that we valued. But as we approach our own times we must be more demanding in discriminating between what is and what is not literature. Once we reach our own age, we are only interested in those writers who cultivate poetry, prose poems, the short story, the novel, and the theater. We only consider essayists insofar as they are men of letters. Had this been an extended history of culture instead of a compressed history of literature, we would also have included critics, philosophers, historians and patrons of art; or even had sociology been our aim, we would have included information about journals, literary gatherings, prizes, and the like. But this book does not aspire to include all. We are fully aware that in Spanish America there are often extraordinary personalities in literary life who study and promote literature, but who do not produce it. Furthermore, at times the men who most influence literary groups are precisely the ones who write neither poetry, nor novels, nor dramas. It may be lamentable, but it is obvious that they do not belong to a history of poetry, novels, and dramas.

The literature of the Americas we are going to study is the one which was written in Spanish. We do not ignore the importance of the masses of Indians; however, in a history of the expressive uses of the Spanish language in America, it behooves us to listen only to those who expressed themselves in Spanish. For this same reason we will not refer to the writers who were born in Spanish-America, but who wrote in Latin (like Rafael Landívar), in French (like Jules Supervielle), or in English (like W. H. Hudson). Nor will we consider those authors who, although they wrote in Spanish, did not write of American experiences (like Ventura de la Vega.) On the other hand, we will include in our history those foreigners who lived among us and used our language (like Paul Groussac).

It is well known that history is a continuous process. We will, therefore, introduce writers in the order in which they came into the world and entered into literary life. But, although history is an indivisible succession of events, we could not represent it without certain conventions which we call periods. In order to be useful, this breaking up of history into periods should adjust itself to historical facts and respect the complexity of each epoch. Thus, a system of periods must be consistent with the principle which it adopts, but it does not need to be regular. On the contrary, excessive regularity would indicate that the historian, through his great desire to embellish his vision, is allowing himself to be carried along by symmetries and metaphors. There are periods of long stability. There are short, rapid periods. In the fear of falsifying literary development through the use of subjective figures, we have chosen an inoffensive criterion: an historical-political classification in three parts, "The Colony," "One Hundred Years of the Republic," and the "Contemporary Period." But within these broad divisions we have shaded in certain generations, attempting to make the external framework of political coincide with esthetic tendencies. The dates heading each chapter indicate the years during which these generations came into being and produced: *"Gestación"* and *"Gestión,"* as Ortega y Gasset put it. In order that the outline might be more useful, we have also indicated the approximate birthdates of the authors. But, when historical sense demands, we shall alter the outline and situate a borderline author on whatever side best suits our purposes.

That we should be arranging the materials of this history into periods does not mean that we are neglecting other regulative criteria: those of nationality, genre, schools, and themes. What we have done is to subordinate these criteria to chronology. In other words, our method is systematic when it groups fundamental literary phenomena chronologically, and asystematic with regard to everything else. It is more difficult this way, but there is less falsification of history.

To have grouped the authors by country would have been to break the cultural unity of Spanish America into nineteen illusory national literatures. To have had recourse to the rhetorical categories of genres would have obliged us to have dismantled the work of any writer who cultivated various types of literature and to have distributed the pieces throughout several chapters under the headings of "poetry," "narrative," "essay," and "theater," not to mention the difficulty involved in classifying the subgenres. To have insisted on schools and "isms" would have caused us to fall into the vice of giving substance to mere ideal concepts, thus, giving more attention to collective styles than to individual ones. To have made our history revolve around certain themes would have been superficial: what counts, after all, is the treatment of the theme, not the theme itself. In spite of what has been said, the reader will find, especially in the last chapters, an arrangement according to nationality (from north to south), in genres (from verse to prose and, within prose, fiction, essay, and theater) and in schools (from the more imaginative to the more realist).

We must remind the reader who opens the book here and there, with the intention not of reading it, but of consulting it, that what he has before him is a history and not an inventory of names. In other words, its value lies in the total interpretation of a continuous process; a series of names, even a series of sentences, only makes sense if it is reached after first reading many pages back. Trusting in the fluidity with which the themes are formed and developed we have boldly incorporated into the text those lists that other historians prudently hide in separate notes. To read just the lists would be tantamount to ignoring the esthetic category to which the names belong. One might ask, why not delete those ugly pieces of census? But they are not pieces of census, they are clouds, constellations, woods, highlands, and dales in an historical landscape. The great quantity of names brings out the fact that, because there is so little communication among the Spanish-American countries, literary values are fixed in local markets: to omit these names would hurt national pride. Now that we have touched on the matter of national honor, the reader must remember that in a history, constructed in one unit as this one is, the number of pages devoted to any particular writer is no measure of his importance. There are writers of really great stature who can be dealt with in brief critiques. On the other hand, other writers of less value require a more extensive treatment if they illustrate a movement, a genre, a theme, or a cultural reality. One final point: there are precocious writers and there are writers who are tardy in maturing. In establishing their place within a period, what we take into consideration is not the chronological sequence of their books but the years that shaped the authors, the historical climate they breathed during their formative period.

An historian of literature cannot read every book (an entire life would not be enough) but neither can he limit himself to commenting only on those books that he has read (if he did this, he would not set down an objective historical process but his autobiography as a reader). In order to offer a complete panorama of what has been written during the past four hundred years in a continent that is now divided into nineteen republics, the historian is obliged to utilize the data and judgments of others. There are several ways of conducting this huge informative enterprise. One way, the most serious from a scholarly point of view, but the least practical from the point of view of a manual, is to interrupt the exposition at every step with bibliographical references, footnotes, citations within the text, appendices, and careful acknowledgement of the works of hundreds of colleagues which are used and reworked. Another way, the one we have risked, is to appoint oneself the Editing Secretary of an imaginary Stock Company of Spanish-Americanists and to invert into a fluid history all that is known among all of us. In this case the historian constructs an optical apparatus, with lenses and mirrors, through which he looks out on the range of letters; and he consolidates his own observations and those of other observers in a book with "form"—a form having unity, continuity, smoothness, and roundness. Composite art. In this way, pages based on a direct knowledge of texts are intermingled and occasionally integrated with others that indirectly summarize scattered studies. The bibliography is only a guide for the reader; it is not a listing of the sources that we have used. These sources are innumerable. We read constantly, and every time we found something that was compatible with the plan of the book, we unhesitatingly incorporated it. There was the searching through overall histories, partial monographs, journal articles, and book reviews. We even went further by writing to critics in different places and using their replies in the systematic construction of this vast synthesis. As we traveled through the countries of Spanish America, we approached literary groups and, pen in hand, took notes which later were utilized. Thus, in some cases, this *History* may be able to give the first fruits of ongoing research that is still unpublished. That is to say that we conceived this *History* as a living and voracious body: the peril lies in our having created a Frankenstein! Our desire has been to render a public service: to bring together dispersed material, to classify the medley of data, to illuminate with a single light the dark corners of a Spanish America inwardly shattered and badly misunderstood, and to present the reader with a *Summa*. Although many have contributed to this *History*, it advances in a single, uninterrupted line. It is a collective yet uniform work. In our desire for verbal economy we have not had room even to cite the most authoritative specialists. We hereby declare our debt to their investigations. We have worked, therefore, in part as architect and in part as bricklayer. In the entire *History* there is not a single citation, not even when the criticism follows other historians closely. Nor do we cite our own scholarly contributions published elsewhere. In those contributions we rigorously analyzed textual styles; but in this *History* we occasionally recast what we have not before analyzed directly. Yet, let us not exaggerate. This *History* is personal in conception, in arrangement, and in a good deal of its commentary. As each new edition appears, we make corrections in it. If we find that, out of immediate urgency, we hastily mended a hole with a piece that did not match, we replace it later upon more accurate, more leisurely and more solid examination. Our *History* is in a provisional stage; some day it will reach a definitive stage. The more its material enters directly into our possession, the more personal it becomes. As we write with an open horizon we see it grow with our growing knowledge.

E. A. I.

TRANSLATOR'S FOREWORD

This *History* is the most comprehensive compilation of studies of the literature of Hispanic America ever written. It is vast not only for the number of pages but also for the breadth of its topics, for the depth of its chronology, for the scope of its geography, and for the magnitude of its philosophic, historical, and cultural framework in which it is neatly ensconced; it is intense for the compactness of its organization and of its prose: all the chaff has been threshed out. The compact prose reflects perfectly the manner in which the author has compressed almost six centuries of literature into such few pages. What is more stunning is that withal it remains a history of *literature,* achieved without sacrificing non-literary data. The key to this accomplishment lies in the richness of the author's language as he dissects literary forms, literally; that is, with the very instruments of the creative artist. The *History* is replete with unexpected vocabulary, turns of syntax, plays on words and ideas, tropes, metaphors which, instead of obfuscating, illuminate the creative process of so many of the writers.

It has been our intention to mirror this prose style in every respect, but all translation-mirrors have their imperfections, and images sometimes yield untrue refractions. (May there not be any distortions!) We tried to trade expression for expression, figure of speech for figure of speech, and if the trading were not possible in one place, we tried to make up the deficiency elsewhere; yet, we may not have been able to liquidate all our indebtedness to the original. If the rhythm of the English prose is not the accustomed or traditional one it is because the original is likewise an unusual and non-traditional Spanish. We hope the readers will become attuned to the new beats.

This is the translation of the greatly augmented third edition of Professor Enrique Anderson Imbert's *Historia de la literatura hispanoamericana* published by the Fondo de Cultura Económica of Mexico City. Since this edition Professor Anderson has added some authors and data pertaining to them, as well as slight modifications of the text. In this respect, the translation has taken one step beyond the original.

Enrique Anderson Imbert, a native of Argentina, is the most outstanding authority in this field, and a teacher revered and admired by many students. Professor Anderson's literary tools, alluded to above, come to him naturally: he is a very respected author in Spanish-American letters, forming part of the very history he writes.

The introduction of this *History* to Anglo-America is propitious at this time because interest in Hispanic-American art and literature is increasing. With the passage of time the artistic and literary production of Hispanic America multiplies at an incredible rate. We need only cast a glance at the table of contents of this *History* to note that the first half encompasses the years 1492 to 1910, while the second half covers the last 50 years or so. The acceleration is patent; the character of the literature, from what once may have been imitative and lagging, now takes on greater variety, newness and autonomy.

As a great number of the works have not been put into English, it was deemed proper to include the original titles with the translated titles. If a title reoccurs after it has been translated, the English title is repeated and not the original. Only Hispanic-American titles are translated; others, including Spanish, are left in their original tongue. Titles of short stories or of poems are translated, but the original is omitted, especially when the full title of the collection is given. Orthodox American English spelling was used throughout the work. In those cases where "ink-saving" orthography appears (e.g. *prolog* rather than *prologue*) it is solely due to the dictates and policies of the Wayne State University Press.

I wish to record here my appreciation and indebtedness to Professor Claude C. Hulet, of the University of Southern California, for having read the greater portion of the translation and to Professor James R. Stamm, of Michigan State University, for having read sections of the work. Their observations, suggestions, and criticisms were well received and of great value. To Professor Harold Murphy of Marshall University go my thanks for his courteous and patient aid in reading the manuscript. Grateful acknowledgment is made to Mrs. Patricia Davis of the Wayne State University Press for her efforts in preparing the text and index for printing. To Professor Anderson Imbert I extend my eternal and humble gratitude for his faith in me, for his patience with me, and for the guiding hand which led me through so many reefs and pitfalls. And finally I wish to thank Mrs. Diana N. Falconieri for the material aid and spiritual comfort that can only be repaid in the heavens.

J. V. F.

PART THREE
Contemporary Period

XII. 1910-1925

Authors born between 1885 and 1900

Historical framework: The social revolution in Mexico opens a new political cycle in our history. In Argentina, new democratic social forces triumph over oligarchy. Effects of the first world war.

Cultural tendencies: The enthusiasm for modernist artifice having mitigated, writers turn toward a simpler, more human, more American form of expression. There is a group which hurls itself into the adventures of cubism, futurism, creationism, and dadaism. Postwar magazines: "ultraism" and its dissolution.

Introduction

As we approach our own era, the number of names becomes greater, facts become disputable, and the critical classifications become entangled. It is only natural—we have stopped writing history to start writing a chronicle. We must now refer to those who have been our own teachers, friends, and even students. These are the drawbacks attending all contemporary criticism of literature—literature contemporary with the critic, that is. Outrageously, the critic acts in the capacity of both judge and judged. Without sufficient historical perspective it is difficult to place writers in hierarchical orders. Nor is there any room for individual studies. These are the years about which most has been written in our America. At the slightest laxness, the critic falls into mere cataloging.

A. MAINLY POETRY

There were poets of normal tastes, of abnormal tastes, and of tastes that were scandalous. We shall review them in this order, within each country. And to avoid repeating the same definitions each time as we go from country to country, we shall explain here, once and for all, what we mean by normal taste, abnormal taste, and scandalous taste.

1. Normality

In the previous chapter we saw how the authors who wrote during the height of modernism (let's say Rubén Darío and his contemporaries) continued to write well into the twentieth century. Death, in its unfailing turn, was making them relinquish their pens. By 1910 they were all consecrated, and almost all were exhausted. At least one of the poetic wells of the modernists was drying up: the Parnassian, with its exterior, visual beauties resembling a museum of art. Some (Darío, Nervo, González Martínez) were drawing from the symbolist well a deep, fresh, and serene liquid. Others (Leopoldo Lugones and José María Eguren) were explorers of verbal fountains of youth and became rejuvenated when surrounded by the admiration of the young writers. The latter, however, were not satisfied: to them would be reserved the task of making incoherence triumph. Rubén Darío, in spite of his cult of mystery, had been a poet of clarity. Had not the poetry from 1850 to 1880 been intelligible even in Baudelaire, Verlaine, and Mallarmé? It was true even in the most hermetic and the most difficult. After all, when Darío's *Profane Prose* appeared, most of the French symbolists were turning toward a clear, limpid, timid, and even almost classical form of expression (Samain, Regnier, Moréas, Jammes). But at the moment when symbolism as an irrational poetry was languishing in France, some of the followers of the old masters, Baudelaire and Mallarmé, renewed their efforts at obscure poetry: Maeterlinck, Gide, Claudel, Valéry. From this flank would come the

expressionists, the cubists, the futurists, the dadaists, the surrealists. In 1910, when Hispanic-American Modernism was sub-
siding, the scandalous writers of Europe were beginning to rave.
Darío met them, mentioned them, but paid them no attention.
Darío was born when Isidore Ducasse, the Count of Lautréamont, published *Les chants de Maldoror* (1868), but he died
without realizing that through this channel would come the inundation of nonsense: Laforgue, Apollinaire, Réverdy, Jacob, and
even Supervielle (in passing: Ducasse, Laforgue, and Supervielle
were born in Uruguay). Not all the young men who entered literature in 1910 came in the same door. They were born together
with the artistic verse and prose of the first *modernist group,*
that is, between the first Parnassian fruits of 1880 and the ripe
Profane Prose of Darío in 1896. They grew up with this estheticist
literature, in close relation with books that had become famous,
and they wished to vie for this fame. The esthetic battle had already been won by their parents: there was no reason for it to be
repeated or exceeded. They accepted as ordinary norms that once
had been extraordinary: the aristocratic function of poetry, the
knowledge of how to insinuate with a slight gesture, the use of
highly finished styles to attain individuality. They succumbed,
however, to that "law of imitation" which does so much damage
to Hispanic-American letters: imitation of European originals;
imitation of Europeanists who managed to express themselves
well; even mutual imitation. Due to the discipline of imitation,
able poets impressed their contemporaries as being great poets.
No one was moved by them, they had no inner illumination, but
they did draw admiration with their cold art of versification and
composition. Undistinguished cliques of poets, specializing in
fashionable tricks, were convinced they stood at the pinnacle of a
Parnassus. Rather than creative imagination, it was a selection
of words, of rhythms, of decors copied in museums and libraries,
of experiments the results of which were known beforehand.
Many soldiers in dress uniform strolling by on festive days, few
captains impassioned by inner combats. Nevertheless, some did
exist.

It is impossible to classify the new poetry. Yet, if one hearkens to the best poets of this generation, he will hear distinctive strains.

Some poets turn to a more direct dealing with life and nature. They are simple, human, sober (Fernández Moreno).

Others have an air of wisdom about them, as if they have traveled far and have returned with many classical secrets (Alfonso Reyes).

Others, the most effusive, sincerely confess what is happening to them, their anguishes, their exaltations (Mistral, Sabat Ercasty, Barba Jacob).

There are those who have a sense of humor, as if the children suspected that there had been something ridiculous and sentimental in the family of traditional Modernists (José Z. Tallet).

There are the brainy, speculative ones (Martínez Estrada).

Or those devout souls (López Velarde).

And the Creolists, the nativists, those who embrace the land (Silva Valdés, Abraham Valdelomar).

And those who are emotional about civics and politics (J. T. Arreaza Calatrava).

2. Abnormality

Let us now pass on to a group which, on leaving modernism, slammed the door thunderously. It cannot be said that they were the best writers of their generation, but they were indeed the most audacious, the ones who best responded to the esthetic changes in all the arts of Europe. Since the first world war (1914–1918) broke out in the middle of this period, literary groups have been spoken of as being prewar or postwar. The war's effect upon literature has thus been exaggerated.

The gestation of vanguard literature took longer than has been assumed. And the effect of the war on it was far less decisive than has been supposed. The war was a concomitant event and not a cause. Long before the war, literature—and all of the arts—had been becoming more and more insolent. Symbolism had taught a kind of revolutionary magic and, when it disappeared, the sorcerer's apprentices were not able to dominate their own revolutions. Not because painting can explain literature, but because it is easier and quicker to see changes in style on the walls of a museum than to disembowel them from the library stacks, the reader is invited to remember what happened in the plastic arts beginning about 1900: "fauvism," "expressionism," "cubism," Italian "futurism," French "orphism," Russian "irradiantism," "dadaism," "surrealism," etc. Think of the prodigious restlessness of Picasso which fills an entire history of pictorial "isms," and you will have an idea of what was happening in European consciences long before the first world war. An analysis of the philosophic theories of the vitalists, irrationalists, neo-idealists, mystics, existentialists—would take us to the same place: the spiritual energy with which the logical scaffolding raised by the common sense of the nineteenth century was demolished, so that the plural dimensions of life might triumph. Ever since the days of symbolism, writers had been convinced that literature was a permanent revolution. We have said already that in Hispanic-America modernism was just that: a feeling that all fashions, all new manners, had their own validity. In French literature Apollinaire, Salmon, Réverdy were demanding new revolutionary processes. First of all, the liquidation of symbolism. They took from the symbolists precious necklaces of metaphors in order to break the thread of meaning: let each metaphor roll where it will, like a loose pearl. Not only had the new writers completed the liberation of the so-called free verse of the symbolists, but they also carried symbolist irrationalism to its ultimate consequence: they denied the logical principle of identity, they denied causality, they denied the a priori concepts of time and space. Prior to 1914 then, there existed a disintegrating literature—in Spain the *"greguerías"* of Ramón Gómez de la Serna. But the first world war, from 1914 to 1918, exacerbated all the new trends. The instability of civilization, the power of political violence, the depreciation of man, the feeling of the absurdity of existence and of the world, the disillusionments with the pretensions of the seriousness of past art, produced an eruption of incoherent forms of expression. The "isms" in the history of painting had their equivalents in literature: expressionism, cubism, futurism and, during the war years, dadaism, the ono-

matopoeia of incoherence. Tristan Tzara, Paul Eluard, André
Breton, Louis Aragon, Paul Morand, Blaise Cendrars, Drieu La
Rochelle, Valery Larbaud, Max Jacob were the best known
writers in Hispanic-America. The dadaists discovered that the
subconscience was a source of esthetic pleasure: if verbal incoherence illuminates abysses of the soul, they used to say, why
look for beauty? Far better to free the obscure and spontaneous
forces. They wanted to touch the very sources of artistic creation,
hence their attraction to the art of primitive peoples. Once this
problem was posited, the dadaists prepared "surrealist" poetry,
poetry dictated by the subconscious—André Breton, Philippe
Soupault, Aragon. The desire for art diminished and the esthetic
pleasure of surprise in the face of dreams and psychic automatisms increased. Many dadaists were swallowed up by this non-
art. Those who survived profited by discoveries of the obscure
for the purpose of constructing works sufficiently clear to mean
something—Cocteau, Morand, Salmon. The surrealist movement
was more orderly and productive than the dadaist, but both con-
curred in their anti-materialism, in their aspiration for a more absolute reality than the one perceived normally, in the rejection of
logical intelligence, in their yearning for escape, travel, adventure, dreams. In Hispanic-America this literature influenced some
of the writers we have designated as "normal." But among the
"abnormal" ones we must separate the most exasperated. In almost all of the poets to be studied in this chapter we will notice
strange things. The truth of the matter is that strange men were
moving about modernism or, at least, men who had a strange
manner of moving. But the strange ones who will occupy our
attention now—Vallejo, Huidobro, Brull, Greiff, Girondo—all
move in the same direction; they meet, conspire, proselytize, and
reach out to take hold of the banner that is to wave in the avant-
garde.

3. Scandal

We have just seen how some of the inheritors of modernism,
having used up their inheritances, began to build up new fortunes.
There were poets younger than these, born without this inheri-

tance, who dedicated themselves to the new industry: that of the metaphor of the ultimate, that of the ultraistic metaphor, that of ultraism. It was a scandal. But even scandals, no matter how sudden and unexpected they may seem, in literature, above all in Hispanic-American literature which is so timid in its experiments, come after exercises, experiments, imitations. In 1918 after the end of the war, some poets who were over forty caught glimpses of the flames from the conflagration in which the expressionists, the cubists, the futurists, and the dadaists had burned the libraries and museums. And, in order to take part in the madness in some way, they leaped in the air, clicked their heels, and cut capers. We have spoken of Lugones and his *Sentimental Lunar Poems*, of Herrera y Reissig and his "Moonlight Gathering," of Eguren and his *Symbolics,* of Tablada and his *Ideographic Verses.* Following the obscure vein of symbolism, they at least came close to the "creationism" that Huidobro was to impose later. There were among the poets who were less than forty years old at the end of the war some who occasionally or belatedly felt the desire to do what the Europeans had done, from expressionism to dadaism: Alfonso Reyes, López Velarde, Peña Barrenechea, Ibarbourou, Storni. Others, who were around thirty years old when the war ended, were more violent, decisive, and conscious of their desire to scandalize: Vallejo, Huidobro, Girondo, Greiff.

But the first poets to emerge completely from the negation of modernism and its styles were those who were less than twenty years old when the war ended: Borges and Co. This movement was concomitant with the one in Spain; and the Spaniards and Hispanic-Americans put their heads together to formulate a new esthetic program, like their brothers-in-law Borges and Guillermo de Torre. GUILLERMO DE TORRE (Spain–Argentina, 1900) imposed the happy word "ultraism" to designate the literature of the avant-garde: his 1925 book *European Literatures of the Avant-Garde (Literaturas europeas de vanguardia)* was the first panorama offering a synthesis of the new tendencies, leveling off and integrating European, Hispanic, and Hispanic-American elements. By 1919 the whole group, Spaniards and Hispanic-

Americans, was called "ultraist." "Ultraism" alludes to a youthful and liberating yonder, a desire to establish new horizons. "Here is our motto: Ultra, in which all advanced tendencies will fit." This word was all that remained as a landmark to indicate, not the birth of a current, nor that the current had passed by, but that that current had existed. The official ultraist group—with the exception of the Spaniard Garfias and the Hispanic-American Borges—did not have any great poet in the few years it lasted, from 1919 to 1922. And even these two were great not during these years but afterwards. From 1919 on, the reviews already in existence became ultraist (*Grecia* and *Cervantes,* from 1919 to 1920) and those that came to light were born ultraist (the Spanish *Ultra,* 1921–22; the Argentine *Proa,* 1922–23, *Prisma,* 1921–22, *Martín Fierro,* first period 1919, second 1924–27; the Mexican *Horizontes,* 1926–27, and *Contemporáneos,* 1928–31; the Cuban *Revista de Avance,* 1927–30; and the Uruguayan *Los Nuevos,* 1920, and *Alfar,* which lasted until 1954). Ultraism was a most happy word. There were many other labels: simplism, creationism, vanguardism, cubism, dadaism, posthumism, surrealism, stridentism, advanceism, and so forth. When new explosive esthetics were lacking, they made simplicity itself explode as "simplism" (Évar Méndez). It was said that ultraism lay "beyond all other 'isms' "—that is, it was an "ism" to end all other "isms." The "isms" that appeared were branches of the great industrial plant situated in Europe. But this time, the Spanish-American writers who had been born around 1900 wrote simultaneously with the Europeans. Never before had we been so close to synchronizing our clocks with those of Europe. But they were clocks bought at local bazaars. Those who were adolescents when the World War ended wound up the clocks, set the alarms, and let them go off noisily so that everyone might believe that a new literary hour had begun.

It is difficult to study these "isms" because, at first, they were not meant to exist as literature. They must be studied in two steps: the first in "little magazines," the second in books. This chapter is concerned with the first, which was the really scandalous one. These magazines are interesting not so much for a history of literature as for a history of literary life. In them are found all the excesses, madnesses, nonsense, badinage, nihilisms, and scandals. Poetry could not go on like this. It had to accept coherence. After all, no matter how irrational a poem may be, it must offer a minimum of sense in order to be generic and understandable. Some poets, obstinate in their folly, disappeared or became shadows or stayed to beat in the drum sections of jazz bands. Others saved themselves in books, seeking an honorable conciliation between fantasy and logic. Those poets who were able to save themselves will be looked at in the next chapter. But it would be unjust to scorn the negation of the literary past by the first vanguardists, no matter how senseless this negation might be. In seeking the naked metaphor and eliminating well-known verse forms, they were fulfilling a necessary function. The bad thing about these inflamed metaphors was that, without being aware of it, they gave in to a superstition: that of believing that metaphors, through some more or less magical virtue, had value in and of themselves. They searched for them rather than found them. And in their search they tended to forgo direct mention of what they wanted to say, which would have been more poetic. The metaphors did not express the intimate being of the poet. This was true because the vanguardists started from a disrespect for literature. They had no faith in poetry. They did not believe it was serious. They were ashamed of it. They preferred badinage. The metaphoric creation, in spite of being essential, occupied a subordinate position. There was a certain insincerity in this because, in mocking serious poetry, they earned a notoriety in reverse: the easy notoriety of those who reject the well known. They wrote *against:* against pleasant perspectives, against the cosmopolitan dreams of modernism. And in writing against, they surrendered to loose verse, to the idolatry of images, and to the grammatical functions of words, to deliberate barbarisms, to the over-production of neologisms. And this excessive preoccupation with forms—negative preoccupation, but preoccupation after all —changed to rhetoric, and the rhetoric corrupted what good they brought to literature, which was the feeling that beauty need not be dreamed of in other lands, but can be seen in the simple, ordinary life of the cities and countryside of Hispanic America. We know that every style is penetrated by a particular outlook on the world; or, if we please, that every outlook on the world prefers to mold its own style. In periods when man sees an integral cosmos, he tends to compose with closed forms, with clearcut limits, with well-defined words, with independent and proportioned details, with clarity and repose. But now there were writers who felt themselves to be in sharp conflict with the world in which they lived.

The result was that forms shook loose from each other, they became disorganized and broken, and sentences began to sound as though they were coming from the mouth of a schizoid. Their eyes saw chaos. That is, there was a kind of blindness, and in this way a literature emerged, less visual than that of the modernists; on the other hand, more visceral, more tactile sensations were projected. Feeling that the universe was hostile or, at least, that it turned its back on human understanding, these writers were anti-realists who preferred to project abstract schemes in which they could distort things with a violence of emotion and a freedom of fantasy. In Europe, during the first world war and the years immediately following, philosophic anthropology advanced in great strides. Thus, at the same time that philosophers, sociologists, psychologists, and biologists were looking for answers to the question "what is man?" the vanguard writers, independent of anthropology, contributed to it with their own explorations, one of which was surrealism. The problem was not posited in anthropological terms, but their purpose was to illuminate the obscure zones that literature had never illuminated before. The style of these writers was as chaotic as the object they were describing: human chaos.

In Mexico the scandal, at least the noise, broke out in 1922 with the "stridentism" of Manuel Maples Arce, Germán List Arzubide, Salvador Gallardo, Luis Quintanilla, and Arqueles Vela. They launched manifestoes and reviews and even left a chronicle of their disdain for the bourgeoisie and for literature in List Arzubide's *The Stridentist Movement* (*El movimiento estridentista,* 1926) and in Vela's *Nobody's Coffee* (*El café de nadie,* 1926). They had heard the stuttering of Tristan Tzara's dadaism and they were enchanted by its irrationality. They were defiant, mischievous youths for whom poetry was a rack on which to hang their hats: hats that buzzed with a mental beehive of metaphors. They wanted to link the literary revolution—futurism, dadaism, surrealism—with the social revolution. Good literature did not emanate from the stridentists, however, but from the group of the *Contemporáneos* review (1928–31), where three excellent poets stood out, Villaurrutia, Gorostiza, and Pellicer, and also Torres Bodet and Salvador Novo. They wrote with classical desires for perfection, but in the final analysis, it is the voice and not the outcry that makes poetry move. And if the stridentists in the end were unable to communicate anything because they relied too much on the notion that communication with the man in the street is easy, the solitary writers of *Contemporáneos,* in interiorizing themselves, converted their ivory towers into lighthouses that radiated messages. They will be received in the next chapter.

In all Hispanic-America, Argentina (or better, Buenos Aires) was in truth the big circus of the vanguard. The world was breaking into smithereens, but the Argentinians felt quite confident of the future in those years of prosperity. That is why the literary vanguard was not a political vanguard. Generally speaking, they wrote to amuse themselves and to make fun of the sacred Lugoneses and Capdevilas. In a letter to Juan Pinto (published in 1958) the refined Carlos Mastronardi said: "In spite of the world war the generation to which I belong knew a stable world. Only later did the pillars of that moral and spiritual world, which went into bankruptcy during the last World War [1939–45], falter. Even up to 1920 the principles that made up a sort of organic system of life were still in force; we inserted ourselves into this system, without violence and without bitterness. The spirit of innovation was able to find fulfillment precisely because it was supported by a sound reality with well-defined boundaries. The aggressive nihilism of the schools in the vanguard that emerged in that period was identified with a certain inclination for careless play. There was still a sense of humor left over from an epoch that stressed progress." Oral, mural, and printed magazines were light-hearted activities.

Borges used to go to printing shops and insert grotesque errata in the poems of his friends. González Lanuza used to write epitaphs to Lugones, and Alfredo Brandán Caraffa to González Lanuza. They would lasso the wildest creatures—an English soap, a patio faucet, the grinding sound of a trolley—and bring them, tamed, into the corral of the printed page. They would twist the language to laugh at the faces of the grammarians. They would invent authors in order to jibe at the pedants. They would invade cafés with masks on. They would stick out their tongues. They were promiscuous in love. Taunts and gags for the professors and for the serious public. Jeering. Carnivalades. Jesting. Confronting these good-humored youths (Girondo, Borges, González Lanuza, Marechal, Norah Lange) were those concerned about the moral decadence of the world and about the suffering of the proletariat (Yunque, Barletta, César Tiempo), but even from here, furious clowns appeared, such as Raúl González Tuñón and Nicolás Olivari.

So, the postwar "isms" planted their fabricated canes in the soil of Hispanic-America; and on occasion the cane sprouted like the branch of a tree. The stick was becoming a plant. It was almost a mistake; but mistake or no, those "isms" transplanted to Hispanic-America were productive. For example, educating an artistic eye for primitive, subconscious, elementally creative and mythical forms made possible the respect for Afro-Antillian folklore and for indigenous arts, although the meaning of the Maya paintings and the Mexican bas-reliefs was ill-interpreted.

A table of the scandals in the postwar literature would include these peculiarities:

1. *Cosmopolitanism.* The language meridian passed through all cities, not only Madrid. Writers continued to look toward Europe, but it was no longer the idealizing Europeanism of the Modernists, but an irreverent Europeanism which made it possible to sing, in any corner of Hispanic-America, of humble local things. The streets of every city formed an international network more true to life than the network of the academies—the academies now served to provoke anti-academism.

2. *Attitude toward literature.* Although they were more productive in theory than in practice, the young writers were in agreement in their desire for insurgence, nihilism, and iconoclasm. Literature was a purposeless game. Refusal to give explanations. Talk for its own sake, without meaning. The abolition of ornamentation. Carefully sought obscurity. Schematic forms.

3. *Ingenuity.* Reality became an arena where one tested his ingenuity and imagination. Aphorisms. The cult of novelty and surprise. They did not clearly define the logical categories they used, but they had recourse to a gradation of analogies that became increasingly vast until they lost themselves in empty symbols.

4. *Sentiment.* The dehumanization of art, thus obliterating the sources of all sentimentalism. They destroyed the "I" by substituting the psychology of man for what they imagined to be the lyricism of matter. They heeded their instincts and, when they gave vent to their feelings, there were feelings of scorn, sarcasm, confusion, and humor.

5. *The cult of the ugly.* In their desire to achieve the maximum of disorder, they cultivated the grotesque, the extravagant, the revolting, the deformed, or things traditionally ugly. Poetry proposed to be a new mode of understanding, uninterested in the manipulation of a beauty already known.

6. *Morphology.* It did not matter to them if language lost its communicative practicality, so they managed to empty it of meaning. Being in disagreement with language, they would rupture it or substitute for it mathematical and musical signs. They reduced it to pure matter (the "letterism" in which each letter of the alphabet was no more than a scrawl); they made it sound like a jester's jinglebells (*jitanjáforas*). In poems, white space was worth as much as words. They abandoned capital letters and punctuation. Typography was set in several planes simultaneously. Words were printed on the page to form the shape of the things they were describing, in calligrams.

7. *Syntax.* They destroyed syntax by setting down nouns according to the accident of their origin. Words set free. Verbs in the infinitive. Intransitive verbs became active. The adjective enlisted as a noun. The abolition of adjective and adverb. The

redoubling of the noun analogically: Man-torpedo, Woman-gulf, Multitude-undertow. Connective words and interlocking phrases were eliminated. A return to medieval script, without capitals or punctuation.

8. *Metrics.* The abandonment of strophic molds, of rhyme, of measure, of rhythm. The loose verse, the loose word, used to give maximum liberty to the poet. In this way the legacy that poetry had inherited from music was renounced.

9. *Themes.* The exclusion of the narrative and the anecdote. The description of the landscape as an artificial backdrop. Inanimate things become protagonists. The introduction into literature of elements until then neglected: noise, weight, smell. The presence of the machine and of social movements.

10. *Imagination.* Instead of the musicality of external things —the rhyme and rhythm of the modernists—the ultraists violently searched for another kind of poetry, one reduced to metaphor. The image for the image's sake, at all costs. They shipped in carloads of metaphoric bricks without constructing the house: the poem's unity—if it existed at all—remained in the mind of the poet, and what was visible were metaphoric fragments. A bombardment of metaphors. The algebra of metaphors. Metaphors in long unconnected series or mixed metaphors.

We have tried to give the theory, the history, and the stylistic traits of the literary scandal that took place during the years of the first world war. The writers born between 1885 and 1900 who took part in it were confused with those who were adolescents or almost adolescents when the next period began: 1925. After all, there was not much difference in age between Girondo (1891) and Borges (1899), between Huidobro (1893) and Neruda (1904). The writers who never deviated from pure scandal belong—we repeat—to the history of literary customs, not to achievements. The others, born from 1900 on, will be passed to the next chapter. A good deal of what we have said in this paragraph is valid also for the next chapter. At times it is proper for historians to mix the chapters: in this way the reader, who was beginning to accustom himself to a conventional scheme, will be obliged to take notice of the fluidity of the historical process.

And now let us travel over the geography of poetry, from the Rio Grande to Patagonia.

(i) *Mexico* / In chapter X we have seen how the language was being rejuvenated with the first Mexican Modernist, Gutiérrez Nájera. It was the epoch of the *Revista Azul*. To the same period belong Salvador Díaz Mirón and Manuel José Othón, solitary travelers. In chapter XI the poets at the pinnacle of modernism were seen: above all Amado Nervo and those who appeared in his *Revista Moderna*. Urbina, Tablada, Rebolledo, González Martínez, Rafael López, Argüelles Bringas, Manuel de la Parra were crepuscular modernists. Urbina was a solitary figure. González Martínez was the great poet of the day. The poet who left the modernist circle in order to seek new ways, and therefore influenced the youth born after 1900, was Tablada. In this chapter González Martínez still dominated the literary groups. But now the generation of the *Ateneo* emerges. In 1909, the *Ateneo de la Juventud* initiated an important renovation in Mexico. The elder poets of the *Ateneo* have been mentioned already: López, De la Parra, Colín, Gómez Robelo, Castillo Ledón, Cravioto. At the beginning of this period, which includes those born after 1885, the finest among the young writers was Alfonso Reyes, who will be studied separately.

The list of all these poets is long and will be of value only to the curious reader: Some went to the bottom during the modernist shipwreck (JOSÉ DE J. NÚÑEZ Y DOMÍNGUEZ, 1887–1959; RODRIGO TORRES HERNÁNDEZ, 1889–1915; PEDRO REQUENA LEGARRETA, 1893–1918; ALFONSO TEJA ZABRE, 1888–1962) and others changed ship in the hope of reaching a port safely (JORGE ADALBERTO VÁZQUEZ, 1886–1959). Some sang the praises of life in the country (JESÚS ZAVALA, 1892–1957; MANUEL MARTÍNEZ VALADEZ, 1893–1935; LEOPOLDO RAMOS, 1898–1956), of religious sentiments (ALFONSO JUNCO, 1896), of evocations of dreams and memories (GENARO ESTRADA, 1887–1937; RENATO LEDUC, 1898) or of historic and civic themes (MIGUEL D. MARTÍNEZ RENDÓN, 1891); CARLOS GUTIÉRREZ CRUZ, 1897–1930; HONORATO IGNACIO MAGALONI, 1898). Others kept up the music of obscure symbolist melodies (JOSÉ D. FRÍAS, 1891–1936), and others analyzed all the effects of stimulated senses, or wanted poetry to be a feast of beautiful and sonorous words (DANIEL CASTAÑEDA, 1898–1957; VICENTE ECHEVERRÍA DEL PRADO, 1898). But toward 1922, the poet who undoubtedly attracted those who, up to then, had given their attention to González Martínez was López Velarde.

RAMÓN LÓPEZ VELARDE (Mexico, 1888–1921) wrote little: the sentimental verses of *Devout Blood* (*La sangre devota,* 1916), the complex and farfetched verses of *Anxiety* (*Zozobra,* 1919) and, posthumously, *The Sound of the Heart* (*El son del corazón,* 1932) which is a collection of compositions representing the styles of his two books, including his best known poem, "Sweet Fatherland," 1921. His prose is not unworthy of his poetry. López Velarde left half-organized a collection of his prose in *The Minute Hand* (*El minutero,* 1923), some of it having high artistic value. Little by little his scattered works in verse have begun to be collected, but up to now these posthumous volumes mix the gold with the dross, and in any case the material is neither complete nor organized with sufficient critical perception.

We should not reduce López Velarde's stature because his lyrical work was not profuse; and we should not be deceived by the apparently elementary map of his poetic domain: the provinces, Catholicism, his loved one, juvenile anguish, death, his ironic commentary on things that are dear to him. In this domain, which seems so simple on the map, things are occurring that are strange, secretive, complex, and mysterious. For example, López Verlarde's religiosity has an erotic root and his "fearful yearning to intermingle earth and heaven" might scandalize his coreligionists; his love, which he declares to be an only one (love of Fuensanta), is shared by many women; his soft provincial landscapes, painted in a language without softness, in a severely sifted selection of extravagant words, unexpected adjectives, and aggressive metaphors; his traditionalism, a screaming war against the commonplace. Yes, López Velarde had more spiritual complexity than his map of poetic themes leads us to believe. It was his esthetic ideal to be able to reveal himself with sincerity in terms that combined originality with an adaptability to the style of Creole themes.

He gained in importance with the publication of *Devout Blood*, and even more in 1919 when *Anxiety* appeared. His work, brief and intense, is among the most enduring since the liquidation of modernism. He showed a desire for renovation, not a superficial renovation, but one of the inner substance of things—he dug deep into the subjective (his soul) and into the objective (Mexico's inner nature). His amorous inclinations are always present. In *Devout Blood* the two extremes of the love sentiment appear: the pure and ideal, directed toward Fuensanta, and the one of carnal temptation, which is most patent in *Anxiety,* his best book. There are verses here showing the poet submitting himself to love; but the most significant ones are those that reveal his disenchantment and even his failure to satisfy the appetite of his senses or to achieve spiritual communication with his beloved. In *The Sound of the Heart* he is more poised because the poet appears to have struck a balance in his spiritual development, but he is less intense. "Sweet Fatherland" speaks to us of his Mexican province, but the poet does not remain there: without leaving his own garden he visits the literary gardens of other literatures. This is curious "interior exoticism." His veneration for Leopoldo Lugones ("the most sublime, the most profound poet of the Castilian language," he used to say) explains his similarity to other poets of his day, also partisans of Lugones. The Lugones of *Sentimental Lunar Poems* had begun a school for Hispanic-Americans born during the years of the emergence of modernism.

Of course Lugones, like Herrera and Reissig, was a lens that concentrated many rays of European literature such as, for example, the tender and ironic rays that emanate from Laforgue. López Velarde, like others, wanted to invent a language that would surprise the reader with unusual images. The danger lay in affectation, in rhetoric, in verbal complexities that lose themselves in obscurity. López Velarde sensed the danger and withdrew in time. Although they radiated surprises, his words respected the traditional character of the language and even the shadings of the region in which it was born. His humble and even prosaic colloquialisms went out to meet the aristocratic verbal inventions, and they embraced happily at the half-way point. In spite of this, López Velarde might have fallen into mannerism, if it had not been for the very personal confessions he had to make to us. López Velarde conversed with himself, in the voice of the flesh and the voice of the spirit. For him the city was a place of violence and sin; the province, a nostalgic world. And López

Velarde wrote "Sweet Fatherland," which is not a poem by a country or city dweller, but by a solitary spirit who tenderly and ironically expresses mellow nostalgias and ironic distances. López Velarde, the most Mexican of the poets of his generation, takes refuge in "Sweet Fatherland," the best civic poem of Mexico.

(ii) *Central America / Guatemala:* Rafael Arévalo Martínez is outstanding, but he will be examined later. Another Guatemalan poet, of modernist origin, is the battling FÉLIX CALDERÓN ÁVILA. Of later development, but still modernist, is ALBERTO VELÁZQUEZ (1891).

Honduras: RAMÓN ORTEGA (1885–1932) was a simple poet, a romantic varnished with modernism. A writer who stood out in his day was ALFONSO GUILLÉN ZELAYA (1888–1947). He was also one of those who, after his modernist capers, returned to simplicity: *The Almond Tree in the Patio* (*El almendro del patio*). He was the first in his country to write social poetry, as in the sonnet "Poet and Beggar." RAFAEL HELIODORO VALLE (1891–1959) published *Thirsting Amphora* (*Ánfora sedienta*) in 1922, which includes "Niña Lola's School," a delight of agile rhythms, images, and lyrical leaps. His ideal is simplicity, as evidenced by his celebrated composition "Jasmines."

El Salvador: Modernism embraced the poets here so strongly that it left them almost immobilized. First, the initiators CARLOS BUSTAMANTE (1890–1952) and JULIO ENRIQUE ÁVILA (1892). Among the more prominent are JOSÉ VALDÉS (1893–1934), the serene author of *Pure Poetry* (*Poesía pura,* 1923); RAÚL CONTRERAS (1896), who carried his modernist devotion to the theater, in *The Princess Is Sad* (*La princesa está triste,* 1925), a scenic gloss of Darío's *"Sonatina."* The book *Mist* (*Niebla,* 1956), signed by Lydia Nogales, is Contreras' work. His last title, *Presence of Smoke* (*Presencia de humo,* 1959). ALBERTO GUERRA TRIGUEROS (1898–1950), a reflexive poet of deep Christian sentiments.

VICENTE ROSALES Y ROSALES (1894), who published his anthology in 1959, abandoned modernism, advanced in search of new forms, and eventually spoke in the language of the vanguard.

Nicaragua: After having given birth to Rubén Darío, Nicaragua needed a long and merited rest. One can speak, nevertheless, of two movements, both more or less modernist. In the first we find the landscapist RAMÓN SÁENZ MORALES (1885–1926), the sober and Christian MANUEL TIJERINO (1885–1936), the disconsolate LUIS ÁNGEL VILLA (1886–1907), the solitary LINO ARGÜELLO (1886–1937), the anecdotic ATANASIO GARCÍA ESPINOSA (1886–1938), the gallant GABRY RIVAS (1888), the emotional CORNELIO SOSA (1886), the elegiac ARÍSTIDES MAYORGA (1889), the effusive JERÓNIMO AGUILAR CORTÉS (1889), the impressionist ANTONIO BERMÚDEZ (1889), the sentimental LUIS (1889–1938), and EDUARDO AVILÉS RAMÍREZ (1896) and the poetesses ROSA UMAÑA ESPINOZA (1886–1924), BERTA BUITRAGO (1886) and FANNY GLENTON (1887?). But the major figures were Alfonso Cortés, Azarías H. Pallais, and Salomón de la Selva. ALFONSO CORTÉS (1887) went mad, and his madness gave absurd subtlety to his verses on such metaphysical themes as time, and to his hallucinatory moods. AZARÍAS H. PALLAIS (Nicaragua, 1886–1954), a priest, sang from Bruges, in Belgium, of his medieval, primitive, and ingenuous world. SALOMÓN DE LA SELVA (1893–1959) also lived a long time outside of his country. He wrote some of his poems in English. *The Unknown Soldier* (*El soldado desconocido,* 1922) was written in Spanish, during his Mexican period. If at times he seemed to approach the vanguard, on other occasions he returned to classicism, as in his *Evocation of Horace* (*Evocación de Horacio,* 1948). In the second modernist movement, more or less from 1914 on, the conquest of flexibility in themes and meters is reinforced. Some of them mockingly resist the first signs of the vanguard. Others prefer, without polemics, a poetic work that is simple and of vernacular inspiration. Outstanding are: NARCISO CALLEJAS (1887?–1917), ROBERTO BARRIOS (1891), ANTENOR SANDINO HERNÁNDEZ (1893), GUILLERMO ROTSCHUH (1894), ADOLFO CALERO OROZCO (1897), JUAN FELIPE TORUÑO (1898).

ANDRÉS RIVAS DÁVILA (1889–1930) was one of the writers who prepared the way for the vanguard, somewhat stridently, in *The Kiss of Erato* (*El beso de Erato*).

Costa Rica: Some of the modernist treasure was inherited by ROBERTO VALLADARES (1892–1933), ROGELIO SOTELA (1894–1943), JOSÉ ALBERTAZZI AVENDAÑO (1892), JOSÉ BASILEO ACUÑA (1897), HERNÁN ZAMORA ELIZONDO (1895). The most brilliant poet was RAFAEL CARDONA (1892). In *Morning Gold* (*Oro de la mañana,* 1916) his preoccupation with the gracefulness of forms was already noticeable. Although he preferred the sonnet, he tried his hand at different meters and strophes, without going as far as free verse. His themes were ambitious—man and his destiny, for example. His impressionism and his initial symbolism yielded later to a more conceptual art. The other Costa Rican poet of significance was JULIÁN MARCHENA (1897), who published his first book in 1941 (*Wings in Flight —Alas en fuga*) but because of his age, his modernist forms, and the clear logical construction that gives unity to his sentiments, he must be placed here.

Panama: The most noteworthy poet in all its literature is RICARDO MIRÓ (1883–1940). His review *Nuevos ritos* (founded in 1907) was one of the principal organs in the modernist renovation after the advent of Panama as a republic. He worked in careful verses—with a preference for hendecasyllables and sonnets—themes of love, of patriotic emotion, and of admiration in the presence of landscapes. He was a poet in minor key, introspective, solitary. His last book of poems was *Silent Paths* (*Caminos silenciosos,* 1929). He also wrote short stories and two attempts at novels. His work has been presented in anthologies: the most recent, *Poetic Anthology* (*Antología poética,* 1951) and *Introduction to the Stories of Ricardo Miró* (*Introducción a los cuentos de Ricardo Miró,* 1957). GASPAR OCTAVIO HERNÁNDEZ (1893–1918) was a modernist poet who combined the tricks of the trade in almost all his production, but also allowed us to see a personal and popular vein, which expressed in a direct manner his social condition as a patriotic Negro preoccupied with injustice. MARÍA OLIMPIA DE OBALDÍA (1891) used her voice as wife, mother, and teacher with dignity: *Orchid* (*Orquidea*), *Lyrical Breviary* (*Breviario lírico*), *Children's Parnassus* (*Parnaso infantil*). The emotional JOSÉ MARÍA GUARDIA (1895–

1941) completes the family portrait of the Panamanian modernists of this generation. There were others of lesser modernist accents such as ANTONIO NOLI B. (1884–1943) and ENRIQUE GEENZIER (1887–1943).

(iii) *Antilles* / In Cuba, poetry was not in the avant-garde either in this period or the following. It may even be said that, after Casal, there was not even an energetic modernism. Rather than great works, the poems of Boti, Poveda, and Acosta—three of the worthiest poets to represent the continuation and renovation of modernism—are a beautiful awakening. Boti, in spite of his rhythmic audacities, was placed in the previous chapter because he was born in 1878. In spite of belonging to an older generation, he was the first, after Cuba won its independence from Spain, to dust off Cuban letters and leave the air clean. For his estheticism, directed toward pure poetry, Boti can be coupled with Poveda (although his work endured longer than Poveda's and thus reached the generation which in 1927 launched the magazine *Revista de Avance*). In JOSÉ MANUEL POVEDA (1888–1926)—*Precursor Verses* (*Versos precursores,* 1917)—there were ostentatious attempts at creating new forms. They are not very new. It was he who was eccentric, not his verses. His eccentricity ("our I above our selves," he used to say) led him to the cultivation of "hysterias," "decadencies," and "satanisms" (these also are his words) and in this way, he restricted himself, together with others, to a cosmopolitan manner. He learned from Europeans (Regnier, Kahn, Stuart Merrill, Laforgue) and from Hispanic-Americans (especially from Darío, Silva, Lugones, López Velarde). The moon to which he sang in a sentimental voice and with ironic little glimpses was the moon that had been seen by Laforgue and Lugones: but the neighborhood from which he saw it, tenderly, was his own. His nervous trembling also made his verses tremble in meters that were freer than those his contemporaries were accustomed to. Like his friend Boti, he too, wanted to renew poetry, but the wise and elegant acoustics of his verses was a thing of sensitivity, not just a part of a program of experiments. Nevertheless, he was a technician more than a revolutionary: he employed unusual words, recondite allusions to mythology, difficult notes. Different from Boti and Poveda, for his greater proximity to the things of Cuba, was Acosta. AGUSTÍN ACOSTA (1886) took flight with *Wing* (*Ala,* 1915) and circled the modernist sky, expressing sentiments of gallant love and feelings of patriotism (as in his song to Martí) which became even more simple in the mellow and melancholic poems of *Little Sister* (*Hermanita,* 1923). Of more national significance was *Cane Harvest* (*La zafra,* 1926) in which he evoked lyrically, but with social sensitivity, the life of the workers in the sugar industry. It is a poem of a great variety of moods—subjective and realist—with effusions and descriptions that exhibit Acosta's skill as an artisan and also—why not say it—his prosaic stumblings. Cuba is converted into one great cane field. "There is a violent smell of sugar in the air," he writes. As the poem proceeds, this smell of sugar cane vaguely suggests warnings, catastrophes, revolutions. Occasionally, a vanguardist image: "on the envelope of night / the moon sets its stamp." But, in general, Acosta's national fervor is frank, realist and even didactic. At the sonorous festivals of rising pyrotechnics that the modernists used to celebrate, Acosta was a moderate. He became increasingly clear, simple: *The Distant Camels* (*Los camellos distantes,* 1936), perhaps his best book, and *The Desolate Isles* (*Las islas desoladas,* 1943). But his orbit was modernism, and in *The Last Moments* (*Ultimos instantes,* 1941) he invoked, irresistibly, the Darío of "It was a soft air." A modernism, we repeat, in which there are declamatory, patriotic, religious, sentimental notes, and even touches of a diffused philosophy. After the impetus given by the three leaders, Boti, Poveda and Acosta—their *Mental Arabesques* (*Arabescos mentales*), *Precursor Verses* and *Wing,* respectively, appeared from 1913 to 1917—Cuban poetry was set in motion. Sometimes in reverse, as in GUSTAVO SÁNCHEZ GALARRAGA (1892–1934) and in the brothers FERNANDO (1883–1936) and FRANCISCO LLES (1887–1921), and sometimes circulating around the main avenues of modernism, as in ARTURO ALFONSO ROSELLÓ (1897), ERNESTO FERNÁNDEZ ARRONDO (1897), RAMÓN RUBIERA (1894). At times it turned to the prose of daily life or, at least, toward ordinary themes. FELIPE PICHARDO MOYA (1892–1957) ran through the geography, the history, and the social activities of the island of Cuba, in "The Poem of the Cane Fields" (*"El poema de los cañaverales"*) or in his compositions on the Negro theme, but he managed to write vanguardist verses in an attempt to place himself within the "new sensitivity" of the postwar days. Prosaic, although lively and ironic, was JOSÉ ZACARÍAS TALLET (1893), whose only book, *The Sterile Seed* (*La semilla estéril,* 1951) appeared to be hanging from an exclamation by Laforgue: "How humdrum life is!" Tallet used to balance himself on the edge of humble, flavorless, plebeian things and from his balancing board moved either to compassion, or smiled with pessimism and sarcasm. Like Pichardo Moya, Tallet announced the poetry of African themes which was to have so much success later. He was a sentimentalist, saddened by the failure of everything, and because of the lucidity with which he faced mediocrity, he achieved the brilliance of the grotesque. A lyricist? At any rate, a lyricist who now doubts his own individual song: "I am one of the last who says / 'I,' tragically / convinced at once that the password / for tomorrow must be 'we.'" RAFAEL ESTÉNGER (1899) also fits into this turning of poetry toward a public reality. At times poetry moved into deep crevices of emotion, as in MARÍA LUISA MILANÉS (1893–1919), MARÍA VILLAR BUCETA (1899). At times poetry advanced toward new forms of expression. The most notable example in this direction of modernism, a modernism that sprang from the Lugones and Herrera y Reissig fountain—was RUBÉN MARTÍNEZ VILLENA (1899–1934). But he was exceptionally gifted, and in *The Sleepless Eye* (*La pupila insomne*)— his only book, a posthumous one—one admires what he was able to do with the prose of life by dint of sentimental sincerity, bitter humor, philosophic reflections, and even political irritations, for he was a Communist. Also in REGINO PEDROSO (1896) we find an evolution from early modernism—*The Route to Bagdad and Other Poems* (*La ruta de Bagdad y otros poemas,* 1918–23)—to a poetry of social emphasis, "Fraternal Greeting to the Machine Shop," 1927. First, sumptuous images and allegories according to fashion: then, the struggles of the worker, machines, anti-imperialism. A writer of the avant-garde, but more for his themes than for the dislocation of his forms. His humanitarian impulse is despoiled little by little of political propaganda and it leads him to affirm the creative forces of the world. In the end he seems to fall back on the Chinese shadows of his race in

Translations of a Chinese Poet of Today (*Traducciones de un poeta chino de hoy*). EMILIA BERNAL (1885), tender, ardent, intuitive, was capable of denying these qualities in herself in order to complicate sounds that brought her close to a poetry which, under the heading "abnormality," will be studied next.

In Cuba it was MARIANO BRULL (1891–1956) whose sails were swollen with the first winds of the new poetry. He began with *The House of Silence* (*La casa del silencio,* 1916), in a lyricism that was serene and disturbed at the same time, like a light reflected in mirror after mirror.

Attracted by the ideals of pure poetry—to liberate verse from anything that could be said in prose, according to Valéry's definition—Brull got into the vanguard with *Waning Poems* (*Poemas en menguante,* 1928) published, significantly, in Paris. (There he followed closely the debate on *poesie pure,* promulgated by Henri Brémond.)

These were the years in which the new poets, gathered to celebrate the third centennial of Góngora, discovered that Gongorism was present, and not past, and that in the light of this high moon they could write better than ever a poetry of pure images and beautiful themes. The lyricism appears in the brief patterns of clear syntax, with metaphors between parentheses and mounted rhythms. Afterwards Brull published *Rotund Song* (*Canto redondo,* 1934), *Rose Solo* (*Solo en rosa,* 1941), *Time in Torment* (*Tiempo en pena,* 1950). There is no evolution in his work, nevertheless—it is monotonic (and even monotonous). Every object Brull touches—the rose, the sea, the stone, the light, the shore, the clouds, the eyes of a child—gives birth, with his help, to a metaphor. Beautiful metaphors, but they leave the womb of the world from which they sprang in ruins. As an example of this, read "Epitaph to the Rose" (*"Epitafio a la rosa"*). Brull allowed himself one indulgence: the free invention of sounds as the dadaists had done. He believed, as the dadaists did, that everything could be said in poetry, provided it sounded different from what older poets had written. But Brull's tenderness, imagination, grace and serenity are unjustly less remembered than the sheer auditory delight of poems like "Green Cajolery" (*"Verdehalago"*). From one of his experiments—*"Filiflama alabe cundre*

/ ala olalúnea alífera / alveolea jitanjáfora / liris salumba salífera"
—Alfonso Reyes took the word *"jitanjáfora"* and made it famous as a reference to those stupid and sonorous sisters of metaphors that erupted in this deliberately infantile poetry.

Other Cubans accompanied the youths in their vanguardist subversion: Juan Marinello and, above all, MANUEL NAVARRO LUNA (1894) who, beginning with *Furrow* (*Surco,* 1928) basted metaphors onto diminutive allegories and drew calligrams.

In the Dominican Republic, the brothers Pedro and Max Henríquez Ureña were the first to openly write frankly modernist poetry in 1901; but both stood out in other genres, so that we will refer to them elsewhere. The truth of the matter is that there was scarcely any modernism in this country. It arrived late, it was weak and it lasted no time at all. Everyone's eyes turned toward the "decadents" of France, but some of them were still sighing over their Romantic troubles (like the elegant ALTAGRACIA SAVIÑÓN, 1886–1942). Others, closer to the Rubén Darian sun, shone more brilliantly. VALENTÍN GIRÓ (1883–1949) was the first, with his sonnet *"Virgínea,"* to ignite one of those polemics so necessary to the triumph of new styles. OSVALDO BAZIL (1884–1946) was a modernist from head to foot, and left at least one sentimental gem: "Little Nocturne." RICARDO PÉREZ ALFONSECA (1892–1950) is remembered above all for his "Ode About an I" (*"Oda de un Yo"*). There were others—such as the tender and simple VIGILIO DÍAZ ORDÓÑEZ, 1895, or FEDERICO BERMÚDEZ, 1884–1921, of social and humanitarian themes—but modernism in the Dominican Republic was timid. Other names: EMILIO MOREL (1887), BALDEMARO RIJO (1885–1939), RAMÓN EMILIO JIMÉNEZ (1886), ENRIQUE AGUIAR (1890–1947), JOSÉ FURCY PICHARDO (1891), JUAN BAUTISTA LAMARCHE (1894–1956).

The Dominican Republic, late with its modernism, received early the tendencies of postwar vanguardism, due to the advent of "posthumism." The word "posthumism," like "futurism" and "ultraism," manifested the impossible desire to write the literature of the-day-after-tomorrow. But the posthumists diluted Dadá's wine. In their tiny country they seemed quite daring to themselves, but in comparison with what was being done elsewhere, they were scarcely extravagant. They thought they were iconoclasts because they neglected the language; they were enthralled with free verse and did not study the great poets of the past. But they lacked the mischievous, playful, and irreverent spirit of the vanguardists. *From the Posthumous Movement* (*Del movimiento postumista,* 1922) came the first anthological pamphlet. The posthumists were legion, and in their stampedes they wanted any ridiculous nonsense to pass as poetry. One of them, nevertheless, the Supreme Pontiff of Posthumism, was the best poet that had been produced up to then on the island of Santo Domingo: DOMINGO MORENO JIMENES (1894). His first booklet of new poetry was *Psalms* (*Psalmos,* 1921). He ignored the traditional forms of the verse, and with his melancholy humor he would soften and work up ideas. Anarchic and uneven, he looked about him, and the landscape of his country entered his poetry, detail after detail. His nativist, landscapist, and folklorist realism is his greatest merit. After all, it was something his predecessors had not done. And as for his elegiac sentiments and ideas, they miscarried because his language was plain, opaque, lax, and poor in imagination. When he does synthesize his ideas in an image, he manages a very personal poem, and at these moments one phrase has the power of an entire poem. Later they bestowed the title of Supreme Pontiff of Posthumism on RAFAEL AUGUSTO ZORRILLA (1892–1937), author of micropoems of keen sensitivity, but only Moreno Jimenes is saved. Despite everything, posthumism has been one of the most consequential, combative, and durable movements on the island. Related to it were: JULIO ALBERTO CUELLO (1898), ANDRÉS AVELINO GARCÍA SOLANO (1899), MANUEL LLANES (1899), RAFAEL AMÉRICO HENRÍQUEZ (1899) whom we shall see later.

Puerto Rico had had its great modernist poet in Luis Lloréns Torres, whom we have already studied. Modernism was belated and short lived. Those who followed Lloréns were ANTONIO PÉREZ PIERRET (1885–1937), somewhat Parnassian in *Bronzes* (*Bronces,* 1914); ANTONIO NICOLÁS BLANCO (1887–1945), of limited scope; JOSÉ ANTONIO DÁVILA (1898–1941), a good sonneteer and a good representative of all post-modernism; and JOSÉ POLONIO HERNÁNDEZ Y HERNÁNDEZ (1892–1922), who ascended, though always a few rungs lower, the lyrical ladder that Bécquer and Rubén Darío had climbed: melancholy in his sentiments like the former, a verbal craftsman like the latter. His two books, *Couplets of the Bypath* (*Coplas de la vereda,* 1919) and *The Last Combat* (*El último combate,* 1919) speak to us of nature, of death, of love. Love was the inspiration for a madrigal, "To Two Astral Eyes," that made him famous.

In Puerto Rico the promoter of new tendencies was EVARISTO RIBERA CHEVREMONT (1896). When he returned from Spain in 1924, where he had been for five years, he diffused the poetry that he had become acquainted with in ultraist circles. His "vanguardist page," which appeared for ten years in *La Democracia,* was an organ of esthetic propaganda and also a laboratory for poetry. His program was to break with the excessively eloquent, solemn, and heavy forms that predominated. But he did not affiliate with the Puerto Rican "isms" nor with Vicente Palés Matos' "euphorism" and "no-ism" nor with Graciany Miranda Archilla's "watchtowerism" (*"atalayismo"*). Ribera Chevremont liked to experiment with new techniques—*Hebe's Glass* (*La copa de Hebe,* 1922) was his free verse experiment—but after *Color* (1938) he felt more attracted to tradition, as is obvious in his *Poetic Anthology* (*Antología poética,* 1924–1950). He was a universalist; he respected what the Parnassians and symbolists had done. Traditionally Hispanic forms persisted in him; and although he did not allow himself to be suffocated by native subjects, neither did he yield to the revolutions that followed dadaism. Ribera Chevremont explored his inner self, the landscape, the existing social system (with sympathy for the people and for the demands of social justice) and enriched decades of the poetic production of his country in its various forms of language and literature with his own strong vocation. MANUEL JOGLAR CACHO (1898) was a sentimentalist, simple, serene, tender, religious: *In a Low Voice* (*En voz baja*), *Intimate Task* (*Faena íntima*). CLARA LAIR (1895) (Mercedes Negron Muñoz) was erotic, passionate, daring in her confidences on surrender to the male and solitude in the midst of such fires: *Bitter Tropics* (*Trópico amargo*).

(iv) *Venezuela* / Now we hear several orchestral combinations. The violins of modernism are muted, but there is still no clear surge of postwar saxophones. Instead, it is the native flutes that dominate. There are romantic and modernist poets who, because they were born after 1885, should have a place here: LUIS YÉPEZ (1889), ISMAEL URDANETA (1885–1914). But the most interesting phenomenon is the transition from modernism, which was declining without having produced a single great poet, to the literature of the vanguard, which was beginning to excite the very youngest.

In Venezuela people speak of the "generation of '18," a generation whose aim was to transcend modernism and raise the cultural level by importing European norms but keep the content Venezuelan. According to some, this was probably the most resonant, the most effective, generation in the nation's poetic history. It was probably a movement united in mutual personal respect, a preference for the same themes (infancy, the landscape, love, civic life) and a common esthetic attitude. The initial group consisted of Mármol, Paz Castillo, and Blanco. LUIS ENRIQUE MÁRMOL (1897–1926) was the first to achieve a certain ascendancy over the others; he was restless, rebellious against all that was false in modernism, serious in his concerns, sentimental and imaginative. But he died prematurely, leaving the posthumous *The Madness of the Other* (*La locura del otro*). FERNANDO PAZ CASTILLO (1895), secure, serene, and gentle; consistent and universal. His poems, *The Voice of the Four Winds* (*La voz de los cuatro vientos*), *Signs* (*Signos*), have an aristocratic air of solitude and culture. The most famous of the group was ANDRÉS ELOY BLANCO (1897–1955), a poet rich in timbre, serious and gracious, brilliant and multicolored, overflowing but intimate, capable of classicism, but at heart a romantic steeped in the juices of homeland and folklore. His many books, from *Lands that Heard Me* (*Tierras que me oyeron*, 1921) to *Moonflower* (*Giraluna*, 1954) present something like an industrial exposition of poetry. Blanco never turned down any business, or any tidings. He changed constantly, but no change ever caused him to repudiate the previous one. He experimented and then built up a collection of his various styles. His versatility seems, at times, to stem from a temperamental romantic source. At times it seems to be the manifestation of a desire to attempt to do everything that others are doing and, if possible, surpass them at it. He chose what he liked and also what was expected of him. He was therefore popular. His multiple accents resounded in America, and resounded in Spain as well. He was a person who crossed geographical frontiers, but was himself a frontier poet. Behind him lay modernism; before him the drive for change. Since modernism came late to Venezuela and lasted longer than elsewhere, the vanguard battle was also going to be delayed.

Other poets were joining the initial group of which we have just spoken. RODOLFO MOLEIRO (1898), a minor poet of moderate sentiment, expressing love for his native countryside; LUIS BARRIOS CRUZ (1898), with his *Response to the Stones* (*Respuesta a las piedras*, 1931), was emotionally moving because of his daring, almost vanguardist, manner of styling native themes; JULIO MORALES LARA (1894–1952) was the most traditional of the group; his poetry is Creole, dwelling on the beauty of the country and the feelings of the people; ENRIQUETA ARVELO LARRIVA established herself with one title, *Nervous Crystal (Cristal nervioso)*. We shall see the younger members of the "generation of '18" in the next chapter. As a matter of curiosity, ENRIQUE BERNARDO NÚÑEZ (1895) novelized the literary life of this generation in *Inner Sun (Sol interior)*, and there we see and hear Blanco, Moleiro, Fombona, etc. But before closing this Venezuelan section we should like to add some other names that for one reason or another do not fit into the "generation of '18" as precisely as those we have mentioned. ELÍAS SÁNCHEZ RUBIO (1888–1931), PEDRO RIVERO (1893–1958) and, above all, JOSÉ ANTONIO RAMOS SUCRE (1890–1929), one of the most outstanding. His books of poems, *The Helmsman's Post (La torre del timón,* 1925) and *The Enamel Sky and Shapes of Fire (El cielo de esmalte y las formas del fuego,* 1929), were famous as lessons in poetry for youths of succeeding movements.

(v) *Colombia /* As if it were carrying a glass filled with precious traditions and it were afraid of spilling them at the slightest slip, poetry in this country is seen moving with a very careful but somewhat belated step. A poet dressed in the old fashion was AURELIO MARTÍNEZ MUTIS (1887–1954), who always worked with the scruples of a good artisan in the different fields of the narrative, the elegy, and the landscape. He had begun, hardly modernistically, with the *silvas* of *The Epic of the Condor (La epopeya del cóndor,* 1913), but his *Marble (Mármol,* 1922) came from the modernist quarry. Although tied to modernism by a rubber band, other Colombian poets withdrew a few steps. They are those of the "generation of the Centenary," so called because they began publishing around 1910. They had more of a civic sense than the Rubén Darío esthetes and they were inspired by their national birthright. Nevertheless, the "Centenarian" poets learned their art from Parnassian and symbolist models and, inside Colombia, they continued the work of the modernists, Valencia, Grillo, and Londoño. The most brilliant were Rivera, Rasch Isla, Castillo, Castañeda Aragón, Gilberto Garrido, Leopoldo de la Rosa, and Seraville.

José Eustasio Rivera was one of the first to rely upon the Colombian landscape, the source of his springing lyricism, but we will deal with him separately below. MIGUEL RASCH ISLA (1889–1951) the confidential poet of *On the Surface of the Soul (A flor de alma), For Afternoon Reading (Para leer en la tarde), When the Leaves Fall (Cuando las hojas caen)* and *The Apple of Eden (La manzana del Edén)*. And, the most influential in this constellation, EDUARDO CASTILLO (1889–1939), a gentle, delicate, sad, resigned poet who presented his message through suggestion. His book: *The Singing Tree (El árbol que canta,* 1938). Thanks to Guillermo Valencia, whom he humbly admired, Castillo traveled all the routes of modernism, always correct, seldom inspired by a personal and powerful lyricism. Rather than a feeling for life, he felt an esthetic theory of life. This theory, of course, came from a European library, rich in French books, poor in Spanish. His readings are more recognizable than his emotions, perhaps because he penetrated his own personality very timidly and, on the other hand, elaborated with great decisiveness a theory of art that became a school in his country.

The Centenarians were about twenty: GREGORIO CASTAÑEDA ARAGÓN (1886) who wrote of the sea and of men of the sea, author of *Corners of the Sea* (*Rincones de mar*); the desolate and recondite ABEL MARTÍN; the soft, musical and enamored ROBERTO LIÉVANO; LEOPOLDO DE LA ROSA (1888–1964), with two wings: one of angel and one of demon; DELIO SERAVILLE [Ricardo Sarmiento] (1885–1936); the melancholy and somber GILBERTO GARRIDO (1887); the brothers BAYONA POSADA (Daniel, 1887–1920; Jorge, 1888; Nicolás, 1902); JUAN BAUTISTA JARAMILLO MEZA (1892), GENARO MUÑOZ OBANDO (1890?); ÁNGEL MARÍA CÉSPEDES (1892), who was acclaimed at the age of sixteen for his poem, "The Blossoming of the Sun," chiseled his poetry in Francophilic fashion; and others. Younger, but still harking back, are DANIEL SAMPER ORTEGA (1895–1943), the restrained CARLOS GARCÍA-PRADA (1898), and MARIO CARVAJAL (1896) of classically religious themes, emotions, and vestments.

This roster, which may annoy readers allergic to the pollen of names, indicates nevertheless the great expanse of the Colombian garden. In the middle of this garden there is a bushy tree, the last in a long line of modernism: PORFIRIO BARBA JACOB (1883–1942). Miguel Ángel Osorio, known by his pseudonyms Ricardo Arenales and Barba Jacob, is in fact a strand in the same thread of poetry to which we previously attached Silva and Valencia. He was not as delicate or profound as Silva, nor as artistic as Valencia, but his themes were romantic, like those of the former, and his forms had a modernistic cut, like those of the latter. He is generally considered a bright light. However, Barba Jacob, for all his restlessness, vehemence and despair, did not succeed in giving poetic utterance to that inner world that was engulfing his heart. In "Light Song" (*"Canción ligera"*) he complained that he could see things right before his eyes and was still unable to give them voice; "and we, wretched poets / trembling before the vertigo of the sea / behold the unhoped-for wonder / and can only sigh." And it was true. Barba Jacob is deeply troubled by great questions, doubts, discouragements, rebellions, desires, lusts, immoralities; but he remains in his cellar, a sick man, and what we hear from him is not so much songs as groans. His lyricism is so dense that at times it is obscured, as in *"Acuarimántima."* At other times he attains clarity in exclamatory poems (the exclamations reveal the poet's emotional charge), poems with form (the symmetries reveal the effect he tries to make), narrative poems (the action of an anecdote or an allegory indicates the direction of the spirit or the idea of the poem). His best songs are about deviation, perdition, solitude. The legend of his life as a homosexual does not concern us (although it contributed to his reputation) but the legend about his poetry should be critically revised. He exaggerated his lacerations, and in his desire to scandalize he would achieve simulations that were artistic, but not poetic. On the other hand, in his moments of sincerity he frequently failed to see clearly into his own depths. Another strange one was JORGE ESCOBAR URIBE (1886–1917), better known as Claudio de Alas. He is so strange that he enters literary history not so much as himself but as a character in a novel, *A Lost One* (*Un perdido*) by Eduardo Barrios. After a tempestuous life, he grew tired of living, and his weariness led him to suicide.

Between the poets of the centennial that we have seen already and the "new ones," whom we shall see, we place LEÓN DE GREIFF (1895) here, all by himself. Complex, introverted, sarcastic, discontented, imaginative, with explosions of rhythms, words, and madness, always lyrical, León de Greiff was, among the best Colombian poets, the one who opened the way for the vanguard. Beginning with *Tergiversations* (*Tergiversaciones*, 1925) he never stopped his contortions. Actually since 1915, in the review *Panida* of Medellín, he had already begun to startle readers with a poetry that resembled nothing known in Colombia. Later, both in Spain and in Hispanic-America, poets appeared that left León de Greiff in the shade—but he came first and what he did came from his own head. Youthful in his lyrical rapture, the years pass, but he continues to enjoy the respect of youths, generation after generation. He is not easy to read, however. He handles words like musical instruments in a carnival orchestra. He had a good musical education, but his verbal music sounded like nothing known. His sound effects consist of repetitions that, although inevitable, are at the same time surprising. The words— archaisms, onomatopoeias, neologisms, cultisms—the capricious repertory of themes—legends, reminiscences of strange authors, Scandinavian landscapes—the sudden changes in mood, and the constant excitement also contribute to the difficulty, not of understanding, but of enjoying his work. One of his self-caricatures: the "Sonnet" which begins, "if a picture of mine is required, let this one qualify" (*"si es un retrato mio, aqueste vala"*). For a full-length portrait, read *Complete Works* (*Obras completas*, 1960).

(vi) *Ecuador* / Modernism struck its spark here in the first decade of the century, though the best of Ecuadorian literature will come later and will appear by preference in prose form. ARTURO BORJA (1892–1912) was one of those who best fanned the new fire. He was sentimental, clear, spontaneous. His influence came directly from French symbolism: in *The Onyx Flute* (*La flauta de ónix*) one hears echoes of Baudelaire, Verlaine, Rimbaud, Mallarmé, and Samain. Perhaps these readings accentuated his melancholy disposition and made him feel tired of life before living it. He was a solitary, inexplicably suffering. ERNESTO NOBOA CAAMAÑO (1891–1927) makes us hear Verlaine and Samain in *The Ballad of the Hours* (*La romanza de las horas*) and *The Shadows of the Wings* (*La sombra de las alas*). More harmonious than Borja, though like him, he felt weary of life. He is elegant and moderate despite the intensity of suffering he wished to express. MEDARDO ÁNGEL SILVA (1899–1920), a humble youth who invented his own aristocratic Rubenian atmosphere and who wished to be what he was not, sang his sad melody. Verses by Verlaine, Moréas, and Samain moved in surreptitiously to mix with those that he composed. In *The Tree of Good and Evil* (*El árbol del bien y del mal*, 1918) it is difficult to distinguish his inspiration from that of others. He reflected on the uselessness of existence and then seemed to have found a meaning in his own harmonious song. Borja, Noboa Caamaño, and Silva committed suicide. The one who wanted to live longer, but could not, was the afflicted HUMBERTO FIERRO (1890–1929). He also produced echoes of symbolism in *The Lute in the Valley* (*El laúd en el valle*, 1919) and in the posthumous *Night in the Palace* (*Velada palatina*). He was one of the most exquisite poets in his melancholy and in his weariness. He made an effort to leave behind the company of Rubén Darío's followers and to overtake the new writers. These are the four major poets of the best choir that sang in the autumnal parks of Ecuador. They evaded Ecuador, reality, and even life. There were others: JOSÉ MARÍA EGAS (1896), with his amorous and mystical breviary, *Unction* (*Unción*, 1925); REMIGIO ROMERO Y CORDERO (1895), modernist in *The Pilgrimage of the Caravelles* (*La romería de las carabelas*); MIGUEL ÁNGEL ZAMBRANO (1895), who showed up late, in 1957, with desolate and nihilist poems. And the oldest: AURELIO FALCONÍ (1885) and GONZALO CORDERO DÁVILA (1885–1931).

HUGO MAYO (1898) imitated the dadaists and the creationists somewhat. Although reluctant to publish in books, he is still respected for his original personality (real name: Miguel Ángel Egas).

(vii) *Peru* / After Chocano and Eguren, a group of modernist poets appeared which was worthwhile as a group, although no principal figure stood out. JOSÉ GÁLVEZ (1885) began to sing beneath the moon, in a closed garden—*Beneath the Moon* (*Bajo la luna*, 1910); *Closed Garden* (*Jardín cerrado*, 1912)—in the manner of Rubén Darío, although he also followed the example of Chocano's narrative, civic, and American poetry. ENRIQUE BUSTAMANTE Y BALLIVIÁN (1884–1937) visited poetry in the attitude of the intellectual: that is to say, he observed, studied, reflected, experimented. And so it is with his work—without being original, it reflects all the comings and goings of those years: Parnassianism, symbolism, Creolism, indigenism, vanguardism. ALBERTO J. URETA (1885) had the greatest tonal unity: from *Sound of Souls* (*Rumor de almas*, 1911) and *Pensive Torment* (*El dolor pensativo*, 1917) there surges a constant melancholy. PERCY GIBSON (1885) composed local poems, with landscapes, anecdotes, and ordinary human types.

Other poets, who had mingled with the preceding ones, separated from modernism in search of more up-to-date formulas. Within this endeavor at renovation stands ALCIDES SPELUCÍN (1897). In *The Book of the Golden Ship* (*El libro de la nave dorada*, 1926) he collected the verses he had written between 1917 to 1921, which spread out like a fan showing the rococo decoration so dear to the modernists; but there are also sallies toward ordinary, humble, real themes, above all, with a sea atmosphere. ALBERTO GUILLÉN (1897–1935) was a chronic individualist and an acute egotist. He was assertive, optimistic, and even ideological in his barbaric exaltation of force: *Imitation of Our Lord I (Imitación de nuestro Señor Yo)*.

For the time being, we close this exposition of Peruvian poets with a few names as suspension points: PABLO ABRIL (1895), ALFREDO GONZÁLEZ PRADA (1891–1943), CÉSAR A. RODRÍGUEZ (1891), FEDERICO MORE (1889), FEDERICO BOLAÑOS (1896), DANIEL RUZO (1900). We have already seen how some Peruvian poets broke lances with modernism. Let us add RICARDO PEÑA BARRENECHEA (1893–1949). In *Flowering (Floración,* 1924) he was still a sentimentalist of the old school, but later he disciplined his poetry and made it move along recently opened trails: *Lineal Canticle (Cántico lineal)*. Like Góngora, whom he admired and emulated, he cultivated cultist and popular lyrics. At times he was seen in the poetic vanguard with those younger than he. His lyricism flitted about graciously telling us about his loves, but was unconvincing when he became serious. He was proud of his poetic licenses and images, inspired by Góngora, "supreme acrobat of Spanish syntax, juggler of hyperbaton, unicyclist of color." Let us also add here JUAN PARRA DEL RIEGO (1894–1925), who during the years of World War I, took possession of the images of the new language of speed, machinery, sports, jazz, and violent action. His "Ode to the Motorcycle" was epoch-making. His "polyrhythms" as well. Nevertheless, all this was still not vanguardism. JOSÉ CARLOS MARIÁTEGUI, an essayist who focused on serious social problems with Marxist lenses, had said in 1924 that futurism, cubism, dadaism, and pirouettes of the decadent bourgeoisie would not emerge in Peru. It is curious that of all the vanguardist reviews—the vanguardism of the first of these, *Flechas,* 1924, could hardly be said to have been impetuous—*Amauta* (1926–30), directed precisely by Mariátegui, was in sympathy with the idea of revolution and it did not matter whether the revolution was in politics or in letters. *Amauta*, in consequence, being leftist, published everything. For many years the books of a Peruvian, ALBERTO HIDALGO (1897), had been coming from Buenos Aires. A "futurist," like Marinetti, he sang to war, energy, violence, anti-democracy, the machine, and speed, extravagant in his manipulations of all the "isms." He believed himself to be a poet of genius. He had less stature than his megalomania led him to believe. After his *Chemistry of the Spirit (Química del espíritu,* 1923) he attained *Simplism (Simplismo,* 1925) through distillation: here he proposed his own "ism," which consisted of reducing poetic substance to pure metaphors. "In the air our glances graze / many flocks of metaphors," he used to say. "Let the world stand on its head; let evil people govern it; let the strong crush the weak: it matters not to me. I am but a poet and only build metaphors! Poetry is necessary, but it is useless, u-s-e-l-e-s-s!" But, in the vanguardism of those years, no one was able to rise as high or go as far as Vallejo did in *Trilce*.

CÉSAR VALLEJO (Peru, 1892–1938) left on his first poetic voyage—*The Black Heralds (Los heraldos negros,* 1918)—

away from the esthetics of his forefathers, Rubén Darío, Herrera
y Reissig, and the Lugones of *Sentimental Lunar Poems,* carrying
in his pockets, like gifts of candy, many verses from the modernist cupboard. But the lad, though he kept eating the candy on the
way, turned away from cosmopolitanism to head toward national,
regional, popular, and indigenist areas. Mestizo the author, mestizo the poetry. His Parnassian and symbolist blood circulates
through his verses mixed with that of Peruvian realism. His
themes are erotic or family love; the daily life in his land of *cholos*
or mestizo laborers; and his mood is one of sadness, disillusion,
bitterness, and suffering. Man suffers fatal, undeserved blows:
"There are blows in the world, so hard . . . I don't know! /
Blows like the hatred of God." He never wanted to be born; and
while awaiting the coming of death, he wept and had compassion
on his fellowmen who also suffered; and when a blow missed him
he felt guilty because he knew it had fallen on some other unfortunate. There was something in him that wanted, in his solitude, to expiate for all the faults of man, something of the
Carthusian monk. And it made his tongue Carthusian, and dry,
and hard, and lean, and humble, and cindery.

This impulse for human solidarity was to take him later to
political rebellion. Meanwhile, his next book was one of pure
poetic rebellion: *Trilce* (1922). It was an explosion. Literary
traditions burst into pieces, and the poet advanced in search of
liberty. Free verse, to begin with, but not only free from meter
and rhythm, but also freed of syntax and logic, with images flying
freely in all directions without exchanging a glance, and with
such speed that at times they are lost in the darkness before the
reader can recognize them. Cubism? Creationism? Ultraism?
Surrealism? Vallejo, the solitary one, would not have written
these demented poems had he not known that he was in the
company of other poets who were at that time cultivating the
same poetic dementia. However absurd, his language was still a
language; it was of no use to him as a medium of communication,
but it was useful as a countersign within an experimental group.
He was a solitary accompanied by other solitaries in a solitude
shared with many. *Trilce* is an unfortunate book. In the worst

instances we come across merely external caprices: grammatical and typographical irregularities; meaningless sounds; unnecessary verbal mechanisms; ugly mixtures of technical and popular terms, hackneyed expressions and obscure neologisms (the title *Trilce* was, for example, a whimsical neologism invented from an insignificant circumstance). But these same caprices become ennobled—that is, they stop being caprices—when they contribute to the expression of a deep intuition of life on the subject of his orphanhood, solitude, helplessness and invalidity.

In these cases the poems reveal the serious, tormented, desolate soul of Vallejo who, convinced of the absurdity of existence, recalls his lost home, his dead mother, and his early sufferings. The poems in *Trilce* are irrational and unintelligible; only those poems move us in which Vallejo has elaborated sentiments common to all men (See for example III, XXVIII, LXI). The value of this book is primarily historical. In 1922 Vallejo was thirty years old, but he exhibited some of the traits of adolescent vanguardism that appeared after World War I. Later on we will refer to this vanguardism. However, Vallejo's poetry is not dehumanized. His feeling, his subconscious shadows, his experiences of poverty, orphanhood, and suffering in prison, his protest against injustice, his feeling of pious brotherhood toward all the oppressed, rise through the crevices of his versification.

After *Trilce* Vallejo left his country (he was not to return to Peru, ever) and withdrew from poetry: he wrote short stories, novels, dramas, and many newspaper articles. He lived in France, Spain, Russia, and other countries. He was now a Communist and wrote literature of Marxist, revolutionary propaganda. The Spanish civil war forced out the *Human Poems* (*Poemas humanos*) which were published posthumously in 1939. (Although it contains poems written since 1923, others grouped under the title, *Spain, Take This Chalice from Me* (*España, aparta de mi este caliz*) refer to the Civil War. The old pity he felt for the underprivileged now turns to action; the old desolation, to hopeful combat. And the poet, as he sings of his own belligerency and that of the masses, reaches, naked and free, the deepest part of his being—his incoherent emotions. Of his prose works the stories were the most significant part. *Savage Speech (Fabla salvaje)* is the story of a neurasthenic, the peasant Balta, who feels himself followed, pursued by the shadow of a human form which he occasionally surprises in the mirror or in the reflections of a stream, watching him from behind. Hallucinations, forebodings, and doubt grow in his mind while in his wife's womb a child is growing: just when the child is born, he, Balta, harassed by the shadow, falls over a cliff and dies. The sad atmosphere depicted with magical realism tends to shine with poetic images. Under the title *Musical Scenes (Escenas melografiadas)* he collected some miscellaneous pages: prison memories, poems in prose, fantastic stories (like *"Los Caynas"*), all in a prose verdant with verbal buds, with dadaist and surrealist phrases, with expressionist fantasies. After his first trip to Russia (1928) he abandoned this artistic attitude and served the Communist Party with a propaganda novel: *Tungsten (Tungsteno, 1931)*. The hero is the blacksmith Huanca, whom we see in the last pages preparing the social revolution with Marxist catchwords. The action takes place a little before 1917. A United States company has bought the tungsten mines in the province of Cuzco. We are presented with the exploitation of the Indians, the political corruption, the brutality of the police, the debauchery of priests and bourgeoisie, the servility of the intellectuals, in truculent scenes of sex, misery, drunkenness, and death. The prose is journalistic, discursive, plain; also conventional is the lineal composition of the story. All leads to one end: to exalt the example of Lenin, to promote world revolution, and, in Peru, to dignify the Indians and to give political power to the workers and peasants. The intellectuals are assigned a role: "to place themselves at our orders and at the service of our interests," says the worker Huanca.

(viii) *Bolivia* / After the three vertexes of Bolivian modernism—at the apex Jaimes Freyre and at the base Tamayo and Reynolds—come a few lines of plane geometry. The most enthusiastic propagator of modernism was CLAUDIO PEÑARANDA (1884–1924), who collected his entire work in *Songbook of Real Experiences (Cancionero vivido, 1919)*. His "Elegy to Rubén Darío" was, similar to Darío's "Response to Verlaine," a poetic definition. It is, perhaps, the most imaginative poem of this group; and the imagination it expresses has romanticist notes of sadness and horror.

José Eduardo Guerra (1893–1943) was also one of the "cerebral" poets of modernism, with philosophic restlessness, and tinges of melancholy and anguish. Others: Humberto Viscarra Monje (1898), Juan Capriles (1890–1953), Nicolás Ortiz Pacheco (1893–1953), Lola Taborga de Requena (1890). Rafael Ballivián (1898), author of *The Illumined Path* (*La senda iluminada,* 1924), is distinguished for a cosmopolitanism open to innovation.

(ix) *Chile* / Chilean modernism had not produced any great poet: barely two, Pezoa Véliz and Magallanes Moure. Suddenly, the wind of poetry freshened. Chile was to bring the only Nobel Prize for literature to our America, Gabriela Mistral; it would bring one of the most clamorous innovators of our letters, Vicente Huidobro, and later, Pablo de Rokha and Pablo Neruda, the latter being one of the greatest poets in our language. However, let us not anticipate, but take things in order. The figure of international stature in this period is Lucila Godoy Alcayaga, known as

Gabriela Mistral (1889–1957). From her rugged, irregular poetry—with "voluntary prose-isms" (her words)—Gabriela Mistral does not appear to derive from the virtuosos of modernism; nevertheless, her metaphors have the symbolist family habit of leaping into the abyss with torch in hand, illuminating as they fall the recesses of the inner life. They are metaphors for readers accustomed to the thrilling spectacle of those mad exercises: anti-intellectual metaphors that do not demonstrate with the slowness of logic but reveal with the rapidity of the immediate gesture and, therefore, require a prepared public. Although different from the modernists, Gabriela Mistral learned from them—from Magallanes Moure, from Carlos R. Mondaca, from Max Jara. At any rate she wrote for those who had read the modernists. In "The Sonnets of Death" (*"Los sonetos de la muerte"*), for which she received a prize in the Floral Games of Santiago in 1914, she was already leaving her teachers behind. She introduced provincial ways of speaking (Gabriela was from the Elqui valley), adverbial forms (as in the verse "evil hands entered tragically in him"), and biblical terms. She never stood out as a revolutionary in poetry, in the manner of Huidobro, Rokha and Neruda, but she too, contributed to the poetry of the vanguard. Her influence was not visible, but like a subterranean river she irrigated contemporary poetry. Her great theme is love; and all her poetry is a variation on this theme. Amorous, amatory poetry, but not erotic. In the first group of these variations, two sad episodes from Gabriela's life are composed in counterpoint. One describes a first love for a man who killed himself for honor and the other, years later, another love that hurt her deeply. These poems were collected under the sections, "Anguish" (*"Dolor"*) and "Nature" (*"Naturaleza"*) of her first book, *Desolation* (*Desolación*)—the first edition, 1922; second, 1923; and the third, 1926, contained additions; the best edition to date is that of Aguilar, 1958. Since neither Gabriela nor anyone else has given the biographical key to these two histories, and the poems are not arranged in two chronological episodes, the reader believes himself to be reading the painful history of a single love; her love for the man who committed suicide. No one has expressed with such lyrical power the awakening of love, the feeling of ecstasy in the presence of the loved man that can find no words to express it; shyness in the awareness that she is seen by him, and shame at the sight of the poverty of her nakedness; the sweet warmth of the body; the fear of being unworthy of her beloved, the dread of losing him, jealousy, humiliation, heartbreak; and then, when he has put a bullet through his head, the consecration of her life to him, the prayer to God to save the soul of the suicide, the anxious desire to know what lies beyond death and through what shadows her dead one moves; the loneliness, the futile waiting in places they used to frequent together, along with an obsession that he is at her side in a supernatural visitation; remorse because she still lives on, the world of remembrance, the stamp of virginity and the yearning for maternity; the passing of time and of her own flesh that is dying under the dust of the bones of her deceased love; the sudden realization, on reaching the age of thirty, that she cannot even remember the vanished face; the utter poverty after this loss . . . But, as we have said, this frustrated love, moving as it is, is the first suite of variations on the theme of love.

On reaching her thirtieth year—"Already in the middle of my life"—Gabriela Mistral continued with other variations of universal love, love of God, nature, mother, good causes of the world, love of the humble, the persecuted, the sufferers, the forgotten ones; and, above all, children for whom she wrote rounds, songs, and stories. In *Desolation* she tells how she came to write for the consolation of others: "Your beauty shall also be called mercy, and it will console the hearts of men," she says in "Decalogue for the Artist" (*"Decálogo del artista"*); and she formulates the "Vow": "Forgive me, God, for this bitter book, and you men, who feel life as sweetness, you too, forgive me for it. In these hundred poems a tormented past still bleeds, a past in which the song, to alleviate me, was reddened with blood. I leave it behind me in that somber ravine and along these simple slopes I move toward the spiritual plateaus where a wide band of light, finally, will fall upon my days. And from here I shall sing words of hope, without turning to gaze upon my heart . . ." In this way Gabriela, after her purification through suffering, rises to a candid, pure, and transparent love for her fellow man. She continues to be desolate, but now sings her tenderness. *Tenderness* (*Ternura*, 1924) is the title of a book of poems, most of which are prunings from *Desolation*, except that these branches have blossomed in a new edition of 1945.

Another of her books—the second original one—*Felling of Trees* (*Tala*, 1938) is a new version of the religious theme of *Desolation*, but here Gabriela's vision is more abstract. After her innocence, her passion, and her sad disillusionment in the first contact with poetry, she brings to poetry colorless flowers: symbols, dreams, ideals. Nature is remembered from a distance, or it belongs to strange countries where Gabriela moves, caught in the net of constellations that are not her own southern ones. In her exile, in her uprooting, her verses become harder. In the poetry of her third and last book, *Winepress* (*Lagar*, 1954) her love of land and man is stylized even more. Most of the poems have the rhythms of songs. The fatigue of old age in a strange land makes her remember and yearn for death, and her verses are hard, dry, opaque, even prosaic: "like copious smoke / I am not a flame or burning coal." In reality, *Desolation* is her best work; it was there that she gave the best of herself, and it is there that we find the themes in her later works. Her vigor—the vigor of a poet rather than a poetess—is not due to the things she writes about. No. Thousands of weak poets chose strong themes. Her strength lies in the reality that she has lifted, taken into her very entrails, converted into her own flesh and blood, and then poured out in her generous and noble song of love. Her Christian sentiment made her sympathize with the cause of social justice. Her *Poem of Chile* (*Poema de Chile*) is posthumous. She has written poems in prose, essays, letters. Her prose, though very abundant, circumstantial, and unstable in quality, on the day it is completely edited, will not diminish the importance of her verses, which will continue to be fundamental in Gabriela's work; but an anthology of that prose will be surprising for its delightful spontaneity. Some prose titles are: *Messages* (*Recados*); *Telling Chile* (*Cantando a Chile*, 1957).

We should mention other significant names. The great Pedro Prado will be studied in another section with the prose writers. Enter MAX JARA (1886), retiring but proud, scanty but neat, severe in a poetry that had few chords: his *Assonants* (*Asonantes*) of "minor tone" shows his simplicity, the result of a profound purification. In a younger group, the first in order of merit is ÁNGEL CRUCHAGA SANTA MARÍA (1893), still illuminated by symbolism, personal in his religious sentiment. Growing less and less effusive, more and more intentional, his most notable collections of poems are *Job* (1922)—an expression of the suffering of all things created —and *Night of Nights* (*Noche de las noches*) which is interspersed with poetic prose. Then we must remember JUAN GUZMÁN CRUCHAGA (1895), intimate, sad, compassionate; he is notable for his simplicity, for his sobriety: *The Fixed Stare* (*La mirada inmóvil*, 1919), *High Shadow* (*Altrasombra*, 1958). His theater is meant to be read rather than acted. A simple listing of other poets will give an idea of the awakening of Chile in this period: the tender and yet modernist ROBERTO MEZA FUENTES (1899), the tremendous and multitudinous inquietude of WINETT DE ROKHA (1896–1951), the reflexive and symbolist JORGE HÜBNER BEZANILLA (1892), the erotic and landscape poet CARLOS PRÉNDEZ SALDÍAS (1892), the priest FRANCISCO DONOSO GONZÁLEZ (1894), and the very human MARÍA MONVEL (1899–1936), whose simplicity in manifesting tenderness, love and home life sharply contrasted with the more sophisticated poetry of her contemporaries.

The most notable Chileans in this panorama of "abnormality" that we are offering are Huidobro and Rokha. When the anthology *Lyrical Forest* (*Selva lírica*) was published in 1917, Rokha seemed to be closer than Huidobro to Marinetti's futurism and other vanguard tendencies. Rokha is better represented in this anthology than Huidobro. Alongside him Huidobro seems insipid.

But with time, Huidobro kept growing until he became the significant Chilean poet.

PABLO DE ROKHA (1894) is a poetic personage more than a poet. Impressive, emphatic, affirmative, and negative, he drowns in his own words. He had an influence on other Chilean writers: one of those influenced was none other than Pablo Neruda (the older Pablo however is a desperate poet whom we shall not take seriously; and Pablo the younger, on the other hand, is a serious poet who will never convince us that he is really desperate). The demoniacal and disoriented Rokha has the voice of a romantic. Like the romantics he confronts what he calls the "infinite," the "eternal." And while he moans and roars he feels like a titan. He howls a foreboding of death. His emphasis qualifies everything as gigantic, tremendous, colossal. A volcanic eruption that releases its pressure in a long enumeration of images broken in pieces, or molten in formless lava. Poetic gems in prosaic slag. The disorder of his poems does not always render, legitimately, the vision of a disordered world—at times it is just a failure in the composition. The undulation of his verses does not always release what is shaking him from within: at times it is just free-versism. For this reason his gigantism tends to resemble the characteristic diffusion of gas. His best poems ("Circle," etc.) combine lenses that make objects appear farther away as well as closer; and as the images are mixed, they superimpose in enlargements and miniatures (century and scarf; world and skirt; God and bottle, and so on). He is very Chilean and understands the obscure meanderings of the Creole soul and the meaning of popular language. Because he loved the people, he wrote civic, political poetry (which he believed to be Marxist). He stopped feeling like the "visionary," "the terrible megalomaniac of metaphors" in order to dedicate his soul to "social service, which is its truth"—"Allegory of Torment" (*"Alegoría del tormento"*). In spite of his love of the populace—manifested in folkloric subjects and communist catchwords—his excessive invectiveness and megalomania have prevented him from being truly popular: *Ode to the USSR* (*Oda a la USSR*), *Morphology of Fright* (*Morfología del espanto*).

VICENTE HUIDOBRO (Chile, 1893–1948) has claimed for himself the honor of being the father of creationism. Not everyone concedes it to him. Be that as it may, he was one of the first poets in our language who was in the vanguard of European literature and, among other happy innovations, he proffered this one: a poetry that magically obliterates the real world and, in the emptiness that remains, creates almost magically a new ideal world. This is poetry, then, as absolute creation—"creationist" poetry. This pride in creation—"The Poet is a little God," says Huidobro —is as old as poetry itself, but it was contained or dissimulated in those styles which for centuries imitated nature or imitated imitations of nature. With symbolism, from Mallarmé to Apollinaire, the poet denies the purely adjectival function of qualifying a reality outside himself and instead affirms energetically his substantive function of inventing objects inside his own mind. Huidobro incorporates himself into the host of poets having this divine vocation; and he was so precocious that in a few years he skipped several stages of a long historical process. At the outbreak of World War I, in the manifesto *Non serviam* (1914) read in Chile, he began to take the road that Apollinaire had opened in 1912 in *Esthetic Meditations*. Apollinaire had spoken of the "servitude" to nature, and said that "it is time we were our own masters." Huidobro says: "*Non serviam*. I shall not be your slave, Mother Nature; I shall be your master . . . I shall have my trees, and they will not be like yours; I shall have my mountains, I shall have my rivers and my oceans, I shall have my sky and my stars. And no longer will you tell me: that tree is bad; I don't like that sky . . . , mine are better;" "Until now we have done nothing better than imitate different aspects of the world, we have created nothing. What has come from us that was not first standing in front of us, all around us . . . ? We have sung our hymns to nature (something that matters very little to her). We have never created our own realities . . . We have accepted, without further reflection, the fact that no reality exists other than the one around us, and have not thought that we too can create realities in a world of our own, in a world that awaits its own fauna and its own flora." During the war, in a lecture given in the city of Buenos Aires in 1916, it seems he said, "all history of art is no more than the history of the evolution of mirror-man to god-man;" a work of art "is a new cosmic reality that the artist adds to nature." And less than ten years later Huidobro remembers: "That is where they baptized me with the name *creationist* for saying in my lecture that the first condition for being a poet is to create, the second to create and the third to create." A month later he published the booklet, *The Water Mirror* (*El espejo de agua*; this edition of 1916 can not be found), in which his famous "Poetic Art" appears: "Why sing to the rose, oh Poets! / Let it bloom in your poem." The composition that gives its title to the booklet beautifully illustrates his esthetic manner. Toward the end of 1916 Huidobro arrived in Paris and joined the group led by Apollinaire and the review *Nord Sud*, which also counted among its contributors Pierre Réverdy, Tristan Tzara, Paul Dermée, and Max Jacob. Huidobro is not just a simple follower because he collaborated on an equal level. Huidobro published poems in French, which are beyond the confines of this history, though in many of them there are definite outlines of his creationism. From the point of view of our Hispanic culture, it is Huidobro who brings us new French axioms, it is he who speaks the new French poetic language. That is, because of Huidobro the new French style becomes Hispanic-American. In 1918 he arrived in Madrid, and immediately his creationism pointed to another direction, the desire to travel new esthetic roads that he urged upon youth. He perturbed some, enthused others; he was envied and feted. After a trip to Chile, (he was in Madrid again in 1921) he was present to assist at the birth of what was to be known as ultraism. The bulk of the Huidobro rockets began to burst in Castilian literature with *Arctic Poems* (*Poemas árticos*) and *Ecuatorial*, both of 1918. It was the musical poets who were disturbed by all the ruckus. The visual poets, accustomed to silent movies, noticed on the other hand that those rockets were signal flares or fireworks which, with their firecrackers, girandoles, sparklers, Bengal lights and pyrotechnic castles, gave the night its festive air. They looked upon the rain of images with an admiring, ah! Thundering rockets, but also sparkling rockets: "A nightingale in his down cushion / beat his wings so much / that he loosed a downpour of snow;" "I made rivers run / that never existed. / With a cry I raised a mountain / and around it we danced a new dance"; "I am the old mariner / who sews the severed horizons" (*Arctic Poems*). "The wind rocks the horizons / that hang from the rigging and the sails"; "Slowly the captive cities pass by / sewn together one by one with telephone lines"; "The black slave / opens his mouth quickly / for his pianist master / who makes his teeth sing" (*Ecuatorial*). Huidobro had rejected Marinetti's futurism—as too muscular and extroverted—and André Breton's surrealism—because its source was mental debility and its medium a feigned automatism

—in order to promote his esthetics of creationism that went deep into the inner self to produce autonomous poetic objects that could not be compared to the objects of nature.

Only the poet, he says, "possesses the vertiginous mirrors that capture the pace of metamorphoses." His formula: "To make a poem the way nature makes a tree." What does this mean? It means that the poet must create, invent new things like the forces of nature but without imitating nature. How? With the metaphor. Things are despoiled of their real being and imaginatively fused with another being. Creationism, then, was a way of making metaphors. He suppressed comparisons and the logical connection of fantasy to reality and he established as truth the fact that "slowly the captive cities pass by / sewn together one by one with telephone lines." What seems to be a simile, becomes real, the image becomes an object. The world that our intelligence accepts and ordains Huidobro cheerfully contradicts with an invented world. This is what poets have always done, but Huidobro surprised everyone with his chaotic enumerations, his neologisms, his manifold deluding images, his free verses capriciously spelled, his cult of meaningless words and unconnected letters of the alphabet, the capers he cut to mock literature. The humor of the dadaists had freed poetry from an excessive weight of melancholy. Huidobro, too, gives freedom to poetry through his humor. His humor is neither comical nor somber: it is poetic. Huidobro continues to grow, and with him grows his ambition. He strives for longer and more confidential poems. The more he confesses, the more surrealist become his creationist images. He tells us of his life, his yearnings, his disillusions. This is the best Huidobro, the anguished Huidobro who, in denying God in order to take his place as a divine poet, finds himself in a void. He can, of course, create his own world of images, but it is a fallacious creation. With his mind full of inventions, in his imagination he feels he is falling toward death. This is the Huidobro of *Altazor* (1931), *See and Feel* (*Ver y palpar*, 1941) and *The Citizen of Oblivion* (*El ciudadano del olvido*, 1941). The *Last Poems* (*Ultimos poemas*, 1948) are posthumous. According to Huidobro he composed those books between 1919 and 1934. Here, through the openings of his Harlequin's mask, Huidobro's eyes are looking at death. Once the things we call real are abolished, Huidobro casts his metaphor-glances to fill the great void; and he casts them —here lies his seriousness—with the deliberate and conscious intent of being "an absolute creator, a god-artist." His metaphor-glances fly, because this flight figures in his theoretical program— poetry as flight—and because flight was the rising impulse of Huidobro's aerial nature. "Flight" and "Travel" are the two beautiful constellations in his metaphoric zodiac: sky, light, wings, angels, airplanes, birds, meteors, wind, arrows, indicate that Huidobro, in nullifying reality, flies through the air to the center of his subjectivity. What has wings is positive: adventure, play, life. What does not have wings is negative: sadness, sickness, downfall, death. *Altazor or Voyage in Parachute* (*Altazor o El viaje en paracaídas*) tells us of this fall down into the depths of oneself, this tumbling toward death. It is one of the worthiest poems of this period; and in his verses, as in the prose of *Satyr* (*Sátiro*), Huidobro proves that creationism is not a game, but the anatomy and physiology of his theory of poetry, a theory lived and not merely thought about. Altazor is Huidobro himself, *alto azor* or hawk on high, "hawk fulminated by the heights," "Vicente anti-poet and magician."

He wanted to coexist with things, but how was he to sustain himself in a world of imaginary creation, of pure vision without meaning, a world dreamed by a small god who does not believe in the great God, a nothing-world, in a word? One afternoon he took up his parachute, he explains in the preface, and leaped into the hollow spaces of the void. "My parachute began to fall giddily. Such is the force of the attraction of death and the open grave." And as he fell he recited his poems, "aerial feats." Throughout seven cantos Altazor-Huidobro renounces the world, falls in "an eternal traveling into the interior of himself," falls to the depths where death awaits him. "Justice," he exclaims, "what have you done with me, Vicente Huidobro?" And the fallen angel, in its "fall without end, of death in death," tragically "challenges the void" and transforms the universe in an incessant metaphoric re-creation. The poet gives us his biography as a magician of words with his anxieties and insurrections. And in the fall, his words, little by little, become mad—"a beautiful madness in the zone of language"—lose their grammar, change into pure sound, break up into separate letters and in the final canto they fuse into chaos: "*Lalalí /* Io ia i i i o / Ai a i ai i i i i o ia." In *See and Feel*, the same tone. In "Song of Livingdead" (*"Canción de la muervida"*) he speaks of the dead who "are exiled from earth and enheavened in the skies." "Let us fly to nothingness / . . . / Fly like a sensitive bird when death comes nigh." "I fall from my soul / and I break into pieces of soul upon the winter." In the first poem of *The Citizen of Oblivion*, when he takes an account of his thirty years, he asks "what madness has made us be born, / from whence this substance of bitterness comes"; and when he remembers his life as the poet who sang within his enigmas, he adds that then "I did not know the weight of my death." In another poem, "In Time's Ear," he says "I contemplate from such heights that all becomes air"; and then the world crumbles into nothingness, a nothingness that only those who agonize can feel. In "Transfiguration": "the universe only discovers its alliances / moving through your own insides. / In this amalgam of echoes / I am living and I will be dead." He also wrote theatrical pieces and novels. Among the former, *In the Moon* (*En la luna*, 1934), "a little guignol," is a political farce which ends with the collectivist revolution in which the intellectual of the 1930's believed. His novels were more interesting. *Cagliostro* was published in fragments between 1921 and 1922; the first edition came out in 1934; we have seen the second edition of 1942. A "film-novel" Huidobro calls it. If this is so, it looks more like a joke played on the movies, since the plot is absurd, truculent, mysterious in the bad sense. Huidobro's ironic sub-titles have not been sufficient to convert Cagliostro's adventures into literature. Then came *Mio Cid Campeador* (1929). But the novel that interests us most for its professional revelations is *Satyr or The Power of Words* (*Sátiro o El poder de las palabras*, 1939). The novel intertwines two themes: the double development in the neurotic Bernardo Saguen of a literary vocation and an unbridled sexual desire for ten-year-old girls. Since in poetry a word creates a reality—this is Huidobro's creationist credo—the word "satyr," hurled unjustly in the face of Bernardo (chapter II), results in creating a real satyr in him. His efforts to be a writer and not a satyr, and the failure of both efforts, are the sum total of the novel. An interior novel, then, in which there are lightning strokes of "creationist poetry." In general, a novel more reflexive than introspective. For a few fleeting moments, nevertheless, Huidobro tries the direct interior monolog that reveals the stream of Bernardo's consciousness.

(x) *Paraguay* / Modernism began to manifest itself here when in the rest of Hispanic-America it was already outmoded. The figure of greatest stature, ELOY FARIÑA NÚÑEZ (1885–1929), approached modernism and entered into it; but the distinctively modernist groups will come later. Fariña Núñez lived abroad, but from a distance sang of themes relating to his country. *Secular Song* (*Canto secular*, 1911) is a long epic poem in blank verse, of pseudoclassical serenity and coldness. He collected his poetic work in *Poems* (*Cármenes*, 1922). In reality, he was not a great poet. He cultivated his mind by reading and studying European or Europeanized books in the literary circles of Buenos Aires. The idealization of his Guaraní homeland in *Guaraní Myths* (*Mitos guaraníes*) was the best he produced. He also wrote narrations of Hellenic inspiration in the short stories of *The Vertebrae of Pan* (*Las vértebras de Pan*) and the novel *Rodopis*, theater, and several books of essays. Modernism, such as Rubén Darío many years earlier had imposed on the rest of Hispanic-America, took hold in Paraguay in two belated movements. The first was formed around the review *Crónica* (1913–15); the second, around the review *Juventud* (1923–25). Prominent in the first of these movements was GUILLERMO MOLINAS ROLÓN (1889–1945). This Bohemian, talented but short on poetic production, was a symbolist made ardent by the metaphors of Herrera y Reissig. The other two interesting figures of *Crónica* were LEOPOLDO RAMOS GIMÉNEZ (1896), a libertarian poet of violent social mettle in *Sacred Pyres* (*Piras sagradas*), tending more to esthetic forms in *Eros* and *Wings and Shadows* (*Alas y sombras*), and PABLO MAX YNSFRÁN (1894), somewhat Parnassian in his desire for formal perfection in exotic and philosophical themes. Later he abandoned poetry for the essay. The most popular poet was MANUEL ORTIZ GUERRERO (1897–1933), popular in part because of the painful legend of his life as a leper, and as a self-sacrificing, idealistic bohemian, without resentment or bitterness. The stamp of Rubén Darío is recognized in his works: *Surging* (*Surgente*), *Eastern Clouds* (*Nubes del este*), *Kernels* (*Pepitas*). This last work (1930) is a collection of imaginative definitions modeled on the *hai-ku*: "I am a thread of water on the plain; / by night, bright stars / I sew singing." He combined exotic and native themes. He also wrote in Guaraní. He collaborated in the development of folklore; for example, he collaborated in the Paraguayan song, the *"guarania"*, composed at that time by the musician, José A. Flores. The bilingualism of Paraguay (Guaraní, Castilian) had affected the country's literary development. Now the first signs of a national form of expression began to appear; but it was only after the war of the Chaco (1932–1935) that a creative impetus was felt that integrated the entire nation. The rebellious FACUNDO RECALDE (1896), author of *Celestial Kindlings* (*Virtutas celestes*) gave himself to social themes. Together with the latter two, we should study Natalicio González, but we prefer to do so when we come to the prosists.

(xi) *Uruguay* / As we have seen in the previous chapter, the miracle of an extraordinary generation had emerged in Uruguay: the "generation of 1900," formed by none other than Reyles, Viana, Rodó, Sánchez, Quiroga, Carlos and María Eugenia Vaz Ferreira, Herrera y Reissig. They were the greatest poets of this generation. Between them and the poets that belong to this period —those born after 1885—there fell, like a shooting star, DELMIRA AGUSTINI (1886–1914). The life of a woman of ardent sex, constantly desiring the arms of men, would have no spiritual importance in itself, if it went no further than to tell us, spontaneously, what happens to her organism. Delmira Agustini was like an orchid, humid and warm; one of the themes she repeated was that of waiting, in her bed, for the visit of the nocturnal lover. But she transcended her eroticism and the delights of the body were converted into esthetic delights. The beauty of her desires acquired independent value; they became art, with the palpitations of biological life, to be sure, but spiritualized in marvelous images. No woman had dared, up to then, to make confessions of the type found in "Vision," "Another Lineage," "The Brook," in short, in all the poems of her books, from *The White Book* (*El libro blanco*, 1907) to the posthumous *The Stars of the Abyss* (*Los astros del abismo*). But these confessions are of value, not for their anecdotes of life, but for their vision of a transcendental life in which voluptuosity is sublimated in poetry. Her imaginative daring is more amazing than her immodesty. And, well considered, did not her immodesty have a good deal of the fantastic? She had experienced desire, but its carnal satisfaction, very little: her marriage had scarcely been a month old when she published her work. Her images sprout when least expected, like "gigantic mushrooms."

The poets we will now present lived longer and therefore left more complete works. They emerged from the ebbing modernist tide and they dis-

banded at times in opposite directions. In spite of disbanding, those who
wore the modernist emblem over their hearts were PABLO MINELLI GON-
ZÁLEZ (1893) and Juana de Ibarbourou. The most philosophical were the
vitalist, Sabat Ercasty, the intellectual, Oribe, and the estheticist, Casaravilla Lemos. With more symbolic intentions, Basso Maglio and Maeso
Tognochi either descended dark cellars or climbed clear allegorical towers.
Inclined toward national roots are the nativists Silva Valdés and Ipuche
and the "Negro-ist" PEREDA VALDÉS (1899). And the declamatory ÁNGEL
FALCO (1885); the epic writer, EDGARDO UBALDO GENTA (1894), the
lyricist with the gentle voice. EMILIO CARLOS TACCONI (1895) and many
others. But to stop slipping from name to name, let us pause before those
poets who will help us to illuminate the atmosphere of those years.

JUANA DE IBARBOUROU (1895) because of the purity of her
song was consecrated as "Juana of America." Whoever speaks
of her finds these words rising to their lips: flower, fruit, harvest,
gazelle, lark; that is, images of vegetable and animal elements
rapt in the joy of living. From these metaphors others emerged;
for example, her poetic work passes through the cycles of birth,
youth, maturity, and old age. At times the cycles are compared
with the four seasons of the year or the four parts of the day.
Thus, it has been said that *The Tongues of Diamond* (*Las lenguas
de diamante*, 1919) was her introduction to life one spring morning; *Savage Root* (*Raíz salvaje*, 1920) youth, one summer noon;
The Rose of the Winds (*La rosa de los vientos*, 1930) maturity,
one autumn afternoon; and *Lost* (*Perdida*, 1950) old age, one
winter night. Metaphors. Because to contemplate oneself is to
contemplate something neither vegetable nor animal, but human,
and all of Juana de Ibarbourou's poetry is persistent narcissism.
She is a female Narcissus who delights in coquetry but is troubled
by the mirror of Time in which we can see ourselves growing
uglier and dying. Young, spoiled, inviting, she felt in her flesh
the power of her beauty. She knew she was admired and desired
by men; and for these men she would describe herself, naked,
ardent, and urgent in the certainty that that supreme moment of
beauty would never be repeated. "Take me now for it is early
still / and I carry new dahlias in my hand," she urges in "The
Hour." And what are "Savage," "As Springtime," "The Afternoon" but invitations? In "Fleeting Restlessness" time is not a
theme for serious meditation, but a sensual message to the lover,

that he should not turn his eyes from that "fugitive and restless moment" in which she feels herself as beautiful as a defiant nymph. She fears old age more than death; because after all, death can fix her in that final esthetic pose. In the sonnet "Rebel" ("Charon, I shall be scandalous in your bark") she sees her naked triumph. She imagines herself dead in "Life-Hook" but, even dead, she wishes to survive as contemplated beauty: "Make my grave just below the surface," she asks her lover; "I foresee / the struggle of my flesh to return above." The mirthful coquettishness of *The Tongues of Diamond*, her best book, persists in *Savage Root* but it is suppressed by the preoccupation of encountering something new to do. In *The Rose of the Winds* the verses are no longer easy, simple, clear, pleasant, musical, but are fanned by the currents of vanguardism, they break into irregular rhythms, they become obscure in mystery, and the images aspire to surrealism. That jubilant narcissism of before is saddened and bitter. There is less feeling, more thinking. Thinking of time—"the heavy owl of time," "the moss-covered branch of time"—and of the flesh that becomes withered. "What can I give you when my youth is gone?" But she has lost her youth, and is losing her beauty. "I feel the weight of each hour / like a sack of stones upon my back. / Oh! I would free myself of this burden / and return to rosy, agile days" ("Days Without Faith"). In *Lost* Juana continues to face her mirror and, melancholy, thinks matters over. Her first poem is named, significantly, "Time" (*"Tiempo"*).

In 1912 CARLOS SABAT ERCASTY (1887) burned his poems (decadent, crepuscular, modernist) and from then on sought a healthy, exuberant, and athletic form of expression. He returned to the primitives, to ancient cultures, and in his first book, *Pantheos* (1917), he sang of the indissoluble unity of God and creation. He was excited at his own prophecies of a powerful Hispanic-America. In the vast series of his *Poems on Man* (*Poemas del hombre*, from 1921 to 1958) man as a problematic animal was its center. He managed to make his poetry a micro-man, in the same way that man is a microcosm. His later books yielded a clamorous, vital, diffuse lyricism that influenced the young Neruda. In 1953 we heard him recite his "Book of Martí" (*"Libro de Martí"*) [the ninth of his *Poems on Man* (*Poemas del hombre*)]. A great crowd was there on that night in the plaza of the cathedral in Havana, and the poet revealed spectacularly the eloquent content of his poetry. EMLIO ORIBE (1893) discarded the cold

Parnassian chisels in order to occupy himself more and more with philosophic problems. His poetry, as well as his meditations—and for him, to poetize and to meditate were simultaneous activities—showed him an interior path, always open, through which he advanced without feeling the necessity of repeating himself as many more sedentary poets do. Because of his lack of confidence in emotions and his reliance, instead, on the intellect, even on logic, poems like those in *Ars Magna* (1960) grow cold and pallid under an abstract light devoid of the colors of intuition. ENRIQUE CASARAVILLA LEMOS (1889) has a lyrical strength that sometimes goes awry, beats its head against a wall, or strays off through a path of concepts, but when it goes just right it carries him to a high plane of beauty. FERNÁN SILVA VALDÉS (1887) dazzled young writers—Jorge Luis Borges and others—with *The Water of Time* (*Agua del tiempo*, 1921), an admirable book because of its felicitous picture of the Creole world seen through the eyes of thousands of unexpected metaphors. In this way he launched an ultraist nativism or a nativist ultraism, of great success in the history of our poetry. His *Book of Ballads of the South* (*Romancero del sur*) was notable. He won renown also in the short story and in the theater. PEDRO LEANDRO IPUCHE (1889), like Silva Valdés, was an explorer of things Creole in his poems and in his short stories. His roots are in the land, and his poetic flowers, no matter how "metaphysical" they appear, come from there: see his *Dilutions* (*Diluciones*). From 1921 to 1930 his work was clearly nativist; afterward, it became increasingly profound and he entered a "metaphysical" dimension. Poetry: *The Key of the Shadow* (*La clave de la sombra*). Prose: *Patrol Island* (*Isla patrulla*). He has also written for the theater. CARLOS RODRÍGUEZ PINTOS (1895) glances about in search of elevated themes—love, fatherland—approaches them with changing styles, although always with an aristocratic attitude. VICENTE BASSO MAGLIO (1889) repudiates real things and submits to severe and at times hermetic symbols: through intuition and reflection he reaches a poetry of depth, which influenced the younger groups. Between the essential qualities held dear by the symbolists and the deep images gleaned by the surrealists lies the language of Basso Maglio, one of the most representative poets of these years. His "Song of Small Circles and Great Horizons" ("*Canción de los pequeños círculos y los grandes horizontes*") is worthy of an anthology. HUMBERTO ZARRILLI (1898) displays a lyricism of the senses in his *Passion of the Image* (*Pasión de la imagen*, 1949). JULIO J. CASAL (1889–1954) broke the soft modernist trend of his early books and from 1921 on became involved in ultraism, but this involvement was more evident in his sympathy than in his verses. From *Tree* (*Arbol*, 1923) to *Hill of Music* (*Colina de la música*, 1933) Casal went about seeking poetry, finding it, losing it, and returning to his search and to his renewed finding and loss.

(xii) *Argentina* / In Argentina, earlier than in any other country, writers purged themselves of modernist artifices. That is, in Argentina, there had been a compact group of modernists, while elsewhere only isolated voices were being heard; and, conversely, when elsewhere compact modernist groups appeared, modernism was dissolving in Argentina, and a group of moderate tone was appearing. Now the precious, the exotic, the morbid, the artistic attracts less attention than immediate human themes. The poets continue to be esthetes but their expression is simpler. After Lugones, two great poets appeared: the unprolific Banchs and the prolific Fernández Moreno.

ENRIQUE BANCHS (1888) published four books of poems— *The Barks* (*Las barcas*, 1907); *The Book of Eulogies* (*El libro de los elogios*, 1908); *The Falcon's Bell* (*El cascabel del halcón*, 1909); *The Urn* (*La urna*, 1911)—and then was silent, except perhaps for a "few pages not published in book form" that some friends gathered together in 1950. He was not an inventor of images; he did not experiment with forms; he did not affiliate with any group nor look for fame; he did not sing at the top of his voice or intervene in the usual literary polemics: and his premature renunciation of letters was his last "no" in this negative series. Yet, positively, he was liked, respected, and admired, even by the youngest poets. Banchs gravitated toward poetry— he says so himself in "The Vow"—"like a pilgrim / full of saintly fears is timid in approaching / the altar, all in linen and light and silver and snow." He wanted perfection, but, stupefied and trembling, would not step past the threshold. His verses, always polished, became thin and transparent until they took on a fragile subtlety. From the modernists he learned the cult of perfection, but without the ornamental tricks that often were sheer substitutes for that perfection. Some of Banchs' sonnets are the best that have been written in Argentina. The one that begins "Hospitable and faithful to his reflection" is of such proficiency that one is impressed that Banchs should renounce this skill in order to write such simple, such elemental, such naked verses as the tender ones in "Stammering" or verses as folkloric as his ballads and songs. He lived in the Castilian, purely Spanish, classical tradition of poetry. He was a pure poet: although occasionally he wrote a verse or two with a social bearing or realist description. As he sang in his first three books of the beauty he saw or imagined, there was a growing buoyant revelation of his inner self. These were the years of wholesome wonder at the harmony of the world, but Banchs still covered himself with symbols, surrounded himself with sumptuous objects, entwined himself in literary language. Then the poet revealed his sadness and his own misfortunes directly. This is when he published *The Urn* which contains one hundred sonnets, a book in which we see him uncomplaining, yet meditative and melancholy.

BALDOMERO FERNÁNDEZ MORENO (1886–1950) wrote steadily from the time he published his first book, *The Initials of the Missal* (*Las iniciales del misal*, 1915) to *Penumbra: The Book of Marcela* (*Penumbra: El libro de Marcela*, 1951). He admired Darío, but from another esthetic perspective. By giving his attention to what lay nearest to him he added themes to Argentine poetry which the modernists, with their eyes fixed on the distance, had failed to perceive. He attained simplicity through discipline. The trait that he had in common with Bufano, Camino, Mariani and Pedro Herreros has been called "simplicity." According to his son, César, the "epoch of simplicity," of sentimental spontaneity, lasted until 1923: *Provincial Interlude (Intermedio provinciano)*, *The City* (*Ciudad*), *Argentine Countryside* (*Campo argentino*); from that time until 1937 the poet went through a "formal epoch," when he was largely concerned with artistic canons: *Décimas* (ten-line stanzas), *Sonetos* (sonnets), *Seguidillas* (dances), *Romances* (ballads). In 1937 the death of a son seriously affected his nervous system. "I am no longer the same," he told me years later, while we were riding through Buenos Aires. His "substantial epoch" dated from this year on, when he synthesized the previous epochs but deepened his insight until he reached the lowest depths of his disillusion and bitterness: *Penumbra*. Perhaps the poet was right in explaining his anthology in these terms: "There is an impressive unity which I certainly never set out to achieve—I simply paid heed to the natural exhalation of my being." What is evident is the uniqueness of its origin. Fernández saw himself as a poet, at times gratified, at times ironic. And his poems generally reflect, with the fidelity of a mirror, this image of a poet aware that he is a poet. Then we catch him in the act of taking a blank notebook and going out into the street or road, to walk and walk, looking at everything with the eyes of an impressionist. "All of my 'art of poetry' can be reduced to going out. When I return home I have something to write [*Last Floor* (*Ultimo piso*)]. "What is important to me / is to see and observe" ("Hexasyllables of the Casino"). "I see the world in lyric fragments, nothing else" ("Argentine Theater"). He went through life in love with humble things and, by simply looking at them, would save them for poetry. Those who could believe that his poetry was trivial because his themes were trivial —the city of Buenos Aires, the country folk, the fields, the home, his literary life, his labors and leisure moments; his memories of childhood in Spain, his inner life, made sweet by love or startled by death, were unable to understand the depth of his imagination. He seems to see only what we all see, but he surprises us [as in "Autumn Sea" (*"Mar de Otoño"*), to mention one of many poems]. His verses appear to be elementary, but they are complex. Simple but not prosaic. Sincere but not ordinary. Fernández Moreno was the type of poet who plants himself where he lives and looks about him, faithful to what he is as a man, and to what things are when seen in their essence. For him there was no one object more poetic than another: all things, the most common, the most insignificant, the smallest and most transitory, had their place in poetry. Each tiny portion of reality excited his imagination; and with two or three strokes he would give it meaningful beauty. Like all good impressionists, he was a fragmentary poet who respected the unique validity of each separate thing. However, on a few occasions his images would continue in a series, in the expressionist style: "Shepherd of Verses" (*"Pastor de versos"*), "Full Moon" (*"Plenilunio"*). The unity of his enraptured vision of the world is truly admirable. There lies the world for him to sing about heartily. The poet may be sad, downcast, and melancholy, but being able to sing gives joy to his life. His sensorial impressions are laid bare by beautiful flashes of light. He had a gift for defining, for drawing in miniature, for synthesizing lyrically. Things take shape in metaphors; the metaphors are softly tinged with the sentimental touch of the poet. There is also ingenuity—and even humor, running the gamut from sarcasm to jocularity—which as strokes of pure genius can be best seen in his aphoristic prose—*The Butterfly and the Rafter* (*La mariposa y la viga*, 1947). His language—learned because of all he had read and heard—was that of all Hispania.

Banchs and Fernández Moreno moved in a traditional, classical, Hispanic current, and in this current was another group—AUGUSTO GONZÁLEZ CASTRO, 1897; CARLOS OBLIGADO, 1890–1949; ARTURO VÁZQUEZ CEY, 1888–1958; EUGENIO JULIO IGLESIAS, 1897; PEDRO HERREROS, 1890–1937; and ANTONIO PÉREZ-VALIENTE DE MOCTEZUMA, 1895—from which we will only select Cané and Marasso. LUIS CANÉ (1897–1957) gave Creole shading to the old voice of the Spanish people. Gracefully, freshly, and sensually he wrote ballads, couplets, and songs on love and adventure, past and present. ARTURO MARASSO (1890), a student of the classics, learned from them how to sing about universal themes, especially those of human destiny.

Some poets still clung to romantic styles, others to modernist styles. Let us look at them in two groups. Among those of romantic tone—because of the intensity of her personal confession —stands ALFONSINA STORNI (Switzerland-Argentina, 1892–1938). She kindled her poetry with the embers of her resentment against men, but she also damaged it by leaving too much esthetic ash. She explained it thus: "I am, in general, superior to the average men around me, but physically, as a woman, I am their slave, their mold, their clay. I cannot love them freely: there is too much pride in me to submit to them. I lack the physical means to subdue them. The torment I feel is superior to my desire to write poetry . . ." She saw herself a humiliated, conquered, tortured woman, but, nonetheless, with a pagan need for love. She searched for it desperately. She had no illusions: she knew what a man was. "Your catacombs inundated by dead / obscure, muddy waters were / by these hands felt." Love of men but at the same time disillusionment and even disgust. An original note, therefore, in erotic feminine poetry. The theme: a disdainful, ironic, and always frustrated love of the male, "master of the world," for whom a woman is nothing but a "feast." The books of this first manner ran from *Sweet Mischief* (*El dulce daño*, 1918) to *Ochre* (*Ocre*, 1925), perhaps her best. In the end, Storni triumphs in her struggle against the male, but at the cost of her sensitivity. It is the triumph that the plant wins over its sap by drying up. The most tale-telling symbol had been, up to *Ochre*

(*Ocre*), that of a violent and almost paradisiacal spring, as if Alfonsina always felt her flesh flowering. She abandoned her eroticism in *The World of Seven Wells* (*El mundo de siete pozos*, 1934) and also the modernist make-up of her verses. Looking for images hidden in things, she disarranged all the drawers of her verse and became a belated companion of the vanguardists. Life is not worth living, she seems to tell us. She had had an easy literary success, because there were people who sympathized with her human struggles. But she, who had valiantly proclaimed her liberty as a woman, was also valiant in literature: she renounced her successes, she renounced her admirers and began a new type of poetry—tortured, intellectual, of different rhythms— that took her away from her old public but brought her no new public. Now she stylized her non-passionate, serenely deceptive experiences in symbols of obscure keys: *Mask and Trefoil* (*Mascarilla y trébol*, 1938). She knew she was through. She wrote a sonnet—"I go to my sleep"—simply and meekly, then went out to sea to drown herself.

Also romantic in tone is ARTURO CAPDEVILA (1889), although more eloquent than lyrical. First there was an accent of anguish (from *Melpomene*, 1912, to *Book of Night—El libro de la noche*, 1917). Then, beginning with *World Holiday* (*La fiesta del mundo*, 1922) he was resigned and even happy, and he spoke of his adolescence, of his voyages, of his civic feelings, of his thoughts. His language—rich in nuances—often flows spontaneously like sincerity itself: then it moves us. In his best instances —e.g., *Melpomene*—his verses quiver with the mystery of human depth.

Let us bring this group to a close with ENRIQUE MÉNDEZ CALZADA (1898–1940), HÉCTOR PEDRO BLOMBERG (1890–1955), and PEDRO MIGUEL OBLIGADO (1888).

In the second group, the poets of modernist style, the best are Ezequiel Martínez Estrada and Arrieta. The first will be studied later with the essayists of this generation. RAFAEL ALBERTO ARRIETA (1889) is a lyricist without excesses, limited, but within whose limits one sees, hears and feels things. He is elegant, demure, cold, and brief. *Soul and Moment* (*Alma y momento*, 1910), *The Mirror of the Fountain* (*El espejo de la fuente*, 1912), *Golden Nights* (*Las noches de oro*, 1917), *Fugacity* (*Fugacidad*, 1921), *Highland Summer* (*Estío serrano*, 1926) and *Captive Time* (*Tiempo cautivo*, 1947) are the subtle and veiled confidences of a distinctive spirit, more Nordic than Latin, who polished the crystal of symbolism without achieving the transparencies of pure poetry. His poetry is tender, sweet and elegiac. This group closes with FERNÁN FÉLIX DE AMADOR (1889–1954) and ÁLVARO MELIÁN LAFINUR (1889–1958). And still another group could be introduced here, those poets immersed in their American regions, such as JUAN CARLOS DÁVALOS (1887–1959), ALFREDO R. BUFANO (1895–1950) and ATALIVA HERRERA (1888–1953). A partial Lugones—the one of the *Sentimental Lunar Poems*—and a complete Macedonio Fernández was the farthest reach of the modernist generation: and this is recognized by the young postwar ultraists. Between these two modernists and the young ultraists, there were poets who were coming and going, and the abnormality consisted in their coming and going. Of those born during the last fifteen years of the nineteenth century, some approached ultraism. Ricardo Güiraldes, in *The Crystal Cowbell* (*El cencerro de cristal*, 1915), had poems which anticipated the watchwords of ultraism —"to drink what comes / to have the soul of a prow," can be read in "Travel"—and, in fact, he joined in the revision of *Proa* and *Martín Fierro;* however Güiraldes will be studied as a writer of prose. The anomaly of ÉVAR MÉNDEZ (1888–1955) is not in his own work—four books of poems that would not have alarmed Rubén Darío—but in his enthusiasm for the work of the younger group. He directed *Martín Fierro,* introduced some ultraist poems, and paraded the banner of an esthetic movement not his own. For his playful wit and his acrobatics, mention can be made of EMILIO LASCANO TEGUI (1887). He made himself a "viscount" for the same caprice that Ducasse had made himself "count of Lautréamont." His verses *The Shadow of la Empusa* (*La sombra de la Empusa*, 1910); *The Singing Tree* (*El árbol que canta*, 1911); *Boy from San Telmo* (*Muchacho de San Telmo*, 1954) and his prose works *On Elegance While One Sleeps* (*De la elegancia mientras se duerme*, 1925) are fanciful, humorous, dextrous. An *enfant terrible* was OLIVERIO GIRONDO (1891). He was not a child when he committed his first act of mischief: *Twenty Poems to Be Read in the Trolley* (*Veinte poemas para ser leídos en el tranvía*, 1922). But he did approach the postwar boys, formed an ultraist gang; and when the boys grew up and became serious, Girondo remained a child. He grew old without growing in ultraist stature. He is the Peter Pan of Argentine ultraism. He edited the manifesto of the review *Martín Fierro* (1924): a nationalist program by a reader of Apollinaire, Morand, and Max Jacob. Girondo is aphoristic, explosive, disoriented, metaphoric, dadaist, and surrealist in verse *Decalcomanias* (*Calcomanías*, 1925) as well as in prose *Scarecrows* (*Espantapájaros*, 1932). In *Persuading Days* (*Persuasión de los días*, 1942) and above all in *Our Fields* (*Campo nuestro*, 1946) it looked as if he might change; but in *The Moremarrow* (*La masmédula*, 1954) he returned to his own, which is a bell-ringing lyricism.

B. MAINLY PROSE

In this generation, daughter of modernist esthetics, there were brilliant prosists (Alfonso Reyes). They continued writing novels and short stories with the ideals of lyrical prose dating from the time of Rubén Darío (Pedro Prado). And even in the realist narratives, there is still the memory of the great parade of artistic prose which had filed by with its torches, its brass bands and colorful streamers, through the streets of 1900, showing everyone how to write with esthetic decorum and impressionistic techniques (Gallegos, Rivera, Güiraldes, Guzmán, Barrios). But realism and naturalism, of course, continued in their own direction, ever more certain, more masters of themselves, more determined to narrate actions that interest everyone (Pocaterra, Latorre). The essayist prose of thinkers and humanists was important (Pedro Henríquez Ureña, Martínez Estrada, Vasconcelos, Reyes).

1. Novel and Short Story

We shall present the production of narrative prose by dividing it into national groups, moving in geographic order from north to south. In each national group we shall speak first of the more subjective writers and then of the more objective ones. Since it would be superfluous to repeat, as we go from one nation to another, the same theoretic distinctions between the two narrative styles, let us define their characteristics now, once and for all.

(a) *Narrators More Subjective than Objective* / Instead of sharing with us a contemplation of the world, these narrators confide in us their contemplation of themselves; instead of a reality unfolded on large surfaces, an introverted reality focused on the depths of the imagination. That is to say, a de-realized reality. Although these narrators cannot help but relate what happens to certain men who dream or struggle in the midst of problematic social situations or in the midst of nature, rather than rely on the reality they are describing, what they do is plunge into themselves.

(b) *Narrators More Objective than Subjective* / Whether they reacted against modernism or ignored it, or while respecting it did not feel it was viable for what they wished to say, the fact is there was a family of narrators of unimpeachable realist souls. Some studied life in the cities, but the majority of them worked with folkloric and regional material. Most of them took advantage of the interest that readers had in these matters: the reader tended to have illusions. His lack of literary awareness led him to believe that the author was sincere; the morose description of customs led him to believe that what the author was saying had the value of reality; indigenous words used profusely led him to believe that the author was giving a correct vision of the Indian. Many novelists, instead of creating persons, used to propose names and then tell us that those who bore these names were living and moving on some part of this earth. They would bring in a "problem" from outside and when they had reached a certain number of pages the novel was done. The reader was deceived into believing that these men existed as persons, that those "problems" converted the novels into vigorous allegations. As he studied the novels and short stories, the critic, assailed by a sudden dizziness—the authors are in the hundreds, the titles in the thousands—seeks some support to lean on to keep from falling. One of these supports might be a thematic arrangement: stories of the city, the country, the jungle, the mountain, the coasts; or stories about work in the mines, in workshops, in fruit mills; or about the Indian, the mestizo, the Negro, the Creole, the *gringo;* or about history, ethnography, sociology, politics, anti-imperialism, psychology. We must remember that what is valuable in literature is not the themes, but what the novelists do with these themes.

(i) *Mexico* / The most brilliant: Alfonso Reyes. Like quicksilver, he escapes through our fingers. He escaped from verse to prose; and, within prose, he escapes from the narrative. We will corner him among the essayists, although he deserves a prominent place as a poet and a narrator. Another very subtle Mexican: JULIO TORRI (1889). He has published very little: *Essays and Poems* (*Ensayos y poemas*, 1917); *On Executions* (*De fusilamientos*, 1940); plus *Miscellaneous Prose* (*Prosas dispersas*) form one volume: *Three Books* (*Tres libros*, 1964). His prose is sharp, intentional, malicious. It represses smiles. But he who does not divine the smile is deceived. Intelligence shows up with such grace that one greets it as if it were the poetry itself. His poetic prose is really constructed with intelligence, an intelligence that controls the imagination. *The Flight of Illusion* (*La fuga de la Quimera*, 1915) by CARLOS GONZÁLEZ PEÑA (1885-1955) was one of the first novels which denounced, directly or via the characters, the unnecessary violence of the Mexican revolution. But the revolution is not its theme, but only one of the circumstances. The theme is—as the title indicates—the evasiveness of the illusions of love that exist in three couples. Pure, frustrated and carnal loves—and in the center the drama of a marriage between a young girl and an old man and the predictable adultery. The time: between 1910 and 1913. The scene: Mexico City. The social class: upper middle class, with glimpses of poor families and of Sofia's rapid progress. What happens is true to life. In minor episodes we even have the appearance of famous personages, like the poet Luis Urbina, who recites one of his sad poems in a distinguished salon. But the novel is not a realist novel. It narrates the events in a logical order and with clear architectonic lines, but the attention focused on the psychological life of the characters, the esthetic quality of the descriptions, and the care given to the sentences, place the novel in the modernist school. González Peña sees things from the point of view of a cultured, elegant European. The destructive fury of the revolution in the final scenes is brought into the novel in the way the forces of nature used to be brought into romantic novels, to create an analogy between that fury and the conflict in human souls and so embellish the tragic end. This is esthetic vision, not political.

The revolution of 1910 in Mexico, one of the few Hispanic-American revolutions to really change the economic and social structure of a country, stirred up a whole novelistic cycle.

The cycle was opened by Mariano Azuela, whom we have studied already. Some narrated the fighting itself; others, its consequences. Novelists of both these phases in this period were Guzmán, López y Fuentes, Romero, Muñoz, Mancisidor, Urquizo (in the following period these will be added: Icaza, Campobello, Iduarte, Rojas González, Magdaleno, Ferretis). After Azuela came JOSÉ RUBÉN ROMERO (1890–1952) with *A Villager's Notes* (*Apuntes de un lugareño*, 1932) and *Disbandment* (*Desbandada*, 1934); both are pictured with autobiographical strokes. Beneath the comicality of his types, the situations in which he puts them, and the language he makes them speak, there is, in Rubén Romero, a bitter undercurrent. In *Anticipation of Death* (*Anticipación a la muerte*, 1939) that underground river of bitterness comes closer to the surface than in his earlier novels; e.g., *The Useless Life of Pito Pérez* (*La vida inútil de Pito Pérez*, 1938) presents, during the years of social dissolution which followed the revolution, a rogue from the lower class who is convincing because of his typical Mexican traits. The malicious novel *My Horse, My Dog and My Rifle* (*Mi caballo, mi perro y mi rifle*, 1936) is perhaps the best.

Only because of the common theme of the Mexican revolution do we include here MARTÍN LUIS GUZMÁN (1887), since because of his more artistic style, he should be treated separately. He published the biography of *The Youthful Mina, Hero of Navarre* (*Mina el mozo, héroe de Navarra*, 1932), *Memoirs of Pancho Villa* (*Memorias de Pancho Villa*, 1940) and *Historical Deaths* (*Muertes históricas*, 1959). (The *Memoirs* are not autobiographical: Guzmán, who never concealed his sympathy for Villa—whom he knew personally—makes him speak as he must have spoken, using his imagination here and there where documents are missing, but using it with so much knowledge of the sources that these *Memoirs,* apocryphal and all, are more authentic than those set down by politicians and militarists.) By then he was famous for *The Eagle and the Serpent* (*El águila y la serpiente*, 1928)' and *The Shadow of the Caudillo* (*La sombra del caudillo*, 1930). *The Eagle and the Serpent* is not a novel but a bouquet of stories, all of them having blossomed from the revolutionary experiences of the author. The prose is vigorous and vigorously resists the very dangerous temptations of this type of literature, that of falling into political chronicle. Stylistic vigor, then, which is the only kind that counts in a history of literature. His impressionism, especially outstanding in its pictorial technique, does not disturb the rapidity of the action. Guzmán carries his theme with the muscles of a well-trained style. *The Shadow of the Caudillo* surpasses this one because it is a more ambitious literary project, better organized as a work of art. But, since it is a novel and not an ensemble of chronicles, like *The Eagle and the Serpent*, one is more demanding. And because of this artistic demand—a demand which tends to remain unsatisfied—the taste of the reader vacillates for a moment and he does not know which of the two books best measures the real talent of the author. *The Shadow of the Caudillo* begins with artistic phrases that are rich in impressionistic word pictures. But the whirlpool of action snatches the prose and drowns it in a chronicle of infamy, treachery, ignominy, crimes, abuses, vices that take place during the political intrigues of the Obregón and Calles era, toward the end of 1927 in the city of Mexico and its environs. The Mexican revolution appears here in its farcical electoral process. There is not a single noble figure: not even Axkaná is convincing, since he is also involved in the shady intrigues of others, though he has more scruples. And one is horrified at the cold precision with which Guzmán describes gun-rule in Mexican politics. He has not created any memorable characters because his interest was more sociological. The novel has no unity. The early chapters suggest a situation (Rosario-Aguirre) that later has no development or importance. Nor does it have stylistic unity: impressionistic preciosity in the early chapters, objective prose later. What is most interesting, and in keeping with the tone of a novel, is the intrigue, the conspiracy, the violence at the end. A good novel, all in all. His novel *The Marian Islands* (*Islas Marías*) has cinematographic rhythm.

Little by little, the novel of the revolution lost part of its violence and attended more to social problems. At times the living conditions of the Indians were brought to light, or the ups and downs of political life, or the revolutionary repercussions in the provinces, and even the uprising of the Catholics against the Revolution, as in *The Virgin of the Cristeros* (*La Virgen de los Cristeros*, 1934) by FERNANDO ROBLES (1897). FRANCISCO L. URQUIZO (1891) was a chronicler of precious style. One of the best novels in this period is *They Took the Cannon to Bachimba* (*Se llevaron el cañón para Bachimba*) by RAFAEL F. MUÑOZ (1899), who relates in episodes that are disconnected but in sequence the revolutionary apprenticeship of a boy of thirteen in the ranks of the "*colorados*" who fought against the government of Madero in 1912. It recalls something of *Don Segundo Sombra*, not only because of the boy's devotion to Marcos Ruiz (the general fighting for Orozco), but also because of the idealization of the landscape and of the military feats, and for the richness of its images. But of course, Muñoz' novel has a violence foreign to Güiraldes'. Here, the civil war is related in the midst of revolution. The character Marcos Ruiz would have been more authentic if Muñoz had not put, especially toward the end, moral, political, and revolutionary discourses in his mouth. The novel's action is rapid, like the war, although the author never surrenders his slow-paced description of things, scenes, fields, and villages. And to be certain, the best of the prose, notable for its precision and for the energy of its images, lies in the description. His imagery is not just adornment but impressions of all his senses, experienced by the author and efficaciously used throughout the story. Thus, together with the military action, we are given always the imaginative visions of the protagonist-narrator. The equilibrium between the novel's action and the poetic contemplation is well achieved. JOSÉ MANCISIDOR (1895–1956) sacrificed the art of his best works to Marxist politics. *The Riot* (*La asonada*, 1931) interprets the revolution from the Communist point of view: his denunciations of imperialism, militarism, and religious fanaticism respond to the aims of political propaganda. His novel *Frontier by the Sea* (*Frontera junto al mar*, 1953) opens with the struggle of the people of Vera Cruz against the United States' invasion. The characters are intentionally scarcely individualized. Then he published *Dawn in the Chasms* (*El alba en las simas*) and *María Kainlová Told Me* (*Me lo dijo María Kainlová*, 1956). GREGORIO LÓPEZ Y FUENTES (1897) has written a number of novels of the Mexican scene; the scene—political, anthropological, folkloric, social—tends to be more interesting than the novels themselves. At times the novels study the characters psychologically: *My General!* (*¡Mi general!*), *Huasteca, The Compliant One* (*Acomodaticio*), *Mezzanine* (*Entresuelo*). But his preference for social study is more obvious: *Encampment* (*Campamento*), *Land* (*Tierra*), *The Indian* (*El indio*), *Muleteers* (*Arrieros*) and recently, *Cornfield, Cattle-Ranch and Mountain* (*Milpa, potrero y monte*, 1951) where he denounces the sufferings of the field worker, the cowhand, and the deer hunter personified by three brothers. *The Indian* (1935) is made up of separate scenes—basted together with a tenuous thread of a plot, which is the history of the Lame One—on the life of an indigenous Indian tribe during the years of the revolution. It deals with ethnography (superstitions, customs), sociology (social intercourse, work and property matters, class struggles) and above all politics (the exploitation of the Indians, their claims and the interplay of vested interests). It presents such an abstract attitude that it blurs the individuality of the characters: they don't even have proper names (the hunter, the old man, the teacher, the girl). But this is not an abstraction that a man of science would deal with, because everything is constructed in the form of a political allegation where one protests—with bitter reflections, or simply in the manner of setting up the episodes—against injustice.

The revolution shook intellectual life to such a degree that many of those who would have preferred to stay on their sun roofs looking over European fashions from a distance had to come down quickly, plant their feet firmly on the ground, travel about the territories, find out what was going on, and understand the people, their customs, their folklore. Among these intellectuals who rediscovered Mexico there were those with the souls of historians. Alongside pro-Indian and revolutionary literature, then, there were those who, about 1917, looked back to the colonial period. They are called the "colonialists": Genaro Estrada, Francisco Monterde, Artemio de Valle-Arizpe, Julio Jiménez Rueda, Ermilo Abreu Gómez. The satirist of the group was GENARO ESTRADA (1887–1937), author of four books of verse, very Mexican in their polished transparency—though the crystal may have tinges of Góngora and García Lorca—published from 1928 to 1934, and of a comely novel, *Pero Galín*, 1926, charming, intelligent in its confrontation of the old with the new. Estrada, an antique collector, a bibliographer, a colonialist, seems to have caricaturized himself in his character, a man with a mania for the archaic, oblivious of the present, who suddenly marries an ultramodern young girl, breaks into the movie world, and is cured of his anachronism. The novelistic elements are minimal; the essayistic prose, sharp and good-humored, is what is most entertaining. ARTEMIO DE VALLE-ARIZPE (1888–1961) never strayed from his rut, painting beautiful pictures with the dust of archives, museums, and libraries of the colonial period. In spite of its dissonances and changes of key, his prose has charm. Of his many books perhaps the most vital one is *The Newsboy* (*El Canillitas*, 1942). FRANCISCO MONTERDE (1894) is a poet, dramatist, and novelist. The scholar within him pulls him toward criticism, and even his personal literature has a historical aspect. His theater is important and has represented the political, social, and psychological themes of the rural environment with fine lyrical intuitions. As a novelist, he began with revolutionary themes; then he wrote novels of the viceregal period—*The Madrigal of Cetina* (*El madrigal de Cetina*) and *The Secret of the "Escala"* (*El secreto de la "Escala"*). He is one of the best cultivators of the historical novel in this generation—*Montezuma, the One of the Golden Chair* (*Moctezuma el de la silla de oro*), *Montezuma II, Lord of the Anáhuac* (*Moctezuma II, señor del Anáhuac*); the narrative of *The Fear of Hernán Cortés* (*El temor de Hernán Cortés*) reveals serious study, a desire for a critical revision of the past, and a fresh imagination. ERMILO ABREU GÓMEZ (1894) began in the theater with themes of colonial Mexico: *Long Live the King* (*Viva el rey*, 1921), *Humanities* (*Humanidades*, 1924), *Ballads of Kings* (*Romances de reyes*, 1926). Later without abandoning the theater—*A Play of Scorn* (*Un juego de escarnio*, 1943); *A Parrot and Three Swallows* (*Un loro y tres golondrinas*, 1945)—he extended his alert and novel prose to other themes and genres: poetic stories on the lives of Mayan heroes—*Canek* (1940); stories for children—*Juan Pirulero* (1939) and *Three New Stories About Juan Pirulero* (*Tres nuevos cuentos de Juan Pirulero*, 1944). Of greater scope are *Quetzalcóatl, Dream and Vigil* (*Quetzalcóatl, sueño y vigilia*, 1947), stories on the life of the indigenous god. One of his best works is *Shipwrecked Indians* (*Naufragio de indios*, 1951), a novel about a little Mexican village that protests the invasion of the French. Maximilian's emissaries arrive in town to recruit troops—the rich cede, the poor resist, youths conspire, women pray. The story advances by means of a savory language. The episodes are like watercolors with incisive lines and variegated quantities of color. The title of the first page alludes to the tragedy of the last page: a French ship sinks with its cargo of Indian prisoners. In *Tata Lobo* (1952) he has created, in a gracious style of archaic and popular flavor, if not one of those anti-heroes of picaresque literature, in any case a rogue-hero lost in the chaos of Mexican life; he trudges along from adventure to adventure, but at times he leaps as though he were flying. In the form of a letter-novel he began his memoirs in *Day Was Dawning . . .* (*La del alba sería . . .*, 1954). In *The Conspiracy of Xinum* (*La conjura de Xinum*, 1958) he novelizes the violence of the indigenous uprisings in the Yucatán peninsula, a class war that lasted from 1847 to 1902. ANTONIO CASTRO LEAL (1896), though better known for his literary studies, wrote outstanding stories of fantasy: *The Laurel Wreath of St. Lawrence* (*El laurel de San Lorenzo*, 1959).

(ii) *Central America / Guatemala:* RAFAEL ARÉVALO MARTÍNEZ (1884), poet and novelist. The simplicity of some of his poems ("Clean Clothes"), the invoking of simple good fortune ("Dream of Good Fortune"), the simple traditional themes (religion in "Prayer to the Lord")—none of this should deceive us; Arévalo Martínez is not a poet of simple soul, but one twisted in nervous and sickly convolutions. More than in his verses—from *Jugglings* (*Juglerías*, 1911) to *Along This Little Path* (*Por un caminito así*, 1947) passing through his celebrated *The Roses of Engaddi* (*Las rosas de Engaddi*, 1927)—he has revealed himself in his stories and novels. Above all in *The Man Who Looked Like a Horse* (*El hombre que parecía un caballo*, 1914), which was the most original story of his generation. It is said that that selfish, strong, arrogant, blasphemous, and amoral man-horse was the caricature of the poet Barba Jacob. But a caricature is judged worthy in relation to its model; whereas the story we are commenting on is valuable in itself, as a delirious vision. It has a nightmarish and poetic atmosphere which we knew in Jean Lorrain and today we recognize in Franz Kafka. He wrote other psychozoological stories, namely, *The Colombian Troubadour* (*El trovador colombiano*, 1914), whose main character is a tame, humble, loyal man-dog.

In them we also have "the man who looked like an elephant," and "the man who looked like a tiger." Many years later Arévalo Martínez tells us that a spiritualist friend gathered, in one of her trips to the world beyond, two stories written by a witness to the events that "date back to olden times, millennia ago, when the earth had but one continent, Atlán, which preceded Lemuria and Atlantis": both these Utopias, *The World of the Maharachías* (*El mundo de los maharachías*, 1938) and *Voyage to Ipanda* (*Viaje a Ipanda*, 1939), are interwoven. The first is the more poetic: just as the shipwrecked Gulliver found among the Houyhnhnms a civilization of creatures that looked like horses, the shipwrecked Manuol finds a civilization of creatures that look like monkeys that are also superior to men. They are the "*maharachías*," whose tails are almost spiritual organs. Contrary to that of Swift, Arévalo Martínez' tone is not satiric. One can picture the good-humored smile, and no more, with which the author lyrically describes the love of Manuol for Aixa and Isabel, the warm land of philosophic monkeys and the beauty of their sensitive tails. The novel is not successful, however. The thought does not keep in step with the fantasy. When in *Voyage to Ipanda*—which is an outgrowth of *The World of the Maharachías*—this thought attempts to construct a Utopia with intellectual and political pretensions, the result is worse. Even less interesting, as a novel, is the political outline of *The Torlanian Ambassador* (*El embajador de Torlania,* 1960).

FLAVIO HERRERA (1892). "I'm of romantic origin," says one of the characters in *Ashes* (*Cenizas*), stories written in 1923. "I have read Bourget," says another. In this sentimental zone, and with a touch of the psychological narrator, Flavio Herrera tells his stories, all about love, with a varied gallery of women as a background. The unraveling of each story throws light on the psychology of the characters. The prose moves rapidly and nervously, but along an old artistic river bed: a Frenchified, modernist river bed, with measured turns. As a poet, his lyrical temperament was put into practice in Japanese *haikus*. In poetic prose he also described peasant surroundings. His works: *The Tiger* (*El tigre*), *The Storm* (*La tempestad*), *Chaos* (*Caos*). The poems in *Crossbeam* (*Solera,* 1962) are from different epochs. CARLOS WYLD OSPINA (1891–1958) forms, with Arévalo Martínez and Flavio Herrera, a trio of the best Guatemalan narrators of the artistic style. Like his colleagues, he was a poet: *The Simple Gifts* (*Las dádivas simples,* 1921) is a serene and elegant song to sowing time and to tillers of the soil. Then he wrote short stories: *The Land of the Nahuyacas* (*La tierra de las nahuyacas,* 1933) and novels: *The Gonzagas' Manor House* (*El solar de los Gonzagas,* 1924) and *The Immigrant's Daughter* (*La Gringa,* 1935). In precise, disciplined self-complacent prose he depicts scenes of the tropics and tells of Creole life. Even the pages that appear naturalistic are measured with an artistic yardstick. Another Guatemalan, JOSÉ RODRIGUEZ CERNA (1889–1952), although not a novelist, deserves a place of honor among poetic prose writers. He is author of the beautiful landscapes in *Lands of Sun and Mountain* (*Tierras de sol y de montaña*). CARLOS SAMAYOA CHINCHILLA (1898), the author of *Mother Cornfield* (*Madre Milpa*) and *Four Chances* (*Cuatro suertes*), seeks the picturesque in the regional scene. He penetrates the Guatemalan reality by several routes: the Mayan legend, the still-active folklore, the country's history, the direct observation of customs, his own experiences. Samayoa Chinchilla moves in whichever of these routes he chooses with a dignified and cultured bearing, making no concessions to plebeian notions. Yet, he is not original: his literature is the same as that cultivated in many other countries, not in the material elaborated, but in the style.

Honduras: CARLOS IZAGUIRRE (1894–1956) used his novel, *Beneath the Cloudburst* (*Bajo el chubasco*), to communicate his political ideas.

El Salvador: ALBERTO RIVAS BONILLA (1891) writes narratives on local customs in rural environments: *Doings and Ill-Doings* (*Andanzas y malandanzas*), *I Mount My Colt* (*Me monto en un potro*).

Nicaragua: HERNÁN ROBLETO (1895), in *Blood in the Tropics: The*

Novel of Yankee Intervention in Nicaragua (Sangre en el trópico. La novela de la intervención yanqui en Nicaragua, 1930), gave us the chronicle of the civil war between liberals and conservatives in 1926. Sandino is absent from these pages. The United States appears as the invading force, on the side of the conservatives. Robleto, who took part in this war on the liberal side, does not dissimulate his partiality. He makes propaganda, not against the people of the United States, but against the influence of Wall Street on the foreign policy of the State Department. The United States is represented as a giant intervening between two quarreling dwarfs (liberals and conservatives) in order to protect one of them. Robleto seems to admire the Americans and even wishes to win their good will. The novel ends with a sentimental episode: Sergeant Clifford Williams, who had raped a little Creole, searches her out at the war's end and marries her. In a political framework, this chronicle—for it is a novelistic chronicle, more than a novel—records the sufferings of men, the violence of the struggle, and what is most impressionable, the devastating action of nature on its social ills. A prose without imagination: communicative, objective, descriptive. In *The Stranglers: Yankee Imperialism in Nicaragua (Los estranguladores. El imperialismo yanqui en Nicaragua,* 1933) he re-accentuated his position. *Fixed Sights (Brújulas fijas,* 1962) is a novel about a Spaniard who comes to Central America to make his fortune.

Costa Rica: FRANCISCO SOLER (1888–1920) was a modernist in his themes of the Italian Renaissance. MANUEL SEGURA MÉNDEZ (1895) was a poet and novelist. MOISÉS VINCENZI (1895), an essayist of philosophic themes, published several novels intellectually conceived, with thematic and technical novelties: they go from *Atlante* (1924) to *Elvira* (1940).

The person who distinguished herself most for her direct observation of local reality and for the use she made of folklore was CARMEN LYRA (1888–1951). She was a school teacher and militant in political movements favoring the working class. Her love for children and for people shows in her books: *The Fantasies of Juan Silvestre (Las fantasías de Juan Silvestre)* and *In a Wheelchair (En una silla de ruedas),* both of 1918, and *The Stories of My Aunt Panchita (Los cuentos de mi Tía Panchita,* 1920). This last book has given her the most fame. It is a collection of traditional stories, from written and oral sources, refurbished in popular Costa Rican language. Worthy of note are GONZALO SÁNCHEZ BONILLA (1884), ANIBAL RENI (1897), GONZALO CHACÓN TREJOS (1896). And separately, for his artistic stylization of the Costa Rican reality, LUIS DOBLES SEGREDA (1891–1956), author of *For the Love of God (Por el amor de Dios), Mystic Rose (Rosa mística),* and *Wild Cane (Caña brava).*

Panama: JOAQUÍN DARÍO JAÉN (1893–1932) published stories and novels filled with morbidities that remind one of Vargas Vila.

The short story was cultivated first, and not until the year 1930 did a group of novelists emerge. On the realist side are JOSÉ MARÍA NÚÑEZ (1894) with his *Creole Stories (Cuentos criollos)* and JOSÉ E. HUERTA (1899) with his stories of local customs in *Peasant Soul (Alma campesina).* Less significant is MANUEL DE JESÚS QUIJANO (1884–1950).

(iii) *Antilles / Cuba:* No one will deny a place in our history to ALFONSO HERNÁNDEZ CATÁ (1885–1940) merely because part of his career was spent in Spain. He is a short-story writer conscious of the formal dignity of his genre, richly observant of external detail and intricate psychological conformations. His sense of pathos brings him close to melodrama, but he has enough discretion to stay on the right side of the dividing line—the side of tragedy. His favorite theme is abnormal psychology, sometimes treated with irony, sometimes with compassion. When least expected Cuba appears in the stories. In his first book, *Passionate Stories* (*Cuentos pasionales*, 1907) he brings to mind Maupassant. His mature works were *The Seven Sins* (*Los siete pecados,* 1918), *Acid Fruits* (*Los frutos ácidos,* 1919), *Precious Stones* (*Piedras preciosas*, 1927), *Insane Asylum* (*Manicomio,* 1931). One of his best books was *Zoo* (*La casa de fieras,* 1919). A lively, sensual, juicy, warm, opulent, noble prose predominates. He writes well; that is, he knows how to embroider and emboss a sentence so as not to confuse it with another. He knows the secrets of the trade of the short story writer, as attested to by these anthological stories: "The Witness," "The Guilty Woman," "The Pearl," "The Chinese," "The Little Galician Girl." As a novelist he was not so outstanding: *Pelayo González* (1909), *The New Death* (*La muerte nueva,* 1922), *The Drinker of Tears* (*El bebedor de lágrimas*, 1926), *The Angel of Sodom* (*El ángel de Sodoma,* 1927). And he achieved even less as a poet and playwright.

Armando Leyva (1885–1940) was a short story writer affiliated with modernism, with an ironic fondness for mysteries *à la* Poe.

Political preoccupations, the spirit of social documentation, the need for protest and reform inspired a series of novels. Luis Felipe Rodríguez (1888–1947) planted in his stories and novels the roots of peasant life with its enchantments, but above all, with its miseries and injustices; more than in his novels—*What Damián Paredes Thought* (*Cómo opinaba Damián Paredes,* 1916), *Swamp* (*Ciénaga,* 1937)—he was successful in the short stories in *Home Town Easter* (*La pascua de la tierra natal,* 1923) and *Marcos Antilla,* 1932, his best book. He is not a creator of characters, but rather an outliner of sections of collective life. His defense of the peasants, his attacks against the latifundium system or imperialist plundering, his bloody endings, his liking for documentation, and his theses give his pages an air of urgency more appropriate to the essayist than to the artist. He influenced the young writers. Federico de Ibarzábal (1894–1953), a poet of dockside themes, also preferred themes of the sea in his narrations. A literary sea, but evoked with sober effectiveness and with a sense of adventure and exoticism. Others: José Antonio Ramos (1885–1946), taken up with Cuban reality: *Coaybay, Caniquí:* CARLOS FERNÁNDEZ CABRERA (1889), and MIGUEL DE MARCOS (1894–1954).

Dominican Republic: ABIGAÍL MEJÍA DE FERNÁNDEZ (1895–1941), author of works of imagination, such as *Dream, Pilarín (Sueña, Pilarín,* 1925) of psychological analysis.

Noteworthy for his historical evocations is MAX HENRÍQUEZ UREÑA (1885), author of a sober series of *Dominican Episodes (Episodios dominicanos,* 1915). He is also an essayist and poet: he collected his verses in *Claw of Light (Garra de luz,* 1958). MIGUEL ÁNGEL JIMÉNEZ (1885) is a novelist in *The Daughter of a Nobody (La hija de una cualquiera,* 1927). SÓCRATES NOLASCO (1884) cultivated the Creole story, of folkloric roots, of rural customs: *Stories of the South (Cuentos del sur,* 1939) and his edition of *Wild Stories (Cuentos cimarrones,* 1958) collected directly from oral tradition. FRANCISCO MOSCOSO PUELLO (1885) documented in *Sugar Canes and Oxen (Cañas y bueyes,* 1936) the hard work of the sugar plantations. More than a novel, it is a succession of objective pictures that follow the manufacturing process step by step, from cutting the trees to clearing the ground, to the most unjust phases of exploitation. RAMÓN EMILIO JIMÉNEZ (1886), a poet and narrator of jovial mood. JOSÉ MARÍA PICHARDO, "Nino" (1888) cultivated the national short story, *Flower Bread (Pan de flor),* and the novel, *Inland (Tierra adentro,* 1917). ENRIQUE AGUIAR (1890) cultivated the Indianist historical novel, *Don Cristóbal,* 1939, and also that of national landscapes, *Eusebio Sapote,* 1938. MIGUEL ÁNGEL MONCLÚS (1893), narrator of *Things Creole (Cosas criollas,* 1929), *Creole Scenes (Escenas criollas,* 1941) and a novelist with *Cachón,* 1958.

Puerto Rico: There is barely room to mention JUAN BRASCHI (1884–1934) for his "short attempt at a realist novel": *The Ulcer (La úlcera;* 1915), and, among the short-story writers, CARLOS N. CARRERAS (1895).

(iv) *Venezuela* / The education of RÓMULO GALLEGOS (Venezuela, 1884) in modernist literature and his perception of crude Venezuelan reality appear contrasted in the themes of his novels —the fight between civilization and barbarism in hamlets, plains, forest, coffee plantations, rivers and lakes—as well as in the double onslaught of his style: artistic impressionism and descriptive realism. He had already published his short stories *The Adventurers (Los aventureros,* 1913) and his novels *The Last of the Solars (El último Solar,* 1920) and *The Creeper (La trepadora,* 1925) when Gallegos established himself with *Doña Bárbara* (1929) as one of our few novelists who satisfy the expectations of an international public. *Doña Bárbara* receives its movement from the traditional springs of the nineteenth-century novel. Against a background of implacable nature the action brings out, romantically, almost melodramatically, the heroic endeavor. The symbols—exaggerated even in the names of the characters: the barbarism of Doña Bárbara; the saintly light and ardor (*"santa luz y ardor"*) of the civilizing Santos Luzardo—are too obvious. The composition with its symmetries and antitheses—which at times lean to allegory—tends to go from the artistic to the intellectual: the mare and Marisela are tamed in parallel and simultaneous processes; the civilized man has all the dexterity of the barbaric one; the "sleeping beauty" is savage and lovely at the same time; the idyl in a counterpoint of voices; Doña Bárbara agonizes between good and evil; the burden of witchcraft, black auguries and curses end by yielding to a happy outcome. The scenes are violent and deliberately sensational: the deflowering of Bárbara; the father who runs a lance through his son and then dies with his eyes open; the burial in the room, with an abominable bat; the drunkenness of Lorenzo and Mr. Danger; mother and daughter fighting; the cadaver hanging from the horse. Yet, *Doña Bárbara* is a great novel. The prose moves like the grazing lands of Venezuela. The author's lyrical, folkloric, psychological, sociological attitudes change in the course of the story, and in each perspective he achieves admirable pages. Who has described better than Gallegos the landscape of the plains, the horse-taming, the round-up? The poetic power of the prose in *Doña Bárbara* was intensified in *Cantaclaro* (1934).

The subject matter of *Cantaclaro* (1934) is a fantasy of the couplets, stories, superstitions, and legends that are heard on the Venezuelan plains. All of these are incarnated in the wandering musician, Florentino, nicknamed Cantaclaro. He is a friendly, loyal, haughty young fellow, infallible in his feminine conquests. Gallegos twists together several threads of plot and the action develops like a braided cord. As omniscient author, Gallegos intervenes constantly with explanations, reflections, and long expositions of preceding events, so that instead of seeing directly what is taking place, the reader learns what has already occurred. At the heart of the action is the conflict of conscience in Doctor Payara, a man of rigid moral precepts, who feels he should remove Rosángel from his life, so that the relationship between them, apparently that of father and daughter, will not end in something that he deems to be incestuous. Actually, Rosángel is not his daughter, but the daughter of his dead wife. Cantaclaro carries the girl off with him, but not for himself: he will give her refuge in his home, and will then continue his life as a solitary, nomadic adventurer. But the novel does not coagulate around a plot; rather, it is a succession of sketches of customs, of descriptions, of psychological portraits, of ethnographic and sociological lessons, of poetic moments. The attitude of Gallegos is that of the intellectual —he even gives an aphoristic quality to the dialog of the plainsmen—but the folkloric quality of this novel does not permit him to offer ethnic or political messages as manifest as those in the earlier *Doña Bárbara* or in *Canaima*, which followed it. *Canaima* (1935) is another of Gallegos' good novels. The scene: the cities which lie near the jungle, and the jungle itself, in the great valley of the Orinoco River. The time: the present. The subject: the grimness of life (corruption, intrigues, murders, the revolutions and despotic acts of the political regime of the bosses; the work entailed in commerce, street transportation, the mines and the rubber plantations; a mixed population of Europeans, North Americans, Creoles, Indians and Negroes, various types of human beings motivated by feelings of love and friendship, hatred and vengeance, fear and daring, envy and neglect; and motivated, too, by vice, sickness and insanity.) The theme: "the Male, semigod of the barbarous lands," against Canaima, the malignant god "of the anti-human, satanic jungle." The protagonist: Marcos Vargas. The novel is constructed in the form of a vast and complex sketch of customs. The first and last chapters ("Portico" and "This was it!") serve as the frame. The first chapter contains an exposition of preceding events: we see the landscape around the mouth of the Orinoco and, emerging from Ciudad Bolívar, the childhood and adolescence of Marcos Vargas, a boy fascinated by the legends and adventures of the jungle. In the middle of the picture (chapters II–XVIII), the action begins when Marcos, at twenty-one years of age, sets out "for the open road, to confront life." He is all male, violent, generous, with a sense of justice that leads him to identify himself with the workers, and later, with the Indians, but he is basically more vital than rational, confused, unadaptable, and without heroic stature. Avenging the death of his brother by killing Cholo Parima is all he accomplishes. He seeks adventure simply for the sake of adventure. Having no clearly defined ideals, he renounces civilization, lives with the Indians, becomes one of them, marries a little Indian girl, and so we lose sight of him when he is twenty-seven years old. The last chapter, which repeats some notes on the landscape from the first chapter, completes the framework with an epilog: twelve or fourteen years have gone by, and we see another Marcos Vargas, a child, on the road to Caracas, where he will be educated. The thesis of the novel, more insinuated than formulated, seems to be in the inverse trajectories of these two children, the child of the first chapter, torn from civilization by the witchcraft of the jungle, and the child of the last chapter, who comes out of the jungle to be saved by civilization. It was also possible to visualize a thesis in the contrast between the two "emotions about himself" felt by Marcos Vargas: the emotion he experiences in Chapter XIV ("Torment") when, possessed by the demon Canaima, he feels denuded of history, an Adam in a green inferno, a relative of the monkey, almost more tree than man; and the emotion experienced in Chapter XVI ("A few words from Ureña") when, on being reproached for wasting his energies in adventures that end miserably, for indulging in a cult of man without transcendence, he understands that he is motivated by sheer impulse, that he is doing moral damage to himself, and that he will be lost if he does not mend his life. "Civilize that barbarous force within you, study the problems of this country and assume the responsibilities that you should assume," his friend Ureña tells him. Sensing that he has failed in the life of a primitive, he realizes, when he sends his mestizo son to Caracas, that only European civilization can save the people of his country. Is this the thesis of *Canaima?* The narrative sequence is lineal, but its continuity is not straight, it digresses. To straighten it Gallego frequently resorts to recapitulations, parallels, symmetries and contrasts, reencounters, looking ahead, and references that quickly link one scene with another. There are too many disconnected episodes, and too many characters, because Gallegos appears to be more interested in the sociology and ethnology of that Venezuelan region than in a well-rounded plot and good psychological characterization. Of course there are pages of outstanding artistic talent. For example, there is the elementary art of telling an adventure in the chapter "Aces and Fortunes"; the highly refined art of illuminating the protagonist from within in the chapter "Torment," and the art of description, rich in imagery, through nearly all the chapters. But the novel as a whole suffers from a lack of unity. Gallegos is more concerned with the problems of his country than with the problem of the construction of a novel. This intellectual attitude is evident not only in the direct judgments the author makes on Venezuela as a reality, but also in the way he intervenes indirectly in the body of the novel. Some examples: putting moral discourses and theses in the mouths of his characters; interpreting an episode in the light of a philosophy, giving it thus a meaning the reader would not have discovered for himself; explaining what has happened instead of presenting us with the action at the moment it is taking place; the use of symbols and allegories to bring out his line of thought and his intentions. Some of these symbols and allegories, however, are legitimate art, expressionist procedures that bring to light an imaginative vision of reality, for example in the scene where Araceli and Aymara pronounce the same words of love and in the scene of the four sticks. Later novels: *Poor Negro* (*Pobre Negro*), *Upon the Same Earth* (*Sobre la misma tierra*), *The Wisp of Straw in the Wind* (*La brizna de paja en el viento*).

Delightful TERESA DE LA PARRA (1891–1936) makes us feel time as if it were a substance. And, in fact, time is the substance of her literature. She describes the backward life of the old society. She tells us how it is falling apart. The aristocratic class to which she belongs is a moment of history already spent. She says good-by to things so cordially that we can see them moving off into the past, wrapped in their hours. Or she evokes her childhood; and landscapes, events, and people come from afar, wrapped in their years. Time, always time. But, above all, it is the subjectivism of her prose, quivering with impressions and metaphors, that makes the passing of time so striking. It is known that the inner life is a temporal flux, a process of lived time; so, whatever Teresa de la Parra speaks of, the subject is always herself. Proust was one of her masters in the art of shading the undulating succession of memories. Her first novel was *Iphigenia: Diary of a Young Girl Who Wrote Because She Was Annoyed* (*Ifigenia: Diario de una señorita, que escribió porque se fastidiaba*, 1924). In whispers—because she is confessing and gossiping about others—but with the fluidity of an elegant conversation, Teresa de la Parra comments on the unjust social position of Creole women. Better yet was her second, and last, novel, *The Memoirs of Mamá Blanca* (*Las memorias de Mamá Blanca*, 1929). It is a novel, because the episodes, scattered as they may appear, cannot be pruned away from the central trunk of the narrative. The branches and twigs would dry up. The characters develop maturity chapter after chapter, as in a novel. The artifice of presenting the *Memoirs* as a manuscript left in legacy to the author by the old woman, Mamá Blanca, is also novelistic. These are the memories of a happy childhood on a sugar cane plantation near Caracas. The tenderness, the melancholy, the vivid imagination, the human sympathy, the sensitivity for registering the gentleness of the world, the charm of the writing and narrating have no equal in our literature. Childhood remembrances, but not naive ones. Her intelligence, smiling and ironic, watches over all. Mr. Emphasis and Madame Commonplace would not be permitted to enter these pages. They were not invited; they would be detained at the door with words of bland mock courtesy, and would have to leave in humiliation, hearing behind them little ripples of derisive laughter. The style seems spontaneous because Teresa de la Parra, wisely, ingeniously, laboriously, has dug deep into the hardness of the language in order to strike an original lode of metaphors.

Although JESÚS ENRIQUE LOSSADA (Venezuela, 1895–1948) wrote some stories on rural surroundings and some with satiric intent, his stories of intellectual problems were more personal, with incredible themes or characters that move from lyricism to delirium. He is the author of *The Happiness Machine* (*La máquina de la felicidad*, 1938).

The novels of JOSÉ RAFAEL POCATERRA (1889–1955) were declarations of war against modernism. He was aware of his power: to put into a novel —as he used to say—"people on the street, on corners, in church, in intimate life, from the sidewalk across the street." He was also aware of his weaknesses: he admitted his "defects in form and composition." Was he aware that his novels failed because he insisted on not "drawing persons, but fixing types?" *Doctor Bebé (El doctor Bebé,* 1917) for example, presents a bourgeois family elevated by the political boss or *caudillo,* Bebé, and subsequently dragged down by him to dishonor and misery. But what is presented are types: Bebé, the political boss, sensual, unscrupulous, abusing; the cowardly, intriguing and servile Pepito; the poor women, ambitious but fearful of scandal, in love but browbeaten—Josefina, with her illegitimate daughter, is the one who is most moving. This corrupt society is heard in typical speech, and not in individual voices. The prose is hard and opaque: only in moments of cruel irony does it acquire expressive vigor, and that is when it strikes one most. Being a naturalist, Pocaterra shows the animalistic, the instinctive, the sordid aspects of life. In their irate and aggressive Creolism, his novels—*Obscure Lives (Vidas oscuras), Beloved Land of the Sun (Tierra del sol amada),* and even the best one, *The House of the Abilas (La casa de los Abilas,* 1946) are not as easily read as his *Grotesque Stories (Cuentos grotescos,* 1922). They constitute a panorama of horrors during the tyranny of Gómez. In sarcastic and contemptuous prose Pocaterra describes the corruption, violence, barbarism, ignorance, poverty and stupidity of the national life. JULIO GARMENDIA (1898) is an excellent story teller [*The Doll Store (La tienda de muñecos), The Golden Tuna (La tuna de oro)*], simple, brief, and good-humored. With the first of his books, published in Paris in 1927, Garmendia started a cycle of stories that were neither Creolist nor regional. Immediately afterwards, the stories of Uslar Pietri would carry on the impetus of the new trend. LEONCIO MARTÍNEZ (1888–1941) wrote humorous stories: *My Other Puppets (Mis otros fantoches,* 1932). JULIO ROSALES (1885) was also a notable story teller. We have already mentioned ENRIQUE BERNARDO NÚÑEZ (1895).

(v) *Colombia* / The excessive respect for European forms had an ill effect even on the best Colombian novels, the romantic ones as well as the realist and modernist ones. Suddenly there sprouted pages of a novel having the strength of native trees: those of Rivera's *The Vortex (La vorágine).* The seeds blew about, and little by little other novels emerged with Colombian themes and individual styles.

JOSÉ EUSTASIO RIVERA (1888–1928) wrote admirable sonnets: *The Promised Land (Tierra de promisión,* 1921). The fixed structure of the sonnet lends itself to a tension wherein, verse after verse, the action develops in a rigorous centralized movement which keeps the reader alert to what is coming. The action that Rivera depicts in his sonnets is that of Colombian nature: animals, plants, rivers, mountains, the colors of the sky. The last verse closes the action and leaves it perfect, like a painting full of color. What one sees in this painting is a virgin territory for poetry —no one, prior to Rivera, had laid it open with such intensity, from such a beautifying angle. But the literary technique of painting the things of nature with such cleanness of profile, of shading, of gesture, and of setting them in an artistocratic form, is Parnassian. The words selected by the poet ennoble the brute substance of nature and transform it into precious material. Rivera was one of the forces of nature. His humanistic culture was poor in comparison to his extremely fruitful temperament. But at least he had a cultured way of contemplating himself: his passions, his peculiarities, his need to live in the country among trees, animals, and rivers were all dressed with the raiment of the sonnet. When Rivera wrote *The Vortex* (1924) he maintained his high poetic tension but changed his perspective. Instead of contemplating pictures, he placed himself within nature itself and disclosed the beauty of fear. Framed, in order to make us believe in its objectivity, between a prolog by Rivera and an epilog by the Consul, *The Vortex* pretends to be an autobiographical book. With the old procedure of feigning to edit the memoirs of another—"I respected his style and even his errors"—he lets Arturo Cova tell the story in the first person, except when he transcribes the tales of other characters. The plains of the Orinoco River and the lowlands of the Amazon form the setting. The action takes place in little more than seven months; it begins with the impregnation of Alicia and ends with the abortion of the seven-month fetus. The action is rapid and continuous, but the story, divided into three parts, advances in intermittent lines.

First part: the exposition. Arturo Cova, a young Colombian poet, already celebrated for his intelligence and for his "sculptured" poems (even in the wilds, the sordid Barrera, the drunkard Gámez, and the prostitute Clarita will admire his fame) has an easy love affair with Alicia. He seduces her, without loving her, and flees from Bogotá with her. He flees from the threat of marriage made by her parents, the judge, and the priest. Then a series of adventures follows, with touches of the crime novel. Alicia and Cova live in La Maporita with Franco and his wife,

"Griselda" (these two also have a police record). Arturo, because of his loyalty to Franco, resists Griselda's sensual overtures and, out of spite, begins to conceive a passion for Alicia. Enter Barrera, a scoundrel who robs, lies, kills, betrays, and wants to seduce the women. A furious Arturo leaves in search of Barrera. Arturo is stabbed in a squabble over a game of dice. A prostitute nurses him to health. On his return to La Maporita with Franco, he finds out that Barrera has gone off taking Griselda and Alicia with him. They set La Maporita on fire.

Second part: the action becomes knotted with social condemnations. Arturo, accompanied by Franco and others, goes into the jungle after Barrera and the two women to avenge himself. He lives among Indians—which occasions ethnographical scenes and a contemporary "Indian chronicle." He listens to the grievances of some of those with him—which constitute a hair-raising documentary on the sufferings of rubber plantation workers. The painful history of the Colombian Clemente Silva takes up more than half this part.

Third part: now comes the denouement. The rubber worker, Silva, ends his story and goes off in search of his son's bones; now Cova is on the move again, not only for personal vengeance, but also to fight against the injustices of the big bosses and to redeem the rubber workers. Illness begins to depress, madden, and paralyze him. He falls into the sensual arms of the Turkish Zoraida. New characters open new circles in the green hell: el Váquiro, Cayeno, Ramiro, the swindler Lesmes. Cova starts to write a sheaf of accusations to send to the Consul of Colombia. It will be a panorama of miseries, an "imposing register of ills in a style seething and precipitous like the waters of a torrent." The threads of the story intertwine and are pulled firmly together. Cova comes across Griselda, who tells of her misfortunes with Barrera and how Alicia has slashed his face. The violent scenes mount until they take away the reader's breath: horrendous tortures, mutilations, pools of blood, Cayeno's cadaver floating in the river while a dog is disemboweling it, Barrera bitten to death by fish, Alicia's abortion, the final march where "the jungle devoured them" without leaving a trace.

The Vortex (the novel of the vortex, that is, the jungle) is built on two levels, one of social protest and the other of psychological characterization. Rivera seems to have written it with a double purpose and even with two distinguishable themes. On the first level he defends the Colombians, prisoners of the jungle, and the sovereignty of Colombia, menaced by invasions and depredations. For this he used historical data, word of mouth experiences, anecdotes that he had read, and others that he had lived, and his own travels to the Orinoco and the Amazon. These pages of obvious social and political intentions are not his best—scenes of local customs, moral reflections, satiric phrases, and deviations from the story damage the unity of composition and style. His best literary achievement on this level is the interesting case of the interior duplication of the novel: that is, that while we read the memoirs, not only do we hear the intimate revelations about the way Cova is inspired by nature and about the difference between the traditional conventions of literature and sincerely artistic expression, but also we see him in the very act of writing them, looking after them, and sending them to the Consul. The second level is superior. Rivera has created a character of singularly complicated mentality, obsessed by his failure: "I am not what I could have been." Since Rivera made Cova a poet, not only his reactions, exaltations, and torments are convincing, but also the lyrical tone of his memoirs is authentic. Cova is passionate, irascible, theatrical, imaginative, bold, hysterical, crotchety, with adolescent and neurotic tendencies. The violence of his actions harmonizes with the violence of his metaphors, and the bloodiest and most macabre things are illumined with esthetic lights: "the frenetic sight of the shipwreck shook me like a wind of beauty," he says. And he composes the most truculent scenes of torture, infamy, death, and human bestiality and filthiness with the eyes of an artist. From Casanare, until he loses himself in the Brazilian jungles, Cova traverses inhospitable regions: from plain to plain, from river to river, from village to village, from tribe to tribe and from rubber plantation to rubber plantation, he learns of the horrors of a most devastating environment and of a most degrading humanity. Serpents, ants, infra-men, all appear in one repulsive mass. Occasionally, there is a prose poem on the beauty of the landscape; but generally, he gives us a lyricism of nightmare, fever, and grotesqueness. He is a refined poet, but his drive is barbaric. He gives nerves to the Colombian landscape and, when it becomes convulsive and tragic, we see Cova's soul as well. At any rate, we see the jungle about to swallow Cova, but we see it through the eyes of Cova himself. Cova's complex personality is expressed in the first person. Rivera, however, does not attempt interior monolog. It is, rather, a long soliloquy in which Cova analyzes himself psychologically. His dreams, feverish deliriums, unbridled fantasies, and abnormal sensations appear, not in the dim stream of consciousness and of subconsciousness, but thoroughly explained, arranged, and illuminated in a prose whose greatest audacities are metaphors, impressionistic descriptions, synesthesias, and expressionistic personifications, as that of the vengeance of the rubber trees against the workers.

There were psychological, fantastic, intellectualist novels and those of lyrical intonation, which also existed, although in small numbers. The three most subjective novelists are López de Mesa, Alvarez Lleras, and Restrepo Jaramillo. The first two were not really novelists—the first an essayist, the second a dramatist. Nevertheless, they must be mentioned here. LUIS LÓPEZ DE MESA (1884) wrote his *Book of Apologs* (*Libro de apólogos*, 1918), related to the parables of Rodó, with esthetic pomp. He also attempted the idealist novel with *The Tragedy of Nilse* (*La tragedia de Nilse*, 1928) and *The Biography of Gloria Etzel* (*La biografía de Gloria Etzel*, 1929), in which there are psychological analyses, a diffused spiritualism, and more or less philosophical chats on individual perfectibility. ANTONIO ALVÁREZ LLERAS (1892–1956) left one of the best novels of this period: *Only Yesterday . . . (Ayer, nada más . . . ,* 1930), on the milieu of the Colombian capital, with studies of decadent characters and strolls through mental labyrinths. More important is JOSÉ RESTREPO JARAMILLO (1896–1945), who has been considered the founder of the Colombian psychological novel. Daring in his experiments with the art of narrating and in his esthetic focus on complex psychologies, he delights in the spectacle of his own creative imagination, novelizes the very act of novelizing. He looks at his characters from multiple perspectives. He takes the obscure, irrational depths of life by surprise and describes them lyrically. Titles: *The Novel of Three (Novela de los tres,* 1924), *David, Son of Palestine (David, hijo de Palestina,* 1931), *My Friend Pocahontas (Mi amiga Pocahontas;* 1945). We close this list with FÉLIX HENAO TORO (1900), author of "the first psychoanalytical novel in Spanish": *Eugeni the Handball Player (Eugeni la pelotari,* 1935); M. F. SLIGER, who dealt in the genre of science fiction: *Interplanetary Voyages That Will Take Place in the Year 2009 (Viajes*

interplanetarios que tendrán lugar en el año 2009, 1936); GREGORIO
SÁNCHEZ GÓMEZ (1895–1942) with his phantasmogoric *Life of a Dead
Man* (*Vida de un muerto,* 1936); and RAFAEL JARAMILLO ARANGO (1896)
with his stories of escape into the unreal worlds of animals and of children.

In returning to the land—in part because of the example of Rivera's
The Vortex—many narrators became mirrors in which local settings and
customs were reflected. When they did intervene in reality, it was to denounce social ills and to take up the claims of the humble masses. Their
optimism in wishing to improve things was clothed in apparently pessimistic preferences for misery, suffering, and pestilence. The sociological
view of this type of novel focused on sordid human groups and on trivial
types. The desire to propagandize led them to seek out the mass public, and
the exaltation of the mediocre led to an unimaginative language. Only the
most outstanding of these works of fiction need be cited here. EDUARDO
ARIAS SUÁREZ (1897–1958) divided *Growing Old and Selected Short
Stories* (*Envejecer y cuentos de selección*) into two portions: "sentiment"
and "humor." His humor recalls that of the sketches of customs, somewhat sarcastic and even critical in intent. Among the stories grouped in the
category of "sentiment" he placed his novelette *Growing Old.* There is also
humor here in the reflection of every detail of life. Arias Suárez observes
and then comments on his observations with intelligence, imagination, and
wit. Until his death he was considered the principal short story writer in his
country, perhaps because he wrote mainly about the life of the people of
Colombia, and of its most visible types: the old maid, the barber, the
teacher.

CÉSAR URIBE PIEDRAHITA (1897–1951) with *Toá* (1933) gave us, rather
than a novel, a chronicle on the life of the rubber workers in the Amazon
basin of Colombia. No character takes on sufficient relief, not even the
protagonist Antonio. And the double action—the fights between the Colombian rubber workers and the intruders from Peru plus the love between
Antonio and Toá—is also insufficient. The jungle—which should be in the
background with its diseases, its beasts, and its Indians—is moved to the
foreground. The book has value as a document for the natural sciences,
ethnography, and a little, very little, for sociology; but its value as a novel
is minimal. The intention seems to be not to novelize the cruelties of nature,
but the cruelties of man that vex nature itself: "the white man, lascivious
and covetous, bestially violated nature and in this way tried to dominate it."
But only the intention remains. The interest in *Toá* is derived from the
natural, social, ethnographical reality it describes, not from the art of
novelizing. The prose is simple, communicative, realist, on occasion like a
chronicle or scientific report. His other novel, *Oil Stain* (*Mancha de aceite,*
1935), comes face to face with the imperialistic interests of the petroleum
industry.

(vi) *Ecuador* / One of the respected prose writers of this generation was
GONZALO ZALDUMBIDE (1885). For many years he was esteemed for his
critical works on Rodó, Montalvo, D'Annunzio. He is also the author of an
extraordinarily chiseled novel on youth, *Tragic Eclogue* (*Egloga trágica*).
He wrote it in 1910–11, published some of its segments in different news-

papers from 1912 to 1916, and it was not until 1956 that he published it as a whole in the form of a book, without retouching the style. The youth Segismundo, after traveling for several years through the capitals of Europe, where he experienced all the refinements of the life of an artist without ever having experienced a real love, returns to his native corner of the earth, Ibarra, and its surroundings. He becomes enthusiastic about the beauties of the landscape, he helps the peasants at work, he observes the customs of the Indians, he reflects on the problems of Hispanic-America, he comes to know the disasters of a political revolution, he ardently enjoys a churlish little Indian girl. His uncle Juan José, a forty-year-old giant, lord of the land, takes him to visit Marta, a pretty young girl, sweet, anemic. Marta lives with her insane mother, Dolores. (Dolores had had a clandestine love affair with a German; one night, on finding them embraced, Dolores' father fired a shot at the German; Dolores, now insane, gave birth to Marta; Juan José, Dolores' cousin, became the protector of the two women.) In view of the civil war, Juan José lodges Dolores and Marta in his house. Dolores dies. Segismundo and Marta fall in love. Juan José feels an incipient, desperate passion for Marta and in the throes of jealousy threatens Segismundo with death. The latter, because of his love for his uncle, decides to return to Europe. On the point of leaving, he receives a letter in Quito from Marta who has guessed what happened between the two men and who is saying good-by before taking her own life. Segismundo returns to his uncle's house to remain. Juan José dies; Segismundo lives on with the memory of Marta, "symbol of the happiness that no one achieves." The story is melodramatic: that is, an action that seeks effects, softened by a musical background. The structure of the novel is traditional: the protagonist Segismundo narrates; the descriptive first part and the second part which sets the conflict are slow; the last two parts rush forward tragically. But the exceptional part of *Tragic Eclogue* is the quality of its prose—a modernist prose, with cadenced phrases and a rare choice of the right word and of the lyrical image. The description of nature and of intimate sentiments is brilliant, impressionistic, imaginative. Zaldumbide does not propose to reproduce real things or to analyze psychological states, but to stylize his poetic vision in admirable prose poems. Because of this vision, *Tragic Eclogue* can give delight even today to the pursuers of images; his literary language, nevertheless, produces a strange effect of mixed epochs, with old romantic structures and modern ones of the beginning of the century. CÉSAR ARROYO (1890–1937) directed the review *Cervantes* in Madrid, which at one time was the organ of the creationists; but in spite of his admiration for everything new, the chronicles and narrations he left us are still modernist.

BENJAMÍN CARRIÓN (1898) in 1926 published a novel about the failure of an intellectual, *The Disenchantment of Miguel García* (*El desencanto de Miguel García*), but later he definitely turned to the essay and criticism. FERNANDO CHAVES (1898?) in his novel *Silver and Bronze* (*Plata y bronce,* 1927) showed the suffering of the highland Indians under the injustices of the parish priests and the feudal lords. Thus, with Chaves, the indigenist novel, which will acquire more importance under the pen of Jorge Icaza, arises in Ecuador.

(vii) *Peru* / VENTURA GARCÍA CALDERÓN (1887–1960) was an artist of prose. He raised it to an even higher level than it had attained under Gutiérrez Nájera, Martí, Darío, Rodó, Díaz Rodríguez. His *Cantilenas* (Ballads) evoked Paris and Venice with precious, morbid and intoxicating artifices. He rendered a good diplomatic service by showing Europeans, who believe Hispanic-Americans to be a picturesque people from whom they expect only regionalism—no matter how unpolished and mediocre it might be—an excellently written regional literature. *The Vengeance of the Condor* (*La venganza del Cóndor*, 1924) contains stories of violence, death, horror, superstitions, and unrestrained passions. His good prose seems to strain all this reality (crude in other narrators) through stained glass, brilliant and cold. This man of Parisian culture relating barbaric episodes, or describing hair-raising regions, is smiling with a refined and almost imperceptible irony. Those rather dull souls who need explanations, theses, declamations, believed that García Calderón had not seen his Peruvian land: indeed he had, and he understood its problems, but with artistic moderation. After him (better said against him) came the pro-Indian narrators. If García Calderón had exaggerated the defects of the Indians, they exaggerated the virtues. However, García Calderón wrote better.

ABRAHAM VALDELOMAR (1888–1919) wrote verses and has a place as a poet among those who inspired the *Colónida* Group. But today it is his narrative work that is preferred. At first he was an esthete, after the manner of Oscar Wilde and D'Annunzio; *The Dead City* (*La ciudad muerta*) and *The City of the Consumptives* (*La ciudad de los tísicos*) (both of 1911) reflect a tormented imagination with their descriptions of ruins by the light of the moon, gloomy mysteries, neurotic psychologies, aristocratic language. Then modernism stripped him of his cosmopolitan and fantastic ornaments and equipped him instead with American topics. He took root in his own country: in the provinces, in family life, in everyday people and scenes. During this rurally oriented stage of his work (his best) he cultivated the short story. *"Gentleman Carmelo"* (*"El caballero Carmelo"*) (which furnished the title for his collection of 1918) is a fighting-cock.

Valdelomar's prose is now more tender, intimate, and sincere in its nostalgia for regional scenes and evocations of childhood. MANUEL BEDOYA (1888–1941) produced police novels, like the French (not detective novels, like the English). AUGUSTO AGUIRRE MORALES (1890–1957), with his experience in archeology, reconstructed the life of the Incas: *The People of the Sun* (*El Pueblo del sol*). CARLOS CAMINO CALDERÓN (1884–1956) also wrote historical novels. *The Cross of Saint James* (*La cruz de Santiago*, 1925), written with evocative power and in excellent style, presents the lives of the young Creoles who broke with the traditions of the colony and prepared the Independence. But he did not stick to history. *The Damage* (*El Daño*) is a novel with a wealth of ethnographic observations dealing with a rural region of Peru. CÉSAR FALCÓN (1892) wrote novels from the standpoint of socialist realism. In *The Godless People* (*El pueblo sin Dios*) he tried to bring himself up to date with the literary trends of his time. Its sociological aspect was more successful than its literary aspect, however. But as a sociologist Falcón took a closer look at the exploiters than at the exploited Indians. *The Good Neighbor Sanabria U* (*El buen vecino Sanabria U*, 1947) relates in ordinary and traditional prose a picaresque story with a political theme: the imperialism and the "good neighbor policy" of the United States as it functioned in Hispanic America. *Along the Road with No Horizon* (*Por la ruta sin horizonte*) refers to the Spanish Civil War. Other realists: ERNESTO MORE (1897), JUAN SEOANE (1899), CARLOS PARRA DEL RIEGO (1896–1939).

(viii) *Bolivia* / ARMANDO CHIRVECHES (1883–1926) began as a modernist (from *Lilí*, 1901, to *Nostalgias* [*Añoranzas*, 1912]) but we are grateful to him for having decided to write novels: *Sky Blue* (*Celeste*, 1905), *Manor House* (*Casa solariega*, 1906) and *Tropical Flower* (*Flor del trópico*, 1926). Because of its exceptional merit, we shall consider *The Candidacy of Rojas* (*La candidatura de Rojas*, 1909) separately. In this novel can be discerned one of the modernist phenomena already noted: once the dazzlement of European artificial lights had passed, there were writers who wrote Hispanic-American literature without rejecting cosmopolitan refinements. The protagonist, Enrique Rojas, says that his favorite authors are the Spaniards, Pereda and Palacio Valdés. That may be so. But it is evident that Chirveches formed his style on French artistic prose, from Flaubert on. The novel is about the abortive political adventure of Rojas, who leaves La Paz with the ambition of being elected representative, and ends up by marrying his cousin Inés in a provincial corner of the country. The Bolivian reality of city, country, intellectual groups, and uncivilized masses, of Spaniards, Creoles, mestizos, and Indians, is masterfully described. Chirveches, as only a few have done, symphonically orchestrates all of the instruments and tonalities of the literature of his time: lyrical and humorous pages, the idealization of things and brutal and malodorous naturalism, mischievous wit, and severe critical thought, satiric and idyllic themes, a conscious intention to create literature while poking fun at it, exquisiteness of landscape, yet rapidity of action. Chirveches knows how to tell a story. He has psychological acuteness. The most significant details of each scene do not escape him. He has created, objectively, a character so much alive that the reader, deceived by the fact that the narrative is in the first person, might believe that Rojas is Chirveches himself. He is not: Rojas is a novelistic creation.

ANTONIO DÍAZ VILLAMIL (1897–1948) kneaded the popular clay of folk legends, stories, theater, and novels. In *The Apple of His Eye* (*La niña de sus ojos,* 1948) he novelized a social situation, in La Paz: the young lady of Indian origin provokes race prejudice and class resentments as she prospers in her social status. ALFREDO GUILLÉN PINTO (1895–1950) wrote naturalist novels in defense of the Indian and the proletariat of fields and mines: *Indian Tears* (*Lágrimas indias,* 1920); *Utama* (1945); *Mina* (1953). Also indigenist, but more conventional, are the narrations of SATURNINO RODRIGO (1894). The novel, *The Sense of Life or The Life of Jorge Esteban* (*El sentido vital o La vida de Jorge Esteban,* 1931) by RIGOBERTO VILLARROEL CLAURE (1890) has a pedagogical purpose. TRISTÁN MAROFF (1898) enjoyed a fleeting success—partly because of his personality as a political fighter of Marxist persuasion—with *Suetonio Pimienta: Memoirs of a Diplomat of the Carrot Republic* (*Suetonio Pimienta. Memorias de un diplomático de la República de Zanahoria,* 1924). Irony, sarcasm, and cynicism run like an open faucet, too easily and too superficially. Since the jokes touch on current matters—the theme: five years in the lives of Hispanic-Americans living in Paris—the novel is boring. Maroff has humor, but no wit. There are attempts at social criticism and political reform, but without originality or keenness. The sentences are short, quick, but unfortunately, for one who wished to be the chronicler of what he had seen or lived, Maroff did not display any inventive faculties. All indications of renovation are seen in the realm of political thought, not in literary matters: denunciation of vanity, prostitution, falsehood, holidays, diplomatic hypocrisy, playboyism, etc.

He wrote other novels as well as essays that were more contentious than lucid. He believed in a social revolution (agrarian reform, nationalization of the mines) that would reject everything transplanted from Spain and base its norms on the ways of life of the Inca civilization. Fundamentally he was a skeptic. He broke with Russian Communism, found the revolutionary dreams of Bolivians deceptive, and ended by retiring from partisan politics. LUIS TORO RAMALLO (1898–1946) novelized the Bolivian Indian in his plateau setting in *Cutimuncu and Inca Gold* (*Cutimuncu y Oro del Inca*). CARLOS MEDINACELI (1899–1949) describes provincial customs as he relates the story of the love of a student for a girl of Indian origin in his novel, *La Chaskanawi.*

(ix) *Chile* / EDUARDO BARRIOS (1884). In his juvenile dramas (from 1910 to 1916) there were thoughts of social reform or, at least, concern for social problems: religious hypocrisy, bureaucracy, politics, and woman's disadvantageous position in family life. Later he abandoned the theater, and in his novels he became more interested in people than in things, and more interested in their souls than in their adventures. In *The Boy Who Went Crazy With Love* (*El niño que enloqueció del amor*, 1915) he was already showing his capacity for psychological analysis: it is the diary of a hypersensitive boy of ten who falls in love with a woman, suffers, becomes ill and finally demented. It had an antecedent in *A Boy's Love* (*Amor de niño*, 1864) by the Peruvian Luis Benjamín Cisneros. A more penetrating novel was *A Lost One* (*Un perdido*, 1917), in which he analyzes the history of the unfortunate Lucho who, from failure after failure, sinks into misery and vice. At the same time that he delves into the psychology of Lucho and many other characters, Barrios constructs his work with the ability of an architect; it is a psychological novel, but so crammed with observations on the social life of Chile that it is also a novel of customs. In *Brother Ass* (*El hermano asno*, 1922) once again the tense narrator of rare psychological cases is seen. These detached, impressionistic pages, written in the present tense and in the first person, take the form of an intimate diary. It is written by Friar Lázaro. When he begins his diary, he has already spent seven years in a Franciscan monastery, but he has not been able to forget the world. In this outer world he was called Mario and had loved a woman, Gracia. When Gracia married a pianist, Mario became Friar Lázaro. One day Friar Lázaro thinks he sees Gracia in church. No, it isn't Gracia: it is her sister María Mercedes. She was eleven, twelve years old when Gracia abandoned Mario, and she was then romantically in love with him. Now she is twenty; between María Mercedes and Friar Lázaro is born a sentiment of friendship, even of love, which he tries to control. Gracia and her mother become alarmed. The pages in which Friar Lázaro records his days are interlaced with others in which he describes Friar Rufino. The latter has shown such proof of abnegation and love that people begin to revere him like a saint. This attribution of saintliness disturbs Friar Rufino. He feels he does not deserve it. He wonders whether there is not deep within him a feeling of vanity. Furthermore, he feels he is carrying "a brother ass," that is, a body capable of baseness and temptation. Finally he assaults María Mercedes in the darkness of the chapel, and before he dies he confesses that he wanted to rape her. Was this the lustfulness of "brother ass"? Could it have been the desire to humiliate himself, to have himself hated so as to destroy the notion of saintliness? Or perhaps a way of saving his friend Friar Lázaro by separating him from María Mercedes? Or perhaps a moral mistake in following the advice of the devil, disguised as a Capuchin monk? Or plain madness? The two threads of the story—and even a third, the description of monastery life and the different types of monks—form a well-wrought braid which ends in a firm knot: Lázaro takes Friar Rufino's guilt upon himself and, ironically, the monastery for its own convenience decides that Friar Rufino is to be venerated in spite of his desires and sacrifices.

Since Friar Lázaro, before becoming a monk, was a man of letters—one of his favorite books was *The Boy Who Went Crazy With Love*, by Barrios himself, and its manuscript begins with some verses of Amado Nervo, making it plausible that his diary should contain beautiful pages of fine impressionism, rich in metaphors of interior and exterior vistas. In two decades, Barrios produced nothing of great value until *Tamarugal* (1944), in which he continued his description of Chilean life in the desolate fields of the north. In *Gran señor y rajadiablos* (1948), Barrios constructed a pentagonal pantheon to the memory of José Pedro Valverde, whom he imagined as having died close to his eightieth year of life. The novel has five parts: evocations of childhood, adolescence, youth, maturity, and old age. In artistic prose—rich in perceptions and in brilliant descriptions—he painted on each tympanum of the vaulted arch scenes from the long life of this rich landowner (*"gran señor,"* in the feudal sense), virile, powerful, violent, cock-brained, Catholic, haughty, donjuanesque, enterprising, fearsome, likeable, intelligent although anti-rational. The character of the protagonist, nevertheless, is seen less clearly than the social and historic panorama of the Chilean landscape from the middle of the nineteenth century until the advent of the "democratic and leftist rabble of the twentieth century." Not that Barrios is more of a sociologist than a psychologist, it was merely that he conceived of his hero as a representative figure of Chilean progressive oligarchy. Unfortunately, those actions which best lent themselves to the novelistic treatment—bandit fights, the raping of women, the wars with Bolivia and Peru, political changes, adventures—were not actually presented, but merely alluded to. We learn of what has taken place, without having seen it happen. Although the novel is well written, there is something indefinably wrong with its composition. And since the creation of a character is conditioned by the creation of a plot, the defects in the composition impair the development of the personality of the hero. One of the few indicative situations developed fails to be convincing: José Pedro and Marisabel love their son, Antuco, but because he was born outside of the Church, before they were married, they do not want to acknowledge him for fear of creating a scandal, and they keep him deceived as to who his real mother is. The rest is a series of disconnected sketches, two-dimensional, like a series of pictures presenting a hagiography. What Barrios tried to do was personify a myth.

We have used the "psychological" concept in connection with

Barrios so much that it would be well to warn that his novels are more subjective than psychological. The fact is that Barrios uses narrative conventions that are not always plausible, and at times they are incredible from a strictly psychological point of view. Barrios' subjectivism in the creation of characters and his impressionism in the creation of phrases go together. His last novel —*Man's Men* (*Los hombres del hombre,* 1950)—re-creates the inner torture of a husband who doubts he is his child's father. "You suddenly get the notion," says another character in the novel, "that Charlie is not your son. Why? Because an English friend, his godfather, dies without heirs and leaves him a million."

PEDRO PRADO (Chile, 1886–1952) was first a verse poet, but prose poetry was his widest and longest channel. Verses: *Thistle Flowers* (*Flores de cardo,* 1908). In 1949 an *Anthology* (*Antología*) and *Old Unpublished Poems* (*Viejos poemas ineditos*) were published. Prado's poetry does not exhibit efforts at formal renovation. Although he was one of those who introduced free verse in Chile, he prefers traditional techniques, the sonnet. In language faithful to grammatical norms, he rouses the reader's attention but does not take him into unexplored worlds. In "Love's Abodes" the dominating motif is the love. During his last years, he gathered poems from different books and with them he initiated a new phase: *The March of Time* (*Camino de las horas,* 1934), *Autumn in the Dunes* (*Otoño en las dunas,* 1940), *This Beautiful Poisoned City* (*Esta bella ciudad envenenada,* 1945), *Just One Rose* (*No más que una rosa,* 1946). Prado is a reflexive spirit, given to meditation and philosophic preoccupations and readings. He poetized a philosophy of life in parables—*The Abandoned House* (*La casa abandonada,* 1912)—and even in prose poems—*The Errant Birds* (*Los pájaros errantes*). His purest lyrical pages are imbued with a thought process refined into tenuous symbols. In applying his philosophic ideas to social life he arrived at a combination of anarchism and Tolstoyism: through the path of simplicity in conduct, confidence in intelligence and the cult of beauty and goodness, mankind would be liberated. His first novel—*The Queen of Rapa Nui* (*La reina de Rapa Nui,* 1914)—is a beautiful fantasy set on a lost island of the South

Pacific. He followed with *Alsino* (1920), a story about a miracle
that happens to a little Chilean boy who wants to fly. He falls from
a tree. He becomes hunchbacked. His hunch sprouts wings, and
Alsino flies. He grows, he loves. But he is not happy. They im-
prison him and cut off his wings. With brutal witchcraft a woman
blinds him. In the end, in a final flight, Alsino disintegrates in the
air. *Alsino* has no value as an allegory, except for a few scattered
philosophical reflections. Nor is there any evidence that it was
Prado's purpose to elaborate once again on the traditional topic
of human flight; or to analyze the psychology of a man inherently
constituted to reach upwards through his imagination and his
dreams. We do see the lyrical trajectory traced by Prado in his
eagerness to look at nature from changing perspectives. But his
aerial novel is too heavy. It is impaired by its lack of unity. Fantasy and reality beat like Alsino's wings, but his preciousness and
modernism and his realistic description of Chilean life do not
dovetail. The action is disconnected and the beauty of the best
scenes is more literary than poetic. *A Rural Judge* (*Un juez rural*,
1924) relates from street level the daily life of a slum, but the
scenes are not realistic: the author has come down to the street
surface but his eyes bring an idealism from above. After *Karez-
I-Roshan*—a literary hoax that attempted to pass off some of
Prado's prose poems as those of a Persian poet—he published
Androvar (1925), a "tragedy in prose" with a metaphysics of
personality: Androvar, his wife, Elienai, and his disciple, Godel,
fuse into a single consciousness; when Godel dies the two others
can see beyond death.

Also in Chile, also in the narrative literature that does not surrender to realism, we must record JENARO PRIETO (1889–1946).
In his novel, *The Bad Judgment of a Dead Man* (*Un muerto de
mal criterio*, 1926) a judge dies and continues to pass sentence
on "cases" in a court in the world beyond: the cases are absurd,
grotesque, phantasmagorical. The rapid parade of farcical scenes
at times sparkles with good imaginative art. The nightmare ends
when the judge is resuscitated (or, if one prefers a realist explanation, when by a series of injections he recovers his consciousness) and begins to write a novel about the world beyond the

grave which is, precisely, the one we have just read. Very superior was his novel *The Partner* (*El socio*, 1928), related by an omniscient author capable of showing us simultaneous actions and of depicting different characters. Nevertheless, Jenaro Prieto is intentionally close to his protagonist, Julián Pardo (notice that the names of author and character have the same initials), and by means of indirect interior monologs, he follows him even in his most intimate thoughts. Julián Pardo, at one time a poet, now a real-estate agent, invents a partner, Mr. Davis, in order to lighten his responsibilities. All Chilean society accepts the hoax, and the ideal Mr. Davis begins to take on life, body, independence, and effectiveness. He humiliates Pardo, threatens him, destroys him. In the end a beaten Pardo becomes demented, believes in his own creation, and commits suicide—Mr. Davis appears to be the murderer. The police, naturally, then look for Mr. Davis. It is possible that the novel's situation may have been suggested by Oscar Wilde, whom he cites (remember how Algernon invents Bunbury in *The Importance of Being Earnest*). The scholar might propose a long list of possible sources, because the variants on interior duplication in works of art are innumerable: the novel within a novel, the character who invents another character, the fictitious situation that becomes real, the imaginary hero who rebels against the author and proclaims his autonomy. When one speaks of this theme people always remember Pirandello (*Il fu Mattia Pascal, Sei personaggi in cerca d'autore*). But the fact is that Spanish literature was one of the first to deal with it (splendidly in *Don Quijote de la Mancha*) and there is no reason to go far from home: remember in Galdós *Misericordia* how Benina invents "Don Romualdo," who suddenly appears and intervenes in the action, or *El amigo Manso*, also by Galdós, or Augusto Pérez from Unamuno's *Niebla*. The hypostatization of the fictitious Davis is part of a more complicated game: Anita and Julián invent a novel of adultery which they eventually incarnate; Anita invents a Madame Duprés just as Julián Pardo had invented a Mr. Davis, and Madame and Mister will have loves from which will be born a child; a fortuneteller predicts that Anita will marry a nonexistent man, and so Anita has to fall in love with Mr. Davis.

Therefore, it is not a psychological novel with Julián as the "case," but rather a humorous and occasionally satiric novel on the symbolic medium in which all men live, on our myth-making capacity, on imagination as the fabric of an ideal world. Everyone believes in the fictitious Mr. Davis, and even sees him. And the reader himself, in certain pages when he has doubts as to whether Davis exists or not, is also converted into a character of the novel. It is an expressionist novel, then, which in the form of a farce shows how the most absurd ideas are objectified. The prose is rapid, alive, natural, of rare imaginative quality. The metaphors —mainly modernist, at times ultraist—are constantly and forcefully catching fire. The book is impudent, original, humorously winking, but it has a serious purpose: to bring to light man's deceitful nature. His book of memoirs, *The Old House* (*La casa vieja*) was posthumous.

The "more subjective than objective" narrators (as we have labelled them) were at times quite realistic, like Barrios in *A Lost One* (*Un perdido*). And those whom we now characterize as "more objective" at times display a great deal of interest in the psychological, like Edwards Bello and Maluenda.

The regionalists used to go out into the open air, and there they noticed that men were less free than elsewhere: man seemed to appear to them determined, molded, or overcome by nature. This is not exactly applicable to RAFAEL MALUENDA (1885), who has eyes for seeing through to souls, and even magnifying lenses for psychological breakdowns. He comes and goes between the short story and the novel—he succeeds when, halfway between, he writes long stories or short novels—and he always probes deeply into his characters. He has created a rich gallery of characters where rare, eccentric, and complicated personalities abound. He is especially excellent in drawing feminine figures—*Miss Ana, Confessions of a Schoolmistress* (*La señorita Ana, Confesiones de una profesora*). He began with *Scenes of Country Life* (*Escenas de la vida campesina*, 1909), but also novelized scenes of urban life—*Urban Beehive* (*Colmena urbana*, 1937?). The social scale on which he places his narratives is also varied—from the humble classes to the powerful. A good specimen of his irony, of his wit, of his art, is the story "The Pachacha," whose characters are chickens. His theatrical works are not unworthy of his narrative talent. Another great narrator is FERNANDO SANTIVÁN (1886). Santibáñez is his real name. He joined D'Halmar, Prado, and Magallanes Moure in the foundation of a Tolstoyan colony (see his *Memoirs of a Tolstoyan* [*Memorias de un tolstoyano*, 1955] and also the *Confessions of Enrique Samaniego* [*Confesiones de Enrique Samaniego*, 1933] which, as it fluctuates between a novel and an autobiography, sheds light on literary history). Santiván does not invent extraordinary things nor select extraordinary cases from country life; he takes a "piece of life" and his literary effort consists in preserving its palpitations. *Palpitations of Life* (*Palpitaciones de vida*, 1909) is precisely the name of one of his first collections of stories; one of the last: *The Forest Starts Its March* (*El bosque emprende su marcha*, 1946). In his novels he made incursions into the city, into the middle class, into artist and writer circles; but he distinguished himself most in the interpretation of rural life with *The Bewitched* (*La hechizada*, 1916). It is a novel of country environment. A city youth visits the country, falls in love with a girl, fights his rival, and wins her—not in a duel, but in a farm feat. But in the end he discovers that she is "bewitched"; in spite of all, she loves the bad man. The conception of the hero Baltasar and his contrast with the villain Saúl is romantic; and so is the "case" of the girl Humilde. And even the descriptions of the landscape would be romantic if it were not that certain decorative metaphors remind us that Santiván, in writing *The Bewitched,* left behind not romanticism but modernism. Nevertheless, despite this romanticism and modernism, *The Bewitched* can be considered as toned down realism. The Chilean novels and short stories that described life in the country in realist modes were the most abundant. They were realist yet preserved something of the descriptive ways of modernism. Because they admired the landscape, the fauna, and the flora of each region excessively, these narrators tended to forget their characters and their conflicts. They formed a regionalist, Creolist school. The leader of this school was MARIANO LATORRE (1886–1955). He observes, he lists, he documents; seldom does his literature give birth to characters that have the vitality of real men.

He has written novels, for example, *Zurzulita* (1920), in which we are told that a young villager, Mateo, goes to the country to take possession of his heritage, runs into a hostile atmosphere, has a love affair with Milla, a young teacher, beautiful and harsh, like one of the *zurzulitas* (little Chilean birds) when caged up; he wants to marry her and is refused in spite of the fact that she is pregnant; and when he decides to leave the country he is murdered for the sake of vengeance. Descriptions, excessive in their realistic detail, drown out the story. The only interesting character is Milla who, though not satisfactorily developed, has more of the instincts of a female than the feelings of a woman. This animalism reflects the author's naturalistic point of view. The sketches of customs do not succeed in giving distinction to this novel. Actually, what is admirable of Latorre's work is his collection of short stories. *Ully* (1923), *On Panta* (1936), *Men and Foxes* (*Hombres y zorros,* 1937), *Mapu* (1942), *Viento de mallines* (1944) and many others. It is as if his long series of volumes wanted, tirelessly, to exhaust the description of the soil of Chile, inch by inch: the landscape of Chile appears in his last book, *Bird Island* (*La isla de los pájaros*).

In the Creolist school headed by Latorre we find LUIS DURAND (1895–1954). His characters are peasants. He surrounds them with landscape. When he hears them speak he reproduces their rustic voices unadornedly. He was a short-story writer, somewhat careless in the art of composition, but prolific (see his anthological *Seven Tales* [*Siete cuentos,* 1955]). He was also successful as a novelist: *Frontier* (*Frontera,* 1949). ERNESTO

MONTENEGRO (1885) is not easy to place. He elaborated the folklore of his land without literarily retouching what was handed to him by tradition: *My Uncle Ventura: Popular Tales of Chile (Mi tío Ventura. Cuentos populares de Chile,* second edition, augmented, 1938). Different from the Creolists, sketchers of customs, and regionalists, there were those who, without renouncing realism, brought a greater complexity to the novel—the complexity of large cities, of political agitation, of spiritual life, of uncommon themes, of new techniques in the art of storytelling, of irony and imagination. The two outstanding figures were Edwards Bello, at the beginning of the period, and Manuel Rojas, at the end. JOAQUÍN EDWARDS BELLO, (1886) is a psychological novelist, though not as artistic as Barrios. He is always on the lookout for abnormal human types, unbalanced because of their impulsiveness or their lethargy, excited by action or by delirium. The social conduct of his characters is observed, nevertheless, through the combined perspective of psychology and sociology. After several attempts he succeeded with *The Down-and-Outer (El roto,* 1920), an "experimental novel" on the bawdy houses and the underworld of Santiago de Chile.

In *The Death of Vanderbilt (La muerte de Vanderbilt,* 1922) the imaginary description of the famous sinking of the *Titanic* in 1912 serves as a background for a tenuous love story and a dense network of observations and metaphors. The style, cosmopolitan, flexible, ingenious, ironic, and sometimes aphoristic, reveals the influence that the literature of the vanguard was exerting on the author at that time. Previously, in *The Useless One (El inútil,* 1910) and *The Down-and-Outer (El roto,* 1920), his style had been naturalistic. After the First World War the breath of ultraism blew on his work. Later Edwards Bello turned his travel experiences into novels: *The Chilean in Madrid (El chileno en Madrid,* 1928) and *Creoles in Paris (Criollos en París,* 1933). In the novels set in Chile, the attack on national vices is merciless. There is, down deep, a love for the country and its people, but on the surface one only sees a discontented and reforming spirit. Whether he is evoking memories of his own life—*In Old Almendral: Valparaiso, Windy City (En el viejo Almendral: Valparaíso, cuidad del viento,* 1931)—or showing a life of false luxury through a woman—*The Girl from Crillón (La chica del Crillón,* 1935)—Edwards Bello is amazing for the ease of his narrative movement. Yet, he was not a great novelist. The carelessness of his hurried writing left his characters obscure and pieces of his story unhinged, not counting what fell beyond the artistic heart of the novel itself, such as social theses, sketches of customs, journalistic material.

We have left for the end, because he is singular in every respect, MANUEL ROJAS (1896). He was born in Argentina but as an adolescent went to Chile. In his epoch, the sketches of customs of Santibáñez and his generation dominated the scene. Though his parents were Chilean, Rojas was not looked upon as a Chilean, nor were his experiences totally Chilean. He therefore remained outside the circle of writers of social customs. He told stories, mixing the Argentinian with the Chilean. Rojas was not worried about being atypical. He was not interested in becoming a sketcher of customs. On the contrary. For him it is not, the mission of the short story or of the novel to overwhelm insignificant men with landscapes. What he wanted was to show what man feels, thinks, and is. And to describe this man he did not turn to linguistic naturalism. Of course, his characters spoke naturally, but he did not insist on putting words taken from the outlying corners of society into their mouths. He aspired to be read by a public beyond the region that he was describing. His narrative material consisted of men as they are, and of the situations they are in. Nature enters only in relation with the characters. The description of nature must be essential to the narrative, not a mere decoration, luxury, or exhibition of virtuosity. But he looks at men as a group on the march. He does not seek to create a great character. Hispanic-American writers have had almost no influence on him (he admired Horacio Quiroga most). On the other hand, some Americans did influence Rojas: Hemingway, and above all, Faulkner. From Faulkner he learned to avoid the heavy novelistic techniques of the nineteenth century, where all the action is explicitly described; Rojas preferred to reveal the action with interior monologs and time shifts without having to explain them to the reader. An able narrator in every setting— sea, country, city—he created in his innumerable short stories a whole population of characters. They are collected in various books, from *Men of the South* (*Hombres del sur*, 1927) to *The Biretta from Maule* (*El bonete maulino*, 1943), and in various novels, from *Launches in the Bay* (*Lanchas en la bahía*, 1932) to *Son of a Thief* (*Hijo de ladrón*, 1951). This last one, in the style of memoirs, is considered one of the best in all Hispanic-America. *Son of a Thief* is the first of a trilogy. The second, *Shadows Against the Wall* (*Sombras contra el muro*, 1964. The third, *Better Than Wine* (*Mejor que el vino*, 1958). *Son of a Thief* relates, in the first person, the life of a boy from his first recollections until his seventeenth year: his poverty, his orphanhood, his sufferings, his trip to Chile, his hunger, his participation in a popular uprising, his unjust imprisonment, his hard labors, his friendships. All the material related is real—even the filthiest scenes—but the narrative manner is not typical of realism. His sympathy for strange lives leads him to paint, with very imaginative tints, a whole gallery of eccentricities. His taste for strange people in strange situations cause the narrator to stray from the line of his memoirs. Moreover, the whole novel is dislocated from the inside. There is no narrative sequence. The narrator follows the flow of his evocations. Capriciously, the action is sent forward or held back. This rupture in the order of events increases the reader's interest, especially if the procedure is a novelty to him. If, on the other hand, the reader is already acquainted with the use of dislocations of planes in the masters, James Joyce, Aldous Huxley, William Faulkner, and others, he may notice the huge difference: in Rojas the technique of looking at one life from different levels of time does not form part of an original and poetic vision of the world, but is, rather, a way of composing a novel in the easiest and most comfortable position. The interior monologs, the indirect free style, the stream of consciousness do not succeed, in Rojas, in penetrating profoundly the intimate being of each character. His *Autobiographical Anthology* (*Antología autobiográfica,* 1962) is interesting because of the information it contains on the author's own literary output, up to his novel *End of the Railroad* (*Punta de rieles,* 1960).

Among those writers who were more complex than the Creolists—we have just named Edwards Bello and Rojas—there is a tendency toward sociological realism. It had come down from Baldomero Lillo; now we see it headed by Edwards Bello. We will see its immediate continuation in González Vera; and, in the following chapters, Godoy, Guzmán, and others will carry on. JOSÉ SANTOS GONZÁLEZ VERA (1897) wrote scanty, sober, delicate works that had the virtue of being directed to minorities, even though his themes go deep into the humble and dispossessed masses. *Minimal Lives* (*Vidas mínimas,* 1923) carries the story of a tenement house; *Alhue* (1928) is a collection of simple stories of a country village; *When I Was a Boy* (*Cuando era muchacho,* 1951) is the autobiography of his poverty. ALBERTO ROMERO (1896), with naturalist tenacity, depicted in *The Tenement House Widow* (*La viuda del conventillo,* 1930) a reality similar to that of *The Down-and-Outer* of Edwards Bello, that is, the slums of Santiago. In other novels his preferred theme was the life of the middle class. Other writers, excited by social and political commotions, were: JUAN MODESTO CASTRO (1896–1943), author of *Stagnant Waters* (*Aguas estancadas*), and WALDO URZÚA ÁLVAREZ (1891–1944), author of *A Man and a River (Un hombre y un río)*. Of those Chilean narrators who belong here because of their age, it suffices to mention EDGARDO GARRIDO MERINO (1888), whose novel *The Man of the Mountain (El hombre de la montaña)* places him in Spanish literature; VICTORIANO LILLO (1889) who is inclined to write about psychological and even fantastic themes; CARLOS SEPULVEDA LEYTON (1894–1944), author of *Nobody's Son (Hijuna)*, etc.

(x) *Paraguay* / LEOPOLDO CENTURIÓN (1893–1922) and ROQUE CAPACE FARAONE (1894–1928), both initiated into the modernist group of the review *Crónica* (1913), wrote short stories in a modernist, colorful prose with precious French brush strokes.

NATALICIO GONZÁLEZ (1897) stands out here. In his country he initiated a poetry directed at vindicating the Indian. His attitude was more nationalistic than esthetic. His poetry, beginning with *Guaraní Ballads (Baladas guaraníes)* up to *Elegies of Tenochtitlán* (1953) passing through *Motifs of the Red Land (Motivos de la tierra escarlata, 1952)* in which he included his Guaraní ballads together with other personal and political compositions, remained hidden, however, under the weight of a larger prose production. As a prose writer—essay, narration—he was more vigorous. He is the author of *Stories and Parables (Cuentos y parabolas, 1922)* inspired by indigenous legends, and *The Errant Root (La raíz errante, 1953)*, a novel that takes place in the jungle on the sociological theme of the divestiture of lands from traditional owners. A prose larded with Guaraní language. JUAN STEFANICH (1889) in *Aurora* (1920) novelized the fight of university students against a petty tyrant, with the bourgeois life of Asunción as a background. Other narrators: LUCIO MENDONÇA (1896) and JUSTO PASTOR BENÍTEZ (1895–1962).

(xi) *Uruguay* / ADOLFO AGORIO (1888) colored with fantasy and exoticism the prose narrative of *Rishi-Abura* (1920), a "voyage to the land of shadows." This swamp witch emanates from the superstitions of the Indians.

ADOLFO MONTIEL BALLESTEROS (1888) is one of the more complex—in genres, themes, intentions, and moods. He was outstanding in his pictures of the life of the soil, with narratives that were true to life, but also rich in good humor, imagination and lyricism. At times his mood is so lyrical that the reader discovers that his narrative material is actually made up of metaphors, as in his *New Fables (Nuevas fábulas)*. He has cultivated fiction for children, fiction built on fantasy, and humorous fiction. His most important works, however, are his stories and novels about town and country. *World in Torment (Mundo en ascuas, 1957)* is one of his latest novels. MANUEL DE CASTRO (1896) has alternated verse with prose. He distinguished himself as a sonneteer: *Meridian (Meridión)* and continued to serve poetry. He gained greater recognition with his urban novels: *Story of a Petty Officer (Historia de un pequeño funcionario)*, *Father Samuel (El padre Samuel)* *The Business of Living (Oficio de vivir)*, and short stories: "The Enigma of Work" (*"El enigma del oficio"*), "Smoke on the Island" (*Humo en la isla*). His stories are like fragments of memories of a versatile man of travel with a rich and prodigal vitality. ALBERTO LASPLACES (1887) writes good short stories on native matters.

(xii) *Argentina* / With the appearance of the verses in *The Crystal Bell* (*El cencerro de cristal*) in 1915, RICARDO GÜIRALDES (1886–1927) presented his credentials as a reader of French poetry and daring poet: as a reader, he preferred the symbolists and, above all, Jules Laforgue; as a poet he tried a good deal, succeeded at times, and managed some advances which later were to be called "creationism" and "ultraism." *Stories of Death and Blood* (*Cuentos de muerte y de sangre*), also of 1915, were in reality "anecdotes heard and written because of our affection for the things of our land." These *Stories* were neither well constructed nor well written. But the "affection for things of our land," for the Argentinian countryside and its folk, was to inspire better works. There were already two interesting novelettes: *Raucho* (1917), in whose protagonist we see the same educational upbringing as in the author who, wearied of Buenos Aires, wearied of Paris, was attracted to the country, and *Rosaura* (1922), a simple, sentimental, and melancholy story of small-town loves. The second is of especial interest because the constructive and emotional unity are much more obvious than in all his other works. Quite apparent, also, is the influence of Laforgue on his poetic, metaphoric, impressionistic language, ironic in its expression of tenderness. Güiraldes appreciated the prose poem —in Baudelaire, Flaubert, Villiers de l'Isle-Adam, Aloysius Bertrand—and in poetic prose he published in 1923 his most characteristic book: *Xaimaca*, which is typical of his double and harmonic aptitude as a lyricist and narrator. The novel *Xaimaca*—a voyage from Buenos Aires to Jamaica, with a love adventure— was forgotten because of the success of *Don Segundo Sombra* (1926). There were factors foreign to purely literary merits that entered into this success, such as the nationalist feelings of the reader, the surprise of finding, in gaucho clothes, a metaphoric language fashionable in postwar literature, and a conception of the novel, also fashionable in those years, according to which the poetic tone was more important than the action and the characterization. The action is contemplated through a curious esthetic lens that retires objects to a distance, yet enlarges them. The cattleman Don Segundo, for example, is a "phantom, a shadow, an idea" that appears to be emerging from tradition. He is not the gaucho of the *Facundo* nor of the *Martín Fierro* epoch, but he does come from those backgrounds and the narrator is overcome with admiration for his aura of historic legend: "What a leader of the bushwhackers (*montonera*) he would have been!" Although we see him as a laboring and civilized cattleman, he is not a contemporary man, but "something that is passing." The novel, in this regard, is in the form of a farewell. It evokes an Argentina that is passing and the narrator takes leave of it with the tenderness of a poet. One by one the scenes of country life make up a poetic of regional customs: the small town, the general store, the saddle-breaking, natural love, the slaughtering of cattle, the square dance, folkloric tales, cockfights, scenes of Creole politicking, fairs, encounters of old friends in the nomadic life of the Argentine plains, horse herding, the round-up, knife duels, horse racing for money, stampedes. Within this body of lyrical evocations of customs, there is the skeleton and musculature of a novel. That is, these lyrical evocations of customs move at a novel's pace, but with a simple, minimal action. In the form of memoirs Fabio Cáceres relates details of his life.

There are twenty-seven chapters that might be divided into three parts, though not all the readers will agree on the location of the divisions of this tripartition. Those who like symmetry might propose three parts of nine chapters each. First: an orphan boy of fourteen, who does not know who his father was and who, up to now, has roamed the streets of a country town like a rogue, is suddenly fascinated by the appearance of the gaucho, Don Segundo Sombra, and decides to hang on to him like a burr. He runs away from home and is initiated into "the most manly of occupations": steer-herding on the pampas. This exposition, into which a family secret is inserted, comes to a close with an interruption in the narrative sequence. Second part: five years have passed, and our protagonist-narrator tells us that Don Segundo Sombra has made a gaucho out of him. From this point, the following nine chapters are nine sketches of rural customs. This part, descriptive not only of customs but also of landscapes, culminates in chapter XVIII, when the protagonist-narrator, on coming to

from a fainting spell, has the rare experience of seeing into the
future: he hears, or believes he hears, what he will indeed hear
in chapter XXVI, that from a cowhand he has become a rich
cattleman. Third part: his labors as a cowboy continue, with a
few adventurous sketches included. The protagonist returns to
his home town and there finds out who his father was. He inherits
his name and property, becomes a cultured man, and has the urge
to become a writer. The book ends with Don Segundo Sombra's
farewell. This symmetrical division, although defensible, suggests
a rigorous structure that the novel is far from having. An asym-
metrical division composed of three retrospective moments is one
that the protagonist-narrator himself proposes: first chapter, in
which, at the edge of a brook, the fourteen-year-old youth evokes
his childhood; tenth chapter, in which, at the shores of a river, he
evokes his five years of living with Don Segundo Sombra; chapter
XXVI, in which, on the banks of a lagoon, he evokes his three
years as the owner of a ranch. There are other structural elements
in the novel: the appearance and disappearance of Don Segundo
Sombra (chapters II and XXVII), both actions occurring at dusk
and described almost with the same words ("I thought I had seen
a phantom, a shadow, something that passes by and is more an
idea than a person"; "What went off into the distance was more
an idea than a man"); the narrator's premonition of the future on
coming to after fainting—encased in another supernatural episode, that of Don Sixto, the invisible devil, and the death of his
son—and the repetition of the scene, nine chapters later; the narrator's family mystery that opens the novel, and its final clarification. But let us not exaggerate: *Don Segundo Sombra* is not a
novel of a complex and harmonic architectural structure. The
order is rather that of a collector of scenes and landscapes who
wants to complete an album of pages linearly juxtaposed. The
action changes pace, it moves slowly, it hurries along, and it even
leaps over time, only to return later to complete itself in a flashback (the separation of the two lovers in chapter VI, which closes
the love scene begun in chapter V); but it never reaches the fluidity of the psychic life of the narrator. "Gradually my recollections
had brought me up to the present," Fabio says in his first retro-

spection (chapter I). How coincidental that recollections should be organized in such a logical sequence! These are memories written like a clear and coherent soliloquy that arranges the episodes with the object of moving the urban reader by presenting him with a stylization of country life. There are no interior monologs to reveal directly the profound life of the narrator. "Brief words fell like ashes of inner thoughts," Fabio tells us; but either we do not hear them or, if we do, they have already lost their fleeting intimacy. Nevertheless, the greatest achievement of the novel is the oneness of its point of view. "Enclosed within a character that did not allow me to pour myself out in him except with great prudence," Güiraldes explained to Valery Larbaud, "I have been obliged to restrain my desires to achieve perfection of expression." And, in fact, what elegant temperance this is, to resist the temptation of displaying his powers as a cultured writer! "I don't wish to speak about that," says the narrator referring to his education and travels to the world's capitals, "in these lines that describe a simple soul." He avoided dissonances between the style and the theme, and his efforts were dissimulated and always subtle. And so, as he fashioned the usual gaucho similes, transforming them into new metaphors, he also thinned down the sulky, malicious speech until it took on literary subtlety, as in "I have lost a ring in the cornfield," spoken by the girl, chapter IV, in which "ring"—as in Chaucer—means virginity.

But the protagonist's change in social position, with his subsequent literary education, capably solves the problem that intrigues the reader from the very first pages: What will happen farther on, he may ask, to make the little gaucho who is telling us his memoirs acquire a perspective on his own life that is so literary, so wise in metaphoric procedures? Because the perspective with which the protagonist is contemplating the countryside, its men, and his own adventures is always idealizingly poetic. At times he looks down upon himself from the sun: "the first look from the sun found me sweeping"; more normally he looks at himself from a moon, high and distant, illuminated by cosmopolitan literature. It has already been noted that among the many refinements that Güiraldes puts into the soul of his protagonist—

metaphors, rare sensations, synesthesia—there is evidence of that
literature that offers cases of parapsychological states, telepathy,
and paramnesias. It is true that the little gaucho Fabián always
had a delicate nervous constitution (with esthetic delights, superstitious shudderings, a propensity to tears, and the imagination of
one who enjoys hearing the stories that Don Segundo elaborated
in his campfire chats), but without that jump from cowhand to
ranch owner—and, consequently, without the time distance between the adventures he experienced and the memories he evoked
—the book would not be convincing. In his evocative flights the
protagonist considers as feats what to Don Segundo were everyday events: to lasso, to break horses, to wrangle steers were feats
for one who, through later education, learns that the cultured
public of the city, having read about them in many books, would
also consider them as such. A stylistic analysis would show the
complicated inventive operations with which *Don Segundo Sombra* was created. Operations that were very subtle, very lyrical,
very cultured; but one of these was intended to objectify the collective soul of the traditional Creole Argentina, and this achievement in descriptive transparency is what gained international
recognition for the novel. It was thought to be a realist novel,
almost a telluric novel. Not at all. Güiraldes, a rich ranch owner,
educated in the latest currents of French literature, did not express the real viewpoint of the cattlemen: as he let Fabio Cáceres
speak, he put symbols of distance in his mouth ("for those old
timers"), extemporaneous judgments, philosophical reflections
foreign to the world of the gaucho and, especially in chapter
XXVII, scorn for the wealth and comfort that falsified the social
reality of the Argentine countryside. But, in spite of this social
falsification, the novel has an admirable stylistic truthfulness.
Fabio Cáceres, now a mature man and writer, relives his cowboy
years and describes them in a language of refined expressive dignity, yet true to the actual vision of country life. The vision is that
of a lyrical poet, but the things he sees are only those that are
there before him. No matter how original his metaphors may be,
they never go beyond the horizons of the pampa: they fuse and
transmute things familiar to cowboys and cattlemen. Even the

most realistic details are doubly artistic: because they are chosen for their starkness and because of their evocative effect. Güiraldes combined the language spoken from birth by the Creoles with the language of the Creolist educated in European impressionism, expressionism, and ultraism. In spite of his realist dialogs, his folklore, his rural comparisons, his pampa dialect of cowhands and cattlemen, *Don Segundo Sombra* is an artistic novel. Cáceres, without leaving his pampa, strives for a style rich in rare and brilliant images.

Before going into realism we should record the fantastic narrations of SANTIAGO DABOVE (1889–1951). A friend of Macedonio Fernández and of Borges, a reader of Horacio Quiroga and of Leopoldo Lugones, he wrote a few stories of horror, neurasthenia, madness, alcohol, and metamorphosis, with themes from science fiction and characters obsessed with death.

There are novels from every region, with European urbanity and Creole rusticity, evocative of the past or belligerent in the present, sweet and bitter, written with careful art or with fretfulness. Here are some of the authors. First, those who narrate the life of the city. VÍCTOR JUAN GUILLOT (1886–1940), in *Stories Without Importance (Historias sin importancia), Terror,* and *The Soul in a Pit (El alma en el pozo).* GUILLERMO ESTRELLA (1891–1943), in *The Egoists and Other Stories (Los egoístas y otros cuentos,* 1923) and *The Owner of the Fire (El dueño del incendio,* 1929), ironically captured happenings of life in Buenos Aires. Other narrators of this type: SAMUEL GLUSBERG (1898), JOSÉ GABRIEL (1898), HECTOR OLIVERA LAVIÉ (1893), ERNESTO MARIO BARREDA (1889), CARLOS ALBERTO LEUMANN (1888–1952). In his *Three Stories About Buenos Aires (Tres relatos porteños,* 1922) ARTURO CANCELA (1892) feigns a subtle and cold humor. Cancela is not laughing as he writes: all the effectiveness of his pages is due to his impassivity. The style seems simple, and no doubt it is; at moments it seems to flow from his pen, in a conversational tone, but suddenly one is aware that an effort has been made—the effort to become serious without reproof, bitterness, or mockery. The first of his stories, "Herrlin's Coccusbacillus" *("El cocobacilo de Herrlin"),* is a caricature of Argentine bureaucracy. The second, "A Week on a Spree" *("Una semana de holgorio"),* is better because the satire is less obvious, and the story, in the first person and in the present time, creates an atmosphere of fantasy and even poetry. Nevertheless, the satire is there: it alludes to the events of the "tragic week in January" (1919), when young patriots, taking advantage of workers' agitation following the Russian revolution, murdered Jews and identified the ideals of Argentina with those of the Jockey Club. But the satirical observations appear as the little bones of an airy literary body that moves with the grace and vivacity of stories similar to those of Chesterton, whom, let it be said in passing, Cancela read in English and whom it is not unlikely that he imitated. The third story, "The Cult of Heroes" *("El culto de los héroes"),* is on its way to being a novel, and perhaps because it promises to be a novel, it is less satisfactory as a short story. Some of the narrators of the city, because of their preference for humble lives and cases of poverty, form the "Boedo group," after Boedo Street which was then a so-called proletarian street. Their organ was *Los Pensadores* (later *Claridad*), and their function, to give literary dignity to the working classes.

To this generation (there were other younger ones who are waiting for us in the next chapter) belong Yunque, Mariani, and Castelnuovo, three readers of Russian literature; the first, of Tolstoy, the second, of Chekhov, and third, of Dostoevski. ÁLVARO YUNQUE (1893) believes that the suffering of one man suffices to make society unjust. His literature is a long lament. During those years, these laments were called "social ferment." Of anarchic mind and apostolic sentiments, he spoke to men in very simple words. His tenderness toward the sad lives of poor children was most moving: *Bichofeo*. Other titles: *Scarecrows* (*Espanta-pájaros*), *Zancadilla, Poor Boys* (*Muchachos pobres*). ROBERTO MARIANI (1893–1946) also wrote to serve man and yearned for goodness and justice, but he was more complex. In *Office Stories* (*Cuentos de oficina*) he observed the lowest and grayest layers of the bourgeoisie, but his preoccupation with death gave his pages a deeper dimension: in *Aggressive Love* (*El amor agresivo*), *Death's Visitations* (*La frecuentación de la muerte*), *In the Penumbra* (*En la penumbra*), *Return to God* (*Regreso a Dios*) he penetrated his characters, even those most trapped by circumstances. ELÍAS CASTELNUOVO (1893) was the most naturalistic of the group. Not only did he denounce social inequality but also the curse that falls on the insane, the lepers, and other shattered humans: *Darkness* (*Tinieblas*, 1923), *The Cursed Ones* (*Malditos*, 1924), *Among the Dead* (*Entre los muertos*, 1925), *Cannon Fodder* (*Carne de cañón*, 1926), *Calvary* (*Calvario*, 1929), *Grubs* (*Larvas*, 1931) are his gay titles. Let us now pass on to those narrators who describe life in the country, provincial towns, and villages. Some move from place to place. ALBERTO GERCHUNOFF (1884–1950) who in *The Jewish Gauchos* (*Los gauchos judíos*) described rural life in an Argentine province, with poetic grace; in the novel, *The Important Man* (*El hombre importante*), he described the life of a contemporary political boss, Hipólito Irogoyen, with satiric humor. The quick and pleasant pen of BERNARDO GONZÁLEZ ARRILI (1892) has evoked, in novels and collections of stories, an Argentina of broad scope, of long history, and of a rich variety of themes: politicking— *Protasio Lucero,* the customs of the northern provinces—*The Calchaquí Venus* (*La Venus calchaquí*), the conflicts between labor and capital in the refrigerator store-houses of Barracas—*The Red Pools* (*Los charcos rojos*), historical episodes—*The Invasion of the Heretics* (*La invasión de los herejes*), Creole devotion—*The Virgin of Luján* (*La Virgen de Luján*), memories of childhood in Buenos Aires—*Corrientes Street Between Esmeraldas and Suipacha* (*Calle Corrientes entre Esmeraldas y Suipacha*). JULIO VIGNOLA MANSILLA (1891) re-elaborated the folklore material of several provinces in a series of short stories. A rare gift of phrase is evident in the *History of an Absurd Passion* (*Historia de una pasión absurda*) by CARMELO M. BONET (1886). From the mountainous region of northern Argentina came some good narrative books. *The White Wind* (*El viento blanco*) by JUAN CARLOS DÁVALOS (1887–1959); *The Regionalists* (*Los regionales*) by FAUSTO BURGOS (1888–1952); *The Long-Suffering Race* (*La raza sufrida*) by CARLOS B. QUIROGA (1887); *The Gold Prospector and Other Stories* (*El buscador de oro y otros cuentos*) by JULIO ARAMBURU (1898); *Wild Horses* (*Baguales*) by JUSTO P. SÁENZ (1892); *The Night Patio* (*El patio de la noche*) by PABLO ROJAS PAZ (1896–1956); *The Water Well* (*El pozo de balde*) by ROSA BAZÁN DE CÁMARA (1892). From the coast area and the pampa: *Wanderers and Capable Men* (*Errantes y hombres capaces*) by HÉCTOR I. EANDI (1895); *Gringo Pampa* (*Pampa gringa*) by ALCIDES GRECA (1896).

2. Essay

We have noticed that verse and prose are like two stories of the same building: the writers who live in it go from one floor to another and write a poem as easily as a novel. And there are houses not of two but of ten stories, where the polygraphers, like Alfonso Reyes, live.

ALFONSO REYES (Mexico, 1889–1959)—like Prado, Güiraldes, Rivera, Arévalo Martínez—overflowed from verse to prose. He is better qualified than anyone else to serve as a link between the first pages in this chapter that deal with poetry and the following pages on prose. Since he is as illustrious in one as in the other, he could be placed in either section. But it would not be proper to sever his work and study it separately because, as in no other writer, his verse and his prose form a crystalline unity. His poetic books appeared so widely interspersed in almost unavailable editions, so overwhelmed by his greater prose production, with such versatility of style, themes, and tonality, that very few readers have a clear image of the poet Reyes. When he finally published his poetic works *Poetic Constancy* (*Constancia poética*) in which he collected earlier books and added unpublished poems, it was patent to all, not just to a minority, that Reyes was excellent. He groups his poetry under three headings. The first is a "Poetic review," then the topical verses, "Courtesy" (*"Cortesía"*) and finally, those books of poetry which have a certain unity: "Cruel Iphigenia" (*"Ifigenia cruel"*), "Three Poems" (*"Tres poemas"*), "Day's Sonnets" (*"Jornada en sonetos"*), and "Deaf Ballads" (*"Romances sordos"*). His first poems, from around 1906, were Parnassian. Having learned respect for verse forms in this school,

Reyes struck out for himself. Like other modernists, he penetrated the obscurities of his own being, sometimes to bring color
to it, sometimes to question, and sometimes even to touch its dark
and silent depths. Serious symbolism alongside of which, after the
first world war, rhythms and images of juvenile vanguardism begin
to come into play. There were even poems describing sensual
African dances. Actually, nothing was outside the pale of his
poetry which was "fickle in theme and style." His themes were as
varied as the stages of his own life: autobiographical evocations,
the homeland, friends and loves, works, and death. His styles
come and go between the laboratory in which the hermetic poets
distill their verse and the clear, open road where the people walk.
Reyes was not afraid to walk along the most dangerous trails: for
example, along the trail of prose (in case they "jumped him" he
was well armed—see his "Prosaic Theory," where he declares "I
prefer to be promiscuous / in literature," "the popular ballad / of
the neighbor / with the rare quintessence / of Góngora and Mallarmé"). Difficult or simple he always demands the attention of
the reader, because earlier, he was demanding of himself and now
extracts the sheer essence.

His poetry is concise, sober, insinuating. His prose is beaten
gold. The virtues of intelligence and esteem that tend to come
separately in people are integrated in Alfonso Reyes into a beam
of gracious and subtle light. He is erudite in the field of philology
and sparkling in witty sallies; he writes stories, chronicles,
sketches, and penetrating critical glosses. His prose is prying and
delightful. The multiplicity of Reyes' vocations (a man of the
Renaissance) is not only measured by the vast repertory of motifs,
but also by the stylistic richness of each turn. Reyes' restlessness
transmits to his style a zigzagging, jumpy, prankish, and sensual
movement. Before leaving Mexico in 1913, his writer's hand was
already trained: from this period, with a single exception, come
the stories and dialogs of *The Oblique Plane* (*El plano oblicuo*,
1920), a most original book in the Spanish language because of
its rapid shifts from the real to the fantastic ("The Supper"—
"*La cena*") and because of its expressionist procedures. From
1914, except for a brief stay in France, he was to live in Spain

until 1924, probably the most productive period of his career: *Vision of Anáhuac* (*Visión de Anáhuac*, 1917), whose pages were collected much later under the title of *The Eves of Spain* (*Las vísperas de España*, 1937); *The Suicide* (*El suicida*, 1917), *The Hunter* (*El cazador*, 1921), *Real and Imaginary Portraits* (*Retratos reales e imaginarios*, 1920), and the five series of *Sympathies and Differences* (*Simpatías y diferencias*, 1921–1926). This is a consummate work that links on different pages, and at times on the same page, impressionist sentences, elegances, narrative flights of fancy, biographical sketches, notes, reflections, and fantasies. His norms appear to be these: to express himself in miniatures; not to rely too much on actual things; to subjectivize everything, whether it be through his sensibilities or through his imagination; to intermingle life and culture; to address himself to a sympathetic reader who possesses the same qualities that the writer possesses, and to converse with him; to watch each word. Later still in the diplomatic service, Reyes continued his travels: France, Hispanic-America (1925–1938), and his final return to Mexico in 1939. From among his personal, imaginative, and expressive prose works, let us mention here, *The Testimony of Juan Peña* (*El testimonio de Juan Peña*, 1930), *A Train of Waves* (*Tren de ondas*, 1932), *The Seven Above Deva* (*Los siete sobre Deva*, 1942), *Works and Days* (*Los trabajos y los días*, 1945), *In Pencil* (*A lápiz*, 1947), *The Literary Experience* (*La experiencia literaria*, 1952), *Fireworks* (*Árbol de pólvora*, 1953), and *Fifteen Presences* (*Quince presencias*, 1955). One characteristic of his fictional work is that he prefers to arouse the imagination of the reader through suggested details rather than to satisfy his curiosity with a plot or a denouement. It is fantasy for sharp readers, already accustomed to and perhaps tired of reading so many novels. His essays are always lyrical, even those of didactic or logical themes, because the manner in which he treats his object is personal, not public. In *Sundial* (*Reloj de sol*, 1926) Reyes confessed: "The historian I carry in my pocket will not allow me to waste a single datum, a single document." But it is not so much a desire to recreate a public past as it is to reconstruct an intimate diary whose leaves had been falling out on the way. Like Echo, the quartered nymph, the diary that was buried here and there by Reyes throughout his work lives on in a constant murmur. No matter how impersonal a Reyes theme may appear, one can always perceive the vibration of a confidence about to be revealed. Even though he was one of our most exquisite, most original, most surprising writers, Reyes founded his work on healthy experiences. Others would like to look at the world upside down, to see if a world askew will tell them something new: they mutilate themselves or give value to their mutilations; they give themselves over to sophistic frenzy or to lethargy; they corrupt honor, deny light, betray the heart. Not Reyes. Alfonso Reyes is a classical writer because of the human integrity of his vocation, because of his serene faith in intelligence, in charity, in the eternal values of the soul. The uniqueness of Reyes' poetic universe is not extravagance, but the refinement of the normal directions in man. Each one of his volumes is a collection of unsurpassed pages. To date, the Fondo de Cultura Económica of Mexico City has published thirteen thick volumes of *Complete Works*. On contemplating this grandiose monument to his effort, a literary critic states a number of problems that should be studied carefully: the problem of a writer who fails in spite of being extraordinarily equipped for success; that of a secret sterility that is disguised by incessant labor; that of an intelligence which, because of its propensity for dialog, kept its face turned toward the best spirits of its time, but its back to its own works; that of a classic writer of our literary history who, nevertheless, left no great books. Is there in the air of Hispanic-America something lethal to literary creation? Why did not the author of *The Testimony of Juan Peña* give us the novel he promised? Why did not the author of "The Supper" give us the collection of stories he promised? Why did not the author of *Cruel Iphigenia*, of *Footprints*, give us the drama, the book of poems he promised? Indeed, the fruits yielded are sufficient. But for those of us who had the privilege of being his friends, it is clear that Alfonso Reyes could have given more, much more than that, to the great genres of literature. Where he did succeed was in the essay. Alfonso Reyes is without any doubt the keenest, most brilliant, versatile, cultured, and profound essayist in our language today.

PEDRO HENRÍQUEZ UREÑA (Dominican Republic, 1884–1946) began as a critic—*Critical Essays* (*Ensayos críticos*, 1905), *Hours of Study* (*Horas de estudio*, 1910)—and this is the most visible specimen of his work, which is so pithy in philological research, in literary history, in the disquisition and synthesis of general questions, in the preparation of anthologies and bibliographies. But he was also an imaginative and sensitive writer: verses of modernist flavor, poetic prose, travel descriptions, the *Birth of Dionysus* (*El nacimiento de Dionisus*, 1916), "an essay of tragedy in the ancient manner," beautiful stories. He did not write enough in this vein to be incorporated into a purely literary history. Nevertheless, his artistic sense puts its seal on everything he wrote including his rigorously technical works. His prose was masterful in precision, economy, and architecture. He was a humanist formed by all literatures, by all philosophies; and in his curiosity for things human, he did not even neglect the sciences. His written work, though important, scarcely reflects the value of his talent. He gave his best to his friends, in conversations, in teachings. Wherever he lived he created atmosphere, intellectual groups, disciples. He had classical, rationalist preferences: and even in his socialist ideas, in favor of a new social order based on economic equality, and on personal and national liberty, these preferences for clear and constructive thinking appeared. See *Critical Works* (*Obra crítica*, 1960).

Let us pay a call on another essayist of this period, VICTORIA OCAMPO (Argentina, 1893). Her education was European to the point that in her childhood and youth she thought in French, not in Castilian. But she assumed the civic responsibility of applying European culture to the improvement of Argentine literary life. The secret of her personality lies in her intense perception of spiritual values, in the special delight she takes in cultivating the friendship of anyone who creates these values and in her firm resolution to insure that these creative souls enjoy the greatest possible freedom. Victoria's essays are hardly anything but chronicles of her spirit in its approach to others, in a free association of fertile minds. Her relativist and aristocratic theory of values moves her to write impressionistic autobiographical chronicles. Victoria is an introvert, dwelling in an inner exposure, who speaks

only of what she has experienced and delights only in what has
been illuminated by recollection. The appeal of her prose lies in
its frankness, its freshness. The reader trusts Victoria. He knows
that if she writes it is to say something profoundly moving. For
this reason the passages with the most productive function in her
body of essays are the revealing quotation, the anecdote, the
landscape shaken by the reflection of a passer-by, biographical
sketches of friends, the evaluation of works of art and literature,
the personal nostalgias, the intimate confidences, The tenderness
of these recollections, as well as their elegiac mood (her passages
are often occasioned by the death of a friend), at times attains
narrative value.

Would it be right to separate EZEQUIEL MARTÍNEZ ESTRADA
(Argentina, 1895–1964) from the poets and place him among
the essayists? His books of poems [collected in *Poetry* (*Poesía*)
in 1947; *Ballads of a Blind Man* (*Coplas de ciego*) appeared in
1959] are penetrating and complex—a tremendous tension between reason and unreason, which at times appears pessimistic
and nihilistic. Strange sounds of Babel, with exoticisms, neologisms, scientific and technical terms. Like Darío and Lugones the
poet practiced—to use his own words—"a gymnastics of the
dictionary," together with a culture that makes easily identifiable
references to mythology, philosophy, literature and the arts. But
his method of alluding to this culture causes a sharpening focus
of the mind, as if confronted with a charade: a culture like a
distorting crystal through which Martinez Estrada contemplated
the world and himself. And sometimes he even squinted to look
at the crystal itself. His culture showed a preference for vitalism
and (probably in search for its counterpart) for orientalisms that
invited the dissolution of personality. His thought is geometric,
but it is the geometry of a cobweb strung together with strands
of twilight spittle. A daemon—possibly related to Socrates' daemon, although more agonizing—had climbed to his mind from
the orgiastic depths of the primitive jungle, with a tragic craving
for survival; and it is this daemon that is responsible for the
originality expressed in both his poetry and his prose. His talent
is that of a poet, but his reputation is that of a prose writer. His

daemon dwelt in the recesses of his poetry, insubordinately free. And from there it assailed the world in subsequent books. In the systematic demolition of the social architecture of Argentina we can recognize the intimate architecture of the demolishing poet—his disconformity, his iconoclasm, his pride in himself as an angry rebel and an apocalyptic prophet, his irrationalism as a man of reason who ceases to reason so that the scream of life might be heard, his subtle capacity to take culture apart and reveal its foundations of clay, his contradictions between a misanthropy through excess of love and a philanthropy through excess of hatred, between his humility and his megalomania, between his tenderness and his aggression. *X-Ray of the Pampa* (*Radiografía de la pampa*, 1933) is the bitterest book that has ever been written in Argentina, and the first great literary testimony of the frightful moral crisis into which the country fell in 1930. In magnificently baroque prose, full of metaphors and ingenuities that keep the reader in a constant state of astonishment, Martínez Estrada drew the picture of Argentine miseries. Nothing in Argentina is spared. The detail and the rapid philosophic reflections that follow each detail about like a shadow give the book an extraordinary poetic quality. Its aphoristic force heaves the reader up and, if the reader happens to be Argentinian, throws him in the air, in a grotesque whirl, and then lets him fall in the mire where he can do nothing but cry in humiliation— a sad book, a saddening one—a book of tragic humor, taciturn, severe, unpardoning. The essays in *Goliath's Head* (*La cabeza de Goliat*, 1940) are heterogeneous, but they are held together by the common theme of the "microscopic view of Buenos Aires." When he attempted theater, he failed. *What We Don't See Die* (1941), *Shadows* (1941) and *Hunters*—published in the volume, *Three Dramas* (*Tres dramas,* 1957)—are verbose, confused, sickly. Although enveloped in a Scandinavian mist, very nineteenth centuryish, they lack Ibsen's or Strindberg's tragic sense of life. As in Ibsen, when the curtain rises, the drama has already taken place, and all we witness is its revelation through the dialog and the final crisis. But this retrospective method (and an occasional situation dear to the heart of Ibsen, like the man who vacillates between two sisters of very different character and fails in marriage for having made the wrong choice) is the only Ibsen trait noticeable. His dialogs do not have dramatic force. The words bubble forth from the author's neurasthenia, not from the tormented conscience of the characters. In *What We Don't See Die* we are aware of Pablo's failure (failure in art, in business, in matrimony), and we are present at the catastrophe: Marta, Pablo's wife, commits suicide; and Pablo, humiliated, runs away from the broken home. But the tortured, mournful confessions of these consciences do not obey a profound analysis of life, but respond to pure morbidity. In *Shadows* and in *Hunters* the same theme of matrimonial failure is also unsuccessful. His stories are bitter, even tragic, with their themes and moods of solitude and despair, written in a natural, massive, direct prose: *Three Stories Without Love* (*Tres cuentos sin amor*), *Holy Saturday* (*Sábado de gloria*), *Marta Riquelme, Examination without Conscience* (*Examen sin Conciencia*), *The Cough and Other Entertainments* (*La tos y otros entretenimientos*). In the tone of a biblical prophet, he thrusts himself into the discussion of the heated political problems of his time. His contributions to literary criticism are important: *Sarmiento, Death and Transfiguration of Martín Fierro* (*Muerte y transfiguración de Martín Fierro*), *The Marvelous World of William Henry Hudson* (*El mundo maravilloso de William Henry Hudson*), *Brother Quiroga* (*El hermano Quiroga*), and others.

Critics, with assets in literary creation, in poetry, in fiction, or in theater are MANUEL ANDINO (El Salvador, 1892–1938); the Cubans JOSÉ MARÍA CHACÓN Y CALVO (1892) and FÉLIX LIZASO (1891), and FRANCISCO JOSÉ CASTELLANOS (1892–1920); MARIO BRICEÑO IRAGORRY (Venezuela, 1897–1958); ISAAC BARRERA (Ecuador); JOSÉ DE LA RIVA AGÜERO (Peru, 1885–1944), who went from positivism to Bergsonism and from there to Catholicism; the Chileans HERNAN DÍAZ ARRIETA, "Alone" (1891), ARTURO TORRES RIOSECO (1897), ARMANDO DONOSO (1887), and DOMINGO MELFI (1892–1946); ALBERTO ZUM FELDE (Uruguay, 1888) and the Argentinians ROBERTO F. GIUSTI (1887), JOSÉ MARÍA MONNER SANS (1896), and BERNARDO CANAL FEIJÓO (1897).

Less concerned with pure literature are the essayists SAMUEL RAMOS (Mexico, 1897–1959); the Salvadorians JUAN RAMÓN URIARTE (1884–1934) and NAPOLEÓN VIERA ALTAMIRANO (1894); OCTAVIO MÉNDEZ PEREIRA (Panamá, 1887–1954); MEDARDO VITIER (Cuba, 1886–1959);

ANTONIO S. PEREIRA (Puerto Rico, 1898–1939); JOSÉ CARLOS MARIÁ-
TEGUI (Peru, 1895–1930); the Bolivians IGNACIO PRUDENCIO BUSTILLO
(1895–1928) and GUSTAVO ADOLFO OTERO (1896); MANUEL DOMÍNGUEZ
(Paraguay, 1896–1935), and FRANCISCO ROMERO (Argentina, 1891–1962),
an elegant prose writer, a philosopher of German formation, preoccupied
with the problem of spiritual life as the supreme level of transcendency
toward truth and value—*Theory of Man* (*Teoría del hombre,* 1952).

C. THEATER

After a long decline, the theater had a resurgence in Mexico with the
works of JULIO JIMÉNEZ RUEDA (1896–1960) and FRANCISCO MONTERDE
(1894), who were placed earlier among the "colonialists." These names
should be added: CARLOS NORIEGA HOPE (1896–1934), CATALINA
D'ERZELL (1897–1950), and VÍCTOR MANUEL DÍEZ BARROSO (1890–
1930); the latter, in *Conquer Yourself* (*Véncete a ti mismo*), played with
the real and the imagined in an ingenious and effective manner.

In Central America, J. EMILIO ARAGÓN (El Salvador, 1887–1938) and
H. ALFREDO CASTRO (Costa Rica, 1889).

In the Antilles the most eminent names are Cuban. Above the heads of
Sánchez Galárraga, Sánchez Varona, Louis A. Baralt, Marcelo Salinas,
and Montes López, stands the robust JOSÉ ANTONIO RAMOS (1885–1946)
with his theater of ideas. The ideological preoccupation of the polemicist
and the reformer stifled the dramatist; in play after play he fought the prejudices against the rights of women, the superstitions of mealy-mouthed people, political corruption, cowardice, hypocrisy, foolishness. His was a
theater of careless forms until he produced his masterpiece, *Tembladera*
(1917), in which he put forth a serious Cuban problem—the sale of sugar
mills and plantations to foreigners and the squandering of the money ob-
tained therefrom. The economic suicide, the loss of sovereignty, indolence,
irresponsibility, and parasitism of the families that live in mansions in the
city, with no love for the land. The thesis rises from the dialogs and the
plot situations, and also the hope for a solution symbolized in Joaquín and
Isolina. His predilection for symbols was revealed more in the daring drama,
In the Hands of God (*En las manos de Dios,* 1932). Of greater psychological refinement was his theatrical sketch *The Legend of the Stars* (*La
leyenda de las estrellas,* 1935), somewhat Pirandellian in its epistemological
relativism.

In Venezuela, LEOPOLDO AYALA MICHELENA (1894).

In Colombia the most important figure was ANTONIO ÁLVAREZ LLERAS
(1892), author of *Social Vipers* (*Víboras sociales,* 1911). For him the
theater is spectacle and also literature, a school that must fulfill the social
mission of analyzing conflicts and proposing theses.

In Peru, FELIPE SASSONE (1884–1954).

In Bolivia, ANTONIO DÍAZ VILLAMIL (1897–1948) and ADOLFO COSTA
DU RELS (1891). The latter, a narrator and theatrical author, has written in
Spanish, and for this reason he appears here, but he achieved his greatest
successes with plays in French.

Three authors appeared in Chile who contributed effectively to the formation of the national theater: Acevedo Hernández, Moock, and Lugo Cruchaga. ANTONIO ACEVEDO HERNANDEZ (1886), of humble extraction, founded the popular and social theatre: *The Broken Song* (*La canción rota*, 1921), *Chañarcillo* (1933). ARMANDO L. MOOCK (1894–1943) began by bringing Chilean topics to the stage; his masterpiece during this first period was the comedy *Little Town* (*Pueblecito*); afterwards he moved to Buenos Aires where *The Serpent* (*La serpiente*, 1920) made its first appearance and won international acclaim. "The serpent" is a woman, Luciana, who crushes her prey until she destroys it and then seeks another victim. But perhaps his best-constructed works are *Monsieur Ferdinand Pontac* (1922) and *Rigoberto* (1935). His novel on the theatrical milieu of Buenos Aires, *The Life and Miracles of a Leading Actor* (*Vida y milagros de un primer actor*, 1926) is interesting. GERMÁN LUCO CRUCHAGA (1894–1936) was meticulous in the construction of his works, and sparing. His best was *The Widow of Apablaza* (*La viuda de Apablaza*, 1928), a rural drama on an amorous passion.

DANIEL DE LA VEGA (1892), fertile poet, good essayist, occasional short-story writer and author of one successful novel—*Cain, Abel and a Woman* (*Caín, Abel y una mujer*, 1933)—produced various plays with ironic overtones.

In Paraguay there was some theatrical production, but since it was in Guaraní it is beyond our scope. However, since JULIO CORREA (1890–1953) also wrote in Spanish we enter his name here. He was a spontaneous, careless, pessimistic poet who spoke as readily about himself and the humble lives that surrounded him as about folklore traditions and social injustice. In the last category he was combative, subversive, and inciting to vengeance. It is said that his merits as a playwright surpass those he had as a poet

In Uruguay, after Florencio Sánchez, the spotlight falls on JOSÉ PEDRO BELLÁN (1889–1930), [even more important as a narrator: *Reality* (*La realidad*)] and especially on ERNESTO HERRERA (1886–1917). Herrera is in the naturalist vein of rural drama. *The Blind Lion* (*El león ciego*, 1911) presents in three acts the unsuccessful life of a political boss who led a faction in the Uruguayan civil wars: he is old, blind, and ridiculed by his own coreligionists. Herrera, with his anarchist ideas, could not sympathize with the brutal customs and passions he was describing; on the contrary, he communicates his repugnance. But unfortunately, he did not sympathize artistically with his sanguinary lion, and therefore, Gumersindo comes out psychologically dwarfed. The realist and lively dialog is of more interest to the philologist than the drama to the critic. *The Morals of Misia Paca* (*La moral de Misia Paca*) was first shown in its definitive version of three acts in 1912: before this, only the embryo in one act and its re-elaboration in two acts were known. It is a drama of ideas, but without revolutionary spirit, dealing with ill-mated women among the Creole bourgeoisie. The plot is not original—a young girl married to a sick old man—but Herrera operates in the "case" with the instruments of a surgeon. It has been said that his best play was *Our Daily Bread* (*El pan nuestro*, 1913?) about a broken-up Madrid family of the middle class.

In Argentina the list is long. Also, in these years the world of theatrical troupes settles in Buenos Aires, noisily, actively, brilliantly, and abundantly: VICENTE MARTÍNEZ CUITIÑO (1887), ARMANDO DISCÉPOLO (1887), ROBERTO GACHE (1892), FRANCISCO DEFILIPPIS NOVOA (1891–1930), JOSÉ GONZÁLEZ CASTILLO (1885–1937), FEDERICO MERTENS (1886), CLAUDIO MARTÍNEZ PAIVA (1887), IVO PELAY (1893), RODOLFO GONZÁLEZ PACHECO (1886–1949).

The most important dramatist of the professional theater was SAMUEL EICHELBAUM (1894). His family, his literary family, came from Russia and northern Europe: Dostoevski, Chekhov, Ibsen, Strindberg. His theatrical style is realist. Eichelbaum's realism, however, does not consist in reproducing on the boards of the theater a piece of real life, but rather in showing how the characters suddenly become aware of the dramatic situation they are in without having been aware of it until then. The perspectives in which the characters see one another in the dramas of Eichelbaum are converted into the spectacle itself. The best scenes are invariably those with dialogs containing dense pauses between two characters. Family life is his preferred raw material. He has created, then, a theater of conflicting consciences, with soundings in the subconscious. Eichelbaum is serious, analytical, concentrated, cerebral, inquisitive, somber. He is not a pessimist because his plays have an ethic nerve that reacts actively in defense of spiritual liberty. Profound? More than profound, he is subtle. He selects a few behavioral motivations, the stranger the better, and then promotes a discussion on them. At times he seeks out exceptional situations in order to sound out sentiments that are also exceptional, as in *Clay Pigeon* (*Pájaro de barro*, 1940): Felipa, a poor peon's daughter, gives herself to the sculptor Juan Antonio: a child is born; when Doña Pilar wants to force her son Juan Antonio to marry Felipa, the latter, out of pride, denies his paternity; since the father engendered the child without love, he was born as if he were "a' orphan." Felipa has merit, but Eichelbaum, determined to present her as misunderstood, paints her with shadings difficult to understand. In *A Turn-of-the-Century Tough* (*Un guapo del 900*, 1940), the moral springs are also surprising: Ecuménico, a professional killer, has placed his knife at the service of a political boss; the latter's wife makes him a cuckold with none other than his political rival; Ecuménico kills this rival because he cannot serve a man who has been dishonored by a woman. All this to make a mythical hero of the assassin. In *Two Burning Coals* (*Dos brasas*) the artifice is even greater; and could only be saved by giving it an expressionistic interpretation. Two coals from hell, two misers, husband and wife, sacrifice their lives to the cult of Mammon. The dramatic structure is weak; the United States atmosphere is false; the plot situation, absurd; the psychology of the characters, abstract; the dialogs, wordy; the denouement—the husband strangles the wife—futilely sensational.

The strange thing about *The Waters of the World* (*Las aguas del mundo*, 1957) is Laureano Martín. Amancia refuses his love and has a son by Leiva. When this Don Juan abandons her, Amancia, frightened, declares that the child's father is Laureano. The noble Laureano does not contradict her. Amancia dies and Leiva claims his son, but Laureano will not give him up. He says that men also give birth to children, and that this child sprang into life from his head, out of his desire for him. Amancia may have given herself to another man, he adds, but she gave her son, which was what he most wanted, to him. "You're a strange man, you know it?" answers Leiva and leaves very peacefully. The locale (Entre Ríos, in 1920) is well evoked in humorous Creole dialogs; but Laureano's pseudo-paternal instinct, which has no explanation, not even that of love for Amancia (he has ceased to love her during the two years of his absence) has neither national nor human color. Could this strange moral conscience of Laureano's be the result of his travels over "the waters of the world" as a navy conscript?

XIII. 1925-1940

Authors born between 1900 and 1915

Historical framework: Political and economic consequences of the first world war: on one hand, greater participation in government leadership on the part of the masses, with Communist propaganda and Fascist conspiracies; on the other hand, "strong governments" which defend oligarchy, especially during the depression which begins in 1929. Also affecting Hispanic-American life are the fall of the Republic in Spain, the triumph of international Fascism, and the outbreak of World War II.

Cultural tendencies: After the first world war "vanguardist literatures" with a "new sensitivity" appear. Modernism being exhausted, styles are now violent and hermetic. The determination to break with all the literary norms of the past predominates. Ultraism and its dissolution. The lost generation of those born around 1910. Pure poetry and surrealism.

Introduction

One of the themes considered here is the disintegration of so-called postwar literature, the literature which after 1918 called itself vanguardist. In the previous chapter we have already outlined the theory, history, and intent of this literature. But, as we said, the most scandalous writers calmed down after their first few books and, little by little, became more serious in their desire to express their true originality. The mere chronicling of this literary effort is difficult enough, not to mention trying to form a critique on it, not only because of its lack of seriousness, its crazy disorder, and the brevity of its duration, but also because there were other

tendencies, and they all ran together. Ultraists unto death, rene-
gades from ultraism, enemies of ultraism. But do not believe that
ultraism was the key signature for these years. There were excellent poets who grew up as though ultraism had never existed.
The prose writers complicate the panorama even more, because
in stories and novels it is possible to have styles with prettily
painted faces, homely styles and—as a most extravagant novelty
—"cult of the ugly" styles; that is, a deliberate poetization of
everything ugly, frightful coagulations of "esperpentic" metaphors, a transition from calology to cacology. Writers lived between 1925 and 1940 as though they formed parts of two opposing groups. No one today would insist on the *raison d'être* of these
groups. As an example of how these groups broke up, of how these
writers changed the label under which they wrote, it suffices to
recall the street of the "stridentists" and that of the "contemporaries," in Mexico; and in Argentina, the two streets, Florida
(with its magazine *Martín Fierro*) and Boedo (with its review
Los Pensadores, afterward called *Claridad*). What we have said
of Argentina and Mexico could be extended to take in the inter-
mediary countries; everywhere the pot of literature bubbled over.
It would be useless to try to trace the outline, the duration of each
bubble. Interesting as they may be to the history of each country,
these activities are insignificant from the point of view of a history
of this type which looks at all of Spanish America and can only
pause for the major figures.

We have already characterized the postwar vanguard in the
previous chapter by referring to the "scandal." To put things in
balance we will now characterize the writers whose works began
to appear after 1930. Those authors immediately preceding had
gloried in a "new sensitivity"; these were to brag about being
"newists." What was this sensitivity? No one was able to distinguish it, much less define it. But by this time Ortega y Gasset had
imposed his idea of "the vital sensitivity of each generation," and
those born around 1910 were determined to belong to a generation. The Generation of the Centennial of the Independence? The
Generation of the Sighting of Halley's Comet? The event, whether

historical or astral, was the least important factor. What was important was to be a generation, a brand new generation. And the desire was so great that, since then, there has been no cessation in the invention of generations: that of "40," of "45," of "50," and of "55." Many more generations than can humanly fit into such a short passage of time. The youths who appeared during the decade of 1930 did not bear the aforementioned "anti's" in their lists as all generations customarily do when they present themselves. They were no anti-modernists because Rubén Darío was already a bibliographical item, dead and buried in the literary curricula of the secondary schools. Modernism was an exercise, a remnant of the classical past, for today's classrooms. Neither were they anti-vanguardists because they did not take the orgy of postwar "isms" seriously. This literature had already denied itself; it was not possible for them to deny it further. The more serious ultraists were showing promise of making amends for their first practical jokes, with solidly constructed works. The youths who were beginning to publish after 1930 could not be in opposition to this promise. Thus, whether the past had become impregnably classical, or whether it had disintegrated of itself until it no longer offered resistance, or whether it had requested a moratorium, the fact is that in 1930 it was necessary to plunge into literature without springing from the "anti" trampoline. Since these youths were not belligerents, they met wth no belligerence. They had the feeling that the others, "the previous ones," had swept and cleaned their house. Excellent servants. They were grateful to them. But they were not going to wield the same broom—What for? The house was clean; it was time to get down to studying. Unfortunately, they studied more than they produced. New philological disciplines, new literary theories, new philosophies, new literatures. And the more they studied, the less they wrote. Literary life? These were not times for playing polite games. They separated into political groups rather than poetic groups. Furthermore, they lacked *esprit de corps* and a sense of propaganda. They ignored one another, and cared little whether they joined the older writers or the younger ones. They ended by approaching the younger writers; but in 1940 the latter were already massed together into their own generation, ignoring the near past, attentive to the distant past, that of the ultraists. A bridge was stretched and the writers of the year '30 were left beneath it (as a generation, because a few persons were incorporated into the generation of the year '40). Thus the generation of '30 was denuded to clothe that of '40. Let us not forget this, if we wish to explain why this group was not clearly distinguishable, that from 1930 onward the skies were filled with ominous portents. The first sign was the great depression that convulsed the entire world, and with it, the crisis of liberalism. Let us take the case of Argentina where the military revolution of that year imposed an oligarchic regime that remained in power through systematic electoral fraud. The leftists failed in their attempt to form a popular front. The rightists propped one another up. Nationalism became Rosist, anti-democratic, anti-liberal. Catholic Action, initiated by the Eucharistic Congress of 1934, repeated formulas from Italian Fascism and learned to make the sign of the cross with the swastika. The growing successes of Hitler after 1934 were enough to make one's hair stand on end. The Civil War in Spain and the downfall of the Republic proved that the cause of liberty in the world was lost and that a new era of violence, tyranny, and stupidity had begun. Then in 1939, the Second World War. In 1943, another military revolution; first theocratic aggression, then demagogic aggression; in any case Argentina went down-hill, society was levelled with the masses, and the minorities were crushed.

This series of blows, in all of Hispanic-America, not just in Argentina, made the creation of literature difficult, and even when created, it was difficult for it to find a public. Such was the uproar of the world. Let us have all those born around 1910 take hands and form a line. Does it not seem to be a dividing line? And though it may not indicate the division between esthetic stages, it does, at least, indicate this division: from here on what we have to say is no longer history. Actually, we should at this point consider that our historical framework for Hispanic-American literature is finished. With this reservation, that our literary his-

tory is finished and that what follows is a gathering of friends—
with exclusions and inclusions that do not always have critical
worth—we continue with our chronicle of the latest years.

A. MAINLY POETRY

Pure Poetry and Surrealism

The historian who would give form to the poetry of these years
finds before him the ungrateful task of fitting together a jigsaw
puzzle from the pieces of many puzzles. Some of the modernist
and post-modernist poets are still active. Some follow their un-
varying path; others attempt to cross over to the vanguardist ranks.
They are not always old men; there are also young ones. The
same thing happens with the vanguardists. There are those who
are consistent to their dying day, and those who abandon ultraism,
either to return to traditional and classical ways, or to advance
toward new neo-romantic and existentialist movements. And, at
the end of this period, around 1930, when only a few fading
echoes of ultraism remain in the air, there are youths, born about
1910, who set out to speak of themselves and of their own patriotic
circumstances in a grave, sentimental voice, but in a language of
pure poetry or of surrealism. That the pieces of this jigsaw puzzle
come from various puzzles can be proved by observing the use of
the metaphor. In the modernist poets the metaphors are like doves
caged in allegories, in apologs, in clear, beautiful images. The
ultraist poets loose their metaphoric doves in order to shoot them
down with rifle blasts, and we are left without knowing the final
course of their flight. The neo-romantic and existentialist poets
began to see that the point was to breed carrier pigeons capable
of returning alive to the intimate dove cote from which they had
flown. We have already mentioned the heading "neo-romanticism." Perhaps because of its vagueness, we may not keep this
heading. But we can understand why some poets called themselves
"neo-romantics." Romanticism never died; it was transformed
into symbolism, into surrealism, into existentialism. The attempt
to transform a state of being into poetry (evident since 1930)

was common to Spain and to the Hispanic-American countries. The advent of the Spanish Republic and the interest in Hispanic literature of a popular and effusive tone were not a casual coincidence.

The Spaniard García Lorca and the Chilean Pablo Neruda will be the two poets who most strongly influence the poets who appear in the 1930's. It is interesting to find, on all sides, the effort to restore the classical forms of Spanish literature (ballads, *décimas*, and sonnets) while using spontaneous surrealist images. What those born in 1910 are doing, those born in 1900 were also doing. As we have said, many of the 1900 group had deserted the ranks of ultraism and had accepted the rigors of rhyme and meter. Before reviewing the lyric contributions of each country, we shall say a few words about the pure poetry and the surrealist poetry of these years, as they stand most in need of clarification since the other types, the circumstantial, the descriptive, the civil, the folkloric, and the epic, which were also being written at this time, are already well known. The Parnassians and the symbolists had already spoken of pure poetry, and Valéry, in 1920, had discoursed upon it with the most talent of all. But Henri Bremond chose the term "*poésie pure*" in order to expound upon his personal theory, and thus, between 1925 and 1930, a debate was loosed in France that had repercussions even in Hispanic-America. The premise was this: that reason cannot explain poetry. We can enjoy a poem without understanding it logically. Poetic experience is analogous to mysticism in religion. In this sense, poetry is the fountain of consciousness. What remains of a poem after we strip it of all that is not poetry is a mysterious, supernatural reality: let us call it "pure poetry." Yet, it is easier to define the impure than to speak of the pure. The impure is the superficial, the human content of a poem: to think, to feel, to desire, to imagine, to teach, to move, that is, the ideas, the themes, the elocutions, the forms, the moral intents, the description of real things. Words are not poetic, but they can transmit a mysterious power of pure poetry. A poem energizes our deepest self and numbs our superficial self: it is the shock of the current that passes through the poem and electrifies us before the impure elements of our ordinary human activities can reach us. The poem which happens to be a good conductor of poetry delivers its essence even before the reader has understood it, and even before he has finished reading it. That which poetry delivers to us is not mere pleasure in the presence of beauty, but a knowledge of the supernatural. The mystic state, the ecstatic union with God, is first in the hierarchy of knowledge. Next comes the poetic state which communicates to us, through a poem, an original experience. Farther down are the lesser poetic states, lesser because they are abortive or superficial. And even farther down the scale is the knowledge of physical things which is better gained through contemplating a landscape than by reading about the same scene in a descriptive poem. Thus, pure poetry aspires to silence.

Other anti-rational theoreticians were speaking at the same time about a poetry not directed toward the supernatural, but toward the super-real. Surrealism saw the universe as being in disorder, and to communicate this vision, it forged a language which itself was as disordered as the universe. André Breton and his companions proposed, through psychic automatism, to plumb the deepest abysses of man and of the cosmos. They gathered awesome sentences, totally destitute of meaning, but poetic because of the subconscious mystery from which they sprang. They did not deny reality: they deepened it in their attempt to seize the spontaneous workings of the life of the mind. From 1919 to 1925 surrealism was a scandalous, nihilist, polemic movement. From 1925 on, surrealism, with a certain gravity, oriented itself toward philosophy and politics. There were convergences with Marxism which attracted through its promises of violence and subversion. The two Utopias: that of economic communism and that of psychic communism. Communism, however, was much more interested in the social condition of man (hunger) than in his human condition (the subconscious). Some surrealists continued to interest themselves in communism's politics of the masses; others, more faithful to their individual esthetics, broke with the party. After 1930 surrealism flourished, submitting itself to the dominion of literary forms. Its technique is that of a composition which allows for the free association of words. There is no need to trouble oneself over language for its own sake. After descending to the subterranean depths of consciousness, language will eventually emerge and in the proper manner. Grammatical syntax is a stumbling block to the free affirmation of things marvelously apprehended in their disconnection. Thus, the language of surrealism corrects the false, logical structure of reality. With the disjointing of the grammar, the musicality and, in fact, all traditional forms become disjointed too. On the other hand, images grow and multiply which can only be assimilated through emotion. Metaphors are freed from the things that are recognizable to us through a process of rational thought; they become detached from the world and reveal an interior reality created entirely by the poet. These two ideals of poetry—pure poetry and surrealist poetry—combined with other less irrational, but equally difficult types, in helping to create in Hispanic-America an art so hermetic that even the critics could not understand it. Many poets, through their excessive admiration for certain surrealist automatisms— the doing away with punctuation marks, the denial of the semantic value of words, the breaking up of syntax, the segregation of stray images—fell into a slumber of expressive irresponsibility: each reader could see what he wanted to in a poem since the poet had not filled his verses with his own precise images, but with a diffuse, vague vapor. That is, each reader was to react in the face of the invisible. It is natural that he should be mistrusting. We all remember the story of the two thieves who said they were weaving a cloth that could only be seen by the well-born. We do not dare say "we do not see anything" for fear of being taken for fools. But neither are we sure that there are others capable of seeing this invisible beauty. There was a certain amount of fraud during the ultraist generation. They poked fun at the reader. Today the reader is wary. In spite of this, some readers sincerely and trustingly like the invisible. What do they see? The definers of "pure poetry" have always given us tautological answers: poetry is what remains after we purify it of its impurities. Well: in the hermetic poetry of these years, at times in the best of instances, we do not find impurities: and this not seeing what is not poetry overtakes us as if it were poetry itself. The reader feels an emotion similar to that of faith. Faith in an absolutely poetic, though invisible, reality. It must be divined, apprehended through the purgative, illuminative, unitive discipline of the ascetic and of the mystic. Thus the reader admires a cryptic poetry. Some beautiful images, a few sagely surprising adjectives, various allusions, which, because we are drawn to them we hunt down on the wing, prove to us that behind the poem there is a poet deserving of our respect. And that is enough for us although we are only intermittently able to profit from what he tells us. Furthermore, we admire the courage of this poet who plays his game of poetry with a single card. After all, this poet, by being so hermetic is risking the sense of that about which he writes. Without timidity, without thinking of the consequences, with no quarter given to reason, blind and delirious, he proceeds toward suicide. Thus many of the poets that we will mention (as was the case with many that we have already mentioned) may leave no other testimonial in history than the admiration felt for them by their contemporaries. The most ungrateful task for any literary critic is to have to face the poetry of these recent years. There are too many poets and all too few of them have realized a finished form. We lack the perspective for distinguishing those values which may become permanent. At times the critic becomes impatient and tends to diminish the significance of this poetry, seemingly less vital than the other literary genres.

(i) *Mexico* / In Mexico the "isms" of the postwar period caught on as they did in the rest of the world. Only, the Mexicans—unlike the writers from the Río de la Plata area—did not deny the past. Each poet respects his elders, and the esteem they feel for the Othón-Díaz Mirón-Gutiérrez Nájera-Tablada-González Martínez-López Velarde-Villaurrutia-Paz string of writers threads the generations together in a rare continuity.

It has already been seen in the previous chapter, when we spoke of the "scandal," how little the stridentism of ARQUELAS VELA (1899), GERMÁN LIST ARZUBIDE (1898) and LUIS QUINTANILLA (1900) left. Its major figure was MANUEL MAPLES ARCE (1900). Ever since *Interior Scaffoldings* (*Andamios interiores,* 1922), he proposed rhyming, not the present, but the future action, and believed that this was to be done by presenting a landscape of machines, industrial products, and technical nomenclatures: motors, propellers, airplanes, movies, automobiles, cables, voltaic batteries, triangles, vertices. And this with calls to labor and political action. Maple Arce gradually lost his mechanical toys, and in *Memorial to Blood* (*Memorial de la sangre,* 1947) he attempted a more human poetry. Stridentism was a fleeting adventure.

Of greater vitality, both in intent and result, were the friends who ended up as a group in the magazine *Contemporáneos* (1928–31): Villaurrutia, Gorostiza, Torres Bodet, Ortiz de Montellano, Jorge Cuesta, Owen, Novo, González Rojo, Barreda . . . and although they did not form part of this group, we must add the names of Carlos Pellicer and Elías Nandino. In comparison with the stridentists, the *Contempóraneos* group had a greater artistic decorum, a surer instinct for appreciating the values of European literature and for selecting its models. They were cultured, moderate, well disciplined. They did not permit social unrest to adulterate their art. For them poetry was a play of images and abstractions motivated by intuition, intelligence, and irony. The first few years of youthful grace gone by, they retired into themselves, and in the depths of their solitude they drank bitter dregs. The more important poets were Pellicer, Gorostiza and Villaurrutia. With the exception of Pellicer, the dominant theme of the group was death—the *Nostalgia of Death* (*Nostalgia de la muerte*) of Villaurrutia, the *Death Without End* (*Muerte sin fin*) of Gorostiza, the *Death of Blue Sky* (*Muerte de cielo azul*) of Ortiz de Montellano, *Mirror of My Death* (*Espejo de mi muerte*) of Nandino. More interesting than studying the movement as a whole is following a few individual trajectories, among the most brilliant of all the continental literature of this time.

The poet who in worth was second to López Velarde was CARLOS PELLICER (1899). In spite of the fact that they belonged to two different groups because of their age, they both brought separate poems to light in the same years. Those books which Pellicer held in the greatest esteem, however, are his last: *The Hour of June* (*Hora de junio,* 1937), *Antechamber* (*Recinto,* 1941), *Subordinations* (*Subordinaciones,* 1948), *Practice for Flight* (*Práctica de vuelo,* 1956). The complete works of Pellicer: *Poetic Papers* (*Material poético,* 1962); his latest book: *Teoti-*

huacán and the Thirteenth of August; the Ruin of Tenochtitlán,
(*Teotihuacán y 13 de agosto; ruina de Tenochtitlán,* 1965). On
reading Pellicer, one has the impression that Pellicer is making
an effort to restrain himself; his good health, his resonant voice,
his sensitivity, his sumptuous tropicalism, his interest in the world
and in men are all submitted to a forced fining down. The poet
puts his lyricism on a diet because he admires the dehumanized
silhouette—impossible to him—of others of his generation: in
"Desires" he beseeches the tropics to "allow me for one moment
only / not to be cry and color." He describes his perceptions of
the landscape with such objectivity that at times they seem to be
faithful descriptions, not of his own impressions, but of something
exterior to him. He rejoices good humoredly in nature like a
grateful drunkard. The joy of being alive, the joy of living; and
beyond this love for the light and air that envelop him with the
natural world, the love of the supernatural heavens. Religious
faith is another of his fountains of happiness. He is witty, agile.
A musician of the word, and his words are always music of the
senses. But not music alone: he brings the brilliant color of
painting, the grandiose volume of sculpture, and even the eloquent
gestures of one who makes a tribunal in his own small corner and
speaks to all the men of his time. A solid builder who, with his
lyrical materials, has erected a beautiful city of great monuments
and delicate miniatures. His scruples as an artisan of verse never
robbed him of spontaneity. His metaphors lend brilliance, veloc-
ity, magic, gaiety, surprise, like birds flying over the ocean, that
suddenly hurl themselves at the sun. A lyric flight in which all of
life is praised, and in life, God. In the religious sonnets of *Practice
for Flight* religion is no mere theme, but a beating of wings and a
celestial journey. Perhaps not quite, because Pellicer is a man, not
an angel; he is not even an ascetic man. His religious sentiment
is that of a man who can only open his arms in the form of the
cross without being able to fly on the spread wings of mysticism:
"May the wind at my back give flight! / I live completely on
earth. You are sky. / You blue, and I in the emptiness of myself."
Very rarely do the eyes of the poet seem to go blind with ecstasy.
This poetry gives us, rather than a mystic union with God, images

of the love of God. His eyes, not bewildered by rapture but open
and perceptive, see in life the azures and rose hues of a Fra An-
gelico, or the shadows of the baroque tenebrists. Thus the intensity of faith does not lead to silence as with the mystics, but to
eloquence: a lyrical eloquence without concepts, without scholasticism, but active in its desire for grace. Each image is concrete
and surprising, like details in a landscape of the soul.

XAVIER VILLAURRUTIA (1903–1950) appeared in his first
poems as though he were going to follow the path of López
Velarde. In *Reflections* (*Reflejos*, 1926), however, he revealed a
more graceful and witty spirit. There were sudden religious invo-
cations or melancholy reflections, but on the whole his images
are flamboyant and gay. There were also unusual metaphors without the hurly-burly of the ultraists. Later he drew closer to intelligent, imaginative masters: Proust, Gide, Cocteau, Giraudoux.
From his varied spectrum of themes—landscape, love, mystery,
goodness, art, travel—he chose, for his lucid analysis, the saddest
band of color. His intelligence observes, selects, and orders the
emotions that are to go into his poetry, emotions which come to
him while contemplating and understanding the secret expressions
of things. His best work: *Nostalgia for Death* (*Nostalgia de la
muerte*, 1939–46). It was a splendid work. Villaurrutia foresaw
that life is a dream and that death will be an awakening: "I doubt!
And I dare not ask / if it is the awakening from a dream, or is my
life a dream." Not at all, Death tells him, life is "the dream in
which you would like to believe you live without me, when it is I
who draw it and who erase it." And the poet in yet another poem:
"The night pours down its mystery upon us, / and something
tells us that to die is to awaken." Instead of being paralyzed by
fear like a man who suddenly discovers that he is only a phantom
in the night, Villaurrutia departs from this basic intuition, and
with intelligence and imagination creates metaphysical hypotheses. There are innumerable plays on words and sounds. But these
plays are converted into plays on concepts. They are the themes
of fantastic literature that other writers, in less anguished tones
are trying out during these same years (Borges, for example).
Themes of the double man and of the unfolding of consciousness,

of mirrors facing one another repeating infinitely the same image, of empty bodies that receive mysterious visitors, of autonomous human shadows, of gods who dream into existence men who are dreaming others into existence, of the absurd fear of nonexistence, of solipsist universes, of corrupt angels, of death that surreptitiously haunts us, of the idea that all men are one man and that we simultaneously are and are not, of metamorphosis and labyrinths. Villaúrrutia disintegrates the real world and falls into the solitude of the abyss, where he begins to invent another world and becomes filled with anguish, not only because he knows it is not real, but also because he doubts even his own personal existence. His hypotheses float on the surface of the mood during which he thinks about death. The ten *décimas* of "The Tenth Death" (*"Décima muerte"*) are classical in construction, baroque in their sharpness of concept, and existentialist in the idea that death is a proof of existence, and that in the final analysis we live for our own death. Villaurrutia, calculating and cold when it came to composing his ideas and his verses, was upset by the presence of death. In his last years—*Song to Spring and Other Poems (Canto a la primavera y otros poemas,* 1948)—his emotions no longer obeyed the reins and simply bolted. In his theater there is no passion, only sentiment—sentiment bound by intelligence. Ironic flashes indicate the design of the plot. We are presented with a world of artifice rather than reality. His *Profane Mystery Plays (Autos profanos,* 1943) are five dramatic sketches, so finely drawn that it can easily be seen that they are directed toward an elite and not the public in general. In his three-act pieces—*Ivy (La hiedra), The Legitimate Woman (La mujer legítima), Invitation to Death (Invitación a la muerte), The Incandescent Error (El yerro candente), Poor Bluebeard (El pobre Barba Azul), Dangerous Game (Juego peligroso)*—the dialogs are richer, and on the lips of each character, intelligence wears the same smile.

JOSÉ GOROSTIZA (1901) is one of the best crystallizers of poetry of this generation: *Songs to Be Sung in Barks (Canciones para cantar en las barcas,* 1925), *Death Without End (Muerte sin fin,* 1939), were collected with additional poems, in *Poetry*

(*Poesía;* 1964). In his clear verses of popular rhythmic sketches there is such depth and lyrical complexity that the reader, coming across the obscure half of his poetry later, goes on, confident that he is not being deceived with false complications—as was the custom of the prestidigitators of this generation—and that he will arrive finally at a subtle and authentic zone of the spirit. So he does. With his wings Gorostiza touches folklore, the cultured poetry of the period from Garcilaso to Góngora, and the pure poetry of Juan Ramón Jiménez, but these wings interest us for their flight, not for the objects they brush against. Gorostiza mounts to a height where what was invisible on the ground because of its excessive subtlety is seen clearly illuminated. *Death Without End* was the most important Mexican poem to appear up to that time in his generation. It is only one moment from an enduring agony. The poet suffers his solitude, lost in a world whose meaning escapes him. He does not know whether he is surrounded by God or by nothing. Upon contemplating himself —"my slow, searching steps through the mire"—the poet recognizes himself in the image of the water; although this water might acquire form in the solidity of the glass, this form gives it neither knowledge nor consolation. On the contrary, life, thus contained by the consciousness, is an unending death. All of the universe disintegrates in this poem which runs like a river, in waves of solitude and time, liberty and death, life and intelligence, impulse and form, God and chaos. The glass (intelligence and the word) molds and throttles the water of life. Disillusioned, the poet ends —prosaically, which corresponds with his disillusionment—with a challenge to death who is lying in wait for him behind sleepless eyes: "Come on, little slut with the frozen blush, / let's go to the devil." In spite of the resistance of language (always inadequate) and abstractions (always logical) this poetry ends triumphantly, making the very philosophy sing with lyricism: *"son et sens"* as Valery said; philosophic poetry of the conscious self as a means of knowing temporality; a difficult poetry, for minorities only.

JAIME TORRES BODET (1902) came on the literary scene with a book of verses: *Fervor,* 1918, containing a prolog by González Martínez. His tastes were still conventional, respectful of French symbolism and of Hispanic modernism. Little by little, in dialogs with his "contemporaries," and leafing through the *Revista de Occidente* and the *Nouvelle Revue Française*, he began to understand the jargon of his time: Gide, Proust, Joyce, Antonio Machado, Dostoevski, Cocteau, Juan Ramón Jiménez, Giraudoux, Ortega y Gasset, Morand, Soupault, Girard, Lacretelle, Jouhandeau, Jarnés . . . From 1922 to 1925 he had published seven volumes of verse: from these he selected the best for *Poetry* (*Poesías*, 1926). Suddenly, without abandoning verse, he became enthusiastic about prose. He wrote essays—*Contemporáneos*, 1928—but his most promising passages we find in narrative form —*Margaret of the Mist* (*Margarita de Niebla*, 1927)—in which a minimum of plot sustains interplays of sensitivity and fantasy between two girls and a young professor, who is the one telling the story; *Proserpine Rescued* (*Proserpina rescatada*, 1931), also "dehumanized art," in which the characters walk like Bengal lights and burn in spark-spluttering sentences; and *The Birth of Venus and Other Tales* (*Nacimiento de Venus y otros relatos*), written between 1928 and 1931, but published in 1941, whose first pages—about the shipwrecked Lidia—have the cold, lovely light of the window of an elegant shop on the most luxurious street in the city. Afterwards, Torres Bodet traveled all over the world with important, official duties. He continued to write books of verse: *Without Respite* (*Sin tregua*, 1957), *The Four Leaf Clover* (*Trébol de cuatro hojas*, 1958), essays: *Three Inventors of Reality* (*Tres inventores de realidad*, 1955), memoirs: *Sand Time* (*Tiempo de arena*, 1955). Each one was more opaque than the other. His best moments were those in which his imagination let its hair down, but with an elegance that equaled any coiffeur's. Disheveled images streaming in the wind of madness. Madness? Let us look at them, one by one. They make sense. They startle, because we had never heard before that "ladies / take from their encyclopedic cases / with the missing fingers of Venus de Milo— / an articulated smile / for the head of what Victory of Samothrace?" They are images that go against the grain of intelligence, with allusions to an artistic culture in good standing, humorously frivolous, ironically lyrical, related to very acute states of the spirit. This poetry, of minor tone, anti-climactic, more European than Mexican, without moral or political contaminations, passes triumphantly from verse to prose.

BERNARDO ORTIZ DE MONTELLANO (1899–1949) has written poems in prose—*Net* (*Red*), stories—*Five Hours Without a Heart* (*Cinco horas sin corazón*), dialogs—*The Big Hat* (*El sombrerón*) and, naturally, verses. The edition *Dream and Poetry* (*Sueño y poesía,* 1952) gathers his books together and adds new verses. He began in a muffled voice, but little by little he dared to speak more firmly on the impure, on solitude, on shadows, dreams, and death. He embarked for the murky country of his *Dreams* (*Sueños,* 1933): he never arrived, at least he never reached the ultimate islands of surrealism. But he was able to communicate the sensation of sea-sickness which is common to those who travel on this ocean. His best compositions have a grave and hopeless intonation like the sonnets of *Death of Blue Sky* (*Muerte de cielo azul,* 1937). He explored, not so much his dreams, but his amazement at these dreams when he was awake: "Hymn to Hipnos." SALVADOR NOVO (1904) is the circumstantial and humorous poet of the group. Like his companions, he was born into letters to fly metaphors. He went, nevertheless, to the very edge of the prosaic and leaned over so far that some of his verses crumbled beneath his feet. His accomplishment was in not falling into the abyss himself. In *Poetry* (*Poesía,* 1961) gusts of irony can be seen, lyricism, impassioned impetus, and bitter desolation. He also wrote stories and theatrical pieces. ELÍAS NANDINO (1903) gathered his verses into *Poetry* (*Poesía,* two volumes: 1947–48) and without pause continued to publish those which occurred to him after that. He excels in his sonnets; their tone—monotonous—is breathless. His themes: love, solitude, death. The tormented JORGE CUESTA (1903–1942) and the skeptic GILBERTO OWEN (1905–1952) bring this group to a close. CONCHA URQUIZA (1910–1945), whose voice humbly seeks dialog with Fray Luis de León and San Juan de la Cruz, came later.

(ii) *Central America / Guatemala:* LUIS CARDOZA Y ARAGÓN (1904) occupies with Asturias the seat of highest honor in letters in his country. While he lived in France, he became familiar with surrealism, an experience which left traces in such works as *Luna Park* (1943), *The Tower of Babel* (*La torre de Babel,* 1930), *Maelstrom* (1926), *The Sleepwalker* (*El sonámbulo,* 1937) and *The Little Symphony of the New World* (*Pequeña sinfonía del Nuevo Mundo,* 1949). He is a difficult poet because of his vertiginous images and his explorations through fugitive worlds, but his awareness of living in one of the critical periods of history and his preoccupation with the destiny of mankind illuminate his work. He is also a brilliant essayist, as can be seen in *Guatemala: The Lines in Her Palm* (*Guatemala. Las líneas de su mano,* 1955). Another poet: CÉSAR BRAÑAS (1900), author of one of the most beautiful elegies of the generation: *Black Wind* (*Viento negro*), also wrote artistic novels.

Honduras: The three best poets of this generation are Barrera, Cárcamo, and Laínez. CLAUDIO BARRERA (1912), through the path opened up by Vallejo and Neruda, went into poetry with political implications, on American themes, as for example, his poem "The Double Song" (*"La doble canción"*). JACOBO CÁRCAMO (1914–1959), also with metrical liberty, sang to the "Pines of Honduras" and to the "Ahuehuete" of Mexico. DANIEL LAÍNEZ (1914–1959) was the most spontaneous, the most popular. Other poets were MARCO ANTONIO PONCE (1908–1932), RAMÓN PADILLA COELLO (1904–1931), JOSÉ R. CASTRO (1909), and ALEJANDRO VALLADARES (1910).

El Salvador: One of the most lyrical presences is that of CLAUDIA LARS (1899). Pleased with life, she gratefully rejoices in the good things of the world: love, the beauty of the landscape, myths, the beautiful creatures of fantasy. And she does it with mastery in verse: See her anthology, *Presence in Time* (*Presencia en el tiempo*, 1962). Her originality has a singing voice of its own; her intelligence subtly sharpens her aim so that her metaphors reach their target.

Other outstanding poets: ALFREDO ESPINO (1900–1928), a landscapist in *Sad Ballads* (*Jícaras tristes*); SERAFÍN QUITEÑO (1906), the vehement poet of *Corasón With an S* (*Corasón con S*); and LUIS MEJÍA VIDES (1909). CARLOS LOVATO (1911) and PEDRO GEOFFROY RIVAS (1908) were involved in political struggles. The latter was the author of an "impure poetry" deliberately impure, because the poet gave himself over to the popular leftist tide.

Nicaragua: There were poets who, although they belong to this chapter because of the dates of their birth, echo the accents of the modernist past (like AGENOR ARGÜELLO, 1902, who was incorporated into Salvadorian literature, or LÉON AGUILERA, 1901), or who approach vanguardism cautiously (HORACIO ESPINOSA ALTAMIRANO, 1903–1945; ABSALÓN BALDOVINOS, 1903–1938; SANTOS CERMEÑO, 1903; ISRAEL PANIAGUA PRADO, 1905–1950; ALÍ VANEGAS, 1905; JOSÉ FRANCISCO BORGEN, 1908). Nicaragua is the home of Rubén Darío. The group of youths that we are about to discuss no longer has any reverence for Rubén Darío. "Our beloved enemy" they called him. José Coronel Urtecho presided over the group and was accompanied in his vanguardist campaigns by LUIS ALBERTO CABRALES (1902), MANOLO CUADRA, Pablo Antonio Cuadra, and Joaquín Pasos. Before pausing to study them we will try to set the scene. Through their literature they poured out the usual sentiments—the feeling for the soil, native experience, personal arrogance—into ametric verses, rich and verbose. Politically, they were Catholic, anti-liberal, and anti-democratic. The literary sheet, *Vanguardia,* dated from 1928. In addition to those already mentioned, there were JOSE ROMÁN and ALBERTO ORDÓÑEZ ARGÜELLO (1914) in the vanguard group. This group had an immediate influence on the national literary movement. In search of a national form of expression, they cultivated folklore, drawing on the Hispanic tradition and elaborating it with their own creations. Some of them disseminated their poetic works in magazines and appear in anthologies without ever having published a book. Other poets of these years: EDGARDO PRADO (1912), NAPOLEÓN ROMÁN (1906), AURA ROSTAND (1908), CARMEN SOBALBARRO (1908). Now let us bring to the fore the most valuable. First of all, JOSÉ CORONEL URTECHO (1906). He is one of the most versatile poetic temperaments of all Hispanic-America: an iconoclast, but hard working in the creation of new icons. Well informed on the latest tendencies in all literatures and determined to scandalize all of the consecrated tastes, he began by sarcastically greeting Rubén Darío: "And so, Rubén / my inevitable countryman, I greet you / with a flip of my derby / that the rats ate in nineteen hundred and 20 / five, Amen." The poetry of Coronel Urtecho is disconcerting because of its ceaseless innovations and changes of direction. The only permanent feature is his Catholic faith: in all else he is an experimenter with forms and modalities. He is simple or hermetic, clear or surrealistic, severe or humorous. In search of a popular expression he cultivated folklore and took rhythms and themes from traditional songs and stories. The "Little Ode to Uncle Coyote," for example, is based on a "wayside tale" (that is, a children's story): Uncle Coyote is an animal who steals fruit from orchards. When he is told that the moon, reflected in the water, is a cheese, he tries to eat it and is drowned. Upon this folkloric canvas, Coronel Urtecho embroiders a comic-lyric figure: Uncle Coyote is to be a deluded figure like Don Quijote or the Chinese poet, Li-Tai-Po. Coronel Urtecho has written very little and has not yet published a book. PABLO ANTONIO CUADRA (1912) is the most active and productive regional poet: *Nicaraguan Poems* (*Poemas nicaragüenses,* 1933), *Temporal Song* (*Canto temporal,* 1934), *A Crown of Goldfinches* (*Corona de Jilgueros,* 1949), *Zoo* (1962). In *The Jaguar and the Moon* (*El jaguar y la luna,* 1959) he wrote about Nicaraguan men, landscapes, and customs; the evocation of the mysterious indigenous population served as an inspiration to him. His plays have been produced. One successful play was *Along the Roads Go the Peasants* (*Por los caminos van los campesinos*), a work with political intent. JOAQUÍN PASOS (1915–1947), a writer who was harsh in his sentences, schematic in form, experimented with new poetic forms: "Choral Poems," was written to be recited by several voices, with such effects as simultaneous and contrapuntal words. His works were posthumously collected in *Poems by a Young Man* (*Poemas de un joven,* 1963).

Costa Rica: The dense ALFONSO ULLOA ZAMORA (1914); the simple FRANCISCO AMIGHETTI (1907); the cordial FERNANDO LUJÁN (1912); the landscapist GONZALO DOBLES (1904); ARTURO AGÜERO CHAVES, the most notable regionalist; he wrote in the manner of Echeverría, even though his inspiration came from new circumstances. FERNANDO CENTENO GÜELL (1908), removed from national themes; RAFAEL ESTRADA (1901–1934), a beautiful promise that died; ARTURO ECHEVERRÍA LORIA (1909), and MANUEL PICADO CHACÓN (1910).

Panama: DEMETRIO KORSI (1899–1957), who observed postwar literary restlessness, took his themes from city life and treated them with irony and easy good humor. His poetic production—begun in 1920 with *Strange Poems* (*Los poemas extraños*)—earned for him one of the highest positions in his country. Nevertheless, much of what he wrote at the beginning and at the end of his career had something of the air of imitative exercises. His intervening work—let us say, that done between the ages of thirty and fifty—is more spontaneous in its reference to the neighborhood, to everyday human types, to the aspects of life as daily lived in the city. Country poets were MOISÉS CASTILLO (1899), SANTIAGO ANGUIZOLA D. (1899?), and in a lesser measure LUCAS BÁRCENA (1906). After 1929 there is evidence that the current of vanguardism has settled in Panama: Rogelio Sinán—whom the reader should look for among the prosists—produced the first wave in this current. *Wave (Onda,* 1929) was his book of poems. Panamanian vanguardist poetry, purer, more universal than that which up to this time had been cultivated, flowed from the pens of ROQUE JAVIER LAURENZA (1910), the most learned in the postwar schools; DEMETRIO HERRERA SEVILLANO (1902–1950), who, with the liberty of the ultraists, gave popular rhythms to his ill-bred muse; and RICARDO J. BERMÚDEZ (1914), more ambitious in his themes, with lyric and declamatory images, was, at the same time conscious of the dignity of his song.

(iii) *Antilles* / In Cuba, vanguardist literature was called "de avance," because one of its organs in 1927 was the *Revista de Avance.* The young men felt weighted down beneath a mental inertia and the moral baseness of their country and they reacted vehemently. Even the apparently playful forms carried a feeling of social rebellion. In the words of Jorge Mañach, one of the founders of *Avance:* "The lower case letters, the outrageous images, the meaningless plays of sound, the typographic capers, the plastic deformations, were merely the concrete expression of that mood"; "vanguardism, as a polemic movement, succumbed among us as soon as our consciences felt that they had found the real opportunity for expression in the field of politics." Beneath the ensign of vanguardism—rebellious but futile—two groups of poets are formed: the pure poets (Eugenio Florit) and the poets of social protest (Nicolás Guillén). There are comings and goings from one group to the other (Ballagas). Even Negroid poetry fluctuates between lyricism and documentation. At the end of this period another group appears: the transcendentalists (Lezama Lima).

Let us pause, as we fill in the course we have just outlined, on a few representative poets from each group.

From the group of pure poets—SILVERIO DÍAZ DE LA RIONDA (1902); RAFAEL GARCÍA BÁRCENA (1907–1961); DULCE MARÍA LOYNAZ (1903)—we are going to choose one of the finest lyricists of his time: EUGENIO FLORIT (1903). In the *décimas* of *The Tropics (Trópico,* 1930), the syntactic thought, vagabond but quick, spins images of the Cuban countryside and sea, images which fuse, also with quick strokes, concrete perception and abstract concept. Traces of Gongoristic poetry, traces of popular poetry. *Double Accent* (*Doble acento*, 1937)—the cold accent, measured and classical; the burning accent, overflowing and romantic—is a complex book. At times, as in "The Martyrdom of Saint Sebastian" ("*Martirio de San Sebastián*"), the descriptive, the narrative, the lyrical, and the mystical are joined: the saint is described at the moment when he is about to suffer his torture, and his lyric monolog is narrated from his invitation to the arrows: "Yes, come to my arms, little doves of iron," "Come, yes, hard angels of flame, / small cherubim with tenséd wings"—until the final arrow, the death arrow, that which will unite him mystically with God—"I know that my last dove is coming . . . / Ah! Now all is well, Lord, I shall bring it to you / buried in a corner of my bosom!" In *Kingdom* (*Reino*, 1938) the poet wishes to render his impression of the landscape—be it a subjective insight or an objective view—exact, in its purest essence, and to do this, he outlines it in brief, clean, tense brush strokes. In the new poems of his anthology *My Poem* (*Poema mío*, 1947) his verse becomes simpler, more sentimental: childhood memories, religious unction, solitude, meditations by the sea. *Final Assonance and Other Poems* (*Asonante final y otros poemas*, 1956) is a conversation, also about memories and meditations. But now Florit, since he is conversing—"Conversation with my father"—broadens out his verse and, no longer having to follow a strict course, his thought wanders along with simplicity and even humor. But this verse, although colloquial, is not prosaic. In "Final Assonance"—where the poet allows the occasional images of his consciousness to flow freely, and, as in a mirror, he sees himself in the act of writing—poetry is a close-knit part of the most ordinary phrases. Poetry of tenderness, goodness, of the sad smile, of resignation, and of confidence in God. Poetry which touches little things with a dart of light; the commonplace, the everyday things, thus touched, light up, marveling. His *Poetic Anthology* (*Antología poética*, 1930–1955, published in 1956) traces the most outstanding features of his art.

Negroid poetry—to which we later make special reference—had at times purely esthetic norms, but at other times, when it denounced the conditions in which the Cubans of African heritage lived, it became social and even political. The best representative of this combative poetry is NICOLÁS GUILLÉN (1902). He began, in *Motives of Sound* (*Motivos de son*, 1930) with the rhythms of the Negro dance, drawn in the manner of the sketchers of customs and with an ironic stylization of popular speech. A circumstance, a deed, a sentiment are commented upon in few words while the musical outline of the *son* keeps time with the laughter and gaiety. In *Sóngoro Cosongo* (1931) Negro folklore is integrated with the Hispanic tradition, but above all it is poetry: verbal creation, lyrical metaphors, serious purpose. *West Indies, Ltd.* (1934) intensified the civic, polemic, anti-imperialist comment which was before only occasional: here are some of his good poems, alive with feeling that comes from the very depths of his sensitivity as a mulatto, in solidarity with the oppressed Negro. His *Songs for Soldiers and Dances for Tourists* (*Cantos para soldados y sones para turistas,* 1937), give vent in the simple speech of the humble people and with the rhythm of the *son* to the aspirations of the dispossessed class. Like Neruda, like Vallejo, Guillén also took the side of the republic during the Spanish Civil War, and from this fighting position—which was to lead him to Communism—came the poems on *Spain* (*España,* 1937). His mastery was affirmed in 1947–48 in two *Elegies* (*Elegías*) —to Jacques Roumain, and Jesús Menéndez. The book which best rounds out Guillén is *The Complete Sound* (*El son entero,* 1947), popular in accent, rarely political, more national than racial, having a rhythmic fruition without the comicality of his first *sons*. Here we have a mature synthesis of the personality of Guillén, with all of his traits as an observer and as a sensitive man, as a singer of tradition and of the lyric cult, as a sculptor and musician, attentive to primitive magic, and at the same time to social reclamation. After years of silence, Guillén reappeared, without any surprises, in *The Dove of Popular Flight* (*La paloma de vuelo popular,* 1958): again, the double face of the political agitator and of the traditional lyricist. We prefer the lyrical Guillén, of course. In spite of his interest in the poor and humble folk, in spite of his enthusiasm for folklore, in spite of his themes of everyday, elementary life, of the false rhythm of popular song, and of his political messages, Guillén is an aristocratic poet because of the delicate obliqueness with which his lyricism cuts the air. We have said that some poets would swing between pure poetry and social poetry. The Afro-Cuban poets also swung between estheticism and protest.

EMILIO BALLAGAS (1908–1954) is extremely notable among those who can be studied in either group. *Jubilation and Flight* (*Júbilo y fuga*, 1931) is pure poetry, angelic in its disengagement and capacity for flight, playful in its sounds without meaning, sensual, but with the sensuality of pastoral poetry. Afterwards, in *Eternal Taste* (*Sabor eterno*, 1939), his emotion is amatory and elegiac, as in the romantics. Classically structured in sonnets, *liras*, and *décimas*, *Our Lady of the Sea* (*Nuestra señora del mar*, 1943) is religious poetry. Along with this theme, although he was not a Negro, Ballagas cultivated verses on the life of the Negro perceived from outside: *Notebook of Negro Poetry* (*Cuaderno de poesía negra*, 1934). In Ballagas, then, we find a poetry of verbal sensuality, a pure poetry, a poetry with a Negro theme. Like other poets of his country, with the same tendencies, the same themes, of the same generation, Ballagas, in writing Negro poetry, shakes words like maracas, evoking the sound of the pips, or invents jingling words, and in the end, we hear babblings, interjections, drum rolls, rhythms, onomatopoeias, melodic stimuli to the conditioned reflexes of a popular choreography, rather than poetry. Ballagas leans toward the picturesque, the exterior, the playful; his sympathy for the Negro is a projection, through social means, of his old desire to attain through poetry, a candid, pure, and primitive reality. It is interesting to follow Ballagas' itinerary from his neo-romantic poetry to his final poetry, so much more serene —that of *Sky of Hostages* (*Cielo de rehenes*) posthumously included in his *Poetic Works* (*Obras poéticas*).

RAMÓN GUIRAO (1908–1949) also wrote pure and somewhat surrealist poetry—*Poems* (*Poemas*, 1947)—but his place in literary history is that of the initiator of Afro-Cuban poetry. "The Rumba Dancer" (*"La bailadora de rumba"*) is from 1928. Nevertheless, he had neither the vital interior force of Guillén nor the exterior descriptive force of Ballagas: his book of Negro poems, *Bongó* (1934). Other poets of Afro-Cuban poetry during these years should be mentioned: lyricism poured into social themes in

MIRTA AGUIRRE (1912), the somewhat Nerudian eroticism of JOSÉ ÁNGEL BUESA (1910), FÉLIX PITA RODRÍGUEZ (1909), who went through the initiation rites of French, Spanish, and Hispanic-American surrealism; and, above all, Feijoo who, because he is a solitary figure, can just as well be put in with the group in this chapter as with that in the next, since no particular group attracted him, and Lezama Lima, who, because of his age belongs here, but should be put with those born after 1915 because of his affinities. SAMUEL FEIJÓO (1914) is a neo-romantic who deals with intimate sentiments and Cuban landscapes. Inner and outer poetry, but with gardens on both sides, and at times we do not know whether these flowers are spiritual or vegetable. Narcissism which contemplates itself in the mirror of nature, or pampered trees, hills, ocean, sky, all asking to be caressed by the poet. The island of Feijoo is neatly ornamented with a veil drawn over it to soften and render it even more enchanting: glance at his books, from *Celestial Comrade* (*Camarada celeste,* 1944) to *Face* and *The Poet's Leaf* (*Faz, La hoja del poeta,* 1956). The poet isolates himself within the landscape and notes down his impressions in an intimate diary of poems and poetic prose; in fact, he published *Travel Diaries* (*Diarios de viajes,* 1958). JOSÉ LEZAMA LIMA (1912) was a promoter of magazines—namely, *Orígenes*—of literary circles, and of a new poetic style. He withdrew from everything that had been done and was being done by the Cuban generation that we have just finished describing, but his solitude was of short duration: his first books of poems—*The Death of Narcissus* (*Muerte de Narciso,* 1937) and especially *Inimical Murmuring* (*Enemigo rumor,* 1941)—had scarcely appeared when they seduced the younger poets, making him, from that moment on the master. The ascendency which he exercises over other writers seems to be due to the example of a life monstrously consecrated to literature. Moreover: a life made up of books, bibliophilistic and bookish. His vast library is cataloged in his essays: *Analect of the Watch* (*Analecta del reloj,* 1953), *The American Expression* (*La expresión americana,* 1957), *Treatises in Havana* (*Tratados en la Habana,* 1958). But even between the lines of his poetry the shelves of books were to be seen, with some volumes more dog-eared than others: baroque Spaniards (especially Góngora and Quevedo), symbolists (Valéry, Rilke), Catholics (Chesterton, T. S. Eliot, Claudel), surrealists (Neruda). His poetry—hermetic—is vital in its impulse, but because this vitality, as we have said, is completely identified with literature, the verses which result are more literary than poetic. He knocks things over in order to discover what is hiding behind them, but he refuses to let us know what he sees. His sight is metaphysical, even theological. Man, through original sin, is exiled from absolute reality: he longs to return, but sees that poetry is inaccessible, an "inimical murmuring." There is therefore something sacred in the act of taking up one's pen. The true poet—Lezama believes—is not one who contents himself with the appearances of things, nor with sentimental effusion, but one who, in spite of certain resistance, advances toward poetry which gazes at us from a distance, always from a distance, like the absolute and pitiless creature that it is. *Steadfastness* (*La fijeza,* 1949)—his most complex and difficult book—alludes to this fixed, transcendental character of poetry. We question poetry: the answer it gives is lost even as the poet tries to note it down. His language is hard in its rhythm, its syntax cracked, abrupt in metaphor, leaving a frozen wake. His poems try to be organs of metaphysical perception, but they do not allow themselves to be perceived; they want to be objective, but are so liquefied in subjectivity that we can no longer make out their profile. Lezama thins himself down to such a point that he weakens, loses authority, and his words give themselves up to a captious madness: *Giver (Dador,* 1960). Other poets: MERCEDES GARCÍA TUDURÍ (1904); GUILLERMO VILLAR-RONDA (1912), ÁNGEL I. AUGIER (1910).

Dominican Republic: Between the posthumism of Moreno Jimenes (which we saw in the preceding chapter) and the magazine *La Poesía Sorprendida,* 1943 (which we will see in the next chapter), arise the first imaginative, novel, complex, generally anti-realist poets, educated, if not in Góngora, at least in the Gongorism of García Lorca. The one to receive and unite, in a cordial reunion, the poets of the generation of Moreno Jimenes with those of the generation of Fernández Spencer is the lyricist, FRANKLIN MIESES BURGOS (1907). Either in his free verse or in the rigorous form of the sonnet, he seduces us with an insinuating melody which uncoils in metaphors. His poetic world is as limpid as a happy dream, with lasses, roses, beams of moonlight, crystals, angels, and mystery. Sometimes, however, his voice swells with emotion and he declaims. It is an elegiac emotion, like that of *Without a World Now and Wounded by Heaven (Sin mundo ya y herido por el cielo,* 1944), which seeks the beloved shadow through death. Other titles: *Climate of Eternity (Clima de eternidad,* 1947), *The Presence of the Days (Presencia de los días,* 1949), *The Hero (El héroe,* 1954). RAFAEL AMÉRICO HENRÍQUEZ (1899)—author of "Earth Rose" *("Rosa de tierra")*—gathers together materials from the landscape, carries them to his ceramic workshop and tries to give them shape, to color and polish them. His baroque grammar sometimes makes his images ugly. In spite of all this, his abundant metaphors are the index of his originality. TOMÁS HERNÁNDEZ FRANCO (1904–1952), who captured life by the sea in *Songs of the Happy Coast (Canciones del litoral alegre,* 1936), stands out for his "Yelidá" (1942), an expressionist poem, half narrative and half allegorical. It is the history of a mulatto girl, the daughter of a Norwegian father and an Antillian mother. His poetic imagination coins itself into sentences, strangely brilliant. His dynamism carried him to the story— *Cibao,* 1951—in which he continued to be an impressionist poet.

MANUEL DEL CABRAL (1907) sings with an unmistakable Antillian voice. One of his most famous books is *Pal Mon (Compadre Mon,* 1943), an epic-lyric poem in which he creates the myth of a popular hero. This book, nevertheless, represents a stage already passed: later, Cabral combined human and metaphysical accents in his poetry: *The Secret Guests (Los huéspedes secretos,* 1951), *Planetary Lapidation (Pedrada planetaria,* 1958), *14 Love Mutes (14 mudos de amor,* 1962). His two anthologies —*Anthology of the Land (Antología tierra,* 1959) and *Key An-*

thology (*Antología clave*, 1957)—reveal a vast gamut of themes and moods. Manuel del Cabral has also created a poetic prose: *Chinchina Searches for Time* (*Chinchina busca el tiempo*, 1945) and *30 parábolas* (1956). He is out of orbit. He gets lost and finds his way again only to get lost and find himself once more. The creative force of his popular lyric vein always pulls him up after one of his falls. His Negroid poetry is important also, but he sings ambitiously too, to the men of other races and, in *Planetary Lapidation,* his Hispanic-American voice shouts into space (*"Monolog of Sputnik I"*).

Another poet of these years was the exalted HÉCTOR INCHÁUSTEGUI CABRAL (1912). He comes out into the world and greets the native landscape and above all his fellow man with a powerful voice. He laments human misery and calls for a more just social order. He has a philosophy of life with an active moral spur, and in his desire to communicate it, he often forces his verse to assume the functions of prose. Eloquent verses, more sonorous than musical. He is saved, however, by his urgent bursts of expressive detail, that appear just in time to give subtle color to what was fading into an abstract ideal. Like other vanguardist poets he disdained the traditional forms: ten books of poems, from *Poems From a Single Anguish* (*Poemas de una sola angustia,* 1940), to *Vegetable Rebellion and Other Less Bitter Poems* (*Rebelión vegetal y otros poemas menos amargos,* 1956). Also associated with this movement, to which we will refer with more detail in the next chapter, were the vanguardists of social accent PEDRO RENÉ CONTÍN AYBAR (1910) and PEDRO MIR (1913).

Puerto Rico: There is something in the atmosphere of this country that curbs, moderates, and smooths out the advances that arrive from the literary world. An example of this is JOSÉ AGUSTÍN BALSEIRO (1900): in *Captive Purity* (*La pureza cautiva*), *Homesickness for Puerto Rico* (*Saudades de Puerto Rico*) and *Eves of Shadow* (*Vísperas de sombra*) unity is gained through love of the native island, through clear song, and through sentiments contemplated in the light of conscience, serene in spite of its preoccupations. In general, the poetic spirit did wave in the breeze of popular fashion. Nevertheless, the "isms" of vanguardism proliferated. First, in 1921, the *diepalism* of JOSÉ I. DE DIEGO PADRÓ (1899) and Luis Palés Matos, a movement which proposed an onomatopoeic poetic language. Afterwards, in 1923, the *euphorism* of VICENTE PALÉS MATOS (1903). In 1925, *noism* (from "no"), also initiated by Vicente Palés Matos. In 1928, the *atalayism* of GRACIANY MIRANDA ARCHILLA (1910), FERNANDO GONZÁLEZ ALBERTY (1908) and iconoclasts and individualists who made up a literary circle with something of the bohemian hermeticism of dadaism and something of pure poetry. Later, Luis Hernández Aquino (1907) founded *integralism,* a tendency toward the vernacular, the autochthonous.

We could point out two tendencies: neo-Creolism and neo-romanticism ("neo" refers to the new techniques of the vanguard—techniques in which the poets were taking lessons). Sometimes the same poet follows both tendencies, so that we cannot expect to see dividing lines in these mixed groups. For example, LUIS HERNANDEZ AQUINO (1907) was a neo-romantic in *Poems of the Short Life* (*Poemas de la vida breve,* 1940), but neo-Creolist in *Island of Anguish* (*Isla de la angustia,* 1943), in which he is not content merely to contemplate the landscape, but aims at giving a poetic voice to the land and its people. His anthology, *A Voice in Time* (*Voz en el tiempo*) is from 1952. Later came *Everyday Time* (*Del tiempo cotidiano,* 1961). In the neo-Creolist tendency we have FRANCISCO MANRIQUE CABRERA (1908), who is both agile and profound in his unrestrained methods of capturing the essence of Puerto Rico; *Poems of My Land, My Land* (*Poemas de mi tierra, tierra,* 1936) transfigure the landscape lyrically with images akin to those of ultraism; but he also cultivates Negro, social and childhood themes. One of the major poets is JUAN ANTONIO CORRETJER (1908); he also followed the line of "integralism." He writes about nature, with compassion for human sorrow. His nationalist ideas are expressed in terms of simple, homely affection. The homeland is for him a beloved woman, and in his lyricism, the dreams, the exhalation of the land, and the vital impulse are all given with admirable unity. He recalls his childhood, narrates, describes, denounces and makes a myth of history. *Genius and Fancy* (*Genio y figura*) is from 1961. FRANCISCO HERNÁNDEZ VARGAS (1914) was also an "integralist," and wrote anecdotes in *The Footpath* (*La vereda*). OBDULIO BAUZA (1907) revealed evocative power in *The Noble House* (*La casa solariega*). Women were conspicuous in the neo-romantic trend.

First of all comes JULIA DE BURGOS (1914–1953), profoundly moving in her unsatisfied passion for life, so deep that she verges on metaphysical themes, with an acute feeling for the nature and beauty of love, from her *Poem in Twenty Furrows* (*Poema en veinte surcos,* 1938) to her posthumous *The Sea and You,* (*El mar y tú*). CARMEN ALICIA CADILLA (1908) is modest in revealing her inner self; she projects her sentimental, amorous temperament into nature itself: *Poetic Anthology* (*Antología poética*). For CARMELINA VIZCARRONDO (1906) love of country is at least as powerful as the other.

AMELIA CEIDE (1908), treating eroticism romantically and modernistically, envisioned the sky and the earth as a couple in love: *When the Sky Smiles* (*Cuando el cielo sonríe,* 1946). And now for a few men in neo-romanticism. SAMUEL LUGO (1905), happy in images of nature: *Yumbra, Round of the Green Flame* (*Ronda de la llama verde*). Modernism continued to exist in ultraism, and ultraism continued to exist, although in moderation, in other poets of these years. CESÁREO ROSA-NIEVES (1901) is among those having the broadest register, which includes erotic, Negrophile, Creolist, political and childhood themes: *Walks in the Moon of Dreams* (*Caminos en luna de sueños,* 1957). CLEMENTE SOTO VÉLEZ (1905) and JULIO SOTO RAMOS (1903) prolong experiments that had been initiated by the vanguard much earlier.

The last "ism" of these years was *transcendentalism,* piloted after 1948 by FÉLIX FRANCO OPPENHEIMER (1912), author of *Man and His Anguish* (*El hombre y su angustia,* 1950), and *Of Time and its Shape* (*Del tiempo y su figura,* 1956). The aim was to "lift man up to a plane of high spirituality, without letting him forget his human reality." In his rejection of matter and science there are romantic and religious overtones. Among all of these movements we find EUGENIO RENTAS LUCAS (1910), PEDRO JUAN LABARTHE (1906) and several others. But one of the fundamental pillars of Puerto Rican poetry, on a par with Llorens Torres, Dávila, and Ribera Chevremont, is Luis Palés Matos.

LUIS PALÉS MATOS (Puerto Rico, 1898–1959) is one of the most original poets of this era. He began by writing modernist poetry—*Azaleas,* 1915—but sought his own course and, after 1926, he published poems in forms which immediately placed him in the vanguard of Hispanic-American literature. They were poems on Negro themes that preceded or, at any rate, were independent of those which were flourishing in Cuba. But Palés Matos gathered his into a book much later, after having displayed them in periodicals. His first book of Negroid poetry was *Shoe-blacking of Kinky Hair and Negro Themes* (*Tuntún de pasa y grifería,* 1937), and it was enough to consecrate him definitely. Whether or not the Negroid content of this literature was authentic or of national significance is an ethnographic and sociological problem outside the pale of literary criticism. The important thing is to indicate its extreme poetic merit. With eminent rhythmic skill Palés Matos makes us hear an entire people, real or not. It is like the verbal imitation of the movements of the Negro dances: rhythms, syncopations, repetitions, onomatopoeias, alliterations, and rhymes accented on the last syllables. The vocabulary gathers together expressions either heard, read, or invented; and the proper names, the geographic terms, the mythological references, the descriptions of beliefs, customs, and Afro-Antillian rites end up by creating the illusion of a magic world. The sensuality is experienced by all the organs of perception, and all the impressions are blended into metaphors that are not simply tinsel ornaments, but deep, lyrical intuitions. In his huge orchestra an ironic contrapuntal melody can be heard; because Palés Matos is not a Negro, but a white man, and he smiles wistfully at the contrasts in both cultures, in neither of which he really believes. It is precisely in this refined note of irony, skepticism, and refined melancholy that he differs from the other poets who write on Negro themes. He does not copy a popular reality exactly as it exists in a particular country, rather he interprets the Negro motifs from his position as an imaginative poet with all the artistry of a distant disciple of the baroque. Although these poems, inspired by the Negroes of the Antilles, brought him fame, they constitute only one aspect of his total work. His book *Poetry* (*Poesía, 1915–1956*, published in 1957) reveals a complete Palés Matos to the reader, not confined to the surface of the Negro theme, but penetrating it in poetry that is more essential, profound, complex and enduring. Thus one understands that those Negro poems—"Negro Dance" (*"Danza negra"*)—are mere episodes in the expression of a sad insight into primitive life and dissolution into nothingness—"The One Called" (*"El llamado"*).

Before leaving the Antilles, we will pause to examine what was most different in Negro and mulatto poetry. Folklore is extremely rich in old rhythms and Afro-Antillian themes, but only after 1925 did all this acquire a worthwhile esthetic value. The stimulus came from Europe. The Afrological investigations of Leo Frobenius; the Afrophilism of Paris in the "fauves," expressionist and dadaist paintings, literature and ballet; examples of Negro art in the United States; the use of the gypsy, the African, the folkloric by García Lorca and others in Spain, indicate that the Negro theme was in style during the years of ultraism. The actuality of Negro race and culture in the Antilles favored the fad. Furthermore, in the Antilles, it was less a fad than a self-discovery. But that the stimulus should have come from European literature explains the surprising poetic quality of Nicolás Guillén, Palés Matos, Ramón Guirao, and Emilio Ballagas, to mention but a few of the masters of a school that is becoming increasingly crowded.

(iv) *Venezuela* / First of all, let us take the youngest members of the "generation of 1918," whom we discussed in the preceding chapter. *Shiftings* (*Virajes,* 1932), by JACINTO FOMBONA PACHANO (1901–1951) was a book of genuine Creolist poems, notable for its freshness and lyricism. At that time his themes centered on childhood, the family, civic affairs; his forms were simple. Years later he composed his most vigorous book, *The Unguarded Towers* (*Las torres desprevenidas,* 1940), in which are reflected the preoccupations and problems of a humanity tormented by a war which was not experienced at first hand, but was felt on all sides. ENRIQUE PLANCHART (1901–1935), French in culture, refined in taste, was capable of respecting the values of modernism as well as greeting the promises of the vanguard. PEDRO SOTILLO (1902), warm, hearty, imbued his *Occurrence* (*Andanza*) with national feeling. LUISA DEL VALLE SILVA (1902–1961) provided a feminine, traditional voice. And one final name, before going on to the vanguard. MANUEL FELIPE RUGELES (1904–1959) in all of his books, from *Pitcher* (*Cántaro*) to *Golden Season* (*Dorada estación*), sings of the neighborhood in which he was born, trying to grasp its spirit in clear images.

In Venezuela the first sign of the postwar literary vanguard was *Aspero* (1924), by ANTONIO ARRÁIZ (1903). He marked the dividing line between the generation of 1918 and the generation of 1928. After Arráiz the trend was to move toward other forms. We shall study him later, among the prose writers. But it is he who has brought us to the vanguard, where all the genres undergo a renewal of form: the novel (Uslar Pietri), the short story (Meneses), poetry (LUIS CASTRO, 1909–1933), JOAQUÍN GABALDÓN MÁRQUEZ (1906), PABLO ROJAS GUARDIA (1909). The first vanguardist thrust broke the meter of poetry, changed its subject-matter and brought confusion to its lyric moods. This is only the first sign of the literature of the vanguard. We have already said that it appeared belatedly in Venezuela. We find it well organized by 1936, in the group surrounding the magazine, *Viernes*. When the dictator Gómez died in 1935 some of the exiled politicians returned, among them RAFAEL OLIVARES FIGUEROA and ANGEL MIGUEL QUEREMEL (1900–1939). The latter had assimilated lessons in literature from the French and brought the latest novelties from Spain. He had been in contact with the vindication of Góngora, with pure poetry, with ultraism and creationism. Up to that time the Spaniards of influence in Venezuela had been Antonio Machado and Juan Ramón Jiménez; now, partly because of Queremel, they are Gerardo Diego, Alberti, Salinas, García Lorca, Guillén. Through his tidings and his own verses [those in the *Trapeze of Images* (*El trapecio de las imágenes*), for example] Queremel therefore contributed to the triumph of a literature that was daring. The magazine *Viernes* was a laboratory of contradictory esthetics, all of them experimental: hermetic lyricism, somewhat surrealistic; metaphysical fever; scorn for the facile writing of the romantic-modernists, etc. The *Viernes* group included, besides Queremel, JOSÉ RAMÓN HEREDIA (1900), ÓSCAR ROJAS JIMÉNEZ, LUIS FERNANDO ÁLVAREZ (1902–1952). Other collaborators were: HECTOR GUILLERMO VILLALOBOS (1911), who gave lyric quality to popular revolutionary ballads in *Jagüey;* MIGUEL RAMÓN UTRERA (1910), AQUILES CERTAD (1914), LUIS JOSÉ GARCÍA. Of all the *Viernes* group, those who grew to become poets of influence were D'Sola, Gerbasi and Venegas Filardo. OTTO D'SOLA (1912) had the soundest of poetic vocations, from *On Solitude and Visions* (*De la soledad y de las visiones*) to *The Tree of Paradise* (*El árbol de paraíso,* 1960), in which old religious myths inspired new poetic images. VICENTE GERBASI (1913) gave his Venezuelan experiences universal meaning and form. For example, there is something in a sweet evocation of childhood that does not merely evoke an early experience, but gives us, through what it says, an awareness of a complex human reality. Because of the purity and sincerity of his voice—*My Father, the Immigrant* (*Mi padre, el inmigrante*, 1945)—he achieved ascendance over younger poets. PASCUAL VENEGAS FILARDO (1911) went from poetry to the essay and criticism, but his early poems shed a radiance of light upon the entire group. There were poets who were opposed to the poetry of *Viernes*, at least to that poetry that was encased in obscure symbols. This opposition came from several fronts (not to mention the fact that around 1940 a new movement arose, which we shall find in the next chapter). One of these fronts, made up of partisans of regular forms, and even of classical forms: LUIS BELTRÁN GUERRERO, 1914, and JUAN BEROES, 1914, who was among the first to give classical structure to his poems, with an ear trained to the measures and rhythms of the golden age. Another front was composed of partisans of an objective poetry, on normal themes: ALBERTO ARVELO TORREALBA, 1904. Another, of partisans of the native soil, folklore and regional themes. Also, isolated voices, some of them from the provinces: J. A. DE ARMAS CHITTY (1908), MANUEL RODRÍGUEZ CÁRDENAS (1912), JOSÉ MIGUEL FERRER (1904).

(v) *Colombia* / The "New Ones"—that is, the poets who formed a group around the magazine, *Los Nuevos*, published by Jorge Zalamea and Alberto Lleras Camargo—drew away from the modernists, but not very far. At any rate, they did not break with them as the youths of other countries had. Colombians have always been very circumspect in the use of language. Modernism, with its respect for good form, had reinforced this traditional feeling for grammar. Thus modernism became a part of this tradition, and the desire for linguistic perfection of the Parnassians continued to be dominant until after the first world war. The vanguardist movements scarcely altered the modernist, Parnassian course of the "New Ones." One of the essayists of this generation, Jorge Zalamea, said: "To suppress the books of Valencia and Silva would be to suppress the current moment of Colombian literature." Thus the "new poets" skipped the immediately preceding generation of "Centenarists" without recognizing their mastery. For example, they felt that José Eustasio Rivera had put political propositions, nationalistic sentiments, and a vague humanitarianism in his book *The Vortex*, but that it was all encompassed by a conservative philosophy. As for his sonnets of *The Promised Land*, the "new poets" found them to be too labored. The "Centenarists" had not familiarized themselves with the literary course from Proust to Breton. The "New Ones," on the other hand, although they also prolonged Parnassianism, at least cast a glance at distant vanguardists, from Europe and from some South American cities. The main poets of this generation were the *decadents:* León de Greiff, whom we have already studied, Germán Pardo García and Rafael Maya. In general, they did not disencumber themselves of the past, but it is enough that there should have been among them a few exceptions for us to be able to distinguish them from the "Centenarists." These few exceptional poets leaped into the future with arrogances, obscurities, music, and challenging ideas. Some were pure esthetes who with childish chatter played with literature, dehumanizing it. Others, won over by socialist ideas, proclaimed bellicose programs of political revindication (Luis Vidales). There was one group of skeptics who remained on the sidelines of ideology and another group that supported order and authority (Silvio Villegas, Eliseo Arango, José Camacho Carreño, Augusto Ramírez Moreno). León de Greiff, in establishing himself in Bogotá, lent force to the "New Ones." He was a unique personality, inimitable in his perpetual youth. He had followers, however.

For example, LUIS VIDALES (1904), who in 1926 disturbed the atmosphere with *Bells Are Ringing (Suenan timbres)*, a book of poetry connected with the power house of electrical and unexpected images that functioned throughout the Western world after the first great war. Vidales was the one who took greatest advantage of the mischievous, *gregueristic* mood which was cultivated in Spanish letters after Gómez de la Serna. But Colombian literature did not allow itself to be seduced by the postwar "isms." Certainly not the two major poets of these years: Pardo García and Maya.

GERMÁN PARDO GARCÍA (1902) saw three stages in the fourteen volumes that went from *Will (Voluntad, 1930)* to *Star Without a Shore (Lucero sin orillas,* 1952). His diagram was complicated by the new volumes published later: in 1961 there appeared a "summary" of his thirty years of poetry; in 1965 *Lightning (Los relampagos)* and *Nocturnal Lips (Labios nocturnos)* were published in Mexico, where he has been living since 1931. His poetry went from the approved forms of the past to verbal audacities. In their depths can be heard the same desolate song. Where he is not clear it is because he has opened his eyes in a zone of shadows, but he wants to see clearly, and even his sorrow comes out in regulated verses. There is something romantic in his tone: his exaltation of mysteries and anguish is that of a Narcissus who feels himself to be a titan, and he shouts his protest against injustice and war. He expresses his vision of man's inner abyss as well as that of the outer abyss of the cosmos. He is deep because he gets down to the roots of the problems of existence. He is complex because his concerns multiply on different levels of self-knowledge and of contemporary life. The poet, increasingly aware of the world's threatening circumstances and of the difficulties attending the survival of man, cries out harshly. At times that cry contains more feeling of his personal importance than of universal suffering.

RAFAEL MAYA (1898), moderate, intelligent, extended the scope of his poetry, without changing its character. His sensations and images became more vertiginous; his rhythms disbanded and there was more liberty and more space in his verses. But all this without exhibitionism. The original contemplation of nature, harmonious, tender, simple, grew deeper with the years without his needing to break noisily with the styles of prewar literature. He is of that classical temperament which reflects upon its emotions and obliges them to assume an equilibrium between the new and the traditional. Without ignoring the French, Maya reads the Spanish classicists with pleasure. His last book, *Nocturnal Navigation* (*Navegación nocturna,* 1959), is an examination of conscience. Maya smashes his soul to pieces, as though it were a time glass, and in each splinter the light of a memory is reflected; afterwards, he tries to reconstruct himself from these fragments, and the image that he recovers is that of desolation. But in this solitude the poet feels that he is beneath the shelter of God and charged with a vocation to create his own world with words. The presence of God gives order, unity, and harmony to what He has created, and the poet admires the beauty of His creation in the landscape. Pain from the thorn that he carries in his heart, agony in his expression, happiness in his contemplation of the world: this is the keyboard of his feelings. The soul of the poet flows in time, undivided, and changing, and his voice joins with those of all other poets in singing the multiple stories of mankind. He longs for ancient clarity, not modern confusion. A confidential and simple voice which, by dint of reflection, clarifies even the darknesses of its own being. Not just to live, but to feel alive. Poetry is for him not impressionism, but knowledge of essences, gathered together in time, ready for death. His images, propelled by intelligence, order themselves into beautiful expressionist allegories, stories, literary glosses and fables—always lyric in tone.

Also outstanding in the group of the "New Ones" were the elegant JOSÉ UMAÑA BERNAL (1899), CIRO MENDÍA (1902), JUAN LOZANO Y LOZANO (1902)—an admirable sonneteer—"To the Cathedral of Colonia" (*A la catedral de Colonia*")—and the crepuscular ALBERTO ÁNGEL MONTOYA (1903). Others: RAFAEL VÁZQUEZ (1899–1963), CARLOS LÓPEZ NARVÁEZ (1897), VICTOR AMAYA GONZÁLEZ (1898).

Toward 1935 other poets appeared who formed a group under the aegis of a periodical called "Stone and Sky" (*"Piedra y Cielo"*). Thus the "New Ones" were succeeded by the "Stoneandskyists." The fact that they took the title of the book by Juan Ramón Jiménez as the name for their poetry journals is sufficient to define them. However, Juan Ramón was not the only influence there. This was a generation that had to make its way through a great deal of literature, rejecting it, revising it, or adopting it in new syntheses. They were disturbed by the excessive traditionalism of Colombian poetry, its verbiage and oratorical flourishes. They even went so far as to denounce the leading national poet, Guillermo Valencia, whose beauty factory they considered antiquated, cold, superficial, equipped with verbal strategies that were too obvious. They were fascinated, on the other hand, by the Spanish poets of 1925 (Alberti, Diego, Salinas, García Lorca, Guillén, Aleixandre, as well as by the Hispanic Americans, Huidobro and Neruda; and by the lyricists, whether rigorous or chaotic, whose influence had been felt throughout Hispanic America, from symbolism to surrealism: Valery, Rilke, Cocteau, St. John Perse, T. S. Eliot. Juan Ramón Jiménez' title, therefore, was rather a symbol of equilibrium—"Stone," "Sky,"— than a source. The "Stoneandskyists" formed a group with a unity of style. Vocabulary and syntax, meters and strophes, and even themes, went to prove that, though each had his individual accent, they all came from the same esthetic position, which consisted of a predilection for the illogical image, a disdain for narrative, a respect for form, an approval of sentiment, attempts to create unreal worlds, adventures in the absolute. The first impulse was aerial, soaring; they were closer to the sky than to the stone. Then the impulse became more terrestrial and serious. They touched the rock of America in all its hard reality. The reason for this change in attitude toward poetry is apparent. Basically, the "stoneandskyists" were following the winds of fashion. Earlier, when aristocracy lent prestige, they had directed their efforts towards the minorities but later, when the dominant emphasis became social, they directed them to the majorities. Without exaggerating the cohesion of "stoneandskyism," of its originality or its purity or its importance, it can be said that it was nobly incorporated in Colombian literary history. The poets' verses were elegant and moved in the air with light and flexible grace. When they rejected pomp and eloquence they did not wind up with magic, fantastic or intellectual language, but cultivated a poetry that had dignity and circumspection, more artistic than vital.

The promoter of the "stoneandsky" group was EDUARDO CARRANZA (1913). In *Songs for Beginning a Fiesta* (*Canciones para iniciar una fiesta*, the Madrid edition is of 1953) he included a selection from his poetic work which he had begun in 1936 with a book of poems of the same title. Carranza is one of the best poets of these years. He jubilantly affirms all things and even exalts them beyond his own inner concerns: "All is well . . . / All of creation, except my heart, all is well." It seems that, mistrusting his own voice, he would like to move things, align them, use them, so that they, thus placed, might speak for him. He sings about the reality that envelops him (the native landscape, the history of the fatherland), he sings of his own reality (memories, loves), he sings to Christ. He has an air of awe before the essence of man and of the world; but his expression is not metaphysics (fortunately), but poetry, and his emotion lets loose a lightning flash of metaphors. JORGE ROJAS (1911) is among the excellent ones. He documented his admiration for Juan Ramón Jiménez in the title of his first book of poems: *The Form of His Flight* (*La forma de su huida*, 1939). It is not the best thing he has written. Later he published tercets and sonnets (the latter are the most faultless of his generation) having strict classical form and impregnated with mysterious meaning. And he continues to mature, creating forms increasingly rich in content. His poetry conjures up the great metaphysical themes. Pure poetry, of solitude and dreams: *Water Rose* (*Rosa de agua*, 1941–48), *The Water Maiden* (*La doncella de agua*,

1948), *Solitudes* (*Soledades*, 1948). While Carranza turned to Hispanic tradition, ARTURO CAMACHO RAMÍREZ (1910) represents, rather, the vanguard in America. Although at times he succumbs to outside influence and his voice is confused with echoes of other voices, his work will endure. The list of names of the "stoneandsky" group is completed with DARÍO SAMPER (1909), addicted to García Lorca, TOMÁS VARGAS OSORIO (1908–1941), GERARDO VALENCIA (1911), and CARLOS MARTÍN (1914). All of these "stoneandskyists" contributed an art of verbal subtleties and esthetic experiences that until then had been resisted by the public. Its renovating function was, then, important. During these years there were other Colombian poets who did not belong to the "stoneandsky" group, nor were they typical of it. On the borderline between the "New Ones" and "Stone and Sky," ANTONIO LLANOS (1905), fervently religious, somewhat formed by St. John of the Cross and Fray Luis de León, has exerted influence because of the poetic delicacy and purity of his sonnets: "Tremor Under the Angels" (*"Temblor bajo los ángeles"*), and his maritime poetry; JORGE ARTEL (1905) exerted influence through his Negro poetry. Above all, there is AURELIO ARTURO (1909), who sings of the landscape of his country and of the events of his days and nights with such simplicity and sincerity that his voice is, during these years, the one most frequently heard by the youth of his country. The poet's native land and the beloved woman confer meaning on each other and merge in lyric metaphors: *Sojourn to the South* (*Morada al sur,* 1963). The cruel political experiences of these years—wars all over the world, including the violence unleashed in Colombia itself—had an effect on the "stoneandskyists" and they even set aside what there was of formal purity in "stoneandskyism." Carranza, Martín, Gerardo Valencia were the most persevering, but Rojas sought a more human and concerned form of expression. Camacho Ramírez and Aurelio Arturo continued to withdraw from the group; and Llanos had never actually been one of them. "Stone and Sky" was thus but a brief historical episode.

(vi) *Ecuador* / Two clear voices: Carrera Andrade and Escudero. Born far from the main highways of the world, JORGE CARRERA ANDRADE (1902) left his corner of the earth and wandered all over the world: he wrote poetry about his travels and, of course, about his return to his homeland. Educated in a primitive country town, he sought out difficult books and disciplined himself in French literature: Hugo, Baudelaire, Francis Jammes, Jules Renard. Romantics, symbolists were his teachers. He did not succumb to the surrealism of Breton or Eluard. He was interested in immediate reality, that of the consciousness and of all things. And, in effect, his poetry is limpid. He experiments, changes, grows young again, but remains clearly sentimental. He can be seen in all these various phases, gathered together in

Registry of the World (*Registro del mundo*, 1940), an anthology from 1922 to 1939, and in *Planetary Man* (*Hombre planetario*, 1963). His poetic impressionism has given us his vision of the landscape in surprising vignettes. GONZALO ESCUDERO (1903) is a poet of great vigor: from *Helices of Hurricane and Sun* (*Hélices de huracán y de sol*, 1934) to *Self-Portrait* (*Autorretrato*, 1957) tonal changes can be noted. That grandiloquence of images and abstractions (at times fused into hyperboles) has become more lyrical and moderate.

ALFREDO GANGOTENA (1904–1945), associated with vanguardist tendencies, wrote in French (from *Orogénie*, 1928, to *Nuit*, 1938) but he also showed us, in Spanish, his *Secret Storm* (*Tempestad secreta*, 1940); JORGE REYES (1905), a carefree and playful spirit, wrote his *Quito, City in the Sky* (*Quito, arrabal del cielo*, 1930) in a climate of vanguardism; the tranquil and sad AUGUSTO ARIAS (1903); the abortive MIGUEL ANGEL LEÓN (1900–1942) and IGNACIO LASSO (1912–1943); the Indianist G. HUMBERTO MATA (1904); the tragic AUGUSTO SACOTO (1910); the abundant but refined CÉSAR ANDRADE Y CORDERO (1902); and JOSÉ ALFREDO LLERENA (1912), also a good prosist.

(vii) *Peru* / When vanguardist tendencies became prevalent in Peru, no one was capable of surpassing Vallejo. A large part of the production of the youths who imitated the dadaists, creationists, and surrealists was more ingenious than poetic. It simulated a new sensibility. Its stridence, of which they were so proud, sounded like that of a large armaments factory. And so it was: a factory of metaphors. The molds of literary expression were shattered with nonsense. Such excess had to be moderated. Something of this habit of excess always remained. Some poetic lines were traced with a heavier hand than others. These lines therefore can be seen more clearly: (a) a line of pure poets; (b) another of Peruvianist poets; (c) another of political poets. Even these lines cross, run parallel, and become one. Do not blame the critic for this confusion.

In the line of pure poetry the program is personal, intimate, disinterested, gratuitous, inactive. Eguren had set the example. CARLOS OQUENDO DE AMAT (1904–1936) followed him with his *5 Meters of Poems* (*5 metros de poemas*, 1927), notable for the sincerity of its vanguardist esthetics. His words came loose from real objects and fluttered through the air of fantasy: "In your dreams, elephants graze with their flower eyes / and an angel

rolls rivers of hoops." MARTÍN ADÁN (1908) [Rafael de la Fuente Bena-
vides] was unusual. He was careful with verbal extravagances from
the beginning and ended by regulating them. Old forms of Spanish
verse—sonnets, *décimas,* ballads—were redressed in vertiginous metaphors, in simultaneous impressions, in uneven enumerations, in a new,
magic lyricism, content with its creative powers. Even in those moments in
which he is most free and seems to be writing against form—his "anti-
sonnets," for example—it can be seen that his verbal torments also have a
grammar, a code of laws. There is something of the affected purist and
symbolist about him. *Voyage Across Far Seas* (*Travesía de extramares,*
1950) was his hermetic book. One of his most important books, *The Card-
board House* (*La casa de cartón,* 1928), was not poetry, but narrative prose
of fresh and surprising novelty. It was exceptional for such a novel of the
vanguard to appear in Peru. The inventive capriciousness and the metaphors (reminiscent of Ramón Gómez de la Serna and the Ultraists of Spain
and America) flash brilliantly with irony or lyricism. The one most conscious of European techniques was XAVIER ABRIL (1903), who not only
practiced them, but formulated them. He was a strange one. Through the
quality of his imagination, through his audacities, through his vitality, he
would have been an effective poet if it had not been for the fact that at
times he slackened in his efforts and fell into vanguardist rhetoric. His
poetry, baroquely or surrealistically hermetic, opens an occasional pore
and allows the oxygen of social feeling to enter. He was more successful in
his elegiac songs, of neo-romantic flavor.

As he is an intellectual, he is also capable of prying into the great past
of Spanish literature, as in his "Vague Elegy in the Ancient Tone of Jorge
Manrique" (*"Elegía oscura en el viejo tono de Jorge Manrique"*). Works:
Difficult Labor (*Difícil trabajo,* 1935), *Discoveries of Dawn* (*Descubri-
miento del alba,* 1937). ENRIQUE PEÑA BARRENECHEA (1904), brother of
the already mentioned Ricardo, took advantage of the calls to liberty of the
new tendencies to bury himself in his dreamy, neo-romantic forms of expression. This "wounded intellect," author of *The Aroma of Shadow* (*El
aroma en la sombra,* 1926), *Cinema of Pure Sense* (*Cinema de los sentidos
puros,* 1931). *Elegy to Bécquer* (*Elegía a Bécquer,* 1936), *Return to
Shadow* (*Retorno a la sombra*) and *Zone of Anguish* (*Zona de angustia*),
was a poet of dreams but not a surrealist poet; and we find him comfortably
established in forms that come from the Golden Spanish century. There are
two poets in the purist stream: JOSÉ ALFREDO HERNÁNDEZ (1910), ultraist
and creationist, who has just presented us with the lyricism of sorrow in
Perfect Absence (*Perfecta ausencia,* 1956), and VICENTE AZAR (1913),
author of *The Art of Forgetting* (*Arte de olvidar,* 1942). CÉSAR MIRÓ
(1907) abandoned ultraism to become a lyric balladeer with Peruvian accents. In Peruvian surrealism CÉSAR MORO is extremely important. He
experienced surrealism in Paris during the time of its excesses and its challenges, and goes beyond the bounds of our history in the books he wrote in
French. He belongs to us only because of his compositions in Spanish: *The
Equestrian Turtle* (*La tortuga ecuestre*), *The Sulphur Spectacles* (*Los
Anteojos de azufre*). Moro lived in that international hotel of poetry which
was surrealism.

In yet another room was EMILIO ADOLFO WESTPHALEN (1911). It seems that he gives us only those splinters that were broken off his poems in the process of writing them. And as we look at each splinter, we can still hear the noise with which his poems had burst. In *Strange Islands (Insulas extrañas,* 1933), we get less than splinters: dust, only dust. Not even the structure of a simple sentence, much less the structure of a verse has remained. No punctuation, no syntax, no images. A dust of words blown about by a dark wind of emotion. In *Abolition of Death (Abolición de la muerte,* 1935) his poetry has more than one corpuscle to lean upon: the imagery offers a wider surface, and at times the face of the poet is reflected in it, serious, contracted, preoccupied with time, existence, and the Beyond. There were poets who took rooms in other houses. We have already said that there was an avenue of Peruvianist poetry. On this avenue, the first predominating theme, after 1926, was the revindication of the Indian, which had been commenced by González Prada, but which was now formulated through a collective style. In general, this style was that of postwar European vanguardism. There is no need to mention the fact that the Indians were automatically left out of this hermetic Indianist literature. The best representative here was ALEJANDRO PERALTA (1899), author of *Ande* (1926) and *El Kollao* (1934). The Indians appear as though sculptured from visual metaphors; but the poet also sees the social injustice.

Other stridently indigenist poets: EMILIO VÁZQUEZ (1903) and LUIS DE RODRIGO (1904). The *"cholista"* poetry of GUILLERMO MERCADO (1904), NICANOR DE LA FUENTE (1904) and JOSÉ VARALLANOS (1908) was an expression of the cult of the mestizo. There was also JULIO GARRIDO MALAVER (1909), somewhat petrified in his *Dimension of Stone (Dimensión de la piedra).* The exaltation of the Indian was in reality false, limited, empty. There were greater possibilities in that of the mestizo or *cholo.* LUIS FABIO XAMMAR (1911–1947) was the best representative of this cult of the *cholo.* He spoke to us simply, in the flavorful language of the people, about his love for the countryside and its men, from *Thoughtfully (Pensativamente,* 1930) to *High Mist (La alta niebla,* 1947). "Cholist" literature followed the depletion of Indianist literature, around 1930 more or less. It was no longer identified with the incoherent European vanguard, but rather with traditional Hispanic forms, touched by the spirit of the vanguard, like the ballads of García Lorca in Spain. LUIS NIETO (1910) wrote "cholist" poetry in the style of the Spanish ballad, drawing increasingly closer to social themes. In the field of political poetry, he takes the part of the oppressed classes, or at least he expresses his feelings on the social struggle he sees. MAGDA PORTAL (1901) and SERAFÍN DEL MAR (Reynaldo Bolaños) (1901) used poetry as they would an instrument, that is to say, their poetry was subordinate to them. Others: JULIÁN PETROVICK (1901), RAFAEL MÉNDEZ DORICH. The following poets had social messages, although they were not politicians: LUIS VALLE GOICOCHEA (1908–54) who revived in his poetry memories of the emotions of childhood and adolescence, of provincial circumstances, landscapes and traditional songs, and has done this in unequivocal terms; MANUEL MORENO JIMENO (1913), whose poetry of broken images dramatizes his compassion for man caught in the crossroads of our time; and AUGUSTO TAMAYO VARGAS (1914), who in *"Lyric Entry to Geography" "Ingreso lírico a la Geografía"* announced a poetry "not about myself, but for us" and, in fact, produced descriptive, lyrical and even epic messages, as in his "Cantata to Bolívar" (*"Cantata a Bolívar,* 1960). In short, Peruvian poetry was centered on the mestizo, the *cholo,* things of national origin, with a preference for traditional styles, sometimes brilliantly imaginative, sometimes written in deliberately muted tones. And the political poetry added to local causes the themes of the Spanish Civil War and the Fascist and Nazi aggression that unleashed the Second World War. Another poet: FRANCISCO XANDOVAL (1902).

(viii) *Bolivia* / After the three most outstanding Bolivian poets—Jaimes Freyre, Tamayo and Reynolds—came a generation of greater numbers. OCTAVIO CAMPERO ECHAZÚ (1900), in the popular and traditional forms of Spain and America, captured the landscapes and loves of his region: *Amancayas* (1942), *Voices* (*Voces,* 1950). GUILLERMO VISCARRA FABRE (1901), who in *Climate* (*Clima,* 1918) preferred to utter vague suggestions, and in *Creature of the Dawn* (*Criatura del alba,* 1949) presented clear images of what he saw in the landscape and in the depths of his own sadness. The good poet ANTONIO ÁVILA JIMÉNEZ (1900) was an exponent of Indianism. Others: JAVIER DEL GRANADO (1913), LUIS MENDIZÁBAL SANTA CRUZ (1907–1946), RAÚL OTERO REICHE (1905), LUCIO DÍEZ DE MEDINA, JULIO AMELLER RAMALLO, the VILLA GOMEZ brothers, and JESÚS LARA.

(ix) *Chile* / Poetry had touched Chile, and since Gabriela Mistral, there has never been a time when there were no poets. We have seen Huidobro and Rokha. And in this chapter we will see the greatest lyricist of them all, the vibrant, famous, and influential Pablo Neruda. After the four names cited above—the most resonant—Rosamel del Valle, Humberto Díaz Casanueva, and others follow at a respectful distance.

PABLO NERUDA (Chile, 1904) has marked off the stages of his poetry. The first is that of the *Song of the Festival* (*La canción de la fiesta,* 1921) and *Crepusculary* (*Crepusculario,* 1923). The second is that of *Twenty Poems of Love and One Desperate Song* (*Veinte poemas de amor y una canción desesperada,* 1924) and *The Attempt of Infinite Man* (*Tentativa del hombre infinito,* 1925). The third is that of *The Enthusiastic Slinger* (*El hondero entusiasta,* 1933), of his *Residence on Earth* (*Residencia en la tierra,* Vol. I, poetry from 1925 to 1931; Vol. II, poetry from 1931 to 1935). The fourth is that of *Third Residence* (*Tercera residencia,* 1947), *General Song* (*Canto general,* 1950). The fifth is that of *Elemental Odes* (*Odas elementales,* 1954). The fourth volume of odes, *Embarkings and Returnings* (*Navegaci-*

ones y regresos), is dated 1959. Since then more than a dozen new books have appeared. The bibliographer loses count.

Let us attempt a characterization.

(1) The tone is still modernist. Conventional language, traditional forms. In *Crepusculary* the original Neruda appears, but he still sings in tune with other voices in the literary chorus which he prefers; moreover, at times he is still, and other voices—that of his admired Sabat Ercasty above all—are heard singing in his verses. In "Final" he confesses that "other voices besides mine are mixed in."

(2) The *Twenty Poems*, in many ways, are a continuation of *Crepusculary;* they seem to come before *The Slinger*. More regulated verses, simple, contemplative; images, not in eruption, but laced together in structures of logical patterns; their impetus suppressed through respect for traditional literary tastes. It is Neruda's first personal book: less literary, more sincere in his intimate revelations as a lover. *The Attempt of Infinite Man* acknowledges the desire to break with the past. Free verse, syntax, and spelling; verbal chaos begins.

(3) We are now confronted with the complete Neruda. He hurls us into his imaginative volcano. Obscure poetry, because the poet has not given his intuitions complete shape. Embryos, larvae, sparks, germs of ideas, attempts, promises of poetic expression. It is useless for the critic to try to analyze Neruda's images, since they are barely sketched. It is better for him to understand how and from where they come. Neruda dives deep into his sea of emotion: each time he comes to the surface for air and joins those of us who are watching him from the shore, he brings a fish-image. These images become more and more monstrous as he dives deeper and deeper into his own depths: first, images which we recognize for their literary value (stars, moon, etc.); next, "ugly" or non-literary images (brooms, rags, spittle, underpants). In *Residence* he confronts his existence and allows his emotion to remain hermetic. He does not objectify, does not externalize his sentiments into a structure which is comprehensible to all. His mood goes from sadness to anguish; and his anguish is torn from a desolate vision of the world and of life: death,

decay, failure, chaos, senselessness, ashes, dust, endless ruin, infinite disintegration. He does not disintegrate reality into literary *greguerías*, rather he sees a reality already disintegrated. And he sees it without literature. At least, without much literature. For this reason there are so many failures in expression in his poetry, so many howls, so much dissatisfaction, so much emotional material not esthetically developed. As a surrealist, Neruda wanted to ensnare profound life, show its spontaneous fluidity, bring to light the irrepressible movements of the subconscious. The act of making a poem gave him more pleasure than beholding the finished poem. The circumjacent world is so demolished and dismal that the poet has to look away. Then he sees himself: he sees himself as a pile of broken and dirty mirrors where his violent feelings are reflected in fragments. That is, the poet neither goes out into the world nor enters into his passion. Stripped and shattered, he bends in sadness over the most subterranean streams of his subconscious. There, he allows his poems to be carried by the current, bearing their desires and memories with them. Words do not aim at extrinsic objects: there are no fixed points of reference. Nor do his metaphors have the clear fullness of a vision: they are ugly phantoms wandering through a disordered night. And all of this poetry horrifies the reader just as the dismantled world must have horrified the poet; and as we read Neruda, we find pieces of wreckage from which we reconstruct, with our imagination, the beauty of the cataclysm. The novelty of Neruda lies in his allowing himself to fall inward, to drown himself, to deform himself. Poets and intellectuals were enthusiastic about his *Residence* precisely because they saw Neruda's soul as a busy workshop, at that moment when sentiment, and the poetic intuition of that sentiment, had not yet reached a state of equilibrium. To read Neruda is to enter into the creative process of a poet.

(4) The spectacle of death and injustice in the crushing of the Spanish Republic by the military awakened the political conscience of Neruda: with *Spain in the Heart* (*España en el corazón*, 1937) his voice began to be heard, less and less hermetic, more and more didactic. From his *Third Residence* to *General Song*, the oratorical breadth in the poetry of Neruda grows wider,

while the weight of lyric images diminishes. Because the poet becomes politically excited, he becomes metaphorically tranquil. There are fewer surprises because now his metaphors are threaded together by universal concepts and sentiments. Neruda becomes a militant communist. One must proselytize, one must defend the party, one must denounce the enemy. Before, the poet, very romantically forlorn, viewed chaos from within: nature was monstrous or, when humanized, it acquired the form of an anguished soul, and culture was a cancer which rapidly multiplied its diseased cells, driving man either to utter madness or to total annihilation. Now, the poet, politically organized, leaps out of the chaos. He leaves his enemies to lose themselves in the debris, while he seeks salvation in the order of the Communist Party, which remakes and implants values in a society, now a fatherland, no longer chaotic, but a springboard from which he hurls himself toward the future. Lyricism was Neruda's forte, not the epic. For this reason he slips into creating heavy chunks of prose in verse, utilitarian broths which have nothing to do with literature, in an anti-historic detonation of Russian names which he includes in his songs to indigenous Hispanic-American themes. His *General Song* (*Canto General*) is a portrayal of America: botany, zoology, archeology, conquerors and liberators, the ups and the downs of politics, the history of the past and the chronicles of the present. In some passages—"The Heights of Macchu Picchu" and "General Song of Chile"—it can be seen how Neruda, a powerful poet even though he is sacrificing his lyricism to politics, is capable of intense poetry.

(5) In *Elemental Odes* and *New Elemental Odes* Neruda's rejection of his own past is definitive. His anguished vision of a world buried in quicksand, his tragic solitude, his proud surrealism are left behind: now the poet wants simply to reach the simple man. Thus, he orders his poetry to march toward the masses. Between the thighs of this marching poetry—that of the passion for the Communist International, that of the passion for the American Indian—are seen themes of ardent sex. In other words, a personal poetry appears intermittently in the midst of the political poetry. A Communist city, for example, is erotically compared to a

woman. The poems he is at present producing are like fragments of an intimate yet public diary which contains impressions and events that sometimes border upon trivia. Has Neruda ceased to be the great poet he was? His conversion to communist realism in his later years causes him to be given to the exaltation of three uglinesses: arrogance, demagoguery, and insincerity. In *Embarkings and Returnings* and in *Far Wanderings* (*Estravagario*), there is a gross and noisy superficiality; nevertheless, his creative force is always impressive. In *Far Wanderings* the poet appears to be taking a vacation from politics to relax in a more personal poetry. What endures in Neruda is his romantic vein; it follows all his themes whether they be of passionate love, melancholic hopelessness, delirious nightmares, or political utopia.

Rosamel del Valle and Humberto Díaz Casanueva should be studied together, in spite of their differences. They are at least joined by friendship, by the vanguardist magazines they founded, by a certain common poetic atmosphere, and by their common devotion to poetry. ROSAMEL DEL VALLE (1901) is the more spontaneous of the two. His free-versifying demolishes the structure of poetry until the poet is left standing amid the nocturnal ruins, singing the hallucinations and mysteries of his solitude. And one of the poems from his book, *The Communicable Vision* (*La visión comunicable*, 1956) is named, precisely, "The Lonely Head." With meters that fluctuate between seventeen and twenty-one syllables, the poet converses with a tired, digressive, and occasionally prosaic air on the affinity between persons and phantoms, and upon the solitude to which the real and concrete existence of those who surround us condemns us. When he wishes to communicate, he does so by prophesying thoughts or myths—like that of *Orpheus* (*Orfeo*, 1944). HUMBERTO DÍAZ CASANUEVA (1908) converts the dark mass of his profound life into ideas and song. He is an inquisitive poet: Who am I, what is this Being that surrounds me? He is open to his subconscious, to his dreams, to the nocturnal side of his being: "I must always write when the stars come out, to write my / marks which, like birds, chirp on the side of death"—*Sleeping Beauty* (*La bella durmiente*). In "The Vision" he tells us how "he lay, in the shadow, with his eyelids closed toward the terrible," and suddenly he understood that his "forehead was formed over a vast dream / like a slow scab over a wound that oozes unceasingly." Unlike the surrealists, who show the current of shadows in all of their spontaneity, Díaz Casanueva leaves his subconscious in order to contemplate what he has seen there, and after thinking about it, packs his images in a sealed coffer of symbols. Among his good books: *The Crowned Blasphemer* (*El blasfemo coronado*), *Requiem*, *The Statue of Salt* (*La estatua de sal*), *The Giddy Daughter* (*La hija vertiginosa*), *The Penitentials* (*Los penitenciales*).

Public recognition has distinguished other poets. We will mention a few. JUVENCIO VALLE (1905) is the pure lyricist, of noble vocabulary, with musical, insinuating, and subtle charms. His world is that of the woods: *The Flute of the Man Pan* (*La flauta del hombre Pan*), *The Game-keeper's Son* (*El hijo del guardabosques*), *Of the Woodland on the Hill-side* (*Del monte en la ladera*). Plants, sap, flowers, and fruits, all lend their forms to a dynamic necessity of growing toward the sky. The freshness of vegetation and the flights of birds, water and land elevated in grace, freedom and beauty. The aerial, ascendant impulse of Juvencio Valle, shepherd of clouds, tightrope walker without a tightrope, is one of the happiest of his generation. OMAR CÁCERES (1906–1943) was one who influenced the younger writers. JULIO BARRENECHEA (1910), sings in a voice that is serious, slow-paced, sometimes melancholy, always profound: *Complete Poetry* (*Poesía completa;* 1958). GUSTAVO OSSORIO (1911–1949), GLADYS THEIN (1911), ANTONIO UNDURRAGA (1911), and ALDO TORRES PÚA (1910–1960) merit more attention than we can give them here.

(x) *Paraguay* / An extemporaneous movement of modernist poets, still influenced by Rubén Darío, gathered, in these years, around the magazine *Juventud* (1923). To it belonged HERIBERTO FERNÁNDEZ (1903–1927) who died just when he was beginning to show evidence of renewal in *Sonnets to My Sister* (*Los sonetos a la hermana*); and JOSÉ CONCEPCIÓN ORTIZ (1900), a poet with inner brightness. There was a nativist poetry—like that of VICENTE LAMAS (1909) with a certain descriptive, if occasionally super-ficial, grace, but always correct in form—and a social poetry—like that of MANUEL VERÓN DE ASTRADA (1903), the author of *Banners in the Dawn* (*Banderas en el alba*). A poetess born in the Canary Islands, but definitely associated with Paraguayan literature, took off in new directions: JOSEFINA PLA (1909). Her first book of poems, appearing in 1934, was *The Price of Dreams* (*El precio de los sueños*). She found a wealth of new experiences in poems of which only a few, more hermetic than her previous ones, were collected in *The Root and the Dawn* (*La raíz y la aurora,* 1960). Later she became prominent in the theater. For Pla, poetry is always free and natural, moving in advance of events, rather than being propelled by them.

But the great Paraguayan figure of these years was HERIB CAMPOS CERVERA (1908–1953). He left only one book: *Ashes Redeemed* (*Ceniza redimida,* 1950). He came late, and for this reason some of his surrealist images failed to surprise anyone but Paraguayan readers; but inside Para-guay, Campos Cervera initiated a movement which would be carried on by Roa Bastos, Elvio Romero, and others. He is a poet without gaiety. Shaken by presentiments of death and wounded by the pains of the world, Campos Cervera vacillated between a poetry of intimate, confessional value and one of social service. He wrote in exile from his native land, torn away from his friends; and his best compositions were not those inspired by episodes of war, politics, labor, collective life, or erotic themes, but those in which he lyrically expressed his nostalgia—"A Handful of Earth" (*"Un puñado de tierra"*)—and his recollection of a lost friend—"Small Litany in a Low Voice" (*"Pequeña letanía en voz baja"*).

(xi) *Uruguay* / There were—it was inevitable—ultraist buzzers, bells, and wooden rattles. Nevertheless, the most common trait of the Uruguayan poets of these years was the desire for a rigorous esthetic form. At times, those values seen in the best light were religious; at times, they were social ones. A wide register runs from the estheticizing sensitivity of some, to the deliberate prosaicness of others. The minstrels were Fusco Sansone and Ferreiro. NICOLÁS FUSCO SANSONE (1904) announced in *The Trumpet of Happy Voices* (*La trompeta de las voces alegres,* 1925) that he had come simply to celebrate the joy of living. His lustrous lyricism illuminated book after book, although life put a shade over him from time to time, and a few shadows blurred his work. ALFREDO MARIO FERREIRO (1899) was a clown—*The Man Who Ate a Bus* (*El hombre que se comió un autobus,* 1927)—with something of the ultraist in his selection of images, and now and then a sad face in the midst of the machines of the modern city. Those who moderate the voice of these times are Pereda, Esther de Cáceres, and Roberto Ibáñez. FERNANDO PEREDA (1900), without having published a single book, was admired for the exactitude of his poems, above all, his sonnets. Never satisfied with words that came to him spontaneously, he drove away the more servile ones, and kept the more egotistical ones. Furthermore, Pereda linked them together according to a secret code that he kept hidden in the coldest corner of his heart. Neither pure poetry nor surrealist poetry, but certainly a poetry enclosed in itself, like a geometric volume. In ESTHER DE CÁCERES (1903) religious faith became song. Her simple, sincere sentences, interrupted by fervor or ecstasy, are directed to God. Thus her books—from *Strange Islands* (*Las ínsulas extrañas,* 1929) to *Footstep in the Night* (*Paso de la noche,* 1957)—are like a musical murmur. ROBERTO IBÁÑEZ (1907), already personal in *The Dance of the Horizons* (*La danza de los horizontes,* 1927), continued to simplify his language, not in order to dehumanize it, but to purify it. His *Mythology of the Blood* (*Mitología de la sangre,* 1939) transfigures his vital experiences—longings for permanence, the snares of fate, the certainty of death—into symbols in which sense and sound harmonize delicately. *The Frontier* (*La frontera*) appeared in 1961. JUVENAL ORTIZ SARALEGUI (1907) gives us a lyricism without surprises, but with lovely figures: all is visible and recognizable, even the manner of setting up the poem. SARA DE IBÁÑEZ (1910?) was already famous for her first *Canto* (1940). The prolog was by Neruda. Therefore, some noted a Nerudianism in *Canto* and in *Blind Hour* (*Hora ciega,* 1943): rapidity and dispersion in the firing of metaphoric fusillade, words in conflict that assailed one another with the energy of voltaic batteries. Only Sara de Ibáñez has the mastery of meter, of accent, of rhyme, of strophe. She submits the madness of her lyricism to the rigor of perfectly formed verses. It is as if life had suddenly become a cold decoration. The obscurity of her images is due not to the fact that they remain in disorder in the depths of her subconscious, just as they appear, but to a process of distillation from which a labored mental process leaves a quintessence that remains in hermetic symbols. Sara de Ibáñez penetrates things and allows them to penetrate her; her verses are hermetic because she refers to this violent interpenetration and allows herself to be caught at a frontier where words change in value. *Pastoral* (1948), in three "tempos," each with its own tone and strophic form, causes a river of lights, flowers, fish, wheat, and dogs to flow musically to this frontier and to pass over it. The poem *Artigas* (1951) comes out more into the open and depends on a more public subject matter; but it does not come out very far, and lyricism is, after all, more powerful than the epic. Here, as a contrast to Sara de Ibáñez, we should mention CLARA SILVA (1905), a poetess bearing a neo-romantic stamp in her intermittent surrender to emotion. Lately she has produced religious poetry—religious but not mystical, in which her soul, tense with inner conflicts, concentrates on God, and God evades answering her. The poet is left thus in solitary confinement, but fulfilled. With an "I" increased in stature, the poet faces God like a character in a novel who lives his own life, all the while aware of the novelist on whom he depends [a situation which, by the way, appears in *The Survivor* (*La sobreviviente*, 1951)], a novel by Clara Silva. See her also as narrator in *The Soul and the Dogs* (*El alma y los perros*, 1962). Books of poems: *Delirium* (*Los delirios*), *Indian Prelude* (*Preludio indiano*), *The Wedding* (*Las Bodas*). A poet concerned with social matters is ILDEFONSO PEREDA VALDÉS (1899). His first book of poems: *The Lighted House* (*La casa iluminada*). At that time, he was still a sentimentalist. Becoming enthused with ultraism, he collaborated in its magazines. In 1929 the sufferings of others became a preoccupation with him. It was then that he decided to sing of the Negro, not as an historical figure, but as a living element of the fields and of the cities. From this feeling of sympathy for the Negro arose the most characteristic trait of his poetry.

It has been said that the continuity of the Uruguayan poetry of these years was interrupted by Falco and Cunha, who were held in more esteem by the youths who came after them than by their contemporaries. LIBER FALCO (1906–1955) left us a posthumous book: *Time and Time* (*Tiempo y tiempo*): poor poetry, gray, clumsy, with themes of friendship, solitude, poverty, death. He confesses his emotions in a loud voice or stammers about them prosaically. JUAN CUNHA (1910) is in the first line of Uruguayan poetry. His variety seems to be due at times to the observation and study of the styles of other contemporary poets (Spaniards like García Lorca, Hispanic-Americans like Vallejo). His forms either change in continuous experiments or tend toward folkloric rhythms and stanzas. Words, verse measures, tones of images are renewed, while the poet, beneath this apparent variety, always pursues the same intuition: that of the fluctuation between the outer and the inner life, between communion with man and solitude. And it is this unity in his vision of life that is most worthwhile in him. Cunha appeared with *The Bird Who Came From the Night* (*El pájaro que vino de la noche*, 1929), but his continued production is rather more recent; after his anthology *At the Foot of the Harp* (*En pie de arpa*, 1950) he published several volumes. In his sonnets *At About Dusk* (*A eso de la tarde*, 1961) the poet reflects in his maturity on his past life. Let us now close this section with ÁLVARO FIGUEREDO (1908), an anthological poet reluctant to publish in book form; CONCEPCIÓN SILVA BELINZON (1901), whose symbols go wild.

(xii) *Argentina* / In 1925—which is the date upon which the doors of this chapter open—the poets who enter these doors come from different neighborhoods. Two neighborhoods, above all, were being mentioned a great deal then: that of Florida Street and that of Boedo Street. Florida, the stylish street, centrally located, elegant, cosmopolitan, was frequented by the "vanguardists" who wanted to reform literature and who created a literature (art for art's sake) that had learned many things from Europe: Borges, González Lanuza, Marechal, Molinari, Norah Lange, Bernárdez, Mastronardi. Boedo, the street of the gray suburb, run-down, of the Creole-immigrant, was frequented by revolutionaries who wanted to reform the world, and who created, with a formula of sociological art, a literature that had learned many things from Russia: Barletta, César Tiempo, Nicolás Olivari, Raúl González Tuñón, Gustavo Riccio, Enrique Amorim, Santiago Ganduglia, Roberto Mariani. The Florida clique made fun of the bad artistic taste of the Boedo clique; the Boedo clique, more resentful, condemned the lack of socialist ideals in the Florida clique. The first group wrote in *Inicial, Prisma, Proa,* and *Martín Fierro;* the second group, in *Los Pensadores* (which later was called *Claridad*). The first group was distinguished for its verse; the second group produced more in the novel and short story. For a characterization of the vanguardism of the first group, see the section on "the scandal" in the preceding chapter. The sects which we have indicated were not homogeneous and ended by intermingling. Ultraists who took classicists and romantics as their models. Pure poets who turned into poets of the sacristy. Poets with a political theme who went over into art for art's sake. Revolutionaries of the Boedo group who became Fascists; aristocrats from Florida who joined up with Communism. Needless to say, each band, in its turn, subdivided into factions, magazines, anthologies and quarreling manifestoes. The dissolution of ultraism began in 1922 when the writers turned from magazines to books: *Fervor of Buenos Aires* (*Fervor de Buenos Aires*) by Borges came out in 1923; in 1924, *Prisms* (*Prismas*) by González Lanuza; in 1925, *The Street of Afternoon* (*La calle de la tarde*) by Norah Lange and the *Falcon's Perch* (*Alcándara*) by Bernárdez; in 1926, *Days Like Arrows* (*Días como flechas*) by Marechal; *Red Mill* (*Molino rojo*), by Jacobo Fijman; *The Violin of the Devil* (*El violín del diablo*) by Raúl González Tuñón; and in 1927, *The Religious Painter* (*El imaginero*) by Ricardo Molinari. Moreover, the military revolution of 1930—which made it necessary to take sides, not only in the Argentinian struggle between oligarchy and the people, but in the ideologies of the world, liberal, socialist, and fascist—ended by undoing the literary ranks and from that time the Florida and Boedo groups lost their meaning. (It should not be forgotten that in the provinces distant from Buenos Aires, although there were also committed and uncommitted literatures, the polemic was not as intense and some poets were not even aware of it.) As they developed in their individual trajectories, the poets grew away from ultraism. Ultraism fell behind: it was regarded as a collective style of the past, a school of metaphors where one could obtain diplomas to hang on one's wall, an institution to be rejected just like any other academy. And, in fact, ultraism was rejected. There were some poets who drowned in the ultraist shipwreck; others swam to safety and appeared on the shore, cured of ultraism.

There were also those who did not run aground. They preferred to follow the solid path of poetry. They were content that Lugones should have followed the same path. Actually, Lugones had pursued the poetry of nature: *Ballads of Rio Seco* (*Romances del Río Seco*) as well as poetry that invented its own reality: *Sentimental Lunar Poems* (*Lunario sentimental*). His diatribe against the partisans of rhymeless verse and poetry reduced to strings of metaphors divided his friends. Lugones defended Rega Molina, Nalé Roxlo, Luis L. Franco, Pedroni; and he was attacked by Marechal, Borges, González, Lanuza. The fact is that all the new poets, grateful and ungrateful alike, were his heirs. As we said before, *Sentimental Lunar Poems* was the first school of the ultraists. Even when they rejected his rhymes, they imitated his metaphoric processes. Little by little the ultraists went from arty metaphor that disdained reality to metaphor that penetrated reality to humanize it. Meanwhile, the independent poets (that is, those who did not rely on watchwords, or art for art's sake, or art as a social function) formed, without meaning to, the following families. The family of those who followed the impulses of the heart: Abella Caprile, María Alicia Domínguez, María de Villarino, Juan L. Ortiz, Silvina Ocampo, José Sebastián Tallón, González Carballo, Pedro Juan Vignale, Horacio Esteban Ratti, Córdoba Iturburu, Estrella Gutiérrez, Ulyses Petit de Murat. The family of those who were not content merely to celebrate their own lives, but who concerned themselves with social problems: José Portogalo, Nydia Lamarque, César Tiempo, Carlos M. Grünberg, Raúl González Tuñón. The family of the heirs of modernism: López Merino, Rega Molina. The family of those knowledgeable in the popular or classical tradition: Amado Villar, Alberto Franco, Salvador Merlino, Ignacio B. Anzoátegui, Elías Carpena. The family of the regionalists: Jijena Sánchez, Pedroni, Carlino, Antonio de la Torre.

Let us pass in review those poets who left a considerable work. We propose that the major lyricists are Borges, Molinari, Nalé Roxlo, González Lanuza, Ledesma, and Bernárdez. In the Argentinian literature of these years, the first name, because of his quality, because of his influence, should be that of Jorge Luis Borges. First in poetry, first in the short story, first in the essay. Because his stories reap equal benefits from his ability as a poet and as an essayist and stand, therefore, at the center of his literary work, we will study Borges in the section dedicated to narrative prose. Let it be known, however, that he would merit the place of honor even in this section.

RICARDO E. MOLINARI (1898) appeared with the ultraist group, close to Borges, but he had roots more eagerly penetrating the earth. He avoided easy regionalisms austerely. His language always gave evidence of a sound education in the Spanish classicists and in the European symbolists. Nationalism rises in his poetry, and to catch its essences his language becomes so refined that it is hermetic. He elaborates his language with extreme care. At times he flows over in odes of free verse, at times he builds his structures in the sonnet form, at times he cultivates the popular verse form. His verbal economy tends to make him monotonous. His insistence on certain images tends to harden them into symbols. His ear sometimes fails him in the measures of his verse. But the series of books which he began with *The Religious Painter* (1927) and those which he collected in *Early Morning Worlds*

(*Mundos de la madrugada,* 1943) and that later reached a high point with those that go from *The Guest and Melancholy* (*El huésped y la melancolía,* 1949) to *Night United* (*Unida noche,* 1957) is poetry of admirable intensity. Intensity in his odes on themes of love and death, intensity in his windings along the shores of metaphysics. Of the group of vanguardists, Molinari is the one most respected by the youths of today: he has taught them to discipline themselves by pursuing rigorous forms and by attending not only to the geography, but also to the history of Argentina.

EDUARDO GONZÁLEZ LANUZA (1900) appeared under the big top of the ultraist circus, but, like the others, he left it in time and straightened out his life. "My poems are worked over," he had written in his ironic manifesto in *Prisma* (1924), and since then it has, in fact, been seen that Lanuza is a hard-working poet who has analyzed himself and set in order the abundance of his imagination. González Lanuza has proven to be one of our good poets, passionate, free, unimpeachable, moody, so individualistic that he has remained alone. Prolonged meditation on what the world is, what life is, and what poetry is, has given González such profundity that he can astound the reader without the need of the acrobatics the ultraists resorted to to attract attention. Something of his initial baroque style, however, stayed with him. A sense of the ephemeral quality of all terrestrial things, of the imminence of nothingness, of the insecurity of our lives and of our knowledge, but also the feeling that men are capable of powerful song when they grasp the time that flows within them, these feelings have found no more lofty expression in Argentina than in González Lanuza. The desire to be obscure is not in him; in spite of the fact that he has taken the enigma of existence as his theme, González Lanuza is clear. Neither does he want to play with his verses, which are in classical form or free verse, according to the melody of each intuition, and always infallible in rhythmic mastery. He did not care to restore what the ultraists had condemned: rhyme, meter, strophe. His purpose, from which he never swerved, was to reveal himself sincerely.

ROBERTO LEDESMA (1901), who wrote simply, identified with

the elemental forms of reality, conversant with the telluric, intense in his elegies and romantic expressions, sings, not of unfixed essences, but of the things from which these essences have become detached. *The Flame* (*La llama*, 1955), a selection of poetic works, is shown as a thing (an admirable thing) which is added to an admired reality. The poet baptizes the world which is born anew within him whenever he looks around him. In *The Bird in the Tempest* (*El pájaro en la tormenta*, 1957) he has continued to go deeper and deeper and to assume increasing awareness of his originality, as in "On the Sand." Some of Ledesma's sonnets are the most beautiful in our literature.

FRANCISCO LUIS BERNÁRDEZ (1900) came into the new poetry with *Sunrise* (*Orto*, 1922), *Bazaar* (*Bazar*, 1922), *Kindergarten* (1924), and *The Falcon's Perch* (*Alcándara*, 1925). Later he abandoned this cryptic poetry of assorted images and sounds— with something of the silent movie and of a broken victrola playing jazz—and cultivated what ultraism had forgotten: the extensive poem, clear syntax, classical strophes, the balanced Thomist idea of the world. *The Boat* (*El buque*, 1935) was a theological poem: it is the theme of grace, which in the form of a boat, visits the spirit. These ascetic stanzas skipping over *Land Sky* (*Cielo de tierra*, 1937) were followed by the amorous lyrics—serene, limpid—of *City Without Laura* (*La ciudad sin Laura*, 1938) in sonnets and other regular forms. In *Elemental Poems* (*Poemas elementales*, 1942)—perhaps his best book—Bernárdez raised his voice even louder, doubtless to reach the heights of his Catholic themes. Elemental poems, because they sing about the elements: "earth," "sea," "wind," "fire." When Bernardez succumbs to scholasticism, his verses become syllogistic, hard, insipid, poor; but when he gives in to the impulse of his love (not that of St. Thomas, but that of St. Francis) his religiosity deepens and reveals to us the faith, the grace, the tenderness of his contemplation of the world. His poems become elongated with the undulation of a prayer of supplication, at times in meters of twenty-two syllables with fixed accents. In his best poems, religious feeling moves like a subterranean river: one feels its freshness is felt without seeing it take shape. In *Flesh and Blood Poems* (*Poemas de carne y hueso*,

1943) Christian humility turns into an asceticism of poetic expression. His repertory of motifs is ennobled (the cardinal loves of man: his sons, his faith, his flag, the tomb of General San Martín, etc.), but he falls into logical, non-poetic mechanisms. His last titles go from *The Nightingale* (*El ruiseñor*, 1945) to *The Flower* (*La flor*, 1951). Bernárdez chose the poetic family to which he wanted to belong: San Juan de la Cruz, the two Luises, Lope, and even the more remote Galician-Portuguese troubadours. Nalé Roxlo, whom we will study farther on, also traveled with these major lyricists. Others to be mentioned: Mastronardi, Marechal, Villar, and Luis L. Franco.

CARLOS MASTRONARDI (1901) was a cautious ultraist. He drew apart from those who, having a poor ear for music, thought it was enough to look at things through all kinds of metaphors. Nor was he seduced by styles that reduced poetry to states of being. For him, to intuit was to attune spiritual and linguistic forms with the material of his recollections. The language of his first books, *Awakened Land* (*Tierra amanecida*, 1926) and *Treatise on Anguish* (*Tratado de la pena*, 1930), was more temperate than that of his companions of *Martín Fierro* and *Proa*, and he displayed a clean pleasure in all the things in his province. In *Knowledge of Night* (*Conocimiento de la noche*, 1937) his beloved province of Entre Ríos is the subject of his poems: with a circumspect lyric tone, in well-ordered poetic forms, he sang of fields, villages, men, beasts, days, labor, seasons of the year, pains, joys. His poem "Light of the Province" is dedicated to anthologies.

LEOPOLDO MARECHAL (1898) also belonged to the ultraistic group during the years of *Days Like Arrows* (*Días como flechas*, 1926), but he later turned to themes of human love and divine knowledge and went over the same paths that had been traversed by Spanish Christian poetry of the Golden Age. Even the forms that appeared in these paths were copied in his verses. After *Labyrinth of Love* (*Laberinto de amor*, 1936) and *Sonnets to Sophia* (*Sonetos a Sophia*, 1940) the poet became a militant Catholic. Even in *Five Southern Poems* (*Cinco poemas australes*, 1937), dedicated to his memories and to his country, preoccupation with religion prevails. He is a poet who imbues abstractions lacking temporal color with human values. He also published a novel, *Adam Buenosayres* (*Adán Buenosayres*), with symbolic intentions; in spite of its ugly aspects, it is important because he makes a myth of his "Martín Fierro" generation. JOSÉ PEDRONI (1899) is the poet of daily life, of work and its tools, of human solidarity: *Our Daily Bread* (*El pan nuestro,* 1941).

AMADO VILLAR (1899–1954), a poet with the values of a colorist and an engraver in *Verses with Sun and Birds* (*Versos con sol y pájaros,* 1927), preferred in *Marimorena* (1934) to capture transparent, almost invisible realities: air, water, crystal. A poet of the joy of living. LUIS L. FRANCO (1898) began as a lyric poet who took his vital and happy inspiration from his peasant life: its landscape, its loves, its bodily health, its people. In *Summa* (*Suma,* 1938) and in *Bread* (*Pan,* 1948) he seems to be more committed to social philosophies, but his concern for liberty and justice, his rebellion, his solidarity with those who suffer, in spite of a few lapses in rhetoric, usually have that fresh lyricism that always vibrates in sincere temperaments. His images are as vigorous as his concepts and also pulsate in his prose: *Small Dictionary of Disobedience* (*Pequeño diccionario de la desobediencia,* 1959). Other poets claim individual commentary. Unfortunately we have no space for any more.

We have said that after 1930—the date of the military coup that caused Argentina to stumble in her march toward liberalism—the literary groups broke up. During this time, political factions were more prevalent than poetic ones. All of the poets whom we reviewed at the beginning of this chapter had produced significant works before 1930. New writers appear after 1930. They are the ones born around 1910. Before characterizing them we should put here, parenthetically as it were, between Borges and his contemporaries, whom we have discussed, and the contemporaries of Enrique Molina and Ferreyra Basso, whom we are about to discuss, an excellent poet who demands a special place: VICENTE BARBIERI (1903–1956). He was late in going into literature, and for this reason his voice, heard from *Fable of the Heart* (*Fabula del corazón,* 1939) to *The Dancer* (*El bailarín,* 1953) is confused with that of the generation of '40. Barbieri had the gift of firing his metaphors with such energy, and from such profound depths of his being, that they awaken in the reader emotional resonances which are difficult to analyze. Many of these metaphors, by dint of repetition, are converted into symbols. At times we do not know whether they are symbols or decorative, scenographic, heraldic, aquatic toys. His words do not flow directly and spontaneously from the dark springs of his being, rather, they have an order; however, this order is not clear and intelligible, but belongs to a rhetoric deliberately disordered. Barbieri appears to write his poems with ideas, with messages; and if we were to compile a "dictionary of symbols," we would be able to decipher them. They are ambiguous. He points at one thing and calls it another. His code is secret. Not for this reason is his poetic world any less well constructed. He does not set free the obscurity of existence but gives us charades instead. He was an elegiac poet, whose themes were solitude, death, time, evocations of childhood, the native countryside, his own vocation as a poet. His versification was according to the rules. He also wrote stories, novels and plays. ALDO PELLEGRINI (1903) founded the first surrealist group in 1928, but his books were late in coming out: *The Secret Wall* (*El muro secreto*, 1949) *Construction of Destruction* (*Construcción de la destrucción*, 1957). OSVALDO HORACIO DONDO (1902–1962), in his religious communication with the world, restrains his feelings (his words) in his desire for accuracy. HORACIO ESTEBAN RATTI (1903), MARCOS FINGERIT (1904).

Writers born around 1910, who appear in the literary field around 1930, were much more moderate than the vanguardists. Cured of fright, they searched for equilibrium. They were familiar with extremes. They proposed to be more serious. A philosophy whose preoccupation was the understanding of man led them to the old theme: the life of the emotions. The first Argentine poets (the "newest generation") to begin to give their generation identity through manifestos, magazines and anthologies were ARTURO CAMBOURS (1907) with his Creolist images; IGNACIO B. ANZOATEGUI (1905), classical and Hispanic in taste; and ALBERTO FRANCO (1903). From those born around 1910 came admirable poets. Important among them is ENRIQUE MOLINA (1910). His vision is desolate. He hugs his wounds. He seeks the confirmation of his suspicion that all is mire and pain. And, naturally, he is surprised to find that from the depths of the ruins, his own life being so sad, he can still admire the beauty of the world. His demoniacal, destructive strength bursts into disordered images. He became more and more surrealistic and spontaneous in his manner of accentuating his impassioned nostalgia, and of baring his dreams and imperious longings. Through long-sustained momentum and powerful images Molina creates tremendously intense climates: *Antipodal Lovers* (*Amantes antípodas*, 1961).

JORGE ENRIQUE RAMPONI (1907), one of the notable lyricists—above all in *Infinite Stone* (*Piedra infinita*, 1948)—wove his harsh concepts and images together with surrealist vapor. JUAN G. FERREYRA BASSO (1910) collects landscapes, especially those of the countryside, into the mirror of his soul. The landscape is real; his love of the land is real; nevertheless, everything seems to have been sketched on the surface of a fantastic dream. Works: from *Clay Rose* (*Rosa de arcilla*) to *The Countryman Who Died in a River* (*Paisano muerto en un río*). CÉSAR ROSALES (1910), a lyricist who gave shape through his cantos to love of country, a love that can be felt in his history, nature, dreams and dramatic enigmas. The verses of *I Come to Give Testimony* (*Vengo a dar testimonio*, 1960) are stormy, profound, and overflowing. FRYDA SCHULTZ DE MANTOVANI (1912) restrains and veils her feelings in an attitude that is more intellectual than lyrical— an attitude that is to take her into other genres. FERNANDO GUIBERT (1912), an ambitious narrator of the tumultuous life of a great city: *Poet at the Foot of Buenos Aires* (*Poeta al pie de Buenos Aires*, 1953). ARTURO HORACIO GHIDA, JAVIER VILLAFAÑE (1910) and others whom we shall study later, like Silvina Ocampo and María de Villarino. Besides these, there are the regionalists: MIGUEL ÁNGEL GÓMEZ (1911–1959), whose

Book of Songs (*Cancionero*) had the intonations of the people. RAÚL
GALÁN (1912–1963), telluric, elegiac, traditionalist. CARLOS CARLINO
(1910); JUAN CARLOS ARÁOZ DE LA MADRID (1910). Some of those mentioned above changed direction in their esthetic voyage, began to publish
late, years later influenced young groups, drew close to the generation that
followed them or were incorporated by the strategists of this generation.
The fact is that the neo-romanticism of which we have seen the beginning
will end by becoming quite audible in the generation of '40 which we shall
find largely in the next chapter.

B. MAINLY PROSE

1. Novel and Short Story

Many novels appeared tranquilly, with a nineteenth-century bill
of lading; and if they were modified at all, it was with such gen-
tility that the modification passed unnoticed. French and Russian
realism still retained its clientele. But around 1930 more or less,
European novelistic changes began to have their effects on Hispanic-America. Because, it must be said, it is an Hispanic-
American trait that our writers do not experiment with new forms,
but apply, late and diffusely, Europeans innovations. France continued to be the exporting center for the new art of novelizing.
From Russia the writer whose stature took on increasing propor-
tions was Dostoevski; but now Germany and England are entering the picture; the United States—Faulkner and Hemingway—
will have its influence a little later on; Italy, after the second World
War; Spain—Benjamín Jarnés and his contemporaries—did not
produce anything of any influence. The French novel pointed in
every direction like a drunken compass; Proust, Gide, Mauriac,
Duhamel, Romains, Thérive, Giraudoux, Cocteau, Green, Jaloux,
Fournier, Martin du Gard, Montherlant offered invitations to
adventure, simultaneously indicating all points on a circular
horizon: the evocation of time from a personal and psychological
viewpoint and the leaps of a tourist-cricket around the planet, the
dreamy lyricism of solitary adolescents in their provincial towns,
and the tumult of the masses in the large cities, the impetus of
imagination and of politics, rightists and leftists, the original sin
of the Catholics, the denunciation of evil by the socialists, pre-

ciosities, ugliness, fragmentary novels, cyclic novels . . . Germany had been, from 1910 to 1920, the laboratory of the expressionist novel. Instead of impressionism, which had attempted to record the impact of exterior reality upon the senses of the writer, now the creative energy of the writer was developed to such an extent that nature was fought back with blows delivered by imagination, intelligence, will, emotions, and instincts. And the writer rebelled against the society of his time, he judged and condemned it and brought its traditions to a crisis; not only the old ones, the religious traditions, but also more recent ones such as nineteenth-century liberalism. Radicalism was not just political, nor did it dwell only on social disintegration; it took cognizance of speculations on the destiny of man, his guilt and his redemption, his tragic condition, his failures and his renewed endeavors. It was not a matter of describing outward appearances, but of causing what the writer "experienced" in the face of these appearances to explode into violent language. It was similar to naturalism in the brutality and fearlessness with which it came into contact with the most ominous things, but what was important was the symbolization of nature, not its photograph.

In the thirties, Hispanic-America was reading the narratives of Franz Werfel, Arnold Zweig, Leonard Frank, Franz Kafka, and in the theater they were seeing the works of Franz Wedekind, Ernest Toller, Georg Kaiser. We have mentioned authors of the German language because it was out of Germany that expressionism had come; but we have already mentioned that this artistic upheaval was universal, and that it arrived in Hispanic-America from everywhere. In some circles, the English novel was replacing the French: D. H. Lawrence, with his instinctive challenge to civilization; Aldous Huxley, the superintellectual; the evanescent and monologous Virginia Woolf with her slow shifts in time; and above all, James Joyce, whose technique of the novel was the most revolutionary, with his Dublin internalized into pure stream of consciousness. Thus, the Hispanic-Americans of these years wrote novels at a time when the general consensus was that the novel had gone to pieces. Its architecture had broken down. Its planes had collapsed. There was no order in its episodes. Its characters had no identity. At times there was nothing to tell. The preoccupation with time converted the space where the novel took place into pure metaphor; or it caused the chronology of events to be sacrificed so that different lives or different moments of the same life could be presented simultaneously. The point of view was mobile, unforeseeable, microscopic and telescopic, localized and ubiquitous. A linguistic empire was established, and not a single word, neither the basest nor the most cultured, nor the most neologistic, was foreign to it. In Hispanic-America no single author presented a complete picture of these technical experiments, but in many of them, various of these experiments are to be recognized: Yáñez, Carpentier, Marechal, Mallea, Uslar Pietri . . . But let us not anticipate. It is necessary to put the work of our narrators in order. How? The most practical order is by geographic location. We shall therefore discuss them in groups, going from north to south; and within each national group we shall speak first of subjective narrators and then of objective ones. We shall begin with those works which most disfigure exterior reality and pass to those which are a more faithful reflection of it.

Is it necessary to insist that literary "idealism" and "realism" are no more than logical categories designed to give order to a disordered mass of books?

(a) *Narrators More Subjective than Objective /* What these writers want is to retreat into the innermost recesses of their souls, detach themselves from the web of natural conclusions, free themselves from the things that surround them. They obliterate the physical, human, social reality on which the novel is based and instead create a purely ideal reality. They give greater emphasis to their personal vision than to the things seen. When it is not pure fantasy, it is an intellectual game or an expressionist allegory. Realism is either magic or is so stylized that things take on a lyric quality. The sense of time—especially in evocations of childhood or adolescence—the characterization of complex psychologies, the description of strange impressions, the anguished analysis of existentialist experiences, the unquenchable flow of bleeding images, and the mobility of the narrative point of view impose a poetic rhythm on this literature. And, in fact, many of the writers who make up this group are poets, and we might well have studied them in the section in which we studied verse. Some of them, although they do not present fantastic characters or situations, enfold reality in an atmosphere so dense with imagination that one sees it from afar, as in a dream. In others, superstitions, myths, and folkloric legends are colored with strange, fictitious flowers. Another non-realist form of expression, one that disfigured reality into fantastic symbols, was that of the bestiaries. Science fiction stories and novels and battles of wits between murderers and detectives balance precariously on the trampolin of reality ready to leap into the air and cut curlicues. There have been narratives in which the imagination journeyed to other times, to other places, and to other animal species. All of reality, finally, evaporates into poetic metaphors.

(b) *Narrators More Objective than Subjective* / These are the writers who apply their vision of the world and of life to a reality that, however imaginary it may be, we can recognize as external, public, and ordinary. Subjective writers presented people who evaded circumstances or who felt tortured by circumstances. On the other hand, the majority of the Hispanic-American novelists accentuated circumstances, and there were even stories and novels in which everything was circumstance. They did not contain men, or, at least, men were unimportant. A great part of this literature implied a materialistic philosophy. At times that philosophy was dogmatic: Marxism, for example. In general, the "committed" but more independent novelists—the liberals, the socialists— were the better writers, although not always the most successful. All, some more, some less, presented a situation barren of men, or, if you wish, full of masses of men rather than individuals. Their descriptive techniques were those of naturalism and realism, although there were those who combined them with a detonator of ultraist metaphors, a taste for allegory, and the "messages" of German expressionism. These novels of protest have been classified by critics according to their central themes. Novels concerned about the position of the Indian in our society. Regionalist and rural novels with their conflicts between the landowner and the laborer, between the laborer and a hostile nature. Novels about the rapid changes in our economic life. Novels about our political disasters: wars, revolutions, dictatorships. Novels about the invasion of foreign capitalists, the exploitation of markets and men, and the evils of imperialism. Novels on the tormented life of the great cities, and the agitations of the bourgeoisie and the proletariat.

(i) *Mexico* / We have already referred to Torres Bodet and other poets of the *Contemporáneos* group who wrote poetic narratives. We add here *A Novel Like a Cloud* (*Novela como nube*, 1928) by GILBERTO OWEN (1905–1952) and the dreamy *Storm Over Nicomaco* (*Cerrazón sobre Nicomaco*, 1946) and *The Dove, the Cellar, and the Tower* (*La paloma, el sótano y la torre*, 1949), by EFRÉN HERNÁNDEZ (1903–1958) collected, along with other titles, in *Works* (*Obras*, 1965). FRANCISCO TARIO (1911) is a story teller of the grotesque, of madness, of painful obsessions, a novelist with a rich and terrible imagination, a huntsman of aphorisms: from *Down Here* (*Aquí abajo*, 1943) to *The Door in the Wall* (*La puerta en el muro*, 1946).

We would like to dwell on AGUSTÍN YÁÑEZ (1904), who has maintained a high level as a narrator. His lyric, poetic tendency feels at home with autobiographic evocations, and even in his most objective works one is conscious of the intervention of the author in the lives that he is creating. In *Passion and Convalescence* (*Pasión y convalecencia;* the text is dated 1938) nothing moves, unless it be the amplifications—sometimes rhetorical—that the author gives to each of his lyric fragments: a feverish invalid; his convalescence; his visit to the family dwelling; vacillation between the country and the city and the final decision to return to the city. Delirious images, evocations of childhood. A poematic novel in which subjective reactions rather than objective actions are recounted. Unfortunately, Yáñez has so many "pretentious phrases" that he cannot make them all felicitous. His most ambitious novel is *At the Water's Edge* (*Al filo del agua*, 1947). The title is a popular expression which, in its figurative sense, alludes to an impending event: in this novel, it is the Mexican revolution of 1910 which is the impending event. Yáñez is describing the collective lethargy of a little southern town whose every crevice is filled with religiosity. It is a negative religiosity, dark, morbid, resentful, ascetic, which undermines life, until life can hold out no longer and topples, crushing all, even Father Dionisio. It is he who ends the novel sadly, as he celebrates his final mass with a heart broken by the awareness of his failure and of the failure of all he represents. The plot—if one can speak of it as such—is loosely knit. Thousands of loose ends. Each character is a loose end dancing grotesquely in the burning wind of superstition. None of them attains the fullness of a vital creation, but occasionally their destinies join—always in order to suffer— and thus they seem to be virtualities of possible novels, whose most oft-repeated themes would be those of eroticism, neurosis, and violence. Yáñez does not propose a thesis. He confines himself to depicting an atmosphere. At most, in this huge impressionist canvas, an occasional brush stroke seems to smile ironically. The structure of *At the Water's Edge*, deliberately broken into parallel planes, intersecting planes, juxtaposed planes, or dispersed entirely, gives a notable fluidity to the action. Basically, it is not the stream of reality, but the stream of consciousness that Yáñez seeks to depict. To this end he uses, and well, the techniques of the interior dialog, direct and indirect, of the soliloquy, of the dialog within a tormented mind, of symbols, allegories, and even suggestive typographical changes. The heaviness of the novel is due to its excessive verbosity; because Yáñez, instead of taking himself out of the picture so that the multiple perspectives of the Mexican Archbishop's flock can be revealed—and instead of inviting the reader to come and see for himself—mixes himself into the batter of the rich, slow prose, and tries to say everything. From *At the Water's Edge* Yáñez chose a situation—Gabriel vacillating between two women, Victoria and María—and he prolongs it into *The Creation* (*La Creación*, 1959). Twenty years have gone by: Gabriel, who under the protection of these two women has studied music in Europe, now returns home with the sole purpose of rooting himself in Mexican reality and expressing himself artistically. The novel proceeds to follow his steps from 1920 to 1935. Gabriel's source of inspiration seems to be the "feminine essence." After succeeding with his "erotic symphony"

(inspired by Diotima of Plato's *Symposium*) Gabriel commences
to work on a symphonic poem in which his numerous experiences
with all types of women will be molded into the image of Helen
of Troy. In the course of the novel we have a parade of well-
known politicians, intellectuals, artists, and writers; and we also
have portraits of Mexican cultural life, from Vasconcelos onward,
with the ideals of each group. The novel is flooded and devastated
by the incessant downpour of names which are dropped from a
facile history of culture. In spite of the fact that the theme is the
creative force of art, Yáñez here fails as a creator. His novel is
more artificial than artistic. Among his artifices are the threadbare
ones of interrupting the story line by frequent introspective passages and criss-crossing interior monologs. Gabriel's character is
unconvincing. *Prodigal Earth* (*Tierra pródiga*, 1960) belongs to
the same cycle, with its theme, so typically American, of civilization against barbarism. *Lean Earth* (*Las tierras flacas*, 1962)
analyzes the psychological changes in the peasant when confronted with the machine and industry. The literature surging
from the Mexican revolution was not, in general, revolutionary
either in its technical procedures or in its style. And at times it
was not revolutionary even in its spirit. We have already seen the
emergence of this thematic narrative. Let us now continue with
other figures.

JORGE FERRETIS (1902–1962), from *Calid Land* (*Tierra cal-
iente*, 1935) to *The Colonel who Killed a Cock-Pigeon and Other
Stories* (*El coronel que asesinó un palomo y otros cuentos*, 1952),
was a keen observer of the conflict between civilizing ideals and
civic degradation in our Hispanic-American countries; he is not
satisfied with a mere description of rural life but posits social
problems, for the purpose of reform. Among the writers on social
themes, the most outstanding was FRANCISCO ROJAS GONZÁLEZ
(1905–1951). He also wrote novels: *The Negress Angustias* (*La
negra Angustias*), *Lola Casanova*. But his collections of short
stories—the last one, posthumous, was *The Beggar* (*El diosero*,
1952)—were more suited to his talent which was better at observing than at constructing. He started writing these short stories
about a big-city milieu, but his best ones deal with country life.

They are, however, weighed down by a good deal of artistically unassimilated ethnographic material.

The realist current ran along the channel of the revolutionary theme, but it also ran over into the surrounding terrains. The least superficial, the most ambitious of these realists is JOSÉ REVUELTAS (1914). *Human Mourning* (*El luto humano*, 1943) contains promise and youthful awkwardness. What he has learned from Faulkner he has not been able to apply properly, and the result is that, because of his experiments with shifts in time and perspective, the structure of the novel is fragmented. The action is simple: some country people, men and women, with a dead baby in their arms, try to save themselves from a flood; some are drowned; the anguished survivors on a roof-terrace are pounced upon by vultures. The complexity is not in the action, but in the interwoven memories (at times backdrops painted with scenes of the Mexican revolution and the new political struggles seem to be hung behind these memories) or in keeping undisclosed until the end what happened at the beginning (like the news that the priest had beheaded Adán), or the insets of narrative sections that seem to have been taken from another novel (for example, the long biography on Adán, related while his body floats on the water). The variations on the theme of death are violent and even macabre. Revueltas creates several characters and he "feels" each of them alive, just as they are. He writes in the third person, but actually he lends his characters his own words so that they can ruminate on his thoughts and recall scenes from his past. But in giving voice to all these interior monologs, Revueltas seems to be moved with pity for his own characters; and then it is his own voice, his excessive author's voice, that is heard resounding, synchronized, to be sure, with that of his created character, but longdrawn-out and distracted. *In a Certain Valley of Tears* (*En algún valle de lágrimas*, 1956) tells about a few hours in the insignificant life of a man in his fifties; but as Revueltas follows him, step by step and thought by thought, the entire novel becomes an interior monolog on the part of his character. Revueltas identifies so closely with the point of view of his protagonist that the only description of his physical appearance is that of the image he himself sees in the mirror. When the character is mistaken about the author of some verses, Revueltas, so as not to intrude in the course of the novel, confines himself to clarifying the matter in a footnote. However, between the lofty (and false) idea that the protagonist has about himself and the judgment of the author, who knows him to be avaricious, cruel, unjust, hypocritical, and almost asexual, it is Revueltas himself who has intervened subtly, selecting those details that reveal the psychological truth. His latest novel: *The Errors* (*Los errores*, 1964).

ANDRÉS IDUARTE (1907), in the terse and moving pages of *A Child of the Revolution* (*Un niño de la revolución*, 1951), and NELLIE CAMPOBELLO (1912), in *Cartridge Belt* (*Cartucho*, 1931) and *Mother's Hands* (*Las manos de mamá*, 1937), gave us the juvenile view of the revolutionary movement. XAVIER ICAZA (1902) novelized the themes of the revolution and, in *Panchito Chapopote* (1928), satirized "Yankee imperialism." Other names: ANTONIO ACEVEDO ESCOBEDO (1909), CIPRIANO CAMPOS ALATORRE (1906–1934), RODOLFO BENAVIDES (1907), ALBERTO BONIFAZ NUÑO (1911). More remote from the revolutionary theme were JUAN DE LA CABADA (1903), author of short stories—*Street of Lies* (*Paseo de mentiras*, 1940)—and RUBÉN SALAZAR MALLÉN (1905), who, in his novels *Waste Land* (*Páramo*, 1944) and *Eye of Water* (*Ojo de agua*, 1949), reflects, respectively, on the life of the lowest levels of the city and of the country. ANDRÉS HENESTROSA (1906)—author of a delicate "Portrait of My Mother" (*"Retrato de mi madre,"* 1940)—collected, re-created, and invented in *The Men That the Dance Dispersed* (*Los hombres que dispersó la danza*, 1929) graceful, theogonic legends of his Zapotecan land. This literature, about Indians or pro-Indian in tone, is a kind of service which was paid to the Indian in order that he might express his vision of things. It is significant that one of the best attempts at this type of literature was not that of a novelist or a poet, but of an anthropologist: RICARDO POZAS (1912), with his *Juan Pérez Jolote* (1948), creates an anthropological study which is similar to literature, and by the way, creates literature which is similar to anthropology. The narrator-protagonist is an Indian who reveals a whole way of life in his own words. RAMÓN RUBÍN (1912), with *The Silent Suffering of the Tzotziles* (*El callado dolor de los tzotziles*), and MIGUEL ÁNGEL MENÉNDEZ (1905), with *Nayar*, are indigenist narrators.

(ii) *Central America / Guatemala:* MIGUEL ÁNGEL ASTURIAS (1899) is a poet and novelist. He published his own anthology, *Poetry: Pulse of the Skylark* (*Poesía. Sien de alondra*, 1949). In it can be seen his esthetic changes: bucolic poetry of village life, fleeting emotion, and the return to the vernacular. Other books of poems followed shortly, such as *Poetic Exercises in the Son-*

net Form on Themes from Horace (*Ejercicios poéticos en forma de soneto sobre temas de Horacio*, 1951). He was a poet of minor tone, visual, concerned with relationships between things, with the essence of the mineral and the vegetable, with a gift for shadings. In *Legends of Guatemala* (*Leyendas de Guatemala*, 1930) he elaborated the magic vision of the Mayas with his own images. They belong to the first stage of his career, when, in Paris, under the direction of Georges Raynaud—translator of *Popol-Vuh*—he specialized in anthropological studies of the Mayan civilization. He also has written theater: *Soluna* (1957). But his novels have brought him more fame. *Mr. President* (*El señor presidente*, 1947) is one of the best of all Hispanic American novels. No particular country is mentioned, but we know that the memories Asturias has put into it are those of his childhood and adolescence in Guatemala under the tyranny of Estrada Cabrera. The title, so ironically respectful, announces the important position that the president will have in the novel. He appears only six times, but he motivates all the chapters, as Satan reigns in all the circles of Hell and a real dictator dominates all the activities in a country. He is, in reality, a Satanic dictator; and the novel is a description of the grotesque, tragic, depressing and shameful situation of a Central American republic. This description, of indubitable sociological value, has the artistic merit of an intensely evocative style, an accurate characterization of numerous men and women, and a skillful composition of plot. Because of the many interwoven characters and episodes, the action is complex but not confused. The idiot Pelele kills the most powerful agent of the dictatorship, and this initial episode sets the dictator's infernal machine in motion. The subsequent scenes grow out of one another in an uninterrupted movement. The idiot's crime was not deliberate, but the dictator's vengeance is deliberate. He has Pelele murdered to hide his own guilt and so be able to accuse two politicans, Canales and Carvajal, who have fallen into disgrace and whom he now wants to liquidate. The dictator orders his favorite, Cara de Ángel (literally, face of an angel) to tell Canales that the plan is to kill him in the act of flight. But Canales manages to flee and Cara de Ángel abducts his daughter, Camila.

The trouble is that he falls in love with her and in marrying her loses the favor of the dictator who prepares an atrocious trap for him. He entrusts him publicly with a mission to the United States, has him secretly detained, replaces him with a "double" (who travels under false documents and pretends to disappear, like a fugitive from justice, leaving false traces behind him), keeps him locked up for years in a loathsome dungeon until he becomes sick. Then he makes him believe that Camila is the dictator's beloved, and Cara de Ángel, the best-drawn character in the novel, dies. This is the main thread of the story, but it is interwoven with several others in a plot that is well rounded and well designed. Apart from the retrospective passages which, since they reflect the mental processes of the characters, do not alter the order of actual events, the narrative moves ahead normally. Asturias has chosen the perspective of the omniscient author, and the eyes of this omniscient author swerve like those of a moving-picture camera to follow first one character and then another to avoid losing sight of the significance of simultaneous or successive scenes. The omniscient author not only shows us everything that is happening in this society, publicly as well as privately, but he also lets us perceive the most intimate thoughts of his characters, even the inarticulate stream of the subconscious during absorption in thought, during sleep, delirium and madness. Whether the author psychoanalyzes his characters, lets them analyze themselves, or reveals them to us in their own interior monologs (at times as direct as those of Joyce), the novel is very subjective. The fact is that the omniscient author has turned everything into poetry. The material is seen and molded by an artist, and this is what gives the novel its poetic flavor. Such material, if we were to think about it in reality, should be ugly. Beggars, drunkards, lechers, misers, the corrupt, toadies, cowards, hypocrites, the louse-ridden, prostitutes, homosexuals, traitors, liars, thieves, imbeciles, murderers, brutes; misery, sordidness, venality; in short, every kind of ugliness that one finds in real life. But the artist takes possession of that reality, penetrates it with his vision, gives it shape and turns it into beauty. The reality

Asturias has made use of in his novel is tremendous; but more tremendous yet is his imagination. And because his imagination pervades everything, it is all transfigured into images. The sentences give off a brilliance because even filth has been put into a state of combustion. With these sentences we could form an anthology, not only of Asturia's lyricism, but also of the vanguard literature that followed World War I: expressionism, dadaism, surrealism. *Men of Corn (Hombres de maíz*, 1949) is a collection of stories in which legendary and real elements are given structure, their counterpoint at times being a bit out of tune, because the author has not clarified his artistic intent in his own mind: one of his aims seems to be to show the conflict between the Indians who plant corn only as a food, and the Creoles who plant it for commercial purposes, impoverishing the soil through their greed. In the trilogy of his last novels there is a predominance of the sociological over the purely novelistic: *Strong Wind (Viento fuerte*, 1950), *Green Pope (Papa verde*, 1954), and *The Eyes of the Interred (Los ojos de los enterrados*, 1960). In the first, there is the struggle between the small banana growers and a large fruit company. In the second, the plunder of the peasants ruined by a large fruit company, the piracy of the North American, Maker Thompson, and the abuses of imperialism. In the third, the efforts of the workers to organize and defend themselves against the exploitation of the big banana company sustained by the dictatorship of General Jorge Ubico, from 1942 to 1944. Asturia's novels are wrapped in a mist of poetry shot through with expressionism and surrealism. That is to say, the social and political reality plus the reality of the sacred traditions of the Mayas and the dreams and fantasies of the novelist are expressed in a "magical realism." *Weekend in Guatemala (Weekend en Guatemala*, 1956) is a collection of stories with a frank political purpose: they refer to the invasion of Guatemala in 1954. *The Little Jeweled Boy (El alhajadito*, 1961), written in a prose that is more poetic than narrative, reconstructs memories of a childhood paradise. *Mulatto Woman (Mulata de tal*, 1963) is a novel with roots in indigenous myths. Asturias is undoubtedly one of our major novelists because of the vigor of his imagination, the daring with which he complicates the internal structure of his story and the violent or tender lyricism with which he evokes the lands of America.

MARIO MONTEFORTE TOLEDO (1911) creates local variations on the theme of the struggle between man and nature, with protests against social evils and the exploitation of the peasant class: after *Anaité* (1940), the vigorous novels *Between the Stone and the Cross* (*Entre la piedra y la cruz,* 1948)—perhaps the best, about an educated Indian in conflict between two worlds, the primitive and the civilized—*Where the Paths End* (*Donde acaban los caminos,* 1953), and *A Way to Die* (*Una manera de morir;* 1957). He has also written short stories: *The Cave Without Peace* (*La cueva sin quietud,* 1949).

Honduras: The most outstanding of the regionalists was MARCOS CARÍAS REYES (1905–1949). He wrote thesis novels, such as *Tropic* (*Trópico*), in which he denounces the political mistreatment of the rural peoples. Others: JORGE FIDEL DURÓN (1902), author of *American Stories* (*Cuentos americanos*) and ARTURO MEJÍA NIETO (1900), an expatriate who barely touched on national themes. ARGENTINA DÍAZ LOZANO (1909) wrote, in a simple prose, stories and novels on national themes, *Mayapán,* and a novelized autobiography, *Pilgrimage* (*Peregrinaje*).

El Salvador: In *Stories of Mud* (*Cuentos de barro*) by SALARRUÉ (1899) there are suffering, sad, superstitious, exploited Indian workers, but the unity of action in these tales is so neatly trimmed that sociology and politics are shunted aside. Salarrué sees reality, but he is no realist; there is something of a somnambulist about him; he seems to be walking in his sleep with his eyes open. Each "tiny tale"—as the author calls them—brings a group of Indians together in a situation so propitiously conceived that when they speak in their terse and sober dialect, their words suggest everything that is going on within them. Then came *Shackle* (*Trasmallo,* 1954), *Tales of Fools* (*Cuentos de Cipotes,* 1958), *The Sword and Other Stories* (*La espada y otras narraciones,* 1960), in which Salarrué continued to interweave reality with mystery. Another narrator of poetic prose is MIGUEL ÁNGEL ESPINO (1904): *Trains* (*Trenes*). Within realism, the following were distinguished for their descriptions of regional surroundings and for their sharp consciousness of social ills: RAMÓN GONZÁLEZ MONTALVO (1908), for his stories in *Pacunes* and his novels *The Jars* (*Las tinajas*) and *Verbascum* (*Barbasco*). In this latter novel there are defrauded Indians, defrauding proprietors, and violence, both in society and in nature. NAPOLEÓN RODRÍGUEZ RUIZ (1910), whose novel, *Jaraguá,* with its lovely, popular dialog and its visible landscapes, calls attention to the problems of the farmer; MANUEL AGUILAR CHÁVEZ (1913–1957) and ROLANDO VELÁZQUEZ (1913).

Nicaragua: The writing of novels was part of a literary exercise undertaken in various genres. There were not, therefore, any pure novelists; neither were there pure novels, because social and political life intervened in them. We could give as an example of this tendency ADOLFO CALERO OROZCO (1899), in the novel *Sacred Blood* (*Sangre santa*) and in the

Aromatic Stories (*Cuentos pinoleros*); EMILIO QUINTANA (1908) in the stories of *Banana Trees* (*Bananos*); MANOLO CUADRA (1907) in his tales *Against Sandino in the Mountain* (*Contra Sandino en la montaña*) and *Starch* (*Almidón*). More concerned with the inner workings of their characters were JACOBO ORTEGARAY (1900) and MARIANO FIALLOS GIL (1907).

Costa Rica: The major novelist of this generation here was JOSÉ MARÍN CAÑAS (1904). He wrote four novels. The first, *Steel Tears* (*Lágrimas de acero*, 1929), has a Spanish background. The second was *You, the Impossible: Memoirs of a Sad Man* (*Tú, la imposible: Memorias de un hombre triste*, 1931), written during those years when novels against novels were being written. The novelist proved to his colleagues that he knew how to write, that he had imagination and sensitivity. He wrote novels without saying anything; or if they said anything, they said it in such an intricate, incoherent manner that the ordinary reader became disoriented. The novelist of these years, moreover, wanted to prove that he was superior even to literature itself: from this stems the humorous tone, the habit of taking everything lightly in metaphors that burst in the middle of the story. The author-protagonist, Juan Arocena, gives the esthetic key of this literature when he speaks of himself as a "mannered writer, seeker of astounding terminology"; "I narrate with a furious emotion, in which images seem to be like shots." The syntax of this prose is normal, but the style is very metaphoric; and the various levels on which it was composed gave the novel of those years a new look. There are several points of view: that of Marín Cañas, of Juan Arocena, and of the heroine, Chidy. These *Memoirs,* then, are disarticulated. Putting them back together, we find a romantic story of love, an impossible love between a poor, married writer and a girl of eighteen rich and innocent. The action takes place in Spain, even though the protagonists are Hispanic-Americans. The lyricism at times crystallizes into poems in prose; more frequently, it laughs at itself with those images that the ultraists used to like. The gift for words is greater than the novelistic gift. More serious was his novel, or rather chronicle, *Green Hell* (*Infierno verde*, 1935). It purports to have been written by a Paraguayan soldier in the Chaco War. A war that was completely South American, but Marín Cañas, in describing it, joins the cycle of anti-war literature that arose after the war from 1914 to 1918. That is, Marín Cañas applied the technique and spirit of European literature to a South American war. Also its style. Some of these novels were written in an expressionist style. Through ultraism in poetry and expressionism in prose, this metaphoric fury came to Marín Cañas. There are, in Marín Cañas, clichés and a certain stylistic monotony, but withal, it is evident that he goes forth to encounter reality as it impresses him, and he fells it beneath the weight of his enterprising personality. One of his enterprises is politics: he does not take sides in favor of either Paraguay or Bolivia, but he shows both nations as victims of international capitalism, of patriotic myths, and of an irresponsible citizenry. Esthetics and politics do not contradict each other in a style that might be called expressionist, because both emerge, without contradiction, from the creative energy of the author. His last novel was *Pedro Arnáez* (1942), with Central American landscapes, through which the hopeless and complex Pedro wanders and suffers. His life is seen—on the three occasions on which

Death stalks him—through the doctor-narrator. He also wrote stories and various theatrical pieces. MAX JIMÉNEZ (1900–1947) has given us a curious Utopia: *The Flea Trainer* (*El domador de pulgas,* 1936). He has concocted a society of fleas redeemed by the blood of the trainer, the Christ of fleas. Poor trainer! He dies bloodless and repentant. He has sacrificed himself uselessly: the freed fleas copy the bad passions of human beings. Unfortunately, these acrobatics built on nonsense failed, because the author based his stunt on a hamstrung prose. Max Jiménez lived in Paris and traveled all over the world. He was one of the postwar subversives in the plastic arts and in fiction. His poems were less revolutionary. His last book, *El jaul* (1937), is a novelistic series of peasant tales, somewhat naturalist in its barbarous personages, in the crudity of their voices, and in the exaggeration of its terrible landscapes. ARTURO CASTRO ESQUIVEL (1904) and EMMANUEL THOMPSON (1908) were not realists—at least only mild ones.

The major novelist, in the direction of proletariat literature, was CARLOS LUIS FALLAS (1911). His political position is to the far left. His novels denounce the working conditions on the banana plantations, in the jungles, and on the farms. *Mamita Yunai* (1941), which organizes chronicles that appeared originally in communist periodicals, is a protest against imperialist action and the exploitation of the rural masses. *People and Little People* (*Gentes y gentecillas*), *Marcos Ramírez,* and *My Godmother* (*Mi madrina*) followed. His style is ironic, sincere, direct, elemental. Another militant is LEÓN PACHECO (1902). In *Eleven Degrees North* (*Once grados norte*) he novelized the first armed encounter during a strike between Costa Rican Communists and the banana company. More stylized is the realism of CARLOS SALAZAR HERRERA (1906), in his *Stories of Anguish and Landscapes* (*Cuentos de angustias y paisajes*), and of ABELARDO BONILLA in *Clouded Valley* (*Valle nublado*).

Panama: It was the globe-trotting ROGELIO SINÁN (1904) who headed vanguardism. He began his campaign in favor of the new poetry with *Wave* (*Onda,* 1929) which was followed by *Fire* (*Incendio,* 1944) and *Holy Week in the Fog* (*Semana santa en la niebla,* 1949). Nevertheless, he stood out more for his narratives: *Full Moon* (*Plenilunio,* 1947), *The Red Beret and Five Stories* (*La boina roja y cinco cuentos,* 1954), and *The Birds of Sleep* (*Los pájaros del sueño,* 1958). Introspective, preoccupied with the problem of personality, a delver into the subconscious, ironic in his treatment of sexual themes (read, for example, his story "All a Conflict of Blood"), Sinán was an experimenter. Another Panamanian of the esthetist group was MANUEL FERRER VALDÉS (1914).

The realist narrators were IGNACIO DE J. VALDEZ (1902), whose *Panamanian Stories of Field and City* (*Cuentos panameños de la ciudad y del campo*) attempted a faithful portrait of the people, using antiquated procedures; GRACIELA ROJAS SUCRE (1904) and GIL BLAS TEJEIRA (1901) had greater literary quality; JOSÉ ISAAC FÁBREGA (1900), who states, although schematically and ingenuously, the national problems; historical novelists like JULIO B. SOSA (1910–1946) and LUISITA AGUILERA PATIÑO (191?); regionalists like CÉSAR A. CANDANEDO (1906), or those who wrote descriptions of city life, like RODOLFO AGUILERA (1909). It was not until after 1930 that the writers of more substance arose. There was less senti-

mentalism and more social feeling; vernacular themes, yes, but with re-
formist points of view that coincide with movements all over the continent.
One of the novelists who has understood Panamanian life in broader vistas
is RENATO OZORES (1910): in *Deep Beach* (*Playa honda,* 1950), the idle-
ness of the rich, with frivolous women and love intrigues; in *Bridge of the
World* (*Puente del mundo,* 1951), the formation of the country, with the
contribution of foreigners; in *The Dark Street* (*La calle oscura*), the humble
life in the lower-class districts; this does not include his shorter narratives,
full of good humor.

(iii) *Antilles / Cuba:* There was a group of narrators who took their themes
from the lives of the Negroes and the mulattoes. Those who faced these
themes as a part of the complex of social problems we will see later, among
the realists. We are only concerned here with the more imaginative writers,
those who interested themselves in Afro-Cuban legends and superstitions,
or, at least, those who wrote with a non-realist attitude. Among them are
RÓMULO LACHATAÑERÉ (1910–1952), RAMÓN GUIRAO (1908–1949),
whom we saw among the poets, and LYDIA CABRERA (1900), who collected
in *Negro Stories of Cuba* (*Cuentos negros de Cuba,* 1940), and *Why* (*Por
qué,* 1948) a rich store of ethnographic material, revealing the magic
concept of the world which the African slaves brought to the lands of
America.

Another narrator who touched on the Negro theme in his early
works but who, on opening out onto a more ample reality, became
the major novelist of his generation was ALEJO CARPENTIER
(1904). He traveled a great deal, not only geographically (Europe, above all), but through culture (music, folklore, literature)
and, within letters, through verse and prose. He narrates, generally, the things of his country—as in *Ecué-Yamba-O* (1931),
"an Afro-Cuban history"—but he does so experimenting with
the style and structure of the novel. *The Kingdom of This World*
(*El reino de este mundo,* 1949) presents the Antillian landscape
with "esperpentic" and surrealist techniques. *The Lost Paths* (*Los
pasos perdidos,* 1953) is a novel in the form of memoirs, or,
rather, of a diary, kept by a Cuban musician, educated in Europe,
who goes to New York (1950), is commissioned by a university
to seek certain indigenous instruments in the Venezuelan jungle,
returns a month and a half later to New York, once again wants
to return to the primitive home of the woman he loves, Rosario,
but cannot find the secret path, learns that she is now living with
another, and ends desolately by taking the path that leads straight
to the civilization he despises. Such a summary gives no idea of

the book's excellence. The contrast between life in modern cities and jungle life, the lyrical descriptions of the landscape, tremendous in their power of imagination, and, above all, the journey back through time—the romantic era, the renaissance, the middle ages, antiquity, the stone age, Genesis, the very Godhead before creation—make *The Lost Paths* one of the exceptional books of this generation. The phrases frequently have an unusual brilliance; but it is not only the ingenious phraseology that is extraordinary, but especially the vision of culture, of history, of the reality of America. The action of the novel, though simple (the narrator and the three women, Ruth, Mouche and Rosario; the vicissitudes of the journey; the weaving together of the scenes and the characters) is sufficient; and it is enriched with pages of essay writing full of intelligent reflections and surprising forms of fantasy. (None of this means that we share the protagonist-narrator's sudden enthusiasm for the primitive.) *The War of Time* (*Guerra del tiempo*, 1958)—the title alludes to the words of Lope de Vega, that man "is a soldier in the war of time"—collects three stories and a novel, all, in fact, penetrated by the obsession of time, either historical or personal, put there as the theme itself or as a form of evocation. The three stories—"The Road to Santiago," "Journey to the Seed" and "Similar to Night"—have an air of a magic game: the most far-fetched one is the second, describing how a life travels back over the course of time in "a journey to the seed" (an old man becomes a child, re-enters the womb, and with a world on his shoulders disappears into the world beyond). The novel is *The Pursuit* (*El acoso*). If we were to remake it into a continuous story-line we would have a novel of violence, betrayal, and vengeance: in the years of the downfall of the dictatorship of Machado and of the political chaos that followed it, a young boy from the provinces goes to study at the University of Havana, he joins a subversive, terrorist organization, informs on his companions, flees, and is hunted down and killed in a concert hall where he has been listening to the Eroica Symphony of Beethoven. But his material is divided into three parts. The first and the third take place within one hour: the action begins slightly before and ends slightly after the performance of the Eroica Symphony.

There are two points of view which shape the narrative material: that of the ticket seller and that of the hunted man. They are two parallel lives, and certain common experiences draw them together. The second part takes place within a period of two weeks, but, thanks to the interior monologs of the hunted man, we are made aware of the preceding events and of the present situation in the novel. *The Pursuit* is a puzzle with its pieces carefully mixed: the reader apprehends, little by little, in each fragment, the total design. The concordance between the interior monologs, direct and indirect, and the objects, characters, and episodes of the central action is admirably thought out. Carpentier does not explain, but he leaves all the clues so that the reader can identify the characters, recompose the chronology, reorder the logical sequences, and find the exit from the labyrinth. In spite of the fact that the material, because it is made up of mental processes, appears to pulverize or evaporate, Carpentier subtly organizes it into an ironic spectacle, to which the Catholic religion, the music of Beethoven, and the *Electra* of Sophocles all have lent symbols and allegories. The novel is not subjective. Instead of analyzing the psychology of his characters, the author confines himself to describing deeds just as they occur, random, partial, harsh: let the reader find their meaning. In this, Carpentier is doing in our literature something resembling that which was being done in Europe, after 1950, with the so-called objectivist novel. *The Century of the Enlightenment* (*El siglo de las luces*, 1962) contains some of Carpentier's best pages: there are promising passages with poetic descriptions intelligently organized by an essayist's mind. Nevertheless, it is not his best novel. The *Century of the Enlightenment* is viewed from its culminating point, the French Revolution; and the French Revolution is viewed from the islands of the Caribbean and French Guayana (except in Chapter II, where they are viewed from France and Spain). The real character is the Frenchman Victor Hughes (and other historical characters, like Billaud, etc.), and the fictitious ones are Esteban, Carlos and Sofía, all Cubans. The action takes place between 1789 and 1808. Chapters and paragraphs are separated by titles from "The Disasters of War" by Goya; and, in the final scene, which takes place in Madrid on May 2, 1808, Esteban and Sofía die in the street fight against the Napoleonic troops, and appear to be entering one of the pictures by Goya. A historical novel with a brilliant atmosphere, an intelligent selection of events, an original perspective, well-drawn characters, a plot filled with adventures, violence, voyages, intrigues and love affairs. The analysis of the confusion of the revolutionary process is impressive; advances and retreats in political action, uneven rhythms in the metropolis and in the colonies, heroes who fall, opportunists who climb, cynics who persist obstinately in their positions, the maimed, the disillusioned, the enthusiasts; in short—a picture which here has a historic frame but which Carpentier must have known personally in the revolutions he witnessed. The omniscient author does the narrating but he does it by approximating the perspective of Esteban (and at times, that of Sofía); because, although Victor is the protagonist of *The Century of the Enlightenment* as a historical novel, Esteban is its protagonist as a psychological novel, and on occasion he speaks in the first person.

ENRIQUE LABRADOR RUIZ (1902) has published "gasiform" novels—*Labyrinth* (*Laberinto*, 1933), *Cresival* (1936), *Anteo* (1940); little, misty novels—*Chimeric Flesh* (*Carne de quimera*, 1947); and a "fabulation"—*Trailer of Dreams* (*Trailer de sueños*, 1949); later, he changed his theme and his manner and wrote *Hungry Blood* (*La sangre hambrienta*, 1950) and *The Rooster in the Mirror* (*El gallo en el espejo*, 1953), narratives in which he no longer evades reality, nor does he allow himself to be dragged along by it. In these two books, especially the latter, the author reproduces the language of the Cuban people, with sympathetic feeling for life in the small towns of the interior. LINO NOVÁS CALVO (1905) does not seem to add imaginative festoons to reality; on the contrary, it could be said that he reduces it to elementary outlines. But he could not be called a realist because the slow shifting of his figures, the suggestive power of gestures, words, and even silences, the disintegration of the plot into planes, startle the reader and oblige him to intervene imaginatively in what he is reading. He has also written *The Ninth Moon and Other Stories* (*La luna nona y otros cuentos*, 1942), *I Do Not Know Who I Am* (*No sé quien soy*, 1945), *Cape Canas* (*Cayo Canas*, 1946), *In the Backyard* (*En los traspatios*, 1946). "I have Faulkner in my blood," he has said. He is a witness buried in the inconsistencies of life and society.

The short story enjoyed a period of exceptional popularity during these years, and one of the directions it took was the fantastic, whether free or lyrical or even existential. We will have to repeat here names that we saw in the paragraph on poetry. FÉLIX PITA RODRÍGUEZ (1909), "esperpentic," magic, poematic, but strong in the blows he strikes at the drama of man in our time. JOSÉ LEZAMA LIMA (1912), hermetic, geometric—that is, a darkness with interior guide lines—that brings the power of his poetry into play in the story. DULCE MARÍA LOYNAZ (1903) went from verse to the novel without diminishing her poetic spirit. After *Verses* (*Versos,* 1938) and *Water Games* (*Juegos de agua,* 1947)—poetry in which an insinuating interior music wrapped the words and impressions received from reality in mystery—she wrote *Garden* (*Jardín;* 1951). The author calls it a "lyric novel," perhaps because it narrates and sings at the same time, so that the very prose moves in a rhythmic dance like poetry. Each step in that prose is an occasion for a beautiful dance figure involving the whole body. And the prose goes dancing through the paths of a garden. For the garden in this novel is not only title, motive, character and destiny, it is also form. Except that in this artificial garden we will not find open adventures, fresh air movements, or continuous action. The plot outline is minimal. Enclosed between a prolog and an epilog (which do not explain the plot but suggest the mental state of the protagonist), the story of Barbara takes place. She is a hypersensitive, over-imaginative woman, obsessed by the garden that imprisons her, a woman phantom-ridden from overindulgence in fantasy. We see her first a little before her twentieth birthday, going over old photographs, thus evoking her life in the family, her ailing childhood, her growth, her solitude. Then we see her reading old love letters between her great-grand-aunt, who is also named Barbara, and an adolescent. As she identifies with a romantic past, she awakens to love. And finally (here, in the second half of the book, the pace of the novel quickens and years fly by in a few pages) we see her in love with a sailor. She runs away with him, sees the world, has children, travels; and years later, after her return to the house where she was born, alone, during a phantom-haunted morning, the vengeful garden destroys her. Judged as a novel *Garden* is impaired because the author has not resolved the problem of point of view (she intervenes in the action with her own comments and at times she abandons Barbara's soul to install herself in that of her lover) or the problem of construction (the narrative proceeds at an irregular pace, the symbols that oscillate between reality and delirium are often confused, the rhetorical complications of certain themes tend to swallow up the novelistic material). However, the weaknesses of the novel as a novel do not detract from its value as a book, a rewarding book, one of the most distinguished of its generation for the relevance of its forms and for the unfailing precision of its poetic images. If style could have sex, this would be feminine, in the sense that Virginia Woolf's style is spoken of as feminine—not to mention the femininity with which the psychology of woman is revealed, especially in the part dealing with love.

Of the novels of CARLOS ENRÍQUEZ (1907–1957), we shall concern ourselves only with the posthumous *The Fair of Guaicanama* (*La Feria de Guaicanama*). Throughout a tale of passion (the impulsive Juan Lope swoops away Palmenia and, with her submissive in his arms, he violently challenges social conventions) Enríquez slowly discloses an obscure message: anarchism, vitalism, and irrationalism. This intervention of the author damages the plot of the novel. The exorbitant exaltation of sexual impulses

—in which we discern the influence of D. H. Lawrence—the belief in supernatural forces and metaphysical phenomena, the extremely romantic manner in which he presents his hero—a hero of the barbaric against the
civilized—the lack of intellectual discipline revealed in the characters' discussions, a style overloaded with images and hyperboles, and a careless
composition are all the more lamentable when we know the author to have
more personality and expect from him a better expression of his fantasy.
The social current is represented by CARLOS MONTENEGRO (1900). He
gathered his stories into *The Offshoot* (*El renuevo*), *Two Boats* (*Dos
barcos*), and *The Heroes* (*Los héroes*). His novel, *Men Without Women*
(*Hombres sin mujer*) is one of the strongest of his Cuban generation. With
strong agility, he leaps from the prison to themes of the sea, from the anti-
imperialist war to psychological probings: in these leaps he assumes intense
realistic postures. ENRIQUE SERPA (1899), who began as a poet of modernist
taste, put his strength into realist narratives. Realist in their subject matter,
but the attention that he gives to the psychological, his preference for interior monologs, and his careful phrasing, polish and attenuate reality. The
novel *Contraband* (*Contrabando,* 1938) is a good example of this. In the
novel *The Trap* (*La trampa,* 1956), he falls, nonetheless, into the writing
of political customs. His stories—from *Felisa and I* (*Felisa y yo,* 1937) to
Night of Fiesta (*Noche de fiesta,* 1951)—attest to a progression toward expressive simplicity. GERARDO DEL VALLE (1918), is the author of stories—
Fragments (*Retazos*)—about Negro and mestizo superstitions and beliefs,
about the lower depths of city life, about ancient legends and myths, about
spiritualist themes. Other realist narrators: ONELIO JORGE CARDOSO (1914),
OFELIA RODRÍGUEZ ACOSTA (1906), DORA ALONSO (1910), MARCELO
POGOLOTTI (1902), ALBERTO LAMAR SCHWAYER (1902–1942), JOSÉ M.
CARBALLIDO REY (1913), AURORA VILLAR BUCETA (1907), ROSA HILDA
ZELL (1910).

Puerto Rico: ENRIQUE A. LAGUERRE (1906) wrote novels
about the soil. When *Sudden Flame* (*La llamarada,* 1935) appeared, some believed that it revealed the sugar cane area of
Puerto Rico, the sufferings of the worker, the force of nature,
collective problems, human insular types . . . What was revealed
was a good novelist. He does not give unity to his book, but with
unconnected episodes and scattered characters he has created an
artistic illusion of real life. In *Montoya Farm* (*Solar Montoya,*
1947) he completed the vision of the Puerto Rican field and proposed a program of agricultural rehabilitation. In *Undertow* (*La
resaca,* 1949) he writes about the conspirators who wanted to
free Puerto Rico from the Spaniards during the last years of the
colony and who were overthrown by the apathy of the people.
Laguerre sees his theme panoramically; and, in fact, the land is

what dominates his novels. The souls of his characters float about like telluric emanations. His novels, one after the other, describe all of the landscape of the island, all of its activities, all of its social classes, and always, at the heart of his work, his concern is for the fortunes of his country. *The God-Tree in the Pot* (*La ceiba en el tiesto*, 1956) and *Dry River Bed* (*Cauce sin río*, 1962) are his latest titles. The action of *The Labyrinth* (*El laberinto*, 1959) does not take place in Puerto Rico but in New York and Santo Domingo.

Other narrators worthy of note are: TOMÁS BLANCO (1900), *The Bards* (*Los vates*, 1930); JOSÉ A. BALSEIRO (1900), *Vigil While the World Sleeps* (*En vela mientras el mundo duerme*, 1953), EMILIO S. BELAVAL (1903), *Stories to Encourage Tourism* (*Cuentos para fomentar el turismo*, 1936), ERNESTO JUAN FONFRÍAS (1909), *Root and Tassel* (*Raíz y espiga*, 1963), VICENTE PALÉS MATOS (1903), *Wind and Foam* (*Viento y espuma*, 1946). And the short story writers, NÉSTOR RODRÍGUEZ ESCUDERO (1914), JULIO MARRERO NÚÑEZ (1910), MANUEL DEL TORO (1911), and WASHINGTON LLORENS (1900).

Dominican Republic: The best storyteller in the artistic field was TOMÁS HERNÁNDEZ FRANCO (1904), whom we have already seen among the poets. JUAN BOSCH (1909) has published the major part of his work outside of the country. He has written a novel *The Cunning One* (*La mañosa*, 1936), but his greatest merits are those of the short-story writers: *The Royal Road* (*Camino Real*, 1933), *Indians* (*Indios*, 1935), *Two Dollars' Worth of Water* (*Dos pesos de agua*, 1941), *Eight Stories* (*Ocho cuentos*, 1947) and *The Girl from El Guaira* (*La muchacha del Guaira*, 1955). He prefers to narrate the simple life of the Antillian peasant. He uses the language of these people with veracity, but he interprets his themes with the tenderness and ironic humor of an observer who has withdrawn to a distance from reality to see it with the eyes of the artist. MANUEL A. AMIAMA (1899) evoked the customs of the capital city in his novel *The Trip* (*El viaje*, 1940). HORACIO READ (1899) novelized with vigor the period of United States intervention, in the *Civilizers* (*Los civilizadores*, 1924). Afterwards, he wrote other narratives in a different style: *From the Shadow* (*De la sombra*, 1959). ÁNGEL RAFAEL LAMARCHE (1900), of impressionist, sentimental prose: *The Stories That New York Doesn't Know* (*Los cuentos que Nueva York no sabe*). VIRGINIA DE PEÑA DE BORDAS (1904–1948), author of *Toeya*, a novel of Indianist theme, and of *Stories for Children* (*Cuentos para niños*). ANDRÉS FRANCISCO REQUENA (1908–1952), wrote, in *The Enemies of the Land* (*Los enemigos de la tierra*, 1936), of the moral suffering of the peasants who want to leave their land to go to the city. In *Path of Fire* (*El camino de fuego*, 1941) and *Cemetery Without Crosses* (*Cementerio sin cruces*, 1949), he denounced political bossism. RAMÓN MARRERO ARISTY (1913) is a short-story writer of strong realism in *Balsié* (1938) and also a novelist in *Over* (1939). The latter is a notable novel in which social problems are stated with reference to the exploitation of sugar cane. The title, taken from the jargon of the sugar refinery, alludes to the extortion which the stores employ to abuse the worker. The author himself is a peasant, unskilled in literature, but has lived through these same experiences with a combative spirit. FREDDY PRESTOL CASTILLO (1913), a Creole story writer of social theme, creates in his novel *Pablo Mamá* a good character, untamed and solitary on the frontier. HILMA CONTRERAS (1913), more of an artist, more surprising in her *Four Stories* (*Cuatro cuentos,* 1953).

(iv) *Venezuela* / The first information on cubism, ultraism, and surrealism arrived in Venezuela very late, in comparison to the other countries. When it arrived, a group of story writers and novelists, headed by Uslar Pietri, not being able to deny reality nor wishing to copy it, hit upon the art of noting down the poetic quality which is enmeshed in all things. ARTURO USLAR PIETRI (1905) set the example with a prose rich in sensual impressions, in lyric metaphors, in symbols which suggest a new interpretation of Hispanic-American reality. His first narratives were in 1928: *Barrabás and Other Tales* (*Barrabás y otros relatos*), a departure from sketches of regional customs and dialog. In the two books that followed, there can be seen an evolution from the cult of the very imaginative phrase toward an art more concerned with descriptions of the terrain: *Net* (*Red,* 1936), *Thirty Men and Their Shadows* (*Treinta hombres y sus sombras,* 1949). The first includes "Rain" (*"La lluvia"*), a good harmonization of poetic melody and vernacular accompaniment. In the second the themes of Creole life and folklore are more powerful. He has written, in addition, an excellent historical novel on the war of independence in Venezuela: *The Red Lances* (*Las lanzas coloradas,* 1931). Historical novel? Bolívar does not appear. Nevertheless, the figure of Bolívar provides the framework for the novel. In the first pages, Presentación Campos, the majordomo of El Altar, gets up, annoyed by the voice of a slave who is relating an adventure of Bolívar's. In the last pages, Presentación Campos falls dead without having been able to appear at the window to see the triumphal entry of Bolívar. But within this elemental framework the novel unfolds in barbarity and chaos. The characters live in psychological plenitude: the belligerent, animal, proud will of Presentación

Campos; the sweet and dreamy Inés; the lethargic Fernando; the curiosity for life and the desire to live it completely of the Englishman, David . . . In addition, there are magnificent figures, like that of Boves, fighters and women. But this humanity, so well outlined in his personal bas-reliefs, is not portrayed as is usual in the traditional novel. Pietri passes by the precipices opened up by romantic literature; but he never falls over the edge. On the contrary. His creatures are lost amidst the furious masses of the war. Destinies do not cross, but separate. Inés wanders over the plains, gone mad, disfigured by the fire, searching for Campos in order to avenge herself: but she will not find him. Fernando will not see his sister, will not fight for the Republic in which he believes; he will not fall with his friends, neither will he avenge himself on Campos. Pietri gives us the movements of crowds, not of heroes. The heroism of Boves, of Díaz, of Campos is—as in the epics— a reddish light scarcely visible in the gleam of the lances, stained crimson with blood that covers the plains like an outrageous death. Incarnations of devastation. This perspective which deliberately confuses everything into disorderly and unattached blotches is that of impressionism. Pietri has put the refinements of impressionist art at the service of a barbarous theme. The metaphors—audacious, pictorial, fresh—save the reality which is evoked from the logical interventions of the novelist. Pietri does not construct a novel along political or moral principles. He is not with Boves nor with Bolívar. The novel thus gains in esthetic virtues. *The Road to El Dorado* (*El camino de El Dorado*, 1948), more than an historical novel, is the novelized biography of the diabolic conquistador, Lope de Aguirre; and it is even poetic geography. *A Picture in the Geography* (*Un retrato en la geografía*, 1962) is a novel about Venezuelan society in the era of the fall of Gómez. His latest novel: *Season of Masks* (*Estación de máscaras*, 1964).

Uslar Pietri was followed by José Salazar Domínguez (1902), Nelson Himiob (1908), Arturo Briceño (1908), and Carlos Eduardo Frías (1906). These narrators accept the reality in which they live, but upon this foundation they build a high and well-constructed literature, full of life, its windows ventilated by a breeze of poetry. The same can be said of those who come later. JULIÁN PADRÓN (1910–1954) wrote some stories with realistic tendencies: *Summer Fires* (*Candelas de verano*), *Peasant Clamor* (*Clamor campesino*), *This Desolate World* (*Este mundo desolado*). But his best works were those in which he gave a poetic tone to his memories of childhood and adolescence: *La Guaricha* (1934), *Dawn* (*Madrugada*, 1939), *Nocturnal Spring* (*Primavera nocturna*, 1950). His perception of the landscape—a little town, a river, a road, a cornfield, the mountains, trees and clouds—is so acute that, at times, responding to it, Padrón forgets the action of the novel and the plot suffers. But his suggestive power, the minuteness of detail, and his introspection save the novel even in those moments when its unity breaks down. There is an autobiographic background to his narrations, especially in *Nocturnal Spring*, a novel of the city which, because of its poetic tension and its wealth of symbols, opened up new paths in the field of the novel in his country. Padrón had pity for people, especially for the peasants, because of their sufferings. The title of his latest novel gives the key to his concept of life: *This Desolate World* (*Este mundo desolado*).

GUILLERMO MENESES (1911) captured sympathetically the lives of the Negroes, mulattoes, and zambos in his three novels, *The Sloop Isabel Arrived This Afternoon* (*La balandra Isabel llegó esta tarde*, 1934), *Song of the Negroes* (*Canción de negros*, 1934) and *Song of the Negroes* (*Canción de negros*, 1934) and *Champions* (*Campeones*, 1939). His portraits of humble men, the way he pictures Venezuelan scenes—popular scenes with natural backgrounds—indicate a firm sense of reality, but we place him among our artists because of the singular vivacity with which he showed the inner, psychological side of his characters. The first-mentioned work, *The Sloop Isabel Arrived This Afternoon*, was a small masterpiece. *Three Venezuelan Stories* (*Tres cuentos venezolanos*) are close to being psychological studies: through a youth of fifteen years ("Adolescence"), a Negro ("Drunkenness"), and an Indian ("Moon") Meneses presents the problem of the need for women and its final satisfaction. Other works: *The Mestizo José Vargas* (*El mestizo José Vargas*), *The False Notebook of Narciso Espejo* (*El falso cuaderno de Narciso Espejo*). JOSÉ FABBIANI RUIZ (1911) is something of a potter in the way he creates his stories in *Salt Water* (*Agua salada*, 1939) and his novels *Deep Valley* (*Valle hondo*, 1934) and *The Swell of the Sea* (*Mar de leva*, 1941). He forms his figures as from clay, squeezing, economizing, smoothing here and there, bringing out the necessary relief. *The Painful Childhood of Perucho González* (*La dolida infancia de Perucho González*, 1946)—told by himself—is a clouded novel. Wisps of novel, like scattered clouds. At times clouds that more or less envelop lyrically scenes from the life of a poor, unfortunate, adventurous, and imaginative child. At times, gray clouds form when the style evaporates, impeding our view of the story. *On the Shores of Sleep* (*A orillas del sueño*) —a novel which won the National Prize for Literature in the biennium 1958–59—presents the lives of adults, children, and adolescents; the latter being the protagonists, whom we see in all their solitude, misunderstood and unprotected. ANTONIA PALACIÓS' (1908) book *Anna Isabel, a Decent Girl* (*Ana Isabel, una niña decente*, 1949) puts her on a plane with Teresa de la Parra, author of *Ifigenia*.

MIGUEL OTERO SILVA (1908) novelized in *Fever* (*Fiebre*, 1939) the student struggle against the dictatorship of Gómez. It was a document, political and literary, on the generation of '28. The first pages were written in an exalted style, when he was twenty years old, living in the midst of the same events that he was describing: the last pages—which are better—were written in his maturity. The structural crack between the two styles is obvious, and even the thematic development is lacking in unity. But the breath of poetry that blows across his landscapes, the vigor with which he describes the agony of his protagonist, the fevered atmosphere of the ending incorporate him with all honors into the body of the Venezuelan novel. Later, in *Dead Houses* (*Casas muertas*, 1955) he came to the forefront of Hispanic American literature. *Dead Houses* is an album of sad prints of the city: the city of Ortiz, once a prosperous capital, has become a dilapidated and desolate cemetery for dead houses. Pestilence —yellow fever, malaria, hematuria—have destroyed the city. But, as the teacher Berenice says, if pestilence were able to destroy it, it was because political decay had already weakened its resistance. These were the years of Gómez' tyranny and in this album, together with the sketches of illness, are those on the abuses and violence of the dictatorship. It contains many characters, caught in moving instances. The character that gives the album a certain novelistic continuity is Carmen Rosa; she appears in the first chapter after burying her lover Sebastián; she disappears in the last chapter, emigrating from the city on her way to land where oil has just been discovered. The intermediate chapters contain the story of the destruction of Ortiz and its population. It is not written in the form of evocations by Carmen Rosa, since the narrator, in disconnected scenes, is the omniscient Otero Silva. His prose is clear, concise, careful, pervaded always by the pathos of so much human suffering. At times his words have a poetic brilliance in his references to love, tenderness, and the beauty of these simple lives. From the town of Casas Muertas Miguel Otero moved to an oil camp in his other novel, *Office Number 1* (*Oficina número 1*). ANTONIO ARRAIZ (1903) is a poet and a capable novelist of naturalist bent, esteemed for his animal stories which, in a magic world, reveal the plebeian Venezuelan soul with more efficacy than do many pages of direct description: *Uncle Tiger and Uncle Rabbit* (*Tío Tigre y Tío Conejo*). Even in his last novels we can recognize the poet's fingers in the hand of the narrator: *Real Men* (*Puros hombres*), in which he documents the experiences of the political prisoners during the dictatorship; *The Sea Is Like a Colt* (*El mar es como un potro*)—whose former title was *Dámaso Velázquez*—describes the life of the fishermen; *They All Were Disoriented* (*Todos iban desorientados*) follows the decadence of several families. LUCILA PALACIOS (1902) novelized the marine environment in *The Sea Divers* (*Los buzos*) and *The Courser With the White Mane* (*El corcel de las crines albas*); her last novel is *The Day of Cain* (*El día de Caín*). RAMÓN DÍAZ SÁNCHEZ (1903), in his novel *Mene* (1936), composed with the technique of the reporter—the theme is the rapid transformation of a rural village into an oil well camp—had demonstrated a restlessness that finally led him toward the psychological theme. He is now more interested in man than in the landscape, and he reacts against Creole primitivism. In his novel *Cumboto* (one of the best in the country), with a Negro setting, Díaz Sánchez delves into the crudest of Venezuelan realities, but with a fine brush paints an atmosphere of poetry, terror, and magic symbols. His description of the customs and geography of Venezuela does not continue the line of Romero García or Picón-Febres, nor that of Gallegos. It is enough to compare the manner of conceiving the landscape in *Doña Bárbara* and in *Cumboto* to see the great difference between styles in the treatment of the regionalist theme. Others: ARTURO CROCE (1907), outstanding in the novel and the short story aimed at social reform; BLAS MILLÁN (1900–1959), author of "Frivolous Stories" ("*Cuentos frívolos*") and PABLO DOMÍNGUEZ (1901), a short story writer.

(v) *Colombia* / EDUARDO ZALAMEA BORDA (1907–1963), in his powerful and original novel *Four Years On Board Myself* (*Cuatro años a bordo de mí mismo*, 1934), tells in the form of a diary of his crossing over and stay at the semiabandoned salt mines of La Guajira. The narrator is a vital and jubilant spectator of himself and of the world, an analyst of sensations: "I like to look slowly at things, little by little, as though I were savoring noises, colors and perfumes, with all the intensity of my senses." Life is lived intensely—one's sexual life is part of this intensity—but a free and blithe imagination converts these vital experiences into lyric language. Zalamea Borda does in prose what the "stoneandskyists" were doing in verse: a new poetry of impressions, symbols, and fabulous figures. ANTONIO CARDONA JARAMILLO (1914) is a story writer saturated with the landscape of his district in Caldas: *Mountain Range* (*Cordillera*, 1945). He penetrates into the spirit of the people and makes them speak in a natural dialog. His descriptive prose is agile, complex, artistic, and imaginative.

The naturalism of JOSÉ A. OSORIO LIZARAZO (1900–1964) has specialized in the sordidness of tenement houses, crime, alcoholism and in degenerative diseases, in the superstitions and ignorance of the peasants, in the vices and evils of the bourgeoisie. His purpose was sociological, didactic, and also one of protest. But this novelist of human failure has failed himself, in the creation of his characters. Perhaps his best work was *Man Beneath the Earth* (*El hombre bajo la tierra*, 1944). It is the life, realistically told, of the miners who dig gold from a Colombian valley. Some details are naturalist—the bestiality of man, his physiological needs, his submission to his surroundings—but there is no thesis of social reform or protest. On the contrary: on one hand he exaggerates the power of the mine to determine the fates of men, but on the other hand its beneficent power is idealized. The author seems to tell us that gold will corrupt civilization but that work under the earth makes men happy, loyal, tolerant, affectionate, virile, obedient, honest. The most violent scenes—knife duels, sex, gambling, drunken sprees, death, and madness—all appear as part of the cult of the "he-man." This is the dominant theme: an adolescent, Ambrosio Munero, having run away from his bourgeois home in Bogotá, hides in the mine and there learns to be a "he-man." His apprenticeship of a few months (which serves as a psychological motif, not as a moral example) opens in the first chapter, when he is intimidated by Pedro Torres' knife, and closes in the last chapter, in which he knifes Pedro Torres, exactly in the same scene. A story line describes a complete circle, but the drawing is weak, because Osorio Lizarazo brings in too many characters without building them up sufficiently. ADEL LÓPEZ GÓMEZ (1901) published some six collections of stories: those of 1956 are his *Selected Stories* (*Cuentos selectos*). He is a realist, not a naturalist (that is, the real, not the repulsive side of the real). He offers an ample gallery of characters: cowardly and courageous, stupid and intelligent. And they are not characters all of one piece, but persons drawn with interior shadings. The plot is not important. At times it is nonexistent. Spiritual states more than action. The art of storytelling adjusts to psychological veracity. He is a balanced author. He does not illustrate any extreme esthetic position, even though all of them are represented. His center appears to be in the emotions.

One of the good novels of this period, *Risaralda* (1935), was written by BERNARDO ARIAS TRUJILLO (1905–39). It is like a film—filmed in reels—on the life of the Negro population and cattle-raising. In the middle of the jungle, mulattoes, Negroes, and zambos work, dream, kill, grow violently impassioned, and smile gently. The ethnography is idealized. The prose is swollen with poetry and also with eloquence. EDUARDO CABALLERO CALDERÓN (1910) has published various novels—*Tipacoque, The Penultimate Hour (La penúltima hora)*—with an occasional experimental technique. There is nothing experimental in the best of them: *Christ With His Back to Us (El Cristo de espaldas,* 1952). A young priest, recently ordained, sets out for the first time from the seminary to serve as parish priest to a little town lost in the Andes. It is as though he were visiting hell or dreaming a nightmare. In less than five days he comes to know all the horrors of infamy, of ugliness, injustice, stolidity, violence, and misery. These are the years of civil war between the conservatives and the liberals. Caught in the middle of that fight (in which neither side is better than the other) a boy is condemned for a crime which he did not commit: he is accused of having assassinated his father, the conservative chieftain. The priest hears—without being able to reveal it—the confession of the true assassin, the sexton. Everyone is against this devoutly dedicated priest, the only honorable person in the whole novel. Even the bishop judges him wrongly. Since the priest has failed, he is punished by being sent back to the seminary. The bishop believes that "Christ has turned His back" on the priest; the priest knows that it is man who has turned his back on Christ. The prose is plain, realist, documental, composed in the old technique of the author who narrates in the third person, following the logical order of events (except for a few pages of exposition and retrospection to tie in the line of the narrative). The first five chapters are vigorous: the last three lose their narrative force because they become too discursive and moralizing. His novel *Manuel Pacho* (1962) comes to grips with the primitive violence that was unleashed in the Colombian countryside. The essayist HERNANDO TÉLLEZ (1908) figures also among the better story writers: *Ashes For the Wind and Other Tales (Cenizas para el viento y otras historias,* 1950). In this collection appears "Foam and Nothing More." It is surprising for the artistic sobriety with which it narrates a violent situation. Others: the regionalists with neo-realist tendencies: HUMBERTO JARAMILLO ÁNGEL (1908), ALEJANDRO ÁLVAREZ (1909), TULIO

GONZÁLEZ VÉLEZ (1906); those with broader vision: OCTAVIO AMORTEGUI (1901), AUGUSTO MORALES PINTO (1912), BERNARDO RESTREPO MAYA (1910); the denouncers and protesters: ANTONIO GARCÍA (1912), JOSÉ FRANCISCO SOCARRAS (1907); ALFONSO LÓPEZ MICHELSEN (1913), the author of *The Chosen* (*Los elegidos*).

(vi) *Ecuador* / PABLO PALACIO (1906–1946), in the stories of *A Man Kicked to Death* (*Un hombre muerto a puntapiés,* 1927), penetrated into human life with irony and a biting humor. He was a strange person, and his literature, strangely artistic. He created a dehumanized, anti-sentimental humor, which accepted without question the "abnormalities" of his characters: "This business of being a cannibal is just the same as smoking, or being a pederast, or an erudite"; ". . . being crazy, just like being a political office-holder, a schoolteacher, or a parish priest." He was a spontaneous monologist. (Years later "interior monologs" would become exercises imposed by school teachers.) Palacio was losing his mind, but before he went completely insane, he was able to publish the novels, *Débora* (1929), sentimental in tone, and *The Life of the Hanged Man* (*Vida del ahorcado,* 1932), exacerbated, anguished. Also a narrator of artistic prose was ALFONSO CUESTA Y CUESTA (1912), notable for his creation of juvenile characters. Stories: *The Arrival of All the Trains in the World* (*Llegada de todos los trenes del mundo*).

This country produced a body of novels compactly realist. Except for Mera and Montalvo—isolated cases—the only notable novelist of Ecuador had been Luis A. Martínez, with the powerful naturalism of *Toward the Coast* (*A la costa*). But only twenty years later, a whole family was to rise from naturalism. The first names to announce a new era in Ecuador's narrative art were Pareja Díez-Canseco, José de la Cuadra, Gallegos Lara, Aguilera Malta and Gil Gilbert, "five, like the fingers on a hand." In only a few years a group of writers, for the most part militant communists and socialists, asserted themselves writing to denounce the living conditions of the people and to protest against the injustices of the social system. Crude language, exaggeration of the dark and the sordid, bravery in the exposé of shameful national conditions, sincerity of combative purpose give this literature more moral than literary value. From the Ecuadorian reality they set aside certain themes that they considered bourgeois and chose others that they considered vigorous and wrote novels filled with suffering Indians, with abominable latifundia, with the miserable peons of the coast and of the mountain, with filthy cities, malignant beasts, local epidemics and disasters.

JOSÉ DE LA CUADRA (1904–1941) was the most able storyteller: *The Love That Slept* (*El amor que dormía*, 1930), *Con-
soles* (*Repisas*, 1931), *Oven* (*Horno*, 1932), *The Sangurimas*
(*Los Sangurimas*, 1934), *Guasinton* (1938). He was a moderate
socialist, comprehensive, flexible, and at times ironic. His themes
were taken from poverty, injustice, suffering, human bestiality,
and hostile nature, but they were not monotonous. The stories of
Guasinton are very diverse in theme, humor, and perspective
(there are even poetic ones like "A Girl Is Lost"), and even in
his most unified collections (such as *The Sangurimas*, whose tales
end with incest, rape, madness, and death), the author does not
allow himself to be dragged down by a facile truculence. His
prose, sharp, rapid, and precise gives a frigidity to the observed
reality. A novelist of international fame is JORGE ICAZA (1906).
He published, between *Clay of the Sierra* (*Barro de la sierra*,
1933) and *Six Tales* (*Seis relatos*, 1952), a series of novels,
dramas, and tales that tried to transmute pieces of coarse matter
into literature. The reading of *Huasipungo* (1934), his most famous novel, which is badly constructed, can only satisfy those
who seek sociological documentation or political feelings rather
than literary virtues. In it Icaza novelizes the exploitation of the
Indian by his masters; the Indian is not a concrete person, but an
abstract mass-man. The title refers, in Quechua, to the parcel of
land that the landowners ceded to the Indian in return for tilling
the rest of the farm. They deprive the Indian of his "huasipungo"
when they sell the land to a foreign enterprise. The novel uncovers
the avarice and despotism of the landowners, the corruption of
the parish priest, the brutality in the use of weapons to put down
the indigenous uprising, bestiality of customs, sex, misery, crude
language. It has, nevertheless, a certain haughty coldness, that of
the critical intelligence of the author. Another of his Indianist
novels, with a political theme, was *Huairapamushcas*. ALFREDO
PAREJA DÍEZ-CANSECO (1908), on the other hand, has novelized
the city: *The Wharf* (*El muelle*), *Baldomera, Three Rats* (*Las
tres ratas*). At times, however, he came out of his urban enclo-
sure: *La Baldaca, Don Balón de Baba*. He does not write political
propaganda, although he is interested in the evils of his country

and describes them. He is more conscious of his technique as a novelist. He draws his figures with agility and makes them speak in lively dialog. If his feminine characters are most convincing, it is because one of his novelistic themes is the impact of social injustice on sexual relations. Among his best novels: *The Wharf* (1933) and *Three Rats* (1944). He has recently begun an all-inclusive novel, *The Nine Years* (*Los nueve años*), of which the volumes "The Warning" ("*La advertencia*") "The Air and Memories" ("*El aire y los recuerdos*,") and "The All-Encompassing Powers" ("*Los poderes omnímodos*") are already known. That long novel reflects the shiftings of Ecuadorian society after 1925. *The Wharf* is a naturalist novel, of improvised style and weak composition, facile, sober, and even agile in its descriptions and dialog. It deals with the misery of Juan and María, two mestizos from Guayaquil, with scenes of prostitution, theft, sickness, administrative corruption, lack of work or work that is hard and ill-paid, abuses, and violence. The first few chapters take place in New York: the depression, workers' protests disbanded beneath the blows of the police, contraband. Conclusion: society is badly constructed, as much in Guayaquil as in New York, and the poor worker has no avenue of escape.

DEMETRIO AGUILERA MALTA (1905) prefers to write about the sufferings of the Indians, mestizos, and zambos of the Ecuadorian fields. However, he has written about life in other countries, for example in *Canal Zone, "The Yankees in Panama."* In general, he chooses moving situations in which the social problem dominates the psychological: *Don Goyo, Canal Zone, The Virgin Island* (*La isla virgen*). He seems to have abandoned the novel for the theater. HUMBERTO SALVADOR (1907) seemed, at the beginning of his career, to be going to dedicate himself to the theater, but what appeared were stories—*Chess* (*Ajedrez*) and *A Cup of Tea* (*Taza de té*)—and novels (on social justice): *Comrade* (*Camarada*), *Workers* (*Trabajadores*), *November* (*Noviembre*); others less tendentious: *The Interrupted Novel* (*La novela interrumpida*), *Prometheus* (*Prometeo*); and the most introspective: *Clear Fountain* (*Fuente clara*), *Flash of Anguish* (*La ráfaga de angustia*). He is a sober, humorless chronicler of the city life of his time. He studies circumstances and psychology. At times this fundamentally urban novelist does both things at the same time and psychoanalyzes the city of Quito. While in his first novels the dialog could be heard, in his later ones, we hear the interior monologs of his characters. ENRIQUE GIL GILBERT (1912) conceived of the novel as a political pamphlet at the service of the revindication of the workers. *Our Daily Bread* (*Nuestro pan*, 1941), is a novel about the exploitation of the rice laborers. He later abandoned literature to dedicate himself entirely to politics. JORGE FERNÁNDEZ (1912), a novelist on the peasant theme in *Water* (*Agua,* 1937) and on the urban theme in *Those Who Live By Their Hands* (*Los que viven por sus manos,* 1951), in which he describes the vicissitudes of bureaucracy and unemployment, mediocrity, vice, and humiliation. JOAQUÍN GALLEGOS LARA (1911–1947?) gave us the painful history of Guayaquil in *The Crosses Upon the Water* (*Las cruces sobre el agua*). GERARDO GALLEGOS used the Antilles—where he lives—as the setting for some of his novels, and Ecuador for others. He is a two-fisted novelist, with some good descriptions of landscapes, and, above all, with a knack for the adventure story. ANGEL F. ROJAS (1910) brought new techniques to the novel: in *Exodus from Yangana* (*Éxodo de Yangana*) he describes how an entire town disbands and buries itself in the jungle in search of justice. *Curipumba* is a novel on life in the mines. There is a social theme, but the narrative prose, more careful and more elegant than is found in other political placard novels, is redeemed by its own merits. LUIS MOSCOSO VEGA is successful in depicting lives rooted in the soil in *What Life Denies* (*Lo que niega la vida*), a novel of the highway. There is nothing stranger than to find humor in the lugubrious climate of the Ecuadorian novel. ALFONSO GARCÍA MUÑOZ (1910) was a humorist in his series of *Sketches of My City* (*Estampas de mi ciudad*). Others: MANUEL MUÑOZ CUEVA wrote his *Stories from the Cuenca Zone* (*Cuentos morlacos,* 1931) with an occasional tender smile, although he was also capable of pathos: *Broken Jar* (*Ánfora rota*). Others: GONZALO RAMÓN (1912?), and ARTURO MONTESINOS MALO (1913?).

(vii) *Peru /* There were few poetic peaks in narrative prose. JOSÉ DÍEZ-CANSECO (1905–1949) administered a scathing criticism of the high society of Lima, to which he belonged, in *Duke* (*Duque,* 1934). Although his prose was influenced by the ingenious and brilliant postwar writers (that was where he got his ultraist images and his ability to leap nimbly from image to idea), he was, nevertheless, faithful to reality in his descriptions. He understood the lower classes [see his *Mulatto Sketches* (*Estampas mulatas*)]. But what was new was his realistic novel on the bourgeoisie of Lima. Actually, DÍEZ-CANSECO and JOSÉ FERNANDO (1903–1947)—who wrote *Panorama at Dawn* (*Panorama hacia el alba*)—were the two first novelists of the city.

What was predominant in the narrative of these years was realism at the service of native (Alegría), regionalist (Romero) and urban (Arciniega) themes. With some narrators this realism was socialistic (Alegría, Arguedas). Others dealt with the regionalist theme with more conventional procedures (MARÍA ROSA

MACEDO, 1912; VLADIMIRO BERMEJO, 1908; ESTEBAN PAVLE-
TICH, 1906; ARTURO HERNÁNDEZ, 1903; FRANCISCO IZQUIERDO
RÍOS, 1910; Vegas Seminario). We shall select only the most important. In the first place, there is CIRO ALEGRÍA (1909). His
sympathy for the outcast, the humble, the Indian, the worker,
flows generously. His prose is always powerful in the impetus it
gives to the mass of the novel. In *The Golden Serpent* (*La serpiente de oro*, 1935), *The Hungry Dogs* (*Los perros hambrientos*,
1939), *Broad and Alien Is the World* (*El mundo es ancho y
ajeno*, 1941), although nature and the masses are visible, artistically created characters also move through the novel. The title
of the novel is explained at the end of the book in a kind of Marxist discourse. It means that, for the poor, the world is wide, and
that is why the privileged class pushes them from side to side, but
the world is also alien because the poor never even receive a salary
sufficient to live on. It deals with the sufferings of a community of
Indians in the hills of Peru, more or less from 1910 to 1928. The
landowner, Alvaro Amenábar strips the Indians of their land, per-
secutes and destroys them. Mayor Rosendo dies in jail, beaten to
death. The rebel bandit, Fiero Vázquez, is beheaded. The social
insurrection of Benito Castro is smothered in blood beneath the
government guns. In order that there should remain no doubt as
to the inhuman conditions to which the Indian is subjected, the
novel takes us for a look at Peruvian geography: valley, mountain,
jungle, coast, even to the city of Lima, and shows us the labor in
the fields, in the mines, and on the rubber plantations. The main
line of action of the novel is simple but irregular: there are disconnected scenes, biographies of Indians, historical episodes,
stories, legends, songs. There is also a chapter (the twentieth) in
which are aired ideas on what social functions art, folklore, and
literature should serve in Peru: the Americans, Dreiser, Sinclair
Lewis, John Dos Passos, and Upton Sinclair appear as models in
the field of literature. And, naturally, the "dialectical materialism"
of Marx is included, taught to Benito Castro by Lorenzo Medina,
a director of the workers' syndicate. The population of an entire
town moves through the novel; yet no one character succeeds in
coming alive with all the force of art, although it can be seen that

Alegría made the attempt with the ancient mayor, Rosendo Maqui. He failed because of his excessive idealization. Interior monologs, soliloquies, flashbacks, and impressionist techniques put the action within the souls of the Indians, but in spite of everything, it is always the mass that is seen. The novel uses clap-trap from the nineteenth century, although there are also spatial-temporal cuttings characteristic of the twentieth. The structural innovations are timid: what dominates is the realist, explicative prose, which in moments of enthusiasm for the beauty of the landscape, or some of indigenous scene, succeeds in being more sentimental than lyrical. A novel of protest, without unity of tone, but readable and efficacious.

FRANCISCO VEGAS SEMINARIO (1903) is a novelist in the old style. He narrates without formal discipline, without any desire to experiment; he reads as easily as a nineteenth-century novel. Whether he is narrating episodes about the country (*Taita Yo veraqué*) or about the city (*Tableaus of the Deluded* [*El retablo de los ilusos*]), his realist program is obvious: he wants to illustrate social problems, and to do so he takes average people and stereotypes them. ROSA ARCINIEGA (1909) wrote, among other novels of exasperated political feeling, *Gears* (*Engranajes,* 1931). The title indicates that human lives are so many gears in the great wheel of labor. First, in the smelting ovens, then in the mines, warehouses, and factories, Arciniega shows the horrors of social injustice: hunger, sickness, prostitution. Arciniega believed that one of the new fields for the novel was "to allow oneself to be taken up by the great, collective conflicts," to present the masses, "the man—millions of men," "the case—millions of cases." But it is not a novel of political propaganda. Manuel, the protagonist-narrator, is a proletariatized bourgeois; and at the end, he wants to destroy the existing order with bombs, not in order to redeem the people, but in order to install nothingness. The novel takes place in Spain. The prose is simple, rapid, elliptic; but since she does not create individual characters nor singular situations, the novel is monotonous. In *Mosko-Strom* she continues her criticism of the machine in chaotic contemporary cities. FERNANDO ROMERO (1908)— *Twelve Jungle Novels* (*Doce novelas de la selva*), *Sea and Beach* (*Mar y playa*)—is a regional storyteller of a tragic vein. His last collection— *Rosarito Says Good-bye and Other Stories* (*Rosarito se despide y otros cuentos,* 1955)—contains a rare and hidden lode of relative good humor.

One of the most highly esteemed narrators is JOSÉ MARÍA ARGUEDAS (1913), author of stories and novels that deal with the Indian theme with sober but intense lyricism. He spent his first years in an Indian community and only later did he learn Spanish. Both languages are useful to him in his literary creation. He began with a collection of short stories: *Water* (*Agua*, 1935). In *Yawar Fiesta* he narrated on the strength with which certain cruel rites have impregnated the customs. *The Deep Rivers* (*Los ríos profundos*, 1959) is an autobiographical novel written in conventional style, with excessive ethnographic and linguistic explanations. Ernesto is the son of a wandering lawyer, always pursued by political enemies (these were the years of Leguía's dictatorship, dating from 1919). Running away from parents who mistreated him, he found protection in an Indian community until his father found him and took him with him for several years from town to town. The action of the novel begins when the father decides to put him into a religious school in the mountains. He is 14 years old (1925?). Now grown into manhood, he tells us about his school days. The separate episodes dissolve like images in a dream, sometimes through lack of artistry in the construction of the novel, sometimes because of an abundance of imagination; on these occasions the atmosphere becomes close and poetry flashes through it like lightning. Ernesto is not an Indian but his sympathy invariably takes the side of the Indians. Furthermore, it is to the Indians that he owes his animistic concept of life. The novel's greatest value lies precisely in this, its inscape of the nature of the Indian. Ernesto sees the Indians from within and expresses himself in the myths and metaphors of the Indian. There is no Indianist thesis or political message (although there is a lively awareness of the sufferings of the unappreciated and the injustice of the powerful). The tone is one of tenderness, sweetness and innocence even in the midst of a somber and at times repugnant reality. The book gains in quality as it passes from sketches of customs to the free elaboration of folklore traditions, to descriptions of the countryside and its people and to revelations of the interior life of the protagonist-narrator. The last part, the death of the idiot Marcelina, a generous meal for the sexual appetite of collegians, and the plague of lice which decimated the little village, is the most impressive. The novel ends when Ernesto chooses the savage but genuine life of the "deep rivers." In *The Sixth* (*El Sexto*), he describes the degradation of jail; but even there, Arguedas knows how to find moral values. Although he can and does describe violent climates with vigor, Arguedas becomes tender with his native landscape or with his brother Indians. There is definitely something positive in his vision of man, no matter how low the social squalor into which he sees him fallen. (*Everyone's Blood* (*Todas las sangres,* 1964).

(viii) *Bolivia* / FERNANDO DÍEZ DE MEDINA (1908) published *The Masked One and Other Inventions* (*La enmascarada y otras invenciones,* 1955), fantastic stories without much originality, in a prose more inflated than poetic; but in his best moments, the author frees himself from reality, either in the form of Aimará Indian traditions or by leaping off into absurd spheres using procedures from poetry and the movies. He is also a notable essayist. The war between Bolivia and Paraguay (1932–35) opened up a novelistic cycle. OSCAR CERRUTO (1907), in *Rain of Fire* (*Aluvión de fuego,* 1935), mixed the reality of the war with revolutionary political ideals and also with ideals of a literary phraseology. AUGUSTO CÉSPEDES (1904) collected disconnected tales on episodes of the war in *Mestizo Blood* (*Sangre de mestizos,* 1936); ten years later he wrote *Metal of the Devil* (*Metal del diablo*), a novel against the tin magnates. AUGUSTO GUZMÁN (1903) in *Prisoner of War* (*Prisionero de guerra*) gives us the memories of a soldier in two parts, the campaign and his capture. Another novel: *The Fertile Chasm* (*La sima fecunda*). Besides biographies of historical characters, he has written *The Living Christ* (*Cristo viviente*), showing personal religious feeling.

(ix) *Chile* / In this country, where the story and the novel have been generally in the realist vein and descriptive of the surroundings, one can note during these years a movement toward obscure, irrational, and subconscious themes. The highest—which is the same as saying the most poetic—example of this literary style is that of MARÍA LUISA BOMBAL (1910), author of *The Last Fog* (*La última niebla,* 1934) and *The Shrouded Woman* (*La amortajada,* 1941), where the human and the superhuman appear in a magic, poetic zone, by dint of vision rather than through tricks of style. The reader sees just what the characters of the novel see. Subjectivity. Things appear in a cloud of impressions. In the first of the mentioned novels, a woman loves in a zone between reality and dream. In the second, a dead woman sees, feels, and evokes the memories of her loves and her family life with a definitive certainty and total understanding which is now useless. Other women, although with not so much intensity, rejected the themes of Creolism and the mechanical reproduction of things. MATILDE PUIG, given to psychopathological revelations, aberrations, surrealism, and Kafkaisms. CHELA REYES (1904), also a poetess, erotic in *Nocturnal Wave* (*Ola nocturna*). *Copy Book Diary* (*Papelucho,* 1947) is by MARCELA PAZ (1904). It is supposed to be the private diary of a boy of eight, mischievous, bright and normal. It is charming. The author has a good understanding of child psychology (or at least of the psychology of the adult reader who wants to remember his own childhood) and is convincing because of her realistic attitude, with no extraordinary events, no sentimentality, no moralizing or preaching.

MAGDALENA PETIT (1900), imaginative in her manner of handling biography and history (cf. *The Pincheiras Family—Los Pincheiras,* 1939) and in her invention of purely novelistic situations (*Caleucha,* 1946; *A Man in the Universe—Un hombre en el universo,* 1951). MARÍA FLORA YÁÑEZ (1898)—who signed her first novels with the pseudonym "Mari Yan"— tended to spiritualize and even to make myths of certain aspects of reality. MARÍA CAROLINA GEEL (1913) was daring in her psychological penetrations, as in *The Sleeping World of Yenia* (*El mundo dormido de Yenia,* 1946) and *The Adolescent Perces Was Dreaming and Loving* (*Soñaba y amaba el adolescente Perces,* 1949). Some writers escaped from reality through the sea, adventure, dreams, science fiction, historical evocations, and stories for children. SALVADOR REYES (1899), for example, in *The Night Crews* (*Los tripulantes de la noche*), relates an adventure of love and contraband in a lyric tone; the poetic images are not very disturbing to the plot because the action is also poetically conceived. Although JUAN MARÍN (1900) is the author, among many other books, of a description of the painful existence on the *53rd Parallel, South* (*Paralelo 53° Sur*), he also has a fantastic dimension, as can be seen in his *Stories of Wind and Water* (*Cuentos de viento y agua*). HERNÁN DEL SOLAR (1901) with his stories for children; BENJAMÍN SUBERCASEAUX (1902), who wrote the slightly historical, slightly philosophical novel *Jemmy Button* (1950), and also the author of several books of short stories, some of them republished in *Child of the Rain and Other Stories* (*Niño de lluvia y otros relatos,* 1962); and LUIS ENRIQUE DÉLANO (1907), with *Port of Fire* (*Puerto de fuego*), complete this group of imaginative writers.

Creolism, such as we saw it in Latorre, degenerates a bit during these years, at least as a school. This Creolism, in filling the narrative with landscapes and documents, deprived the characters of freedom of movement; or, when it presented social problems, it simplified them with facile political formulas. Now it will be seen that the realist writers insist on representing our turbulent epoch in all of its shades. Man, struggling between nature and society, seems integrated into a total reality; and this totality is changing, menacing, confused. Of course, as understanding as these realists might be, for them, the connection between man and his environment is always more important than man himself.

In the Creolist direction, MARTA BRUNET (1901) is prominent. She has a powerful dramatic, and even tragic, vision; she is daring and one of her daring acts was to create good literature out of shocking material; she stylizes—as artists do—the material that in the hands of the naturalists remained shapeless. Her *Toward the Mountain* (*Montaña adentro,* 1923) was the masterful beginning of extensive narrative works on peasant themes.

In *María Nadie* (1957) and *Amasijo* (1962) Brunet abandoned the affirmative country environment to enter the city and analyze solitary souls psychologically (like the homosexual Julián in the last novel mentioned). DANIEL BELMAR (1906), in his best novel, *Coirón,* harmonizes an artistic evocation of the landscape, man, and his customs, with a just feeling for social problems. There are countless writers who originate from the people, observe social evils, and write to denounce these evils. They are so conscious of the collective social process, and so concerned with the consequences of industrial changes, that they generally propose political catchwords. In the preceding chapter, we saw that sociological realism, which recognizes the elder Lillo as its master, continued through Edwards Bello, González Vera, and Alberto Romero. In the period that we are now reviewing, this direction is confirmed by those whom we shall mention here. Let us say in advance that *Ranquil* by Lombay and *Blood and Hope* (*La sangre y la esperanza*) by Nicomedes Guzmán are among the novels that best illustrate neorealism. FRANCISCO COLOANE (1910) wrote about what he had observed and lived through in the southern regions of South America, on land and at sea. Although disorderly, his literature is truly estimable, in stories, from *Cape Horn* (*Cabo de Hornos,* 1941), to *Tierra del Fuego* (1956), as well as in the novel, from *The Last Cabin Boy of the "Baquedano"* (*El último grumete de "La Baquedano,"* 1941) to *The Track of the Whale* (*El camino de la ballena,* 1962). NICOMEDES GUZMÁN (1914–1964) made a novelistic study of a poor district in *Dark Men* (*Los hombres oscuros,* 1939) and of a family of laborers in *Blood and Hope* (*La sangre y la esperanza,* 1943). Pestilence, rape, death, human filth do not disgust him. He approaches ugliness burning with faith in the proletariat, with hope for the regeneration of the people; in his prose, naturalism is mixed with lyric metaphors, as in *Light Comes From the Sea* (*La luz viene del mar*). JUAN GODOY (1911) also concerns himself with the lower classes in *Gluttons* (*Angurrientos,* 1940). In his work, more than in the work of Guzmán, can be noted the stamp of a style common to many Hispanic-American novelists of these later years: naturalist and socialist material written with a poetic rhythm, seen with the eyes of many metaphors, glimpsed in visions pleasing to surrealism, moved by hidden resources which, at least in the time of Joyce and Aldous Huxley, were anti-conventional. ANDRÉS SABELLA (1912)—author of *The Great North* (*Norte Grande*)—braids together successfully a literature of protest against social injustice with a literature of lyric imagination: naturally, he ties little bows of allegory to that braid. Let us add to this paragraph a pedestal of names and titles: LAUTARO YANKAS (1902), *The Flame* (*La llama*); RUBÉN AZÓCAR (1901), *People on the Island* (*Gente en la isla*); EUGENIO GONZÁLEZ (1902), *Farther Out* (*Más afuera*); DIEGO MUÑOZ (1904), *Coal* (*Carbón*); JACOBO DANKE (1905), *The Red Star* (*La estrella roja*); GONZALO DRAGO (1906), *Purgatory* (*Purgatorio*); NICASIO TANGOL (1906), *Huipampa;* OSCAR CASTRO (1910–47), *Mine-Dust of Blood* (*Llampo de sangre*); LEONCIO GUERRERO (1910), *The Cove* (*La caleta*); REINALDO LOMBAY (1910), *Ranquil;* LUIS MERINO REYES (1912), *Bitter Bosom* (*Regazo amargo*).

(x) *Paraguay* / We have already said that the Chaco War (1932–35) provoked, in Bolivia, a narrative cycle. Paraguay did not produce novels and stories of high esthetic quality on this theme. ARNALDO VALDOVINOS

(1908), with more passion than art, wrote tales on the war with Bolivia in *Crosses of Quebracho Wood* (*Cruces de quebracho*, 1934); even more militant was his narrative *Beneath the Boots of a Blond Beast* (*Bajo las botas de una bestia rubia*, 1932). In this genre, JOSÉ S. VILLAREJO (1907) produced the best work: *Eight Men* (*Ocho hombres*), a novel of personal experiences, with good descriptions. He is a correct prosist and also writes stories: *Ojhóo the Sayoiby* (1935). Among the depicters of customs, the nativists, we could also mention EUDORO ACOSTA FLORES (1904), CARLOS ZUBIZARRETA (1903), JUAN F. BAZÁN (1900), RAUL MENDONÇA (1901), PASTOR URBIETA ROJAS (1905).

We close this paragraph with the best Paraguayan novelist of this period: GABRIEL CASACCIA (1907). He published stories— *The Well* (*El pozo*, 1947); *The Guahú*, 1938, and novels—*Men, Women and Marionettes* (*Hombres mujeres y fantoches*, 1930); *Mario Pereda*, 1939. In *The Driveler* (*La babosa*, 1952) he has made an inventory—since naturalism does not allow him to invent —of the drivel of gossip, moral corruption, physical misery, and the degradations of a little town near Asunción. The characters, who speak in Spanish and in Guaraní (with translations at the foot of the page), form part of a large, collective body. With this implacable, cruel denouncement of bad citizens, Paraguay made its first contribution to the continental novel and attracted the attention even of people of other languages. Another novel of criticism and protest: *The Ulcer* (*La llaga*, 1964).

(xi) *Uruguay* / FELISBERTO HERNÁNDEZ (1902–1963?), a concert pianist, was also praised for his short stories in *No One Was Lighting the Lamps* (*Nadie encendía las lámparas*, 1947). One of them, "The Balcony" (*"El balcón"*), in which the narrator is, precisely, a concert pianist, is a good example of his story-telling art. In a prose style that is deceptively simple and colloquial Hernández analyzes sensations until he turns them into metaphors; and through these metaphors, which are poetic and ingenious, he gradually disintegrates reality until he has it going like a somnambulist through corridors of madness. With a wry humor he turns the tapestry of the world over and points out the absurd texture of the other side; an example: *The Sunken House* (*La casa inundada*, 1960). GISELDA ZANI (1909), in her short stories *Through Subtle Bonds* (*Por vínculos sutiles*, 1958), criticizes highclass society but gives a free hand to her fancy.

One of the most vigorous writers of later years figures just as strongly in Uruguayan literature as in Argentinian literature: JUAN CARLOS ONETTI (1909). His novels were about enclosed lives: the confinement of the city (Montevideo, Buenos Aires), of enclosed spaces (rooms, cabarets, offices); if life comes out into the open air, the action is again enclosed by nightfall; circumstances enclose the characters with their stains of filth . . . These characters are solitary failures. They have been thrown out upon a hostile world, which from waste to waste precipitates itself toward death. There is nothing remaining for them but to encounter reality, torture themselves, or try to escape by drawing into themselves. The more they escape into the memories of a lost childhood, into their dreams, the deeper they are thrust into solitude. There is an air of pessimism, fatalism, demoralization. Ideals are moth-eaten; friendship is a misunderstanding; love is converted into sex. The similarity between some of Onetti's novels with others of Sartre has been noted. But he set out on the road to existentialism through reading Celine and the North American novelists, Dos Passos and, above all, Faulkner. The raw materials of his first novels open out into introspective meanderings in his later ones. In *Short Life* (*La vida breve*) even fantastic meanderings are revealed. They are novels made up of fragments, each fragment having an interior eye. Thus, the novelistic vision is multiple, simultaneous, or contradictory in various narrative stages and in various temporal stages. *The Well* (*El pozo*), *No Man's Land* (*Tierra de nadie*), *For Tonight* (*Para esta noche*), *Short Life, A Dream Realized and Other Stories* (*Un sueño realizado y otros cuentos*), *Good-byes* (*Los adioses*) all show Onetti to be a novelist of the senselessness of city life. *Short Life* (1950) seems to be written in a turbid, pasty prose: a paste of language with globs, mentally translated from foreign literature. The unctuousness and heaviness of these sentences contribute to the reader's sensation of being inside a nightmare. The novel *Short Life* is that nightmare, and the reader, lost among the crevices and rubbish, suddenly feels it incumbent upon himself to write the novel which Onetti did not want to write. As in all nightmares, this effort to give order to the disordered fails time and time again. The narrator—Brausen—lives several lives, and the story weaves them together. Brausen becomes Arce in order to possess another woman. Brausen fabricates a character Díaz Grey. A heavy atmosphere of sexuality, sadism, prostitution, perversion, crime, cancer, morphine addiction, madness, and ugliness sordidly disfigures things and men. These men, always seeking to put themselves into a horizontal position, in bed, seem to be reptiles. Nevertheless, there are lyric moments, in part because Onetti—using the literary procedures of the interior dialog and showing reality from different perspectives and spatial and temporal planes—is able to lay surprising intimacies bare. Peevishly written in a very Río de la Plata vernacular (as though he were saying to the reader: "If you understand me, fine; if not, tough: I'm not going to knock myself out for you.") his *Short Life* is a curious case of ill-used talent and theme. His creative imagination—capable of originality—is weakened through neglect and through the lack of discipline. Now it appears that his best novel is *The Shipyard* (*El astillero,* 1961).

JUSTINO ZAVALA MUNIZ (1898), bombastic in his theatrical plays—*The Cross on the Highways* (*La cruz de los caminos*)—showed more vigor in the novelized chronicle: *Chronicle of Muniz* (*Crónica de Muniz*), *Chronicle of a Crime* (*Crónica de un crimen*), *Chronicle of the Window Grille* (*Crónica de la reja*). FRANCISCO ESPÍNOLA (1901) in *Shadows over the Land* (*Sombras sobre la tierra,* 1933), a novel about low social classes, created exceptional characters or, rather, characters exceptionally well-conceived, characters shaken by violent bursts of passion and described with dramatic vision (Espínola's dramatic instinct led him to experiment with the theater in *The Flight in the Mirror* [*La fuga en el espejo,* 1937]). He was a distinguished short-story writer, careful, conscious of his craft. In *Short Stories* (*Cuentos,* 1961) he collected all that he had published since 1926 (seventeen): not many, certainly, but their quality is extraordinary. The scene is usually rural, the anecdotes convincingly real, the themes tied up with death. However, Espínola's imagination works from within reality as known, and because he lays bare the temperaments of his characters or reduces their lives to dynamic structures, he raises his narrative material to a level of art. JUAN JOSÉ MOROSOLI (1899–1957), who began with two books of verse, proved that his real talent lay in the short story. Even his novel *Boys* (*Muchachos*) is merely a series of disconnected episodes. Beginning with *The Bricklayers* (*Los albañiles de "Los Tapes,"* 1936), especially, Morosoli captured the lives of people of the field, more superficially than from within. His characters are usually people of little spirit immersed in ordinary situations. He gives us more chronicles than inventions, in fact, more chronicles than beauty. Other realist narrators: SANTIAGO DOSETTI, ELISEO SALVADOR PORTA (1912), and VÍCTOR DOTTI, Author of *The Wire Makers* (*Los alambradores*); and ALFREDO GRAVINA (1913), who seems to be the most important one in this group, and whose novels reflect his social, political and even partisan opinions. On purpose we have left the greatest of them all for last:

ENRIQUE AMORIM (1900–1960), a Uruguayan who also belongs to Argentine literature. He was a novelist of fields and cities, although he gained his greatest success with a series of rural novels. After *Tangarupá* and *The Cart* (*La carreta*), he attained a good reputation with *Countryman Aguilar* (*Paisano Aguilar,* 1934). The theme of this novel is simple. Aguilar, brought up in the country and educated in the city, returns to the country, as the owner of a small ranch. He feels insecure, frustrated in the face of the enticements of the two different kinds of life that he knows so well, until little by little he gives in to the inertia of the surroundings, vegetating in the end, like a gaucho. This simple theme, however, is fragmented into disconnected episodes. A novel, then, without a solid structure; neither are the inner workings of Aguilar clearly illuminated. The best part of the novel is the sharp observations scattered through it. Many of these observations are formulated in metaphors that belong to the literary family of "vanguardism." However, in Amorim these new metaphors, even the most audaciously expressionist, enter into the narrative naturally, without a change in tone of voice, without disturbing the storyline. Amorim is an intelligent observer, moderate but concerned about the lack of spiritual orientation of his time: this is the theme of *The Uneven Age* (*La edad despareja,* 1939). In *The Horse and Its Shadow* (*El caballo y su sombra,* 1941) the action goes at a gallop, as though it were following the "splendid golden sorrel" that comes, with its biological potency, to enrich Azara's ranch. Azara is a landholder of the old style, a cattleman, not a farmer, who tries to impede the progress of agriculture. By prohibiting the people's crossing his fields, he causes the death of a child. The father of the child, an Italian, fights with Azara and stabs him to death. The Italian, who in *Martín Fierro* never fought, here, stands face to face with the Creole and defends himself. In *The Moon Was Made From Water* (*La luna se hizo con agua,* 1944), the author regards the rural area from the perspective of today's city. In *Victory Does Not Come By Itself* (*La victoria no viene sola,* 1952)—notice that the title is taken from a statement by Stalin—Amorim attempts to write a political novel. Social injustice suggests an abstract problem to Amorim; and this is why his characters are also excessively abstract. His crude novel, *Open Corral* (*Corral abierto,* 1956) has value as a document: juvenile delinquency in the filthy, corruptive districts. Indefatigably, Amorim constructs his tower of novels, from which he observes the social structure of South America. None of them is excellent; all are impaired by the clumsiness and the speed with which he wrote and composed them. His last novel was *The Outlet* (*La desembocadura,* 1958), an economic history of Uruguay as reflected in the saga of a family. The narrator hears it from the ghostly lips of his dead great-grandfather while he is gazing at his tomb at the mouth of a stream. It is a hastily contrived novel with a faulty perspective written in a prose without distinction.

(xii) *Argentina* / We have already seen in the preceding chapters (and shall continue to see in the chapters to come) that non-realist prose was more vigorously cultivated in this country than in any other Hispanic-American country.

JORGE LUIS BORGES (Argentina, 1899). As we explained before, Borges is one of the major writers of our time and, if we place him here and not among the poets or essayists, it is precisely because his stories, combining as they do the essences of his lyricism and his intelligence, give us the key to his entire work. Borges had lived in Switzerland (also in Spain) during the war years: he returned to Buenos Aires in 1921. He contributed to the high jinks of *Prisma, Proa,* and *Martín Fierro.* But during his stay in Geneva, he had become acquainted with German expressionism, which struck him as being much more serious and renovating than the frivolous esthetics of the avant-garde which were being voiced and practiced in the Hispanic world. His literary knowledge was amazing, his lucidity, even more so. Over the years this knowledge and this lucidity have become so enriched that we are more troubled than amazed at the spectacle of a new kind of madness. He began with two rites: the funeral of "Ruben Darianism" and the baptism of "ultraism"—childish things. When he became more mature and decided to bury even ultraism, he did not wish to have recourse to any other rite: he simply let it fall into a pit, covered it with the best literature he was capable of—he was the most capable writer of his entire generation—and cultivated an orchard of strange fruit on the site. When he spoke, in 1932, of the "dead ultraist whose ghost continues to haunt me," we were not sure exactly when it had died. We do know that he repented having written "arid poems of the sect, of the ultraist mistake." His first formula had been this: "the reduction of lyricism to its primordial element: the metaphor." Fortunately he did not follow it in his books of poems *Fervor of Buenos Aires* (*Fervor de Buenos Aires,* 1923), *The Moon Across the Street* (*Luna de enfrente,* 1925), *San Martín Notebook* (*Cuaderno San Martín,* 1929): books of poems which were selected, retouched, and gathered together with "other compositions" in his volume *Poetic Works* (*Obra poética:* see the second edition enlarged—1923–1958—in *Complete Works,* 1964). Metaphors, yes, stacks of them; and each one with "its unedited vision of some fragment of life," to put it in the words of the ultraist Borges. But these metaphors were neither primordial nor reductive of the lyricism of Borges. There was something else. Like all lyricists, Borges sang to and of himself. And he chose the traditional genre for lyricism, which is verse. But it was soon seen that, although he sang to himself, Borges did not stick to the old themes: love, death, pain, solitude, nature, happiness, the past of his own country, the reality of his own city; rather, he included in his range of themes preoccupations more appropriate to metaphysics: time, the meaning of the universe, the personality of man. One could see that Borges was singing to himself and thinking at the same time. An intellectual lyricism, then. Even those poems which were humbly Creole in theme were reinforced with an inner framework of universal philosophy. He said it in *Fervor of Buenos Aires:* his lyric was "made of spiritual adventures." From this book of poems comes *"El truco"* [a card game] that contains the idea—a favorite one with Borges—that all men are but a single man. In Borges, metaphysics and lyricism are one and the same thing. Dissatisfied with the limits which tradition imposed on verse, Borges sought himself in the essay and later in the short story. The same breath of lyricism blew across all these genres. His richly inquisitive essays and, above all, his stories assure him of the highest of places in contemporary literature. Essays he had written from the time he was very young: *Inquiries (Inquisiciones,* 1925), *The Size of My Hope (El tamaño de mi esperanza,* 1926), *The Language of the Argentinians (El idioma de los argentinos,* 1928), *Evaristo Carriego* (1930), *Discussion (Discusión,* 1932), *History of Eternity (Historia de la eternidad,* 1936), *Other Inquiries (Otras inquisiciones,* 1952), and so on. But his work as a short story writer—to which he owes his definitive glory—was late, timid and experimental. They were at first merely narrative sketches, almost essays. In *Universal History of Infamy (Historia universal de la infamia,* 1935) he borrowed and even translated the stories of others, although there was at least one original story, the admirable "Man on the Pink Corner." Little by little he affirmed himself in the mastery of the new genre, and soon he amazed everyone with the stupendous stories in *The Garden of Bifurcated Paths (El jardín de senderos que se bifurcan,* 1941), *Fictions (Ficciones,* 1944) and *El Aleph* (1949). The edition of his "complete works" adds some new stories. Others are found in *The Maker (El Hacedor,* 1960) and in *Personal Anthology (Antología Personal,* 1961). Reading the works of Borges in order, one can see how his style is decanted: from a baroque aggressiveness, sarcastic and disorderly, to a terse simplicity in which intelligence and admiration are as direct as light. In his later years, losing his sight, he had to dictate, and his stories are penetrated more and more by the framework of oral language. Borges' theory of literature has progressed through various stages. First, an ostentatious period: the cult of the metaphor for the metaphor's sake. Later, a playful period: expression by transforming concept into image or image into concept. And, lastly, a reflexive period: limiting himself to allusion or mere mention, as if the writer were trying to say something but not saying it ("this imminence of a revelation which does not appear"—states Borges now—"is perhaps the essence of esthetics"). If esthetic value were like economic value, which grows with scarcity and diminishes with abundance, it would be a simple thing to explain the exceedingly high artistic merit of Borges. What he gives us is rare. In fact, if we glance at narrative all over the world from 1918 to 1949—the date *El Aleph* was published—we can verify the rarity of Borges' work. His originality could be studied in his moody metaphysical cavils, in his poetic intuitions, and in his logical rigor.

Borges, at heart, is a skeptic, but the keen critic should be wary of placing him in all the forms of skepticism which are recorded in the history of culture. There are skeptical positions which are definitely alien to Borges. Not being a scholar of philosophy, but rather a hedonistic reader, Borges sometimes uses terms that do not correspond to his essential skepticism. He does not contradict himself, but the reader is often left confused by Borges' verbal complications. For Borges, the essence of truth does not lie in the relation between thought and the object, but rather in the agreement of thought with itself. Sometimes he adopts epistemological idealism and, even its most extreme form, solipsism. Berkeley, Hume, Kant, Schopenhauer, Croce, and all the idealists in general are his favorite philosophers—which is not to say, however, that he identifies himself with any of them. What interests Borges is the beauty of theories and myths, beliefs that he really disbelieves. It is "an esthetics of the intellect," to say it in his own terms.

Borges belongs to that lodge of writers who have always disbelieved in the established, universal order, and remained at the mercy of the elements. The world is for him an absurd chaos. But his vision of that chaos is diaphanously communicated. He is not a surrealist trafficking in the bird-droppings of the subconscious, but an expressionist who re-creates reality with the energy of a consciousness illuminated by all the lights of reason. Neither is he an existentialist: he does not feel himself hurled into life once and for all, committed to realize one sole project from a given circumstance, but rather he is free to choose—within his mind, which for him is the absolute—a multiplicity of simultaneous paths. Instead of crying out his anguish, like the existentialists, Borges prefers to reason out his suspicions. His greatest suspicion is that the world is a chaos: and that within this chaos man is lost as though in a labyrinth. Except that man, in his turn, is capable of constructing his own labyrinths. Mental labyrinths made of hypotheses that seek to explain the mystery of that other labyrinth, the one in which we are wandering, lost. Each mind fabricates its own reality and tries to give it meaning. There are thinkers who propose simple hypotheses: God, matter, and so forth. Borges prefers to complicate his. He is a radical skeptic but he believes in the beauty of all theories; he collects them, and on stretching them to their farthest inferences, he reduces them to the absurd. The dogmatists, who believe that their personal metaphysical ideas, or their myths, are universally true, tend to be annoyed at the agility with which Borges leaps from one hypothesis to another. The agnostic outlook of Borges is expressed in a good-humored dialectics. He encloses the reader in a linguistic labyrinth and plays with him until he defeats him. In his esthetic fruition, nevertheless, overtones of anguish can be distinguished, an anguish which springs from his knowledge that he is unique, solitary, raving, lost, and perplexed inside of a blind being. Aware of his originality, Borges renounced popularity. He created a literature that ignores the common reader. Not through vanity, but through discipline. Discipline in the selection of the theme and even in the choice of words; discipline in the structure of the story; discipline in his dialog with the reader. If he writes something on so popular a theme as the detective story, he takes it to such a high plane that it reaches a rarefied atmosphere where the reader cannot breathe. A game which delights the intellectual but which humiliates the ingenuous realist. The stories of Borges demand a great deal of knowledge: a knowledge of culture (because of their allusions to the history of literature), a knowledge of philosophy (because of their allusions to ultimate problems), and a knowledge of the work of Borges himself (because of their allusions to this or that page of his works). Let us pause a moment on this requirement: that of having to have a knowledge of the complete work of Borges in order to understand one of his stories. In his stories the same themes constantly reappear: the universe as a chaotic labyrinth, the infinite, the eternal return, the transmigration of souls, the obliteration of the I, the biography of one man coinciding with the history of all men, the changes which unreal ideas impose on real things, pantheism, solipsism, liberty, and destiny.

His stories are all connected to each other, and all, in turn, to his essays. For example, the essays, "The Total Library" (*"La biblioteca total"*) becomes the story "The Library of Babel" (*"La biblioteca de Babel"*). From his essays we could extract explanations to put as footnotes in his stories, and from his stories, illustrations to clarify his essays. One story is placed within another. The same outline is repeated or inverted. Here, he merely sketches what there he completes. He attacks a theme from two different perspectives; thus the stories are complementary. The precision of Borges manifests itself in the structure of each narrative, in which each piece is knowledgeably accommodated to the others. He challenges the reader to an intellectual competition, and if it is he who always wins, it is because he does not allow himself to be distracted even for a moment. Part of the perfection of the framework of a short story is the stylistic perfection of each sentence. He startles us by using just the right word. Whoever proposed to do so could point out the constellation of writers to which Borges belongs. Ideas, situations, denouements, the art of deceiving the reader, yes, all these have the same family traits: Chesterton, Kafka, and ten more. But Borges, in this constellation, is a star of first magnitude. He has written stories that do not have a match in our literature: "Tlön, Uqbar, Orbis Tertius," "Funes, the Man with the Prodigious Memory," "Death and the Compass," "The Secret Miracle," "The Dead Man," "The Aleph," "The Circular Ruins," "The Library of Babel." No one would take the sophisms of Borges seriously; but his malicious dialectics fertilize his stories, which no one could help but take seriously. Borges' is a powerful mind. A powerful lyricism of the intimate beauty which he discovers in Argentine life, in the houses, patios, and streets of Buenos Aires, in historical incidents, in wanderings through the suburb, in the pampa that is still present in the city, in the rose-colored general store, or in a vestibule. A powerful imagination which lives each impression of its senses until it is prolonged into a fabulous and allegorical plot. A powerful intelligence which comes and goes without getting lost, through the maze of sophistry. A powerful metaphysics which triumphs over the problems of chaos, mind, and time. A powerful gift for words which our language had not seen since the Baroque writers of the seventeenth century. A powerful moral sense, capricious when viewed from a distance, but always sincere, daring, and consistent if we watch Borges' behavior as a writer. A powerful intellectual knowledge, which is hedonist, because Borges reads only what gives him pleasure and enriches him, without yielding to the reputations established by the handbooks of literary history, yet as strict and serious as that of any scholar.

Before we raise the curtain on the live tableau of Argentine narrators of this period we remind the reader of what we said about the generation that, born around 1910, began to publish after 1930. Here, however, we shall not follow a system of genres, but rather one of esthetics. We will occupy ourselves first with writers of inner lives and moods. A five-pointed star: Villarino, Lange, Sofovich, Gándara, and Levinson. María de Villarino (1905) wandered up an *Out of the Way Street* (*Calle apartada*) (verses written in 1930), and came out in a *Town in the Mist* (*Pueblo en la niebla*) (stories written in 1943), followed by *A Rose Should Never Die* (*La rosa no debe morir,* 1950). Norah Lange (1906) turned up another street: *The Street of Afternoon* (*La calle de la tarde*), her first book published in 1924. She was one of the ultraist poets of the *Martín Fierro* group. Modes of expression from her poetry reappeared years later in her prose—evocations of childhood, literary memories—even in novels and quasinovels, such as *People in the Living Room* (*Personas en la sala,* 1950), in which an adolescent author-protagonist magically projects her own phantom and feminine personages; in *Two Portraits* (*Los dos retratos*) the atmosphere is dusty with poetry, as though Lange were declaring her love for ordinary things at the instant in which they fall into dust. Luisa Sofovich (1912), in the novel *The Bouquet* (*El ramo,* 1943) and in her *Deer Stories* (*Historias de ciervos,* 1945) is one of those who renovated from within (from the retina, from the skeleton of the sentence) the forms of the story. In Carmen Gándara (1905?) psychological explorations go beyond the natural and touch an almost metaphysical depth, from which a vapor of mystery rises and envelops and obscures the narrative action: *The Place of the Devil* (*El lugar del diablo,* 1948); a novel—*The Mirrors* (*Los espejos,* 1951). Luisa Mercedes Levinson (1912?) has recently published a novel, *In Me—A Concert in E Flat* (*Concierto en mí,* 1956), which is an intense soliloquy, and short stories, *Pale Rose in Soho* (*La Pálida Rosa de Soho,* 1959). One of these stories, "The Haven," is a jewel in which the light is violently polarized. Three introspective narrators: Bianco, Sábato, and Mujica Láinez. Jose Bianco (1911), already esteemed for his stories *The Small Gyaros* (*La pequeña Gyaros*), gained even more esteem with *The Rats* (*Las ratas,* 1943). In this psychological novel (in the sense in which the novels of Henry James can be called "psychological") a soul advances by degrees toward the poisoning of Julio Heredia. What is worthwhile is the complex personality of the protagonist-narrator: no less worthwhile, nevertheless, is the complex action and the premeditation of each step, up to the final surprise. Ernesto Sábato (1911) went from science to literature, and within literature, from the essay to the novel, but he always remained more of an intellectual than an artist. In *The Tunnel* (*El túnel,* 1948) the protagonist, Castel, announces that he has committed a crime of passion and proceeds to tell about it. His confession is interesting, not because of the crime, but because each word is a symbol of the progress of his madness, and his madness is the symbol of a desperate metaphysics. The madness of Castel is rational, at times, intellectual: at bottom it is that he can no longer communicate with the world, not even with his beloved, María (who is, incidentally, the first heroine of an Hispanic-American novel to read *Sartre*). He is like a man lost in a tunnel: at times the walls of the tunnel become transparent and he can see the movement of other lives, but it is his solitude, his inability to communicate, which is the anguish of the confession of the painter, Castel. The world is seen through the eyes of an unattached "I," almost pure subjectivity, incapable of communicating with its surroundings. The style is also fast-moving, unpleasant, temperamental and unbalanced. His novel *On Heroes and Tombs* (*Sobre héroes y tumbas,* 1961) is more ambitious. The primitive, intelligent and tormented Sábato seeks his own identity and with awkward movements of his searchlight imparts a striking flicker of light and shadow over Argentine actuality.

MANUEL MUJICA LAINEZ (1910)—in *The Idols* (*Los ídolos*), *The House* (*La casa*), *The Travelers* (*Los viajeros,* 1955)—has novelized with the nostalgia, irony and elegance of Marcel Proust, the search for a lost golden age, that age of wealthy people, in an oligarchic Argentina. Not only does he create an impressionist and metaphoric style, but in the second of the mentioned novels, he reaches the point of creating the image that is the house itself, speaking in the first person, that narrates its history. His latest novels: *Bomarzo, The Unicorn* (*El unicornio*).

Unfortunately, we must now draw back from the window—although a parade of the following narrators is coming down the street: MANUEL KIRSCHBAUM (1905), author of *The Exasperated Diversions* (*Las diversiones exasperadas*), ALEJANDRO DENIS-KRAUSE (1912), MARIO A. LANCELOTTI (1909), LUIS MARÍA ALBAMONTE (1912), HÉCTOR RENÉ LAFLEUR —in order to converse with one of the most important novelists of these years: Mallea.

Existentialism, or at least that anguished meditation which we associate with the existentialism of Kierkegaard—meditation on the human creature, concrete, singular, tormented by the sense of his responsibility—inspired stories and novels. It was neither idealist nor realist literature; its originality lay precisely in the fact that it refused to separate consciousness from the exterior world. It was interested in seeing human life as mobile existence, not as static essence. Oriented in this direction, our America contributed a great novelist: EDUARDO MALLEA (Argentina, 1903). He began playfully with *Stories for a Desperate Englishwoman* (*Cuentos para una inglesa desesperada,* 1926), but after ten years of silence, he reappeared with a tremendous seriousness. *European Nocturne* (*Nocturno europeo,* 1934) was a confession in the third person; in this person—Adrián—Mallea commenced to go deep into his anguished conception of life. In *The History of an Argentine Passion* (*Historia de una pasión argentina,* 1935) he revealed his anguish in its Argentine setting. An autobiographical book, vibrant, heated, with curses for the fraudulent and tenderness for the nation's profound voices. A "visible" Argentina of evil people; and an "invisible" Argentina of good ones. (The Argentina of the values in which the liberal upper bourgeois believed—was this Argentina invisible for Mallea in 1935?)

In *The City Beside the Immobile River* (*La ciudad junto al río inmóvil,* 1936) Mallea attempted to describe the secret of Buenos Aires: characters conscious of their solitude and desperation, with their moral roots in the air. After *Fiesta in November* (*Fiesta en noviembre,* 1938) Mallea, who until that time had expressed himself in monologs, began to construct his novels with dialogs in counterpoint, with multiple personages, each with his own perspective. But in all of the novels that followed, beginning with *The Bay of Silence* (*La bahía de silencio,* 1940), the characters and their attitudes toward life, as varied as they may be, are always inhabited by Mallea who, from each created soul, continues to probe into what it means to be a man, to be a woman, in a living Argentinian situation. Ágata Cruz, the protagonist of *All Greenery Will Perish* (*Todo verdor perecerá,* 1941), is a good example of how Mallea creates his characters. What happens in the novel is less interesting than what is happening inside of Ágata. Ágata, motherless, in a little town in the south of the province of Buenos, Ingeniero White, grows up at the side of an odd person— a Swiss doctor, an insatiable reader of the Bible—marries a man she does not love: the taciturn Nicanor Cruz, who is beaten year after year in his agricultural battle against nature. Each failure separates them more. In the distance, hate begins to grow. When he is ill with pneumonia, she, in order to end everything, opens the doors and windows of the house to the cold wind. But only he dies. Ágata survives. She goes to Bahía Blanca; she feels the necessity of leaving her doldrums, of knowing a man, of loving.

In an atmosphere of frivolity and luxury—in Bahía Blanca—she falls in love with a lawyer, Sotero. They become lovers for several weeks. Then Sotero goes to Buenos Aires. She falls once more into solitude. She returns to her home town, Ingeniero White, growing more insane day by day. She ends by going completely mad and perhaps committing suicide. But, contrary to what this clumsy resumé leads one to believe, Ágata's solitude, which is described in the novel, is not a solitude determined by circumstances; rather, it is the solitude of human existence or, if you wish, that of the personal, unique existence of Ágata. Mallea will describe the flow of that existence; and even more, he will describe its stream of consciousness. In order to do so, he disconnects the novel into two temporal planes: the present action, which takes place within the space of little more than a year, and the evoked action, thanks to which we are familiar with the life of Ágata from the time of her earliest memories. The action, the present as well as the evoked action, follows a successive line in the order of the calendar and of the clock. Mallea, the omniscient author, intervenes between the character and the reader. Not only does he gather together the interior monologs of Ágata, but he also explains and even judges them.

In *The Eagles* (*Las águilas,* 1943) Román Ricarte returns, a failure, to what remains of his ranch, and with his memories—plus flashbacks that Mallea adds—the novel of three generations of rich Argentinians (from 1853 until the present) takes shape. The protagonist is Román, an indecisive, weak person with a noble but unhinged soul. The entire novel appears to be made up of the weaknesses of Román, victim of the social ambitions of his wife and children. Mallea is a shy narrator. Each time he comes to a point in the narrative where it would be propitious to accelerate the action, he veers off into long psychological disquisitions, or more or less philosophical reflections. His style is also evasive, indirect; and although in these digressions he succeeds in creating a few good passages, in general his sentences are clouded. His tone of preoccupation, of sadness, and, at times, of grief over the conditions in which the Argentinians live, is the same which dominates his other novels.

The Enemies of the Soul (*Los enemigos del alma,* 1950) is an attempt to comprehend several lives in provincial Bahía Blanca, especially the lives of the Guillén brothers—lives led astray by motives of opportunism, sensuality and resentment. In spite of its theological title and of the fact that the M for Mario might stand for M for *Mundo* (the world), C for Cora for C for *Carne* (the flesh) and D for Débora for D for *Demonio* (the devil), this novel is not allegorical, but psychological. At any rate, in the psychological analysis of the characters a certain philosophical purpose can be distinguished. Mario and Cora, a worldling and a voluptuary, choose evil freely. Débora, a demoniac, hates them both and in the end sets fire to the house and burns to death there, because her own nature is essentially negative and she is condemned to non-existence, to non-being. The trouble is that none of these characters has been strongly created—nor have any of the others, including the Ortigosa couple, Sara, Ida, the student. They appear more as projections of life than real lives, partly because Mallea delineates them from the outside but does not let them reveal themselves directly in the action or in the dialog. The reader grows increasingly dissatisfied as he goes along, because of chapters that are not constructed like chapters in a novel. An episode is interrupted at a culminating point; when we begin to be interested in one kind of life there is a jump and we find ourselves standing before another human phenomenon. We are asked to believe that someone is an ingenious conversationalist, but we don't hear him speak or, if he does speak, he does not turn out to be ingenious. Only a few scenes are completely described, among them the one in which Consuelo saves herself from adultery and the one in which Debora falls into her flaming inferno. The prose is no common prose, either in its syntax or its vocabulary, but its deviation from normal speech is lost in a zone of glimmering shadows.

Chaves (1953) is a short story more than a novel because of the unique situation it offers us: Chaves, whom suffering—failures, the deaths of his wife and children—has refined spiritually, giving him a distinguished superiority, works as a laborer in a sawmill where he is surrounded by the hostility and hatred of his fellow workers who mistake his silence for proud disdain. Only at the end of the story, in the last line, do we hear a single word from Chaves: when he is asked "Aren't you ever going to say anything?" He answers, "No." Pain has eaten up all his words. The narrative, in which Mallea has installed himself inside of Chaves (indirect discourse) is a braid of two threads of action: the present action from the time Chaves arrives and asks for a job, and the underlying, evoked action from his adolescence to the death of his wife.

Simbad (1957) is a novel about Fernando Fe, a playwright. It is also the drama that Fernando is writing—identification of the playwright's life with that of his hero: "it was as if life, having impeded that work, had condemned him to live it." There are two temporal planes. The first relates the days of Fernando's solitude after his separation from Magda; this portion, from the twenty-eighth to the thirty-first of December, 1952, is written in italics and is divided into fragments, each one of which will head one of the five parts of the novel. The second temporal plane is the actual body of the novel—composed of flashbacks with which Fernando, during these secluded days, reconstructs his past— from the time he was twelve way back in 1914 to the moment that Magda returns and his confidence that he can finish his "Simbad" is reborn. In the last pages, both temporal planes are mingled. The three main themes—the promiscuous amorous life with both Magda, who needs protection, and Lea, who inspires him; the endeavor to dignify with a classical repertoire the Argentine theater; and a description of the process of dramatic creation—are woven together chronologically. Mallea places himself within the novel in the figure of Gustavo Villa, character and witness. In *Simbad,* we find some of Mallea's most beautiful pages. Yet, judging it as a novel, it is not nearly as convincing as *All Greenery Will Perish,* probably because the dissonance between Fernando's moral tone and his double adultery is not compensated for by a concrete analysis of the artist's psychology. The narrative method, much too vague and abstract, robs Fernando Fe of his authenticity.

Those subversive to the real order of things we have left for last. We have already mentioned the poets who, in abandoning verse for prose, continued to disfigure reality so that the figures of their free imaginations could be better seen. From among those not mentioned, let us bring forth SILVINA OCAMPO (1905?). She has alternated books of verse with books of short stories. Her verses—collected in *Small Anthology* (*Pequeña antología,* 1954)—are desolate, but without the rhetoric of desolation; made up of bright memories, but without our being able to tell whether they have been lived in a dream or while awake. She relates and sings at the same time in poems that frequently project her personal feelings into situations experienced by others, and thus she turns an objective reality into a subjective one. In fact, she tells fantastic tales in *Forgotten Voyage* (*Viaje olvidado,* 1937), in which the lyricism, at times metaphysical in origin, is moving because of its naked presence, although the author tends to be a little careless in her narrative composition. In *The Fury and Other Stories* (*La furia y otros cuentos,* 1959) Silvina Ocampo has chosen to tell about cruel situations. She seems to have taken them from reality which she has either lived through or observed. However, we see them as though distorted by thick lenses. MANUEL PEYROU (Argentina, 1902) cultivated the short story in the manner of Borges, although he did not need Borges in order to read Chesterton. His stories from *The Sleeping Sword* (*La espada dormida,* 1944) charm the reader, opening caves in reality, full of ingenious characters, enfolding these characters in situations whose secret the author retains until the end. *The Thunder of Roses* (*El estruendo de las rosas,* 1948) is a detective story (in which the order of discovery is given) although it begins as a police story (in which the order of criminal events is given). In fact, we see a man assassinated; only it turns out that this man is the double of another, who was already assassinated the day before. The uninterrupted and exciting accumulation of events demonstrates very quickly that Peyrou, unlike Chesterton, is not interested in the philosophy nor in the psychological motives of his characters, but in the game. A chess game in which each move on one side of the board is counterarrested by one from the other side. His stories from *The Repeated Night* (*La noche repetida,* 1953) also play at being literature, although they are more successful as a game than as literature. In *The Rules of the Game* (*Las leyes del juego,* 1959) a man kills another in self-defense. Afterwards, he learns that the woman who caused this misfortune is unworthy of him. Prompted by a feeling of remorse on one hand and a bit of vengeance on the other, he decides to confess the crime to the police. The accent of the novel, thus, is placed on the criminal's psychology and Peyrou analyzes it with sympathy, but without idealization. The major artistic merit, however, is in the composition. Just as the rules of the game of life plot the destiny of the characters, so the rules of the narrative game plot the novel. Two rules, two games, two plots: on the one hand, circumstances which become tangled and complicated by the irrational impulses of the protagonist; on the other hand, episodes which are ordered and simplified by the logical plan of the author. In this logical plan upon which the novel's plot is constructed, we can see a reflection of Peyrou's interest in detective stories. The action is linear and is recounted in realistic prose, rapid in its characterizations and in its dialogs. Buenos Aires is seen as a diorama with its streets, restaurants, cafés, movie houses, etc.; and above all we are given a documentation of the moral prostration of Perón's Buenos Aires. The bitter and indignant tone, the irony and sarcasm with which Peyrou criticizes the immorality of the Peronist regime is tempered by his love of Buenos Aires and by his recognition of at least one Argentine virtue: the cult of friendship. *The Tree of Judas* (*El árbol de Judás,* 1961); five stories of intrigue, crime or mystery that either take place in Buenos Aires or have characters from Buenos Aires. They are related by a boy born at the beginning of this century, who in turn heard them from his godfather; the atmosphere, therefore, is redolent with history. The strategies in the art of narration recall those of Chesterton; there are surprises, deceptions, subtle psychological moves, cases of mistaken identity, concealments, and revelations. Except that in Peyrou these tricks do not appear artificial or gratuitous because they fit in normally with Argentine society, which is more arbitrary and less legalistic than London society.

It was in Argentina that fantastic literature appeared more conspicuously than anywhere else, with its preference for lyric and sophisticated play of imagination. The fantasies of Borges and Silvina Ocampo responded to a new enthusiasm, an enthusiasm for a difficult, anti-realist, analytic literary art, which proposed problems in order to then solve them according to set laws. The great reputation of Borges has led to the belief that he had a direct influence on this group; nevertheless, the influences which Borges himself received from French, English, and German literature are the same which acted directly upon the others. By the side of Jorge Luis Borges, it is necessary to put his friend and collaborator, ADOLFO BIOY CASARES (1914). He was an admirable inventor of fabulous worlds constructed in accordance with strict laws. In his novel *Morel's Invention* (*La invención de Morel,* 1940), he tells us of an apparatus which captures the appearances of reality and then, with a projector, reproduces that reality in space and time. But in narrative literature, absolute originality is impossible: Horacio Quiroga in "The Vampire" and Clemente Palma in *XYZ* had already spoken of similar apparatuses. In France its antecedent is *The Future Eve* by Villiers de L'isle Adam. *Plan of Evasion* (*Plan de evasión,* 1945) was the twin of his previous novel: the same implicit philosophy—absolute idealism— the same setting—an island—the same conception and the same art of giving verisimilitude to the absurd. The stories in *The Celestial Plot* (*La trama celeste,* 1948) are so intellectual that the ideas in it do not even take the precaution of disguising themselves. The same thing could be said of the stories collected in *Prodigious History* (*Historia prodigiosa,* 1956). Here we notice that his fantasy ironically accentuates the psychological factors rather than the magic ones. The farther Bioy Casares moves from the short story toward the novel the better he dissimulates his distaste for construction.

In *The Dream of Heroes* (*El sueño de los héroes,* 1954) a magic adventure is embroidered on a realist framework. Guana, a worker in a mechanic shop, and some undesirable friends celebrate the festivities of the 1927 carnival over a period of three days and three nights. Gauna, drunk, will scarcely remember a few disconnected scenes of that dark adventure. He seems to remember, for example, fighting, knife in hand, with a tough of the old school. Three years later, when carnival time comes, Gauna decides to go over the same route with the same companions to see if he can capture the meaning of the adventure. Suddenly, as though a miracle had occurred, the years 1927 and 1930 converge, and what in 1927 had been a mirage in Time—the fight with a knife—now comes to pass: Gauna dies in a knife fight. The force of destiny? Bioy insinuates that it is rather the evil spell of a demiurge or blind god that the wizard Taboada—a friend of Gauna—was able to break the spell in 1927, but which in 1930, when the wizard has already died, must be fulfilled. In a sordid atmosphere, the voyage of Gauna through the districts of Buenos Aires flashes fantastically like that of Jason and the Argonauts: these are the heroes that Gauna has dreamed of. The novel proceeds on two levels, like a mischievous child who walks with one foot on the curbstone and the other in the street. The style is as careless as that of a friendly chat, but with smiles and ironic winks. He wrote, together with Borges, *Six Problems for Don Isidro Parodi* (*Seis problemas para Don Isidro Parodi,* 1941), under the pseudonym of Bustos Domecq. Parodi is a prisoner who, from his cell, solves the crimes that are brought before him with the deductive procedures of the classical criminal detective. They are ingenious stories, notable for their parody of detective-type stories and above all for their satire of Argentine types and situations, told in a language that imitates the commonplaces and affectations of the intellectuals and pseudo-intellectuals. In collaboration with his wife, Silvina Ocampo, he wrote a "whodunit," *Those Who Love, Hate* (*Los que aman, odian,* 1946), without distinction within the genre, other than a biting humor: all of the investigators fail, only the narrator's hypothesis is correct and is confirmed by the written confession of the criminal, a neurotic child. It can be seen that this type of analytic, chess-game literature has nothing to do with the science fiction, the mysteries, or the detective stories which, in the United States, are directed to the mass public. Borges, Peyrou, Bioy Casares, and others write for readers with alert minds, informed on metaphysics, with an enthusiasm for analysis, disciplined in the rules of a refined game. These writers are familiar with all literature, especially the Anglo-Saxon literatures; but if they were to be translated into English, they would not be popular among the masses. We have almost forgotten another Argentinian writer of this group. In *Vigil* (*Vigilia,* 1934), the provincial city appears poetic as seen by the eyes of an artistic and ironic adolescent. In *Fugue* (*Fuga,* 1953)—a musical fugue, a real fugue—a light love adventure dissolves in sensations of "false recognition," "eternal return," and "interior unfolding." Both novels were re-edited, revised, and amplified in 1963. The lyric and magical stories in *The Proofs of Chaos* (*Las pruebas de caos,* 1946) were added to a new score of stories, also fantastic (or, if they have realistic themes, they assume a ludicrous form), and all of them together appear under the title of *The Book of Magic* (*El Grimorio,* 1961). *The Cheshire Cat* (*El gato de Cheshire,* 1965) is a collection of very short tales, improbable but possible in a universe as free as that of the imagination. This writer has compressed himself into a thin line of expression. His narratives are like those Chinese feet, tortured into tiny shoes which take their art from their very torture. But although there is always pain in them for the author, there is not always beauty in them for the reader. Like Velazquez in *Las Meninas,* this writer has painted a historical portrait of his generation and left a blank space on the canvas where he paints his own

portrait with brushes in hand. It is like his signature, and the name is
ENRIQUE ANDERSON IMBERT (1910).

Let us go now to the realist narratives that helped to point out
the social peculiarities of a prosperous and democratic country,
without Indians or Negroes, populated by European nationalities,
of a fundamentally agricultural and cattle-growing economy, but
with powerful industrial centers. Although its reality was cleaner
and more pleasing than that of other countries, many of its novelists sought its more harrowing aspects. The novels that proposed
a documentation of nature or society as well as those that went
deep into the motivations of its characters and into their moral and
political reactions, prided themselves on their veracity more than
on their art. And if these novels did not comprehend the whole
truth, there is no doubt that in their observations they were sufficiently direct to be of service to scholars. They are useful to geography and ethnography, since they describe the life of all the regions of the country.

Buenos Aires had always been the center of literary activity, and from its
streets the following gathered their novelistic materials: JULIO FINGERIT
(1901), ISIDORO SAGÜÉS, JOAQUÍN GÓMEZ BAS (1907), MARCOS VICTORIA
(1902), ENRIQUE GONZÁLEZ TUÑÓN (1901–1943), ARTURO CERRETANI
(1907), and ROGER PLA (1912). Writers also emerged from the inner corners
of the country: from the islands of the Delta (ERNESTO L. CASTRO), from
Patagonia (LOBODÓN GARRA, 1902; ENRIQUE CAMPOS MENÉNDEZ, 1914).
From the shores and jungles of the Chaco (RAÚL LARRA; ALFREDO VARELA);
from the pampas (ARISTÓBULO ECHEGARAY, 1904); from the provincial
towns and cities JUAN MANUEL VILLARREAL, 1905; ABELARDO ARIAS, 1908;
ANTONIO STOLL, 1902; WALTER G. WEYLAND, 1914). At times it was a
case of the same author changing his locale. These novels are useful as history and sociology also, because they describe the successive moral breakdowns that were weakening the national fiber. And finally, they are useful
to political science because they put into action traditionalist, liberal, fascist,
anarchist, and communist ideologies and platforms. Among the many
narrators, whom should we single out?

Above all, ROBERTO ARLT (1900–1942). He was the one
with the greatest amount of originality, who continued the work
begun by the "Boedo Group": Alvaro Yunque, Roberto Mariani,
Elías Castelnuovo, Lorenzo Stanchina. He was considered the
little Dostoevski of the family. Neurotic, irritable, disenchanted,
he appeared with *The Furious Plaything* (*El juguete rabioso*,

1927) in the years when the masses were beginning to take over the country. From this tumultuous life in which he was spectator and actor he took his novels. He attracted attention with *The Seven Madmen* (*Los siete locos,* 1929), wherein he created the personality of Erdosain, and its continuation, *The Flamethrowers* (*Los lanzallamas,* 1931). They were followed by *Love, the Sorcerer* (*El amor brujo,* 1932), the chronicles and stories of *Etchings of Buenos Aires* (*Aguafuertes porteñas,* 1933) and *The Little Hunchback* (*El jorobadito,* 1933). His theater is also interesting: *Africa, 300 Million* (*300 milliones*), *The Desert Island* (*La isla desierta*). For Arlt "human beings are monsters waddling in the shadows," overwhelmed, lost, failures in the murkiest spots of a vulgar city. He created exasperated characters as a pretext for airing his own hate and protests in the face of a Buenos Aires which he regarded as one huge brothel. He was the novelist of the frustrated hopes of the Argentinian middle class during the historic pathfinding days of 1930. But he was no mere chronicler of social events. He was a tortured person, and he tortured the reality of his novels. He believed in evil, and his imagination elevated a world of panderers, perverts, and prostitutes to art. They seem to have been dreamed rather than seen. Dreamed with resentment, with bad words, in a nightmare from which Arlt suffers. These scrapings of humanity eat themselves up and at the same time are the termites of the world in which they live. Arlt's endeavor, unfortunately, had serious artistic failings. He wrote badly, he composed poorly. In *The Seven Madmen* (*Los siete locos*), for example, it is impossible to tell who is doing the narrating. At times it is the omniscient author, at times it is a chronicler who comments on the oral and written confessions of Erdosain, at times it is Erdosain himself; until what happens is that the narrative is broken up, with notes at the bottom of the page and references to a second part which will some day be written. This disintegrated novelistic eye also appears to belong to one of the madmen in the novel. The prose is torpid and at times unreadable. But because of the nervous power of his rough temperament, his paroxysmic rebellion, and his daring scenes, Arlt was popular and, far from being forgotten, he has gained new readers. He has thus reaped benefits from the faulty lenses of young critics. Because after his death Argentina fell into ignominy and the depravations that he had painted in clandestine corners of the city were seen by light of day; because all over the world the novel was coming apart at the seams, torn with multiple points of view and delirious interior monologs; and because of neo-naturalist and existentialist reflux brought in after the war themes of hatred, violence, sex, crime, sickness and cynicism, it was thought that Arlt had been a prophet. There were plenty of disgruntled critics who praised him just to depreciate more cultured writers. Nevertheless, Arlt did not represent the masses; he was an individualist who considered them grotesque. He offered no revolutionary way out, only an unconfined masochism.

LEONIDAS BARLETTA (1902) is another of those who form the "Boedo Group." His debut as a writer with *Royal Circus* (*Royal Circo*) was as mediocre as the things which he was describing, but in *The City of a Man* (*La ciudad de un hombre*) he successfully created a good realist novel. He wrote his stories and novels in a slow, popular, simple, unpretentious prose, which was nevertheless powerful because it was the vehicle of his love for the most humble lives. More humanity than literature, more nobility of spirit than esthetics, but in spite of his unprepossessing theme—people of the poor districts, without refinement, huddled in depressing little houses—Barletta is capable of converting poverty into poetry. Although he is afflicted by the grief of his characters (the consequences of social injustice) and by their loneliness (the consequence of a lack of solidarity between men) his mood is not pessimistic. He believes that man is fundamentally good, and he assumes that a proletariat revolution (Russia, which gave him his literary models, also provides his political direction) would assure complete human dignity. Meanwhile, he describes in a gray tone the contrasts of black and white that he sees in his photographic negatives. Others among the biographers of human misery: LORENZO STANCHINA (1900), author of *The Bedeviled* (*Endemoniados*) and *The Eccentrics* (*Excéntricos*), in the caves of the city. MAX DICKMANN (1902) has a more imaginative realist technique. His selection of detail forms part of his interpretation of social life and his understanding of his characters. The novels—*Mother America* (*Madre América*), *People* (*Gente*), *Bitter Fruit* (*Frutos amargos*), *This Lost Generation* (*Esta generación perdida*), *The Mutiny of the Deluded* (*El motín de los delusos*), *The Inhabitants of Night* (*Los habitantes de la noche*), *The Ragged Ones* (*Los atrapados,* 1962) have a complex and dynamic structure. JUAN GOYANARTE (1900), the vigorous novelist of the struggle of man against nature in *Argentine Lake* (*Lago argentino*), is also a novelist of the moral horrors of the city of Buenos Aires in *Carnival Monday* (*Lunes de carnaval*) and *Three Women* (*Tres mujeres*). An agile, sparkling narrator with a deep sense of humanity: LUIS GUDIÑO KRAMER

(1898), author of *Fond Solitude* (*Aquerenciada soledad*), *Foreign Land* (*Tierra ajena*), *Horses* (*Caballos*). FERNANDO GILARDI (1902) is a careful prosist who in *Silvano Corujo* captured the spirit of the old suburb. AUGUSTO MARIO DELFINO (1906–1961) narrates from within himself situations, things come from the city, but he absorbs them into psychological material. *Márgara Who Came from the Rain* (*Mágara que venía de la lluvia*), *End of the Century* (*Fin de siglo*), *Stories of Christmas Eve* (*Cuentos de Noche Buena*) and *In Order to Forget the War* (*Para olvidarse de la guerra*) have a rhythm of interior time. The realist writers who lived between the two revolutions, the oligarchic fascist revolution of 1930 and the popular fascist revolution of 1945, with the spectacle of the second world war before them, were completing, with broad brush strokes, the mural of Argentina. BERNARDO VERBITSKY (1907) describes the customs of the city with a preference for adolescent characters and always concerned with the social situation: from *It Is Difficult to Begin to Live* (*Es difícil empezar a vivir*, 1941) to *Misery Village Is Also America* (*Villa Miseria también es América*, 1957) and in the novels that followed he has redeemed for art a real Argentine section of humanity that escaped many of his contemporaries. One humorist, at least, in all this group: FLORENCIO ESCARDÓ (1908), with an elaborate, intellectualized humor, very personal in its content and form: *Oh, New Ohs* (*Nuevos Oh*), *Things of Argentina* (*Cosas de argentinos*). Others: MARGARITA BUNGE (1913), SILVIA GUERRICO (1909).

2. Essay

Thanks to the achievements of André Maurois, Stefan Zweig, Emil Ludwig, and others, the novelized biography came into vogue in Hispanic-America, as did essays of the historical or sociological type. Prominent along these lines was LUIS ALBERTO SÁNCHEZ (Peru, 1900), author of *Don Manuel* (1930) and *La Perricholi* (1936). MARIANO PICÓN-SALAS (Venezuela, 1901) appeared with Uslar Pietri in the vanguardist group shortly after the first world war. Like Uslar Pietri, he was a narrator: *Night Dealings* (*Los tratos de la noche*), his novel, was written in 1955. But his narratives, which are very intellectual, occupy a minor spot within his vast work as an historian, critic, and essayist. His cultural histories are excellent, for instance, *From the Conquest to the Independence* (*De la conquista a la independencia*, 1944). He has also cultivated the novelized biography: *Peter Claver, the Saint of the Slaves* (*Pedro Claver, el santo de los esclavos*, 1950). His collections of essays reveal one of the most alert intellects of the continent. GERMÁN ARCINIEGAS (Colombia, 1900) is an agile and brilliant essayist, with points of view which are always unforeseen. He tried to write a novel, *Halfway Along the Road of Life* (*En medio del camino de la vida,* 1949), but it is obvious that he only feels comfortable when he takes the floor and gives opinions. A journalist with a tremendous grasp of things, his opinions usually appear in the form of short articles. Later, he gathers them together, and in this manner he puts out collections of miscellaneous essays, such as the admirable *The Student of the Round Table* (*El estudiante de la mesa redonda,* 1932), *America, Terra Firma* (*América, tierra firme,* 1937), and *In the Land of Skyscrapers and Carrots* (*En el país del rascacielos y las zanahorias,* 1945). At other times, his pages follow a central theme and are organized into unified books, such as *The Commoners* (*Los comuneros,* 1938), *The Germans in the Conquest of America* (*Los alemanes en la conquista de América,* 1941), *This American People* (*Este pueblo de América,* 1945), *Biography of the Caribbean* (*Biografía del Caribe,* 1945). Whatever the exterior form of his writings, Arciniegas' work reveals a profound unity: that of a lucid, original mind, preoccupied with this America of ours. With a sympathy for the Indian and for the lower classes, with a lively sensitivity for the historic past and for its heroic figures, with a militant faith in the good purposes of democracy, culture, and progress, he has been progressively writing a versatile encyclopedia of America. In Arciniegas, knowledge is not mere erudition: it is combined with a vision, rich in good humor, in lyricism, and in meaningful anecdotes.

One of the favorite essay topics is the clarification of the essences of each national reality: within this class, the following stand out: the Mexicans DANIEL COSÍO VILLEGAS (1900), FERNANDO BENÍTEZ (1912), also a novelist of note, and LEOPOLDO ZEA (1912); the Cubans JORGE MAÑACH (1898–1961), JUAN MARINELLO (1898), FRANCISCO ICHASO (1900–1963), RAÚL ROA (1909), and JOSÉ ANTONIO PORTUONDO (1911); the Puerto Ricans ANTONIO S. PEDREIRA (1899–1939) and TOMÁS BLANCO (1900); the Venezuelans HUMBERTO TEJERA (1901?) and EDUARDO ARROYO LAMEDA (1902); the Colombian JORGE ZALAMEA (1905), (important also in poetry, the theater, and fiction); the Ecuadorians BENJAMIN CARRION (1898) and LEOPOLDO BENITES (1909); the Peruvian HÉCTOR VELARDE (1898), whose humorous essays are as lively as narratives; Bolivians, after the fall of the liberal regime in 1920 and later grieved by the Chaco war (1932–35), sought the essence of Bolivia's historic personality in the telluric (the nationalists ROBERTO PRUDENCIO, FERNÁN DÍEZ DE MEDINA,

HUMBERTO PALZA, FEDERICO ÁVILA), in Indian lore (the militant ethnographers CARLOS MEDINACELI, 1899–1949, JESÚS LARA) and in economic aspects (the Marxists JOSÉ ANTONIO ARZE, RICARDO ANAYA and ARTURO URQUIDI); the Argentinians CARLOS ALBERTO ERRO (1903), JOSÉ LUIS LANUZA (1903), DARDO CÚNEO (1914), ROMUALDO BRUGHETTI (1913)—who, in *Prometheus (Prometeo, 1956)* made this mythical person speak in such a manner that his autobiography is converted into the history of liberty.

There are notable essayists, critics, and students of literature. Mexico: JOSÉ LUIS MARTÍNEZ (1918). Puerto Rico: CONCHA MELÉNDEZ (1904), NILITA VIENTÓS GASTÓN (1908), MARGOT ARCE DE VÁZQUEZ (1904). Venezuela: JOAQUÍN GABALDÓN MÁRQUEZ (1906), PEDRO PABLO BARNOLA (1908). Chile: RICARDO LATCHAM (1903–1965). Argentina: LUIS EMILIO SOTO (1902), RAIMUNDO LIDA (1908), MARÍA ROSA LIDA DE MALKIEL (1910–1962), ANÍBAL SÁNCHEZ REULET (1910), JULIO CAILLET-BOIS (1910), ANA MARÍA BARRENECHEA (1913?), MARÍA HORTENSIA LACAU, RAÚL H. CASTAGNINO (1914). In philosophy, GUILLERMO FRANCOVICH (Bolivia, 1901) with his theory of autonomous, universal and absolute values.

C. THEATER

The theater of these later years lives from the professionals who seek economic success, from the authors who, with nobility and dedication, give themselves entirely to experimenting with new forms in small halls before reduced audiences, and from the outstanding novelists or poets who, on writing comedies and melodramas, are apt to lend dignity occasionally to the field of dramatic literature. There were autonomous theatrical movements, particularly in Argentina and Mexico.

(i) *Mexico:* These were years of maturation for the existing realism and for experimentation with European and United States techniques. History and the Mexican political revolution fed the theatrical renovation which JUAN BUSTILLO ORO (1904) and MAURICIO MAGDALENO (1906) undertook together in the Teatro de Ahora [Present-Day Theater] group. Being antiindividualistic, one might expect this problematic type of theater to be of scant psychological value. This is not so, however. Magdaleno, who in his novels of social protest showed himself to be a good observer of human conflict and very capable of creating his characters from it, brought psychological insight to his *Mexican Revolutionary Theater (Teatro Revolucionario Mexicano): Pánuco 137, Emiliano Zapata, Tropic (Trópico).* But it is undeniable that his purpose is socio-political, and not that of delving into the soul or creating theatrical contrivances. The same could be said of *Shark (Tiburón), Those Who Return (Los que vuelven)* and *A Lesson For Husbands (Una lección para maridos)* by Bustillo Oro.

Of all of the Mexican authors, the most professional, the most often translated, is RODOLFO USIGLI (1905). Plays about customs, social and political satires, psychological and historical dramas reveal Usigli's scenic mastery and also his intellectual restlessness. The action of *The Child and the Mist* (*El niño y la niebla*, 1936) is weakly interlaced with certain episodes of Mexican political life: the assassination of Venustiano Carranza and the designation of De la Huerta as president in 1920. Unfortunately, the technique of the drama itself antedates its historical reality: Usigli has recourse to the spent procedures and themes of the nineteenth century (hereditary madness, the armed sleepwalker . . .). In *The Impersonator* (*El gesticulador*, 1937), "a piece for demagogues," using a situation that Pirandello would have treated as a farce (he dealt with a similar one in *Enrico IV*), Usigli wrote a melodrama, that is, drama in which the improbable intervention of chance is more important than character traits. César Rubio, a professor of history, passes for César Rubio, a general of the Mexican revolution who has been assassinated many years before. At first, it is merely an impersonation entered into to get money and to avoid poverty; but later, it becomes a patriotic identification with revolutionary ideals. Ironically, Professor César Rubio dies at the hands of the same person who had assassinated General César Rubio. This tidy duplication of destinies is part of a complicated set of forms that Usigli has described in his *Itinerary of the Dramatic Author* (*Itinerario del autor dramático*): the dramatic action is divided into three acts, with unity of action, place and, if not time, perfect symmetry in the time intervals; the exposition, the climax and the denouement are worked out in ascending and descending curves, with synchronized rhythms at their critical and culminating points, with alternating family and political scenes, with successive variants in the discussion on what is truth, using symbols and a counterpoint of "theatrical effects" and "symbols." A well-constructed drama, undoubtedly, whose value would depend on the interpretation we would give it; it is either a "Mexican case" of social hypocrisy (which is what the author prefers) or it is a universal case showing the boundary between truth and falsehood in the human conscience. If it is the latter, *The Impersonator* can modestly assume a place in the theater of doubt, with roots in epistemology. The figure of Miguel, for example, uttering his last line, "the truth!" changes in accordance with which of the two criteria we adopt. Usigli did himself harm when he publicly acknowledged his admiration for Bernard Shaw. One can see this admiration in *The Family Dines at Home* (*La familia cena en casa*, 1942), but the comparison of Usigli with Shaw is cruel. Usigli begins his career at the point where Shaw ended his: pure dialog, without construction. Furthermore, Usigli lacks a philosophy—at least, an original philosophy—a capacity for dialectic, and even a sense of humor. On the other hand, he has too much of what Shaw had no appreciation for: sentimentalism. *The Family Dines at Home*, although it takes place in Mexico, contains little that is Mexican. If he presents a problem, it is that of mixing different social classes at cocktail parties: an aristocracy of the rich, the diplomats, and the old families; the *nouveau riche*, and the lower social level of prizefighters, bullfighters, and cabaret dancers. The problem, in Mexico, presents itself in a different manner. Neither is the central plot convincing, because Usigli is careless with detail and fails to make it believable. *Crown of Shadow* (*Corona de sombra*, 1943) is one of his most ambitious works. It is an anti-historical work, he says, with an historical theme: the tragic trajectory of the lives of Maximilian and Carlota. It is not, in truth, anti-historical. In any case, we could call it defectively historical. Usigli at times uses known events as a point of departure or interprets them in a manner which would be of little satisfaction to an historian. His work would indeed be anti-historical if he had shown irreverence for historical truth, or if he had resorted to anachronisms in order to illuminate his theme with the light of a personal philosophy. But Usigli has written scenes using effects from historical melodrama and dialogs in which the sentences follow the conventional lines of an historical melodrama. The most anti-historical feature of his work lies in the fact that his characters speak in an altogether too solemn manner, as though they had read a treatise on the Empire of Maximilian written by Rodolfo Usigli. It is a shame, because the scenic conception of *Crown of*

Shadow—the title alludes to the madness that sat upon the brow of Carlota for sixty years—calls for a more novel, original, and brilliant treatment. The action is well multiplied into planes of times: it occurs in 1927, the date of the death of Carlota, and agile flashbacks evoke scenes from the Empire of Maximilian. The thought, however, was not as felicitously complicated into dialectic planes. His latest work is *Crown of Light* (*Corona de luz,* 1965).

CELESTINO GOROSTIZA (1904) began by writing about subtle psychological and intellectual conflicts, but later turned to dramatizing Mexican social life. One of his more celebrated works is *The Color of Our Skin* (*El color de nuestra piel,* 1952). His technique is that of the old realism: a mimetic scenography, flat, dry dialogs, exaggerated sensationalism, character-rationalizations, with their store of reflections and theses. The theme also appears to be a realist theme: the color of the skin of the mestizo seen as a social problem. It is a problem—rather, a pseudo-problem—because it produces an inferiority complex in those whose skin is dark, and a sense of pride in those who are fair-skinned; it is a problem because, according to Manuel, who is the rationalizer of the work, Mexico feels insecure, and by disdaining the Indian, it falls into a stupid admiration of the foreigner, who could not care less about the growth of the nation. A simple thesis, an affirmation of the mestizo base of Mexican nationality. It is likewise defended in a simple manner. There is nothing ingenious, brilliant, paradoxical, or surprising in the point of view. It is the type of thought expected from any well-meaning person. Moreover, what is surprising is that Gorostiza, who shows evidence of such good sense, should not have realized that his theme, although a true one, is altogether obvious. It is especially obvious in Mexico. EDMUNDO BÁEZ (1914), in his play *A Pin in the Eyes* (*Un alfiler en los ojos,* 1950), dramatized with only a few symbols—one of them is the bird whose eyes were pierced with pins so that it would sing better—the forbidden passions of love and hate: the love for one's brother-in-law and hatred for one's mother, passions which lead Quintila to suicide. Neither the plot, nor the characters, nor the dialog is sufficiently convincing. Other playwrights: FEDERICO S. INCLÁN (1910), MARÍA LUISA OCAMPO (1907), MIGUEL N. LIRA (1905), MAGDALENA MONDRAGÓN (1913), and RICARDO PARADA LEÓN (1902).

(ii) *Central America:* The Guatemalan MANUEL GALICH (1912) and the Costa Rican MANUEL G. ESCALANTE DURÁN (1905) stand out.

(iii) *Antilles:* In Cuba, JOSÉ MONTES LÓPEZ (1901), PACO ALFONSO (1906), JUAN DOMÍNGUEZ ARBELO (1909). In Puerto Rico, EMILIO S. BELAVAL (1903) and MANUEL MÉNDEZ BALLESTER (1909).

(iv) *Venezuela:* CÉSAR RENGIFO (1905) is the most fertile, significant, and successful author in his public presentations. Another: LUIS COLMENAREZ DÍAZ (1902).

(v) *Colombia:* RAFAEL GUIZADO (1913).

(vi) *Peru:* JUAN RÍOS (1914), who is the poet of social emotion, brings classic themes to today's world: *Don Quixote, Medea,* etc.; JOSÉ CHIOINO (1900).

(vii) *Bolivia:* JOAQUÍN GANTIER (1900).

(viii) *Chile:* DINKA DE VILLAROEL (1909).

(ix) *Uruguay:* JUAN CARLOS PATRÓN.

(x) *Argentina:* Among the better professional writers in the theater are ENRIQUE GUASTAVINO (1898) and ROBERTO A. TÁLICE (1902). There were authors who were prominent in independent theaters, like AURELIO FERRETTI, a writer of farces. Others who contributed valuable works to the theater were not professionals, but came from the fields of poetry, the novel, or other literary activities.

Let us single one out. CONRADO NALÉ ROXLO (1898). We will study him here as a playwright, but he is above all a poet, and before referring to his theater we should mention his poetry. *The Cricket* (*El grillo,* 1923) has youthful grace, lyric mischief, freshness, innocent gamboling: "My eclogic and simple heart / awakened as a cricket this morning." This Nalé Roxlo is still charmed by Lugones, his literary father, and Darío, his literary uncle. As he grew, he lost his resemblance to his father and uncle. Instead, he preserved his similarity to his literary grandfather, Heine: lyric tenderness and pungent humor. In *Clear Vigil* (*Claro desvelo,* 1937) the mood is more grave, reflexive, melancholy, and even bitter. Surrealism lends him something from its dark cupboard. This man, who just yesterday had told us that his heart "awakened as a cricket," now tells us: "I do not know who I am, nor do I know why I exist." He tells us that he is "pointlessly writing vain words." In *From Another Sky* (*De otro cielo*) the poet, already mature, continues to grow, producing ever sadder fruit. The three books that we have already mentioned seem to be a single book; and, in fact, the first of them was perfect, and the other two only added to that perfection. Nalé, so serious in his poetry, has left us a series of humorous books: he signs them "Chamico." What interests us here is his theater. In *The Mermaid's Tail* (*La cola de la sirena,* 1941), Nalé plays up and down his entire keyboard: the lyric and the humorous. As a lyricist, from the joy of living to bitter disillusionment: as a humorist, from the joke to subtlety. A siren, in love with Patricio (the theme of a story from Andersen), throws herself into the fishermen's nets and allows herself to be caught after Patricio comes to believe in her. She is so in love that she wants to be a woman and allows herself to be operated upon to become a woman. But Patricio loves what was wondrous in her, not what was human. Now Alga—so the siren is named—can no longer sing nor swim. Patricio falls in love with another woman—an aviatrix—because she seems to him to be a marvelous bird. Alga, understanding that she has lost the battle, throws herself into the sea, where she will be punished. At bottom, the theme is the impossibility of love, or, at least, the impossibility of man's loving. Men fall in love with their dreams; when these dreams become real, they become mutilated, and are pushed aside with displeasure. A Difficult Widow (Una viuda difícil, 1944) is a "farce" because the accumulation of so many abnormal situations is improbable, but upon this base, Nalé has constructed a fine comedy about colonial Buenos Aires shortly before the Revolution of 1810. In the drama Cristina's Pact (El pacto de Cristina, 1945) the theme appears elemental: Cristina, in love with a crusader who is leaving on a mission to reconquer the Holy Sepulcher, makes a pact with the Devil in order to gain the crusader's love; Cristina and Gerardo marry, but when she realizes that the price she must pay to the devil is the son who will be conceived on her very wedding night, she commits suicide, a virgin still. Nalé Roxlo wanders among themes, situations, and traditional characters; nevertheless, he does not allow himself to fall into common pitfalls. His paradoxical wit surprises us just at the moment when we were beginning to recognize an old medieval scene. That the love of Cristina, human rather than divine, should be so pure that the devil should not want to buy her soul is a new touch; that the miracle of the fallen beech tree should appear to Gerardo to have come from God, and to Cristina, from the devil, is another; that the pact should have been useless, since Gerardo loved Cristina anyway and the intervention of the devil was superfluous, is an able variation on folklore; that the devil hoped Cristina would give birth to the antichrist is an unusual theological conundrum. Thus could we continue to enumerate the lively intelligence, the lyrical innovation, with which Nalé Roxlo composed the details of his drama. A beautifully worked gem. The last plays of Nalé are *Judith and the Roses* (*Judith y las rosas*), *El neblí* (1957) and *Reencounter* (*El reencuentro*). JUAN OSCAR PONFERRADA (1908) used folklore materials for his melodrama, *The Devil's Carnival* (*El carnaval del diablo*, 1943). It begins well: the Carnival (Pucclay) and Fate (Chiqui) exchange costumes and, so disguised, they transpose the destinies of people, and the feast ends in tragedy. (Many years ago María Selva had given herself to a peon. The daughter born to her, Isabel, is now a woman and she falls in love with the Foreigner, who turns out to be her own father.)

XIV. 1940-1955

Authors born between 1915 and 1930

Historical framework: The second world war ends with the victory of the liberal nations, but in Hispanic-America some totalitarian dictatorships continue. They do not fall until the end of this period. The "cold war" between the United States and Russia forces new political alignments. In general, under the dictatorships as well as under the democratic regimes—which alternate in successive revolutions—the new phenomenon seems to be an evolution toward planned economies.

Cultural tendencies: Surrealism. Existentialism. Neo-naturalism. Committed literatures and gratuitous literatures, with neo-naturalist and existentialist styles predominating on one hand and classically inspired styles on the other.

General Characterization

Those who were born after 1915 had to become writers in the midst of horrors. The second world war had a different effect on them than the first world war had had on the ultraists. Those of the 1914 postwar period showed up as acrobats and clowns. They made fun of literature. They wanted to dehumanize it. They cultivated the absurd. They despoiled verse of all rules and regulations. Later they repented and tried to justify their nihilism. They discovered that at the bottom of their defiance of all literary conventions there was a pathetic sentiment: nothing less than the unhappiness of the world. The youths born after 1915 did not experience this early stage of frivolity; they appeared on the scene pathetically. They even made a great fuss about the acrobatic contortions of their elder brothers. Poetry, no matter how obscure it may be, now aspires to deliver a message. Earlier poetry had been absurd; now, without ceasing to be absurd, it proposed to demonstrate that existence itself is absurd. An almost tragic accent was heard in the new literature. The young people were preoccupied with moral problems because when they had first opened their eyes they had seen human values discarded.

Surrealism, which the ultraists had reached only after becoming serious, was the point of departure for these young writers. The fact is that the embers of surrealism had just burst into flame again in France and everywhere. But this surrealism now was combined with existentialist philosophies. In the Spanish language we had our own existentialism, Unamuno's Antonio Machado's, and Ortega y Gasset's. But it was Heidegger, Sartre, *et al.* who colored the thinking of the youth. Style strove to be "essentially lyric," it strove to express "the truth of being." In addition, there were stylizations of popular elements (like those of García Lorca in the preceding generation). Between personalism and popularism surged neo-romantic and neo-naturalist tendencies. They wrote "gratuitous literature" and "committed literature," with spiritualisms and materialisms, with the beautiful and the ugly, with hopeless anguish and revolutionary ire. Babel years. Has not literary life always been this way? Indeed it has. The historian knows very well that in putting his ear to each epoch, he will hear the confused Babel of literary languages. Nevertheless, the years to be reviewed here have been more Babel-like than ever. Literature was now becoming complicated by new phenomena. The greatest demographic density in the republic of letters—never have so many persons written so much in our America as now—provided an example for every taste. It was as though an earthquake had unearthed all the geological strata and had juxtaposed them. Without perspective, we do not know which is the topmost. Furthermore, the culture of the world has been restructured with violent changes in national prestige, with a multiplicity of creative centers having conflicting values among themselves. The techniques of communication each day offer a complete universal panorama. Literature no longer depends on Paris, not even on

London, New York, Madrid, Moscow, or Rome: it is planetary. The result is that in every minor literary circle there is a microcosm where everything is found. Nor is it even possible to exclude "badly written" literature, because to write badly—to indulge in the cult of the ugly, the "what-do-I-care" shrug, the open sewer emitting filth—does give expression to the desperate spirit of our times. In the three directions of contemporary literature—a literature committed to non-literary realities, a literature directed from outside of literature, and a literature regulated by purely literary laws—all stylistic attitudes are struck.

A. MAINLY POETRY

Introduction

The poets who make their appearance during these years, in general, have a melancholy, elegiac, serious, pessimistic, introspective tone. These could be called neo-romantics, provided we quickly add that their favorite poets were not romantics, but surrealists like Neruda, symbolists like Rilke, concentrated poets like T. S. Eliot, fabulists like Saint-John Perse and, if they looked to the past, it was to admire the Spanish poets of the Renaissance. These influences, in themselves contradictory, are even more complex if we observe them more closely. Surrealism, for example, in some is transformed into a kind of existentialism; in others, because of the social and political views of Neruda and Vallejo, it is transformed into a more or less lyrical communism; in still others, into a Catholicism which, because of its cult of tradition, leads to a cult of one's country.

Respectful of the innovations of vanguardism, they preferred to follow them in earnest. Hence, they admired Neruda, who did not play with literature—the Neruda of the last period, from *Third Residence* on, the Neruda who affirmed the existence of real things, who did not propose or intend to create them. It is a return to reality, but not directly, rather through the suburbs of metaphysics. The result is that many of those who claimed they were affirming human, national, and vital elements became lost

on the road and never reached reality. Instead of creationist metaphors, they stated the things themselves: they believed that this
was "founding poetry ontologically," although it was evident that
these statements were also metaphors, basically. For example, it
is a metaphor to affirm that "poetry does not create," but that "it
discovers and salvages what is being shipwrecked in the dark
waters of our being." The Catholic poets, for their part, affirmed
life in an attitude of concern and even love for man and all his
goods. Reality was there for them to incorporate and celebrate
in their songs. In the very reality that they set up, however, they
recognized the supernatural, the link with mystery. To judge this
poetry is impossible in a brief history. It is easier to point out
mutual praise, collective evaluations, the energy with which some
poets shed radiation on others, discharging on their contemporaries rays that, like uranium, would perhaps shortly lose their
radioactivity and turn to lead. The feeling of the critic in reading
these poets, is similar to the sensation of "*déjà vu, déjà lu*"; it is
quite natural, for we are looking at an abundance of material not
yet sorted, from which the dregs have not been sifted. Since our
story has come to an end we should not be reproached for our
closing enumerations.

(i) *Mexico* / In this country of uninterrupted and diverse poetic
production, none of the roads of the new poetry remained deserted: pure esthetes, contemplators of the world, worriers about
social problems, explorers of the subconscious, those proud of
their hermeticism and those having transparency and classical
tastes, the religious ones, the new romantics. The poets of the
generation of *Contemporáneos* are followed by the generation of
Taller (1938–41); Paz, Huerta, Quintero Álvarez, Beltrán. They
move through the same paths: European culture, artistic conscience, technical rigor. Their experiences nevertheless are different. Marxism, surrealism, the desire to revolutionize man and
society by means of love and poetry.

One of the leading poets of this generation is OCTAVIO PAZ
(1914), a profound poet determined to explore his own depths.
He began as an adolescent with *Savage Moon* (*Luna silvestre*,

1933) and matured quickly during the civil war in Spain with *They Shall Not Pass!* (*¡No pasarán!*, 1936). The books that followed were definitive: *Root of Man* (*Raíz del hombre*, 1937), *Under your Bright Shadow* (*Bajo tu clara sombra*, 1937), *Between the Stone and the Flower* (*Entre la piedra y la flor*, 1941), *At the World's Shore* (*A la orilla del mundo*, 1942), *Parole* (*Libertad bajo palabra*, 1949), *Seeds for a Hymn* (*Semillas para un himno*, 1952), *Sun Stone* (*Piedra del sol*, 1958), *The Violent Season* (*La estación violenta*, 1958). In 1960 he collected what he liked best of his poetry in his own books into *Parole: Poetic Works* (*Libertad bajo palabra. Obra poética, 1935–1958*). The title of one of his books ("at the world's shore") and the keynotes of his poems ("shore," "limit," "frontier," "mirror," "river," "instantaneous") indicate, not an indifferent withdrawal from the world, but the tragic and painful feeling of wanting to identify with it. These are the pathetic poems of an exile who, feeling the world beyond himself, re-creates it with the ardor of an anguished flame. Paz gives body to the languid mists from which other poets of similar language never emerge. His imagination—and not all is imagination, there is an intelligence disciplined in devising metaphysical themes—is profoundly serious. He feels that his existence emerges from being, but he cannot know anything about being. It is the obverse, the zero. His existence is the only illuminated part of being. Between being and existence there is an immense mirror, the last wall of consciousness, against which we stumble and despair. But this desperate solitude of our existence is pure time; and we can objectify and eternalize each instant of our existence in poetry. In poetry, as in a mirror, we find ourselves and lose ourselves. In his most ambitious poem, *Sun Stone,* Paz gives us a synthesis of his lyricism. With a continuous river of images that twists along a cyclical bed, as fully shaped as a human personality, intuitions flow that only seem contradictory if we think them out logically: deep-rooted solitude and the transcendence that seeks companionship, the world of subject and the world of object, rebellion in one's intimate galleries and rebellion in the ruins of society, the minute and the millennium, oneness and wholeness, and love, through which a woman and a land proffer their forms and move away like a single wave, along the undulating river of Paz's lyricism. A lyricism whose secret lies in a desire to resolve thesis and antithesis in a synthesis that might re-establish the lost unity of man. Between solitude and communion, Paz sings lyrically to each instant of his experience, but he is concerned with society, he is introverted and extraverted, hopeless and hopeful, given to blasphemous impulses toward destruction, but having faith in salvation. His effort to transcend to other lives tends to assume erotic intensities. He has passed through the intellectual experiences of our time: Marxism, surrealism, the discovery of the Orient. But his thought seeks new paths. This thought is displayed in penetrating essays: *The Labyrinth of Solitude (El laberinto de la soledad)*, *The Bow and the Lyre (El arco y la lira)*, *The Pears of the Elm (Las peras del olmo)*.

EFRAÍN HUERTA (1914), who began by writing poems of love, went down to the street, mixed with the masses, spoke to them in verse, and incited them to proletarian revolution. His political purpose at times is precipitated into unfortunate messages, which outer circumstances swallow whole leaving not a crumb. In *Star on High (Estrella en alto,* 1956) his two notes are heard, love and hatred. NEFTALÍ BELTRÁN (1916) poured out in his well-turned sonnets many lyrical wines: love, death, forlornness. His book: *Inimical Solitude (Soledad enemiga,* 1949).

A new group, centered in the review *Tierra Nueva* (1940–42), took up the lessons of pure art that had been given by Villaurrutia and his colleagues. They bolted the door against the din of social struggles and celebrated the pleasure of the naked poetic word. The most important is ALÍ CHUMACERO (1918). He offers an intelligently constructed poetry; he is a lyricist concerned with his feelings but he knows that a poem must appear with an austere structure. The cultured themes he mentions are not disguises, but classical moments in which the substance of his poetry will crystallize. The spontaneity of *Waste Land (Páramo de sueños,* 1944) is guarded in *Exile Images (Imágenes desterradas,* 1948) and, now totally disciplined, it was concentrated in *Words at Rest (Palabras en reposo,* 1956). As a poet he is more essential than sensual, more confidential than imaginative, more pensive than frenzied. His desire to enclose his meditations within strict measures is the cult of a solitary poet. The enamored impulse, the dense perception of time, the scorn for vulgarity, the knowledge that death is with us, the lacerations of the soul are reflected in the intelligent mirror of his consciousness and from there classically organized images emerge. Chumacero finds himself in his poetic form and his content. It is a hermetic form, difficult of access because his words, symbols encased in symbols, retreat in long phrases into an excessively private abyss, a metaphysical abyss where the theme of time and death abide. (When the theme is love or, rather, the erotic sentiment, Chumacero's images become more and more sensual.)

JAIME SABINÉS (1926) is also among the personal ones, that is, among those not easily grouped. Bitter, skeptical, derisive, suffering, unadaptable, pessimistic, he speaks to us of himself, especially of his enamored flesh. His eyes seem rather to touch things than merely see them. He is, then, a poet with his eyes open to reality (the enchantment of his provincial birthplace and the disenchantment of the city, carnal love, etc.). *Collection of Poems* (*Recuento de poemas,* 1962) is a collection of his first books and contains previously unpublished compositions.

RUBÉN BONIFAZ NUÑO (1923) began with a poetry of impeccable classical cut—*Images (Imágenes,* 1951). His taste for Latin poets, his preoccupation with form, his studies and exercises, kept him out of the irrational, dreamy, hermetic or automatic current of the poetry of the vanguard. His poetry did not overflow like a river, but flowed in an orderly fashion along a channel of well-constructed verses. While he was writing his poetry, in painstaking forms, he was also building up his image of life. Thus he came to a remarkable change of attitude beginning with *The Demons and the Days (Los demonios y los días,* 1956), when he conversed with the reader in free verse. It was like going down to the people with verses of social content and occasional prose forms. Bonifaz Nuño feels that man in his solitude or in the midst of the evils of contemporary society becomes deformed and loses his wholeness. His bitterness, which at times reaches the point of vociferous indignation, is basically optimistic since it affirms a future in which man will stand completely erect and proud in a society rebuilt on new foundations: *The Mantle and the Crown (El manto y la corona), Fire for the Poor (Fuego de pobres,* 1961).

ROSARIO CASTELLANOS (1925) goes to her poetic confessional with one of the most sincere, serious, and interesting voices of this generation. Her confession tells us about herself—her amours, lamentations, nostalgias, heartaches—and also of her origins, of the whole land and race of Mexico. Although solitude is one of her themes, the dominating note in her work is that of participation in the life of her people: *Poems (Poemas:* 1953–1955, 1957), *To the Letter of the Law (Al pie de la letra,* 1959), *Livid Light (Lívida luz,* 1960). In addition to her poems she has written short stories: *Royal City (Ciudad Real,* 1960), *The Guests of August (Los convidados de agosto,* 1964); drama: *Judith and Salome* (1959); and novels, *Balún*

Canán and *Business of Thunder* (*Oficio de tinieblas,* 1962). If TOMÁS SEGOVIA (1927) is not a pure poet, he is at least a poet of great purity, having achieved this purity through communion with his soul until he was able to bring it serenity and the ability to participate in the spirituality of the world: *Provisional Light* (*La luz provisional*), *Seven Poems* (*Siete poemas*), *Light From Here* (*Luz de aquí*), *The Sun and its Echo* (*El sol y su eco,* 1960). MARGARITA PAZ PAREDES (1922) is a poet who writes about interior penumbras (love, motherhood, human solitude and social betterment). These themes fill eight volumes of poetry, among which *Scaffolds of Shadow* (*Andamios de sombra*) and *Dimension of Silence* (*Dimension del silencio*) are outstanding. Other poets of these years: JAIME GARCÍA TERRÉS (1924), deep but circumspect, constructs his verses with clarity of thought, in contrast to poets of fluid obscurity: *Kingdoms in Combat* (*Los reinos combatientes,* 1961); GUADALUPE AMOR (1920), religious in accent, traditional in form; JESÚS ARELLANO (1923) began with poems of distress, but later others flourished that were more optimistic and combative; JORGE GONZÁLEZ DURÁN (1918), who with daggers of ice dissects his soul, scorched with disenchantment; the nostalgic and elegiac JOSÉ CÁRDENAS PEÑA (1918); MANUEL CALVILLO (1918), one of the most delicate in the nuances of tenderness and memory; MIGUEL GUARDIA (1924) who descends to everyday prose—as he descends his verses become accordingly prosaic—complains of social oppression and, in sympathy for his fellow man, seeks dialog with possible comrades; MARGARITA MICHELENA (1917), JORGE HERNÁNDEZ CAMPOS (1921), EDUARDO LIZALDE (1929).

(ii) *Central America / Guatemala:* During these years the review *Acento,* organ of the "generation of '40," broke out fighting. Its contributors had formed their tastes reading Rilke, Joyce, Valéry, Kafka and in Spanish, Neruda, Alberti, García Lorca; but their tone was one of open democratic affirmation, of clear human optimism. Prime movers: RAÚL LEIVA (1916), the most productive, came out of desolate and obscure poetry into the streets of a more popular poetry—*Anguish* (*Angustia,* 1942), *Ode to Guatemala* (*Oda a Guatemala,* 1953) and *Never Oblivion* (*Nunca el olvido,* 1957); CARLOS ILLESCAS (1919), author of *Autumn Frieze* (*Friso de otoño,* 1959); his stories are usually psychological; ENRIQUE JUÁREZ TOLEDO (1919), author of *Dianas for Life* (*Dianas para la vida,* 1956); OTTO RAÚL GONZÁLEZ (1921), inspired by noble human causes: *Clear Wind* (*Viento claro,* 1953), *The Forest* (*El bosque,* 1955), and various books of poems of like distinction. Then came another wave: the Saker-Ti group, more militant in its leftist movement, more oriented toward the people. HUBERTO ALVARADO (1925) was the standard bearer and he was accompanied by RAFAEL SOSA, MIGUEL ÁNGEL VÁZQUEZ, WERNER OVALLE LÓPEZ, MELVIN RENÉ BARAHONA, ÓSCAR ARTURO PALENCIA, ABELARDO RODAS.

Honduras: One can distinguish the voices of CARLOS MANUEL ARITA and DAVID MOYA POSAS.

El Salvador: CLARIBEL ALEGRÍA (1924), of a sincere and simple lyricism —*Vigils* (*Vigilias,* 1953); *Aquarium* (*Acuario,* 1955)—was also a prose writer with *Three Stories* (*Tres cuentos,* 1958). DORA GUERRA (1925),

who has become silent lately. ALFONSO MORALES (1919). OSWALDO ES-
COBAR VELADO (1919–1961), was first an amatory poet, then turned to
social poetry. In social poetry, committed to leftist political parties, are such
figures as JORGE A. CORNEJO (1923), EDUARDO MENJÍVAR (1920?),
MATILDE ELENA LÓPEZ (1923), and various others.

Nicaragua: Continuing enthusiastically the vanguard tendencies unleashed by Coronel Urtecho and others studied in the preceding chapter, a
new generation appeared concurrently: the one made up of Cardenal,
Mejía Sánchez, Martínez Rivas, and M. T. Sánchez. ERNESTO CARDENAL
(1925) is a spontaneous poet with the clarity of a prose writer. He has determined to frame his sentiments so as to be understood, rather than to
win admiration with his pure form: *Zero Hour (Hora 0), Gethsemany Ky*
(1960), *Epigrams (Epigramas,* 1961). He lives in a monastery. ERNESTO
MEJÍA SÁNCHEZ (1923), one of the most penetrating and severe poets: *Anthology (Antología: 1946–1952,* 1953), *Poems (Poemas,* 1963). In his
acuteness and severity there is also a game of complex meaning and surprises that oblige the reader to respond with his intelligence, not just with
emotion. CARLOS MARTÍNEZ RIVAS (1924) with deep, inner well-springs:
The Solitary Insurrection (La insurrección solitaria). Others: MARÍA TE-
RESA SÁNCHEZ (1918), delicate in quality; ERNESTO GUTIÉRREZ (1929),
nocturnal, desolate, moving; FERNANDO SILVA, popular in attitude and
theme; and RODOLFO SANDINO (1928).

Costa Rica: The most remarkable poet of this period is ALFREDO CAR-
DONA PEÑA (1917). His production, in verse and prose, is copious: his most
important books were published in Mexico, where he lives, although the
memory of his childhood, of his native land, continues to inspire him: *First
Paradise (Primer paraíso,* 1955). He is a cultured, emphatic, eloquent poet,
versatile in traditional and free rhythms. *Major Harvest (Cosecha mayor)*
is the title of his anthology covering the years 1944 to 1964. Other names:
EDUARDO JENKINS DOBLES (1926); ARTURO MONTERO VEGA (1915) of
social cares; MARIO PICADO UMAÑA (1928), an original and disconcerting
seeker of new ways; SALVADOR JIMÉNEZ CANOSSA (1922).

Panama: The new poetry offers these names: the monotonous EDUARDO
RITTER AISLÁN (1916) and the polytonal ESTHER MARÍA OSSES (1916);
the precise TOBÍAS DÍAZ BLAITRY (1919); the vital STELLA SIERRA (1919);
and the withdrawn TRISTÁN SOLARTE [Guillermo Sánchez] (1924), author
of a good novel, *The Drowned One (El ahogado).* Also there are HOMERO
ICAZA SÁNCHEZ (1925), JOSÉ DE JESÚS MARTÍNEZ (1928), JOSÉ ANTONIO
MONCADA LUNA (1926).

(iii) *Antilles / Cuba:* The young people of Cuba were anti-realists; in other words, they wanted to go beyond what we call reality
and approach the absolute. As one of them, Cintio Vitier, said,
they were not determined to advance, like those of the *Revista de
Avance* of 1927, but to submerge in search of origins—and *Orígenes* (1944–56), in fact, is the name of the review around which
they gathered. They gave their esthetic credo the name of "transcendentalism" because they did not enjoy those immediate ex-

periences easily expressed in words, but set out into the unknown in search of absolute entities. The first prominent ones were Gaztelu, Piñera, Baquero, and, as part of the group, Rodríguez Santos. They entered the ranks of literature in two platoons.

The first was led by GASTÓN BAQUERO (1916). He reluctantly writes to tell us that he and we, and all of us, are undergoing constant transformamation, and that we take part, as in dreams, in the metamorphosis of the world, but the final form will be that of death. Not even forms of art will save us. After *Poems* (*Poemas*) and *Saul on His Sword* (*Saúl sobre su espada,* both of 1942) the poet abandoned his vocation prematurely. He had already told us about his disillusionment with poetry in the "Sonnet For Not to Die." Learned in Latin and Spanish classics, Father ÁNGEL GAZTELU (1914) gave us in his *Lauds Gradual* (*Gradual de laudes,* 1955) a poetic exercise on Catholic themes, on Cuban landscapes, and on his readings. JUSTO RODRÍGUEZ SANTOS (1915) is more of an esthete than any of those mentioned. He makes fewer departures from the lyrical tradition, and spells out beautifully the way the world visits us through our senses, and also the spirit in which we received it. Rodríguez Santos has an elegiac spirit. And others: ALCIDES IZNAGA (1914), ALDO MENÉNDEZ (1918):

The second platoon was led by CINTIO VITIER (1921). All of his work from 1938, published and unpublished, was collected in *Vespers* (*Vísperas,* 1953). His work is harsh, craggy, irregular, with shaded precipices (in whose depths Cintio Vitier broods) and sharp pinnacles that raise things (places, nostalgia) until they are lifted to a sky of beauty. The theme of his poetry is that of estrangement in the world, the futile desire to capture it and, within this desire, a recourse to his most obscure experiences. *Plain Song* (*Canto llano,* 1956) is reflective poetry—that is, a poetry written on reflections of what the poet sees within himself. It is like a game of mirrors that multiply objects: the Cintio Vitier who is writing the poetry reflects on the Cintio Vitier who is living. The images, as they ricochet from mirror to mirror, tire and weaken. Because of its reflective attitude *Plain Song* is rich in definitions, esthetic programs, theories on literary creation, confessions, and professional secrets. We could use this "plain song" as a key to his earlier books. The key, in itself, is not hermetic— it serves to open up his hermeticism.

Certain of her own poetic visions, FINA GARCÍA MARRUZ (1923) in *Lost Glances* (*Miradas perdidas,* 1951) allows herself the luxury of expressing herself in terms that are plain though not simple, natural though artistic, human though not common, always sincere in her religious beliefs, in her memories, and in her impressions of the landscape: "Who shall gather thee, fleeting dust, lost afternoon / that leaves in my soul the sensation of the lily." OCTAVIO SMITH (1921) feels the presence of God in the quiver of all things. Each thing is an adjective indicating the substance of God: Touched by this universal radiation, the poet's verses also ascend to vibrant adjectives: *Of the Furtive Exile* (*Del furtivo destierro*, 1946). Others: RAFAEL CHACÓN NARDI (1926), ELISEO DIEGO (1920), LORENZO GARCÍA VEGA (1926). The last two will also be found among the narrators.

Dominican Republic: The most important event in this period was the founding of the review *La Poesía Sorprendida* (1943–47). Its originators, directors, and collaborators belong to three generations. The Chilean poet Alberto Baeza Flores, together with Rafael Américo Henríquez and Franklin Mieses Burgos, already mentioned, and Freddy Gatón Arce, who will be mentioned, founded it. It was also edited by Lebrón Saviñón and Fernández Spencer. Among others, the editorial board was formed by MANUEL LLANES (1899), AÍDA CARTAGENA PORTALATÍN (1918), MANUEL VALERIO (1918), MANUEL RUEDA (1921), learned and possessing an encompassing, integrating vision, and JOSÉ MANUEL GLAS MEJÍA (1923). The tone of *La Poesía Sorprendida* was esthetically demanding—it got rid of the weight of local themes and the coercion of traditional forms, not to yield to easy ways but to impose upon itself a new rigor. It took heed of novelties in the literary world and in this way it refined its imaginative modalities. Surrealism passed through its pages, but there was no one single esthetic that prevailed. On the contrary, it sought the integration of ancients and moderns, of Europeans and Hispanic-Americans, of symbolists and existentialists. It respected anything that incited effort and coordinated Dominican culture with that of the world.

One of the more famous poets in these years is ANTONIO FERNÁNDEZ SPENCER (1923). He opens his mouth with a naive gesture and sings of his wonder at life, nature, love, and death. He is plain, frequently prosaic, always spontaneous and affectionate. "To relate what happens in life" was his definition of poetry. Fortunately, he recited more than he related in *Interior Winds* (*Vendaval interior*, 1942) and *Beneath the Light of Day* (*Bajo la luz del día*, 1952). FREDDY GATÓN ARCE (1920) began in *Vlía* (1942) with obscure, bubbling, demoniacal prose poems. But in passing on to verse, without encountering serenity, he stepped up to an illuminated podium and there recited his lyrical meditations. MARIANO LEBRÓN SAVIÑÓN (1922), an inspired musical poet, also tried a drama. The desolate MANUEL RUEDA (1921), masterful sonneteer and theatrical author, is one of the most interesting personalities. Among the poets of the so-called "generation of 1948": RAFAEL VALERA BENÍTEZ (1928), RAMÓN CIFRE NAVARRO (1926) and others who will appear in the next chapter. In other poetic groups we find poets as dissimilar as SÓCRATES BARINAS COISCOU (1916), RUBÉN SURO GARCÍA GODOY (1916), MANUEL DE JESÚS GOICO CASTRO (1916), HÉCTOR PÉREZ REYES (1927), CARMEN NATALIA MARTÍNEZ BONILLA (1917), JUAN SÁNCHEZ LAMOUTH (1929).

Puerto Rico: One of the most enraptured voices, not only for his lyricism, but also for his patriotic ideals, is that of FRANCISCO MATOS PAOLI (1915).

His is a poetry that at times surprises us with its purity and hermeticism— *Inhabitant of the Echo* (*Habitante del eco*), *Theory of Forgetfulness* (*Teoría del olvido*)—and at times, for its profound grasp of things Creole —*Peasant's Thistle, Song to Puerto Rico* (*Cardo labriego, Canto a Puerto Rico*). Sometimes he puts them all together: *Light of Heroes* (*Luz de los héroes*). No sooner do we see him sensually yielding to the solicitations of the flesh and of the tropical landscape than he is singing to his solitude, his chaste spiritualism, his deep religious preoccupations. A great poet in all his moments. His latest: *Song to Madness* (*Canto a la locura*, 1962). Other poets worthy of consideration: FRANCISCO LLUCH MORA (1925), co-founder with Oppenheimer of "transcendentalism." With manifest concern for form (and with a preference for the sonnet) he expresses a lyricism that is sometimes jubilant, sometimes elegiac: *Of Siege and Closure* (*Del asedio y la clausura*), *Desperate Song to Ashes* (*Canto desesperado a la ceniza*), *Notebook of Love* (*Cartapacio de amor*, 1961). JUAN MARTÍNEZ CAPÓ (1923) reveals himself as a poet of nuances and essences in *Voyage* (*Viaje*, 1961). VIOLETA LÓPEZ SURIA (1926) has published poems and short stories. As a poet she is among the best in the neo-romantic trend of those years. She has expressed a rich gamut of amorous feeling in *Lovingly* (*Amorosamente*, 1961). In her work there is a religious spirit, a delicate perception of nature, an attentive consciousness of the way people live. She has an ample series of books of poems, ending with *The Clouds Cast Shadows* (*Las nubes dejan sombra*, 1965). Other feminine poets: MARÍA GLORIA PALMA (1922)—erotic themes—, ESTHER FELICIANO MENDOZA (1917)— children's themes—, LAURA GALLEGO (1925)—introspective themes. JOSÉ EMILIO GONZÁLEZ (1918) is a neo-Creolist poet, from *Prophecy of Puerto Rico* (*Profecía de Puerto Rico*) to *Parable of Song* (*Parábola del canto*, 1960).

(iv) *Venezuela* / Those who appeared in 1940, though they may not have formed a single group with a single program, had at least a common desire to get away from nativist, vernacular poetry as well as from the surrealism and free versism of the generation of the review *Viernes*. They aspired, instead, to the expression of universal human values in poetry that followed formal patterns. They cultivated the sonnet, the *lira*, and other forms that they admired in the Castilian classics. They were cultured youths, most of them having a university education, who prepared themselves intellectually for the creation of their poems. They first gathered around the magazine *Suma* (1943); then, toward 1946, they formed a friendly group who were later to found their own magazine: *Contrapunto*. Besides those who later collaborated in the pages of this periodical, there were other groups formed in university halls, or in the editorial offices of newspapers, not to mention those writers who were reluctant to join any group. The list of poets is impressive. We could assemble them all under the heading "generation of 1942." There are symbolists, surrealists, existentialists, poets committed to politics or religion, cultivators of classic and baroque forms and free verse. JUAN LISCANO (1915) comes out into the world, with which he communicates easily. His poetry is concerned with the meaning of life and human destiny; it is a poetry of protest, of aspiration to absolutes, descriptions of nature and civic songs taken up with history and folklore. One of his most ambitous poems is *New World Orinoco* (*Nuevo Mundo Orinoco,* 1959), made up of songs inspired by the magical concept of the Indians, the history of the conquest, the frenzy of sex, the fusion of the races, and the surge of new societies, the independence and the social struggles. Imaginative songs, at times spread out, even typographically, to encompass simultaneous action —external and mental. JOSÉ RAMÓN MEDINA (1921) is a serene poet, deep, lucid, home-loving, at times dwelling tenderly on sweet recollections of childhood, at times voicing concern over present-day conditions of life; he exhibited complete mastery of his style in *Text on Time* (*Texto sobre el tiempo,* 1953) and *The Hills and the Wind* (*Las colinas y el viento,* 1959). JUAN MANUEL GONZÁLEZ (1924), author of *The Property by the Wind* (*La heredad junto el viento,* 1959), adds a new voice to the old repertory of the lyric: love, sadness, solitude, death. Interesting women poets: LUZ MACHADO DE ARNAO (1916), PÁLMENES YARZA (1916), LUCILA VELÁZQUEZ (1929), ANA ENRIQUETA TERÁN (1920), JEAN ARISTEGUIETA (1925), MORITA CARRILLO (1921), notable for her childhood themes. One of the most original of the women poets, IDA GRAMCKO (1925), is noted for the expansive power of the lyricism that radiates in her verse: *Poems* (*Poemas*), *The Magic Wand* (*La vata mágica*), her theater: *Juan Palomo's Daughter* (*La hija de Juan Palomo*), *Belén Silvera,* and her narrative: *Fearless John* (*Juan sin miedo*). Even her most intense emotions (such as love) are sublimated, delicately, into metaphysical material. Her imagination elaborates freely on myths, dreams, and living experiences, but she has respect for forms. Her creative power is extraordinary because of its abundance and the facility with which she converts the slightest occasion (a memory, a word overheard, a stone or a bird) into a motif of lofty poetry. After a long period of mental illness she returned to her writing with *Poems of a Psychotic* (*Poemas de una psicótica*) and with the mysticism of *The Greatest Thing Murmurs* (*Lo maximo murmura*). AQUILES NAZOA (1920) is a poet of the people. He comes from the people and he sings to them with joyful good humor, and occasionally also in a serious tone of voice: *The Flute Playing Burro* (*El burro flautista*), *Poems for Coloring* (*Poemas para colorear*). And now I ask the reader's pardon for the list that follows: CARLOS GOTTBERG (1929), CARLOS AUGUSTO LEÓN (1914), PEDRO FRANCISCO LIZARDO (1920), BENITO RAÚL LOSADA (1923), FRANCISCO PÉREZ PERDOMO (1929), RAFAEL ÁNGEL INSAUSTI (1916), J. A. ESCALONA–ESCALONA (1917), RUBENÁNGEL HURTADO (1922), ELISEO JIMÉNEZ SIERRA (1919), RAFAEL PINEDA (1926), MANUEL VICENTE MAGALLANES (1922), RAFAEL JOSÉ MUÑOZ (1928), MIGUEL GARCÍA MACKLE (1927), PEDRO PABLO PAREDES (1917), PEDRO LHAYA (1921), FRANCISCO SALAZAR MARTÍNEZ (1925).

(v) *Colombia* / After the "Stone and Sky" group, but without the same cohesion of style, a new generation of poets appeared, whose only common denominator was their desire to be different from the preceding group. They reproached the Stone and Sky group with having fostered a regeneration rather than a renewal, with having put too much confidence in the virtue of repetitive poetic preciousness. Nevertheless, some of the newcomers continued to follow to a certain extent the style of those already established: Jaime Ibáñez, Andres Holguín, Meira Delmar, Helcías Martán Góngora and, somewhat detached, the excellent Eduardo Mendoza Varela. JAIME IBÁÑEZ (1919) has continued after *Tacit Damsel* (*Tacita Doncella*) to reveal many other facets of his personality. He told about episodes of civil wars in *Where Dreams Dwell* (*Donde moran los sueños*) and, in a more poetic style, about human suffering in the face of self-destructive nature: *Every Voice Carries its Own Anguish* (*Cada voz lleva su angustia*). ANDRÉS HOLGUÍN (1918) insinuates his pantheism into the poems in *Canticle to There is Only One Blood* (*Cántico a solo existe una sangre*). MEIRA DEL MAR (Olga Chams) (1922) is Alpha in a vast feminine constellation: MARUJA VIEIRA, 1922; EMILIA AYARZA; OLGA ELENA MATTEI. HELCÍAS MARTÁN GÓNGORA (1920), poet of the sea and of his coastal birthplace. EDUARDO MENDOZA VARELA (1920), a good poet and a good prose writer: *The City Near the Country and Other Poems* (*La ciudad junto al campo y otros poemas*), *Parable of Ganymede* (*Parábola de Ganimedes*). FERNANDO CHARRY LARA (1920), author of the yearning but serene *Nocturnes and Other Dreams* (*Nocturnas y otros sueños*, 1949) and of the pessimistic but resigned poems in *The Farewells* (*Los adioses*, 1963), is a poet of deliberately vague and disintegrating reminiscences. He dreams about phantoms, and so his inner world becomes populated with distracted souls, sleep-walkers and ghosts made of "dust and nostalgia." Appearance, vacuum, dissolution, death, nothing. Others: the elegiac GUILLERMO PAYÁN ARCHER (1921), LUIS ENRIQUE SENDOYA (1917), and the experimenter VIDAL ECHEVARRYA, with his *Guitars that Sound Inside Out* (*Guitarras que suenan al revéz*). Afterwards came the "*cuadernícolas*" ("notebook poets") and the "*nadaístas*" ("*nothingists*"), to whom we shall refer shortly. But first we would like to say that, on the whole, the poets of this chapter, although they were less brilliant than the Stone-and-Sky group, were more concerned with the condition of man in the world. They read Antonio Machado more than they did Juan

Ramón Jiménez. They also read the surrealists. And the English poets. And the theorists of poetry. They examined the problems of existence in a more critical spirit, using everyday colloquial language. Because they wanted to communicate with the public they refused to assume the haughtiness of the hermetic poets. Let us look at the last group that belongs in this chapter. An ironic tone and a conversational idiom seem to prevail in these poets, with the accent on the positive rather than on the fantastic. JORGE GAITÁN DURÁN (1924–1962) is at times limpid, at times surrealist, at times a bearer of social messages. *If Tomorrow I Awake* (*Si mañana despierto,* 1961) brings us verse and prose, both penetrated by an intelligence of poetic caliber, by intellectual emotions artistically elaborated. The subjects that are most evident are eroticism and death. HÉCTOR ROJAS HERAZO (1920) is a poet who comes face to face with an objective world and speaks to us directly about his harsh experiences. His "Psalm of Defeat" (*"Salmo de la derrota"*) which we have read, is a hoarse lament: "We fall, yes we fall / we fall within ourselves / Without charity toward ourselves we contribute to our destruction." EDUARDO COTE LAMUS (1928–196?) pursues his meditations with sad languor; meditations that adhere so closely to personal experiences and things that he describes that, while fortunately they do not completely desert poetry in their incursion into the area of philosophy, they frequently become conceptual and even prosaic. *Daily Life* (*La vida cotidiana,* 1959), *Storax* (*Estoraque,* 1963). He is a poet who relates anecdotes, but is still a solitary. Cote Lamus formed part of a group that has been called "the generation of notebook poets" (because of the scantily paged notebooks in which some of them printed their first poems). Important among them is CARLOS CASTRO SAAVEDRA (1925), who sings with verbal abundance about the life of man in all of its circumstances and achieves some fine poetic moments: *Selected Works* (*Obra selecta,* 1962), *Every Day is Monday* (*Todos los días son lunes,* 1963). ÁLVARO MUTIS (1923), author of *The Lost Labors* (*Los trabajos perdidos*) expresses his thoughts through channels of responsible words; he is a good example of the creation of a disciplined poetic style.

Others: FERNANDO ARBELÁEZ (1924), among the best; ÓSCAR ECHEVERRI MEJÍA (1918), JAIME TELLO (1918), ROGELIO ECHAVARRÍA (1926), JAVIER ARIAS RAMÍREZ (1924), JORGE MONTOYA TORO (1921), DORA CASTELLANOS (1925).

(vi) *Ecuador* / On the first level: CÉSAR DÁVILA ANDRADE (1918), a lyricist of great imaginative intensity, even with something of the magician, has also written some good short stories; FRANCISCO TOBAR GARCÍA (1928), Catholic, original in his human impetus, *Shipwreck and Other Poems* (*Naufragio y otros poemas*, 1962)—is also a dramatist; JORGE ENRIQUE ADOUM (1926), a leftist, Nerudian, vital, and overflowing; and ALEJANDRO CARRIÓN (1915). The latter is a disillusioned soul who gives us the chronicle of his disillusionments. But he reasons, enumerates, and repeats; and under these weights his lyricism becomes slow-paced. There is a noble lyricism, nevertheless, in *Poetry of Solitude and Desire* (*Poesía de la soledad y el deseo*, 1946)—defining title—and in *Agony of Tree and Blood* (*Agonía del arbol y la sangre*, 1948). He collected his work in *Poetry* (*Poesía*, 1961). As a prose writer he collected in *The Damaged Apple* (*La manzana dañada*) stories of childhood evocation. He is ironic, of facile phraseology, though in his novel *The Thorn* (*La espina*, 1959) the theme of solitude is treated with black turmoil. Other poets: ALFONSO BARRERA VALVERDE (1925?) and EDUARDO VILLACÍS MEYTHALER (1925?). JACINTO CORDERO ESPINOSA (1925), EUGENIO MORENO HEREDIA (1926), TEODORO VANEGAS ANDRADE (1926).

(vii) *Peru* / The pure poets now write with seriousness, with gravity, with responsibility. They write of all the emotions they feel worthwhile, without limiting themselves to fashionable themes, without mutilating the totality of man. They write in all modes, whether traditional or very new. At times, very free verses; at times, verses measured in every aspect. Furthermore, one notes in them a respect for well-structured poetic forms. Some of them came from surrealism or from a form of esthetics that demanded that the poet perform verbal sorcery or indulge in the fine art of appearing to be afflicted. JORGE EDUARDO EIELSON (1921) is an esthete concerned with the beauty of the *mot juste* and the suggestive image: *Song and Death of Roland* (*Canción y muerte de Roland*, 1959). JAVIER SOLOGUREN (1922) has a sober and melancholy lyricism. He is distinguished for the sweetness of his poetry, a sweetness inspired not by literary styles (even though he began with surrealism), but by his sincere love for his country, for the Indian, and for tradition. He is successful in pastoral poetry, not in his moments of social protest: *Stanzas* (*Estancias*, 1960). BLANCA VARELA examines herself and the world in surrealistic symbols. FRANCISCO BENDEZÚ (1928) was a surrealist at first and then went on to more severe and even hermetic forms: *The Years* (*Los años*, 1961). There was a constant wavering between a style that was formalist, estheticist, or whatever you may want to call it, and a style concerned with social ethics and politics. It is impossible to follow the transitions here. In general, even the poets richest in fantasy used their literary gifts to serve a collective function. In doing so, some sacrificed themselves. For example, there was ALEJANDRO ROMUALDO (1926), who had attained prestige for his poetry which, although realistic, was ingenious in its expression of human values and its verbal selectiveness. His social fervor was strained to such a point that in *Special Edition* (*Edición extraordinaria*) he ended by writing journalism in verse, full of news, denunciations, notices, and calls for political action. It was poetry converted into an instrument, a weapon, a publicity apparatus, a utilitarian work. Another poet who came down from his ivory tower to go screaming through the streets was GUSTAVO VALCÁRCEL (1921). He abandoned his initial delicacy to discharge gloomy prognostications in Vallejo's shadow. He is also a novelist. *Prison* (*La prisión*) is a document on the sufferings of youths pursued by reactionary forces. CARLOS GERMÁN BELLI (1927), who toyed with pure forms in which there was a mixture of archaic voices and surrealist echoes, later produced, unforeseeably, poetry in which there were exasperated grimaces as well as humorous winks: *Oh, Cybernetic Fairy!* (*¡Oh, Hada Cibernética!* 1962). In WASHINGTON DELGADO (1927) there is a meeting of pure lyricism and social unrest that achieves admirable unity: *To Live Tomorrow* (*Para vivir mañana*, 1959). JUAN GONZALO ROSE (1928) is a social poet, not merely an imitator of Vallejo, but his peer because of his personality, which is both tender and vigorous, with the gift of an imaginative style that is elegiac, sweet, and direct. Poets today no longer think of the Indian or the mestizo as a racial class but as a "new American," the crucible of all ethnic metals. And they also acknowledge a willingness to use classical meters and strophes. Indigenist or *cholista* poets suddenly decided to be "revolutionaries" and subordinated their poetry to the social theme and the ideological testimony. We shall now give the names of a few poets without attempting to classify them: ALBERTO ESCOBAR (1929), a neo-romantic of harmonious and careful forms; CARLOS ALFONSO RÍOS (1919), who contrived a cosmopolitan fabric out of strands of symbolism and surrealism; MANUEL SCORZA (1929), a poet of social imprecations, bitter about injustice but romantic in spirit; EDGARDO PÉREZ LUNA (1928), a pastoral poet; EFRAÍN MIRANDA (1925); ANTENOR SAMANIEGO (1919).

(viii) *Bolivia* / Let us first speak about YOLANDA BEDREGAL (1916), a lyricist of religious accent who writes about children and laments human suffering in daring images, like those in "Uselessness" (*"Inutilidad"*): *Nadir*, 1950, *Of the Sea and Ash* (*Del mar y la ceniza*, 1957). The novelty of these years is the springing up of a generation which is the most numerous in the history of Bolivian poetry: it is called *"Gesta Bárbara."* Let us draw aside at least three significant poets. JULIO DE LA VEGA, making a way for himself between classical forms and the form of surrealism, entertained the noble causes of the world in a Hispanic-American sense. No sooner does OSCAR ALFARO appear with his tenderly lyrical poems of childhood recollections than he disappears in poems of political passions: *Alphabet of Stars* (*Alfabeto de estrellas*). ALCIRA CARDONA TORRICO is a deep, sincere voice, preoccupied with human destiny. One might add the names of ENRIQUE KEMPFF MERCADO (1920); GONZALO SILVA SANGINÉS, of tormented tonality; CARLOS MONTAÑO DAZA, who cultivated children's poetry; JORGE ALVÉSTIGUE, soft, delicate; CARLOS MENDIZÁBAL CAMACHO and JACOBO LIBERMAN, a part of the social theme.

(ix) *Chile* / After 1938 (Neruda and Rokha were already fixed in the firmament, the Alpha and Beta of Gemini) two new constellations appeared. One we will identify with the surrealist, Braulio Arenas, and the other with the popularist, Nicanor Parra. Braulio Arenas was the leader of the group gathered around the hallucinatory magazine, *Mandrágora* (six issues from 1938 to 1941), which sought a weird marriage between an unreal world and an irrational poetry. In its labyrinth, geography lost its frontiers, history only evoked deeds of invented creatures, literature proclaimed that the melting of forms was necessary for human liberty. At times their tricks turned out to be magic, at others, failure. The Mandragorists elbowed their way through, savagely breaking everything: screams, taunts, insults with no concern for good form. The other principal figures who accompanied Arenas were ENRIQUE GÓMEZ CORREA (1915) and JORGE CÁCERES (1923–1949). Gonzalo Rojas joined the group. Without becoming part of it, Gustavo Ossorio collaborated with *Mandrágora*. Among the Mandragorists one could name TEÓFILO CID (1914–1964) and JORGE ONFRAY (1922).

The leader, BRAULIO ARENAS (1913), does not construct objective images, like the creationist Huidobro, nor does he envelop his spontaneous images in a full-blown emotion, like Neruda; but he inebriates his speech and lets it ramble, ragged and stammering, incapable of communicating anything to anyone. His initial forms were violent, but other poets accepted them with such tranquillity that in 1941 Arenas, unhappy over the peace that had settled, broke with *Mandrágora* and founded *Leitmotiv* (three issues from 1942 to 1943). These were wrenching years for Europe. Hitler had invaded France; France became mute; the surrealists took refuge in the United States and, guided by Duchamp, Breton, Char, and others, they invented a new letter of the alphabet, the triple V, not the simple V for Victory, and founded the review *VVV*. Braulio Arenas, fighting against the provincial spirit, becomes one with international surrealism. In order to prevent the death of the Spanish language, he converts it into the true agent of poetry, daringly and with greater liberty. See *Poems* (1960). An offshoot of surrealism is observed in *The Phantom House* (*La casa fantasma,* 1962).

In his nocturnal strolls between Huidobro and Neruda, GONZALO ROJAS (1917) occasionally joined the somnambulists in the *Mandrágora* group. Then without leaving the darkness which is his element, he began to speak more about his emotions than about his nightmares. A matter of accent, because everything was present in his introspective poetry: romanticism, creationism, surrealism, existentialism. And even the handling of viscera, organic functions, things that are repugnant and ugly. Outside of beautiful erotic moments, his moods are dejected, with the exception of some beautiful, erotic moments: he feels lost in a stupid and cruel reality, without knowing what his destiny is or who lent him his body. It is not the certainty of death that torments him, but the uncertainty of living in an indissoluble solitude. Thrust into the void, he feels ephemeral and writes poetry while he himself, "a worm," is undone in the "beautiful darkness," "daughter of the abysses." The title *The Wretchedness of Man* (*La miseria del hombre*) is the key to his book dated 1948. When he reappeared later in *Against Death* (*Contra la muerte*, 1964), he was clearer, more coherent, more critical.

While in the *Mandrágora* movement, freed images beat their wings and gave poetic intensity to the darkness, poets of the other movement gave us a clear poetry, clear, not because it was shaped by reason, but because it was aware of the continuous sentiment that inspired it. In general, the clear, natural, and popular poets turned to the native landscape and, as with the romantics, they converted it into a sweet confidante. They were Nicanor Parra, Luis Oyarzún, Oscar Castro, Jorge Millas, ALBERTO. BAEZA FLORES (1914), Venancio Lisboa, Vicario. They did not advance on the trail of artistic renovation: rather, they backtracked so as to be better understood by the mass public. Nevertheless, they were different.

OSCAR CASTRO (1910–1947), connoisseur of the Spanish ballad, produced a provincial, nativist poetry with noble overtones. JORGE MILLAS (1917) and LUIS OYARZÚN (1920) attempted a philosophic poetry; Oyarzún is, in addition, a notable essayist of philosophic and esthetic themes. NICANOR PARRA (1914) is the most complex. His lyrical score is made up of chords containing popular and humorous notes; that is why his lyricism sounds at times like a folklore guitar. He began with popular and picturesque ballads—*Song Book Without a Name* (*Cancionero sin nombre*, 1937)—and increasingly emphasized his disgust and sarcasm at the absurdities of daily life—*The Long Dance* (*La cueca larga*, 1958). His most famous experiment was that of the antipoems. They consist of traditional poems composed of narrative material which, after drinking several glasses of surrealism, are stood on their heads. The everyday world, seen feet up, appears grotesque. "Life has no meaning," he concludes prosaically in "Soliloquy of the Individual." Colloquial phrases deliberately ordinary, and an imagination that prefers to be ingenious rather than lyrical, communicate the pessimism and the irony of the antipoet (Huidobro had called himself "antipoet and magician"). The first edition of *Poems and Antipoems* (*Poemas y antipoemas*) dates from 1954. Now the title *Salon Verses* (*Versos de salón*, 1962), having nothing to do with the content of the book, indicates Parra's disdainful attitude. We have seen Gonzalo Rojas emerge from nocturnal poetry with alabaster words and Nicanor Parra from diurnal poetry with ebony words. The fact is that there are not poetic groups: there are poetic destinies, and their individual trajectories, no matter how much they ignore each other, end by crisscrossing. On the margin of these groups, then, we should study the Catholics EDUARDO ANGUITA (1914), the more important, and VENANCIO LISBOA (1917). We should also mention the egotistical and disoriented MAHFUD MASSIS (1917). While the generation of 1938, which we have just characterized, matured in poets like Braulio Arenas, Nicanor Parra, and Gonzalo Rojas, another youthful generation was growing up. Some of the young poets are still close to the older ones. They are JOSÉ MIGUEL VICUÑA (1920), ANTONIO CAMPAÑA (1922), RAQUEL SEÑORET (1923), ELIANA NAVARRO (1923), and JUAN LANZA (1925).

Then came poets who firmly manifested their disagreement with what had been done by the immediately preceding generation. For these young writers the free versism of Huidobro, Rokha, Neruda, Díaz Casanueva, and Rosamel del Valle, the nightmarish babblings of Braulio Arenas, and the guitar-twanging of Nicanor Parra were subterfuges to escape from the only responsibility of the poet: to compose poems with maximum formal rigor. What these youths wish is to continue the great tradition of Hispanic poetry, to respect rhythm, rhyme, and strophe and to renounce the non-esthetic activities of the spirit, to withdraw from themes appropriate to prose and to preserve the lyrical grace that wells up from one's inner self. Poetic pressure must be disciplined until it acquires a clearcut visual and linguistic structure. Even free verse must have an interior architecture. The meaning of the composition can be executed in regular as well as irregular verses: the important thing is the unique projection of a worthwhile vision, that the images remain secured to a central nucleus.

One of the most decisive—and lucid—in the theory and practice of this program was MIGUEL ARTECHE (1926), a formalist poet of great purity and intensity in the expression of religious feelings, he has collected three books, the lyrical labor of fifteen years, in *From Absence to the Night* (*De la ausencia a la noche,* 1965). Arteche represents the cult of form that is reminiscent of the Golden Age of Spanish literature, even to his religious themes. Alongside Arteche are ROSA CRUCHAGA DE WALKER and DAVID ROSENMANN TAUB (1926): the latter does not disguise his artful artisan's trade. Our eyes, moving like a pendulum, could follow the formalist poets who, sometimes colloquially, express their passion, solitude, anguish and affliction in free verse. It is not their poetry that moves like a pendulum, but our critical eyes. It is more to the point to add to Arteche other significant poets. Above all, ENRIQUE LIHN (1929), whose slow-paced and scarce poems are more reflexive than emotional, more intellectual than exclamatory: *Poems of This Time and of Another* (*Poemas de este tiempo y de otro*, 1955). He is also a short-story writer. Others, more direct, sang as all poets have sung who feel themselves close to the land, to the people, and to common speech: ALBERTO RUBIO (1928), author of *Vessel of Clay* (*La greda vasija*, 1952) is tender, and we might say humorous if his sad humor could be so called. Another: PABLO GUÍÑEZ (1929).

(x) *Paraguay* / Various poets appeared after Campos Cervera, whom we have already studied. They are Augusto Roa Bastos, who will be found also among the prose writers: HUGO RODRÍGUEZ ALCALÁ (1919) who in *War Prints* (*Estampas de la guerra*) gave us a type of chronicle in verse on the Chaco War; JESÚS AMADO RECALDE (1921), taken up with social problems; JOSÉ ANTONIO BILBAO (1919), given to eclogues; EZEQUIEL GONZÁLEZ ALSINA (1922), culturally oriented toward France; RODRIGO DÍAZ PÉREZ (1924), with his love for all things human. Another group followed immediately with ELVIO ROMERO (1926) in the forefront. Elvio Romero, following in the footsteps of Ortiz Guerrero and Julio Correa, writes about the Paraguayan countryside, its people and their customs and sufferings. He is a social poet with a command of his craft that is exceptional in his vast American group. All of his books of verse—from *Broken Days* (*Días roturados*) to *The Unnameable Ones* (*Los innombrables*)—are represented in his 1965 *Poetic Anthology* (*Antología poética*), from which comes a strong aroma of the soil of Paraguay. His vision is dramatic, that is, it animates the conflicts between nature and man, and in man between the forces of good and evil. He denounces, he insults, he calls for violent action, and then his poetry is not only social but also partisan. But it is still lyrical poetry because even his political desires are part of his identification with the land and with human suffering. At the margin (or within the margin) of "poetry of utility" another group can be distinguished. RAMIRO DOMÍNGUEZ went from concern for society to metaphysical perplexities and esthetic forms of expression: *Sap* (*Zumos*, 1962), *Psalmodious Dishonor* (*Salmosa deshonra*, 1963), *Dithyramb for Chorus and Flute* (*Ditirambo para coro y flauta*, 1964). JOSE LUIS APPLEYARD (1927), familiar with Spanish forms of poetry, is a nostalgic and an esthete in *Then it was Always* (*Entonces era siempre*). ELSA WIEZELL (1927), who wrote *Time of Love* (*Tiempo de amor*, 1965), was another who did not cultivate social poetry. Others: RICARDO MAZO (1927), JULIO CÉSAR TROCHE (1928).

(xi) *Uruguay* / PEDRO PICATTO (1914–1950) keeps alive a poetic language of images which have always been celebrated for their beauty and for a language that is tender, soft, and occasionally doleful. CARLOS DENIS MOLINA (1917) began as a poet surrounded with surrealist decorations, similar, in his self-demanding attitude, to his countryman Fernando Pereda, and then he turned to the theater—*If the Murderer Were Innocent* (*Si el asesino fuera inocente*) and the poetic novel—*It Will Always Rain* (*Lloverá siempre*). LUIS ALBERTO VARELA (1912) diagnosed his heart in the book entitled *The Saddened Side* (*Costado triste*, 1958). In his readings of the surrealist poets he discovered the possibilities of the symbol and the meta-

phor, but he knew how to reject verbal facility and withdrew into his sadness in order to arrange it ever more poetically. Others: ALEJANDRO
PEÑASCO (1914), WALTER GONZÁLEZ PENELAS (1915), GONZÁLEZ POGGI
(1915), BELTRÁN MARTÍNEZ.

The poets who made themselves known when the world war
ended were neither optimists nor pacifists. On the contrary, with
impassioned souls they decided to carry on their own war against
reputations and styles that up to then had been respectable. This
common negative attitude united them. Their mood was elegiac
and hopeless. For this reason they were displeased with the overflowing vitality of Sabat Ercasty, Ibarbourou, Silva Valdés, and
from the poets of the past, they only tolerated the taciturn ones,
like Basso Maglio. The Uruguayan roots of this new poetic bloom-
ing are to be found rather in Cunha and in Liber Falco. In general,
the postwar poets withdrew from society and, immersed in their
inner selves, disdained or ignored the Church, the political party,
and the state. Their style is human, direct, rugged, unarranged;
it seems they feel that to insist on the perfection of esthetic forms
is an insincerity. They absorb all the humors, even the prosaic
ones, of everyday life and avoid rhythms, rhymes, strophes, and
sumptuous metaphors. Time ticks tragically in them; as they ramble through ruins and rubbish they stop occasionally to write of a
happy moment, but suddenly they stumble and think of death
(Vilariño, Vitale, Brandy, Paseyro). Even the least afflicted are
far from the optimism of the preceding generation (Sarandy
Cabrera, Ariel Badano, Hugo Emilio Pedemonte, Silvia Herrera,
Dora Isella Russell, Orfila Bardesio).

Perhaps it is IDEA VILARIÑO (1928) who best illustrates the poetic mood
of this generation. She appeared in 1945 with *The Suppliant* (*La suplicante*)
and since then, in poetic booklets, she has given us the poetry which leaves
us with a bad taste, the taste of death. Yet the voice intones its discouragement with broken and moving rhythms. It is hard, intense, obsessed with
the impassioned hold that death has on us, tortured by sickness, suffering
and desolation. IDA VITALE (1925), since she wrote *Light of This Remembrance* (*La luz de esta memoria,* 1949), has been registering the strong
tones of her sensitivity: *Each in His Own Night* (*Cada uno en su noche*)
appeared in 1960. CARLOS BRANDY (1923), when he disposes of affected
surrealist manners and when he is able to discard certain stylish formulas,
denudes his body of its original feeling of existence and goes ever deeper,
ever more melancholically, into its experience. He also poured poetry into

social themes. RICARDO PASEYRO (1927), melancholy, tortured, caretaker of his flame and his form. *Tree of Ruins* (*Árbol de ruinas,* 1961) is a collection of his first four books of poems. SARANDY CABRERA (1922), though he wrote in the manner of Neruda and Vallejo in his first book (*Onfalo,* 1947), he fixed his eyes on things with such a determination to recognize them, one by one, as familiar objects of a universal disorder that he ended up by creating a convincing lyrical world. When later he delved into social themes, he did not break the unity of that world. See his 1960 anthology, *Pool* (*Poso*). SILVIA HERRERA (1922) is quick and precipitate in her confidential verses of sadness and tenderness. AMANDA BERENGUER (1924) who in *The River* (*El río,* 1952) had achieved an inimitable poetry of living experience (memories, travels, loves) is manifestly concentrated, intractable, wearisome in the eight poems of *The Invitation* (*La invitación,* 1957). She is a despondent woman conscious of her despondency in the midst of a life that invites her to be festive. Opaque images, deafening sounds. Because she knows her own sincerity and her own unmistakable tedium, she is not afraid of prose and allows it to be expressed in terms of ordinary language: *Countersong* (*Contracanto,* 1961); and later: *Joint Declaration* (*Declaración conjunta*). DORA ISELLA RUSSELL (1925) is copious and adheres to traditional forms. The classical architecture of her poems is aired by a breeze from her inmost being. Her subjectivity—desires, presentiments of love, heartbreaks—at times touches a metaphysical depth. A careful technique holds her feelings in check, and rather than describe them she suggests them to us. ORFILA BARDESIO keeps watch over her love poetry by fleeing from the episodic. CECILIO PEÑA (1925) decants metaphysical essences into images and symbols with uneven success. WASHINGTON LOCKHART (1914), author of *The World is Absurd* (*El mundo es absurdo,* 1961), incorporated himself with the younger poets. We close this section with MILTON SCHINCA (1926): *This Urgent Hour* (*Esta hora urgente*), *World under Question* (*Mundo cuestionado*); and HUGO EMILIO PEDEMONTE (1923).

(xii) *Argentina* / In 1940 a group appears—the "generation of '40"—which finds the immediately preceding poets too formal and too balanced, and from the past, it esteems only the Lugones of *Ballads of the Rio Seco* and certain random devotees of Martín Fierro: Borges, Bernárdez, Molinari, Mastronardi, Marechal. Some turned to Argentine sources; others preferred to examine their souls in a universal mirror. In other words, while the breaking with established forms had been a primary obligation in the ultraist program, among the youths of " '40" it was not so much a formal imperative as a desire to auscultate the palpitations of the country through its geography and the heartbeat of man in his existence. In general they were grave, melancholy, elegiac, prudent. They had seen the world in shambles, and had no desire to play at literature. They complained with the word "heart" on their lips and in their verse, in a kind of neo-romanticism. They did not cultivate wit for wit's sake nor the metaphor for metaphor's sake. They preferred traditional forms (like the sonnet) and at times popular inspiration. They created no innovations in the art of verse because they were closer to colloquialism than to virtuosity. They knew existentialism and when they were not writing about what they saw in their proximate visions they wrote on the universal themes of existence. They were well educated—even university people—and they tended to have a feeling for philosophy. Some of those in the group of the year '40 we have already seen in the preceding chapter. We shall see here only those born after 1915. Later, other poets began to appear, who went on with the work of the initial group. They also wanted to belong to a generation, and they spoke of the generation of '45 and that of '50. But the historian cannot consider so many generational subtleties. What seems to unite poets of different groups is not so much age but concepts of literature and mental climate. We would be satisfied if we could succeed in classifying poets in the manner suggested before: those poets who turn to Argentina for their sources and those who prefer to look at their souls in a universal mirror. (We could say it in other words: poets who spread their poetry out over the landscape, and poets who draw their poetry into their inner recesses.)

National poets, landscapists, conservatives, traditional poets (this trend will be well served by provincials). LEÓN BENARÓS (1915), indifferent to the ingenious diversions of those who played with forms and metaphors to provide elements of surprise in their work, turned to his own life and to the lives around him, from which his poetry emanated, rich in inner vision as well as in popular traditions and historical episodes, from *The Imperishable Face* (*El rostro inmarcesible,* 1944) to *River of Years* (*El río de los años,* 1964). MIGUEL DE ETCHEBARNE (1915); his intent in *John Nobody: The Life and Death of a Tough* (*Juan Nadie: vida y muerte de un compadre,* 1954) (which is more of an ethology than an epic) is abstract, universal and even allegorical. Although the subject makes no claim to grandeur, many of the strophes have an extremely vivid impact through images that are colorfully descriptive, ingeniously defined, and fairly sing with lyricism. Borges' enthusiasm for this poem ("It is one I would have liked to write, but could not," he told me in 1959) is proof, not so much of the value of the book itself, but of the value he placed on the effort to do for the *"compadre"* (tough guy, roughneck, hoodlum, gangster) what Hernández had done for the gaucho. Juan Nadie is to the city what Martin Fierro had been to the country. JORGE CALVETTI (1916), with his recollections of childhood, landscapes, and historical evocations. JOSÉ MARÍA CASTIÑEIRA DE DIOS, chaste and popular. ALFONSO SOLA GONZÁLEZ (1917), melancholy, deep, confidential, lyrical. MANUEL J. CASTILLA (1918), author of the celebrated *North Within* (*Norte adentro*). RAÚL ARÁOZ ANZOÁTEGUI (1923). NICANDRO PEREYRA (1917). ÓSCAR HERMES VILLORDO (1928). AMELIA BIAGIONI. HORACIO ARMANI (1925). MARIO BUSIGNANI (1915). EMMA DE CARTOSIO (1924). LEDA VALLADARES (1920?). JULIO CARLOS DÍAZ USANDIVARAS (1926). HUGO ACEVEDO (1925). ENRIQUE VIDAL MOLINA (1926). HORACIO JORGE BECCO (1924), with no juvenile displays of vanguardism (although he made use of the freedom won by that vanguardism) wrote in *Country Poems* (*Campoemas,* 1952), with tranquillity and with a sincerity that did not even attempt to be musical, his impressions and feelings about the Argentine countryside. He evokes figures from the past as readily as he reaches forward to things to come in an attitude of expectancy. He takes the material of the country into his hands and shapes it into surprising miniatures, metaphors independent of one another, rich in ingenuity or visual effects. Some poets (those from the city more than those from the country) express anxiety about social problems, like ATILO JORGE CASTELPOGGI (1919).

Learned poets, European in their thinking, reformers, philosophers, with experimental tendencies. One of those we have read most is DANIEL DEVOTO (1916). He has grace, imagination, culture, technical mastery and abundant lyricism, from the dark roots within the depths of his solitude to the bright flower that blossoms at the peak of his song. *The Archer and the Towers* (*El arquero y las torres,* 1940) was his most metaphoric moment. The inter-

mittent, hard, obscure and provocative images in it demand imagination and sensitivity of the reader, which may finally penetrate
them like an electric current; whereupon image after image lights
up in the flash of a volcanic battery, illuminating the poet's solitude and melancholy.

In *The Book of Fables* (*Libro de las Fábulas*, 1943) we can
see that Devoto has learned by meditating on his own sadness
that if we go deep within ourselves we touch fear, and deeper
still we find a void. Shadows permeate his memories. Feverish
shudders of shadows. But his mounting lyricism washes the
wounds and heals them. Reverently, kindly, optimistically, Devoto seeks whatever beauty there is in things and tries to save it.
In his "Canticle of David" he is grateful for what is a source of
anguish to others. Later, Devoto applied himself to formal problems. In *Songs Against Change* (*Canciones contra mudanza*,
1945; *Disheveled Songs* (*Canciones despeinadas*, 1947), *Two
Rondels for Xylophone* (*Dos rondeles con maderas del país*,
1948), *Summer Songs* (*Canciones de verano*, 1950), *Hexasyllables from the Three Realms* (*Hexasílabos de los tres reinos*,
1959), he reconciled extremely complicated forms with maximum
facility of expression. It is a program of technical severity, with
acrostics ciphered in a code of difficult keys, surprising cabalisms,
counterpoints of short and long verses, regular and free verse,
criss-crossing of rhymes, experiments and manipulations that mis-
chievously flaunt precepts. But from the bottom of this creation
and re-creation of metrical procedures we can hear the sorrowing
voice of the poet converted into pure song. Love awakens sorrow
in him, on one hand, and on the other, poetry. In *Songs for No
One* (*Canciones para nadie*) his verse is more closely bound up
with pure intuition. JUAN RODOLFO WILCOCK (1919) sets out
with a romantic impulse to express his own feelings, but out of
respect for classic canons, he regulates them accordingly; a rare
equilibrium for one who is ashamed neither of the intensity of his
nostalgia nor of the power that ancient metres and rhymes have
on him in molding his expression. His neo-romantic accent, which
began with *Book of Poems and Songs* (*Libro de poemas y canciones*) and reached its fulness in *The Beautiful Days* (*Los her-*

mosos días) gradually became more ironic and bitter. He has also
written for the theater and a book of short stories: *Chaos* (*El
caos*). MARÍA GRANATA (1923), withdrawn and anxious, agonizing, and full of pallid fears. OLGA OROZCO (1920), who wrote
long dissolute verses, dark with the strong emotions of a solitary.
MARIO BINETTI (1916), dissatisfied with his own epoch, travels
through the centuries: the Greco-Latin classics, Dante and Pe-
trarch, Garcilaso and Fray Luis, the great European romantics,
the symbolists; and as he travels he writes about his own solitude
in ten books of confidential poetry from *The Good Shadow* (*La
sombra buena,* 1941) to *The Book of Returning* (*El libro de los
regresos,* 1959). JORGE VOCOS LESCANO (1924) has celebrated
feelings of human and divine love in architectural tones, conscious
of belonging to an illustrious family of Spaniards, from Garcilaso
and St. John of the Cross to Góngora, Bécquer and Juan Ramón
Jiménez, as well as to the family of Argentines from Banchs to
Bernardez and Molinari. GUILLERMO ORCE REMIS (1917) has a
double theme: man, tormented and helpless; and God, waiting for
us. ROBERTO PAINE (1916), an elegiac who begins with landscapes and draws them into himself, interiorizing them. The exquisite DAMIÁN CARLOS BAYÓN (1915). Two final poets, Murena
and Girri, are among the best of this generation. Murena we shall
study later among the prose writers. ALBERTO GIRRI (1918), with
none of the expressive automatic mechanisms of surrealism, but
crouching against a background of deliberate ambiguities, seeks to
reveal himself in images that capture essences. They tend to be
hermetic; they tend to freeze up; they tend to harden. "I refuse to
become tender," he says in "The Test." But behind the images we
can glimpse that the poet is apprehending the temporal sense of
existence. He focuses his thoughts, has doubts, and lets his imagination go to work. From *Deserted Beach* (*Playa sola*) to *Italian
Elegies* (*Elegías italianas*) he has sought the exact, hard, cold
word in which his vision of himself as an impassioned and tragic
solitary soul could be engraved implacably. CÉSAR FERNÁNDEZ
MORENO (1919), who evoked his nostalgia with simplicity in
Blind Rooster (*Gallo ciego,* 1940), allowed his voice to fall
into the broken, inarticulate murmur preferred by surrealists in

Twenty Years Later (*Veinte años después,* 1953). EDUARDO A. JONQUIERES (1918) began by writing serene poems: *Permanence of Being* (*Permanencia del ser,* 1945), *Growth of the Day* (*Crecimiento del día,* 1949), *The Monsters* (*Los vestiglos,* 1952). In *Song Trials* (*Pruebas al canto*) his language writhes in grimaces of inner torment. By plunging into the sources of his own existence the poet comes to know himself, and so his poetry becomes philosophical. ALFREDO A. ROGGIANO (1919) also became prominent in this effort to capture the meaning of being, that is, to reach objective thought through subjective channels, in *Illuminated River* (*El río iluminado,* 1947) and *Uncertain Vòyage* (*Viaje impreciso,* 1958). NORBERTO SILVETTI PAZ (1923), NICOLÁS COCARO (1926), and HORACIO NÚÑEZ WEST (1919) tend to be subjective and estheticist, but they have ontological roots. After the "generation of '40" there were other poets, less elegiac, more vital, nonconformist, anti-conventional, who moved back and forth between creationism and surrealism. Those who felt most keenly the need to be inventive called their movement Inventionism. They were RAÚL GUSTAVO AGUIRRE (1927), EDGAR BAYLEY (1919), JUAN JACOBO BAJARLÍA (1914), CARMELO ARDÉN QUIN, and GYULA KÓSICE (1924). Inventionism implied an attitude of artistic purity, fantasy in the initial impulse, and much linguistic labor in the construction; a preference for the autonomous image to the descriptive image, for indifference to personal anecdotes, for real objects and even for the logical meaning of the written material. Ardén Quin y Kósice detached himself from all of them to promote "madism"—*Ma-terialismo Di-aléctico* or "Madi Art" (Dialectical Materialism), which was exaggeratedly technical. Aguirre, one of the most important poets of these years, tried to integrate the poet's imagination with his life and even with his social milieu, and he did it by combining surrealism and creationism: *Signs of Life* (*Señales de vida*). Surrealism put out new shoots in the poems of JORGE ENRIQUE MÓBILI (1927), CARLOS LATORRE (1916), OSVALDO SVANASCINI (1920), JUAN JOSÉ CESELLI (1914). MARIO TREJO (1926), ALBERTO VANASCO (1925), and FRANCISCO MADARIAGA (1927) belong to these vanguard movements. We close our panorama

with the names of HÉCTOR EDUARDO CIOCCHINI (1922), JOAQUÍN
O. GIANNUZZI (1924), EMILIO SOSA LÓPEZ (1920), OSVALDO
ROSSLER (1926), JUAN CARLOS GHIANO (1920), CARLOS VIOLA
SOTO (1922), RAÚL AMARAL (1918), SIMÓN KARGIEMAN
(1926), GUSTAVO GARCÍA SARAVÍ (1920), JULIO LLINÁS (1929),
ROBERTO JUARROZ (1925), FERNANDO LORENZO (1923), NAR-
CISO POUSA (1926), DAVID MARTÍNEZ (1921), BETINA EDEL-
BERG (1921).

B. MAINLY PROSE

1. Novel and Short Story

A new realism, a new naturalism appears. It will be remembered that in the previous chapter the dissolution of the novel was
discussed—the novel such as it had been practiced up to 1910.
Proust, Joyce, Mann, Faulkner, Kafka, Woolf, Huxley, and others
broke its framework. And in Hispanic America novels appeared
that seemed to aim only at going counter to reality. But now, after
those experiments, there was a willingness, once again, to grasp
reality. Except that one could no longer return to the naturalism
of the nineteenth century. The young novelists of 1940 to 1955
read the Italian, French, and American neo-naturalists. Especially
the Americans. Instead of describing reality, they wanted to
transplant it in their books as something objective; to present it
as something alive, unruly, rough and unpolished, something that
is taking place between the novelist and the reader. That is, the
novelist no longer aspires to control the reader. The narrator as
the omniscient witness, as the operator who arranges things from
the inside in order that we may understand them better, as pro-
ducer and impresario of a spectacle to which we are invited for
our entertainment, disappears. The novel seethes, like life itself.
The characters are scarcely glimpsed because there is no one who
sees them totally. And since the characters only see one another
and do not clarify for us the mobile situations from which they
see one another, the chronological and spatial orders become confused. Reality is like this: absurd.

Although this realism does not look like that of the nineteenth century, it is realism. Furthermore: it is a daring, raw, aggressive, shocking naturalism. Things are not narrated or described by an author who feels the esthetic form of the novel, but presented by an author who feels the formless anti-novelistic ugliness of everyday life. Something is presented and something is hidden at the same time: a reality is presented but the artistic connections are hidden. The experiments that a few had undertaken earlier now are repeated as if they were not experiments but established modes of novelizing: representation of time, alteration of the narrative sequence, multiple perspectives, the technique of the stream of consciousness, and simultaneous, retrospective, crisscrossing actions on various planes. Novels, then, with a minimum of plot, characterization, and description. It is as if the novelistic structure had disintegrated. Either the stuff of the narrative is deposited in the mind of the author or of the characters—as was done in James Joyce's generation—or psychology is eliminated and autonomy is given to the objects themselves—as is done in Alain Robbe-Grillet's generation. It goes without saying that in these novels, or anti-novels, that resemble pieces of chaos, Creolism is abandoned. Creolism seemed to identify Hispanic-America with an agrarian reality. This could have been convincing up to the second world war; but then literature had to become aware that the cities had grown at the expense of the countryside, that the tone of life was that of the industrial society, that realism had to reflect class struggles in more urban styles.

One interesting phenomenon is the emergence, at the end of the fifties, of a Catholic group of narrators who, without deviating from the traditional beliefs, illuminate with a crude light and experimental techniques the sinful state of man (in Argentina, for example, Dalmiro Sáenz, Helen Ferro, Federico Peltzer, Bonifacio Lastra, and others). There is no bigotry in them. On the contrary, they often dare to treat themes of sex, crime, violence, and infamy, and they accomplish this with free ingenuity and good humor. Rooted in an ancient Catholicism, but displaying avant-garde techniques, these narrators resemble an opposing group, the Marxists, who also explain reality dogmatically, but who now practice ways of writing they had considered "bourgeois" and "decadent" in the thirties and forties.

(i) *Mexico* / JUAN JOSÉ ARREOLA (1918) has a preference for fantastic short stories and for intellectual games rich in humor, problems, and paradoxes: *The Whole Fabulous Book* (*Confabulario total,* 1962). He also published a theatrical farce, *Everyone's Day* (*La hora de todos,* 1954), in which he satirized the life of a potentate, in mobile scenes, full of innovations. His novel, *The Fair* (*La feria*) came out in 1963.

JUAN RULFO (1918) molded regional life with its landscapes, its names, its words and its situations of innocence, crime, adultery, and death—in his short stories *The Plain in Flames* (*El llano en llamas,* 1953), notable because of the way they present the inner life of peasants. Later, in *Pedro Páramo* (1955), he worked on his rural themes with a complicated novelistic technique which owes something to William Faulkner. The complication is due to the fact that the story is told in leaps, forward, backward, to the sides, and from several points of view. The eye that knows all and sees all belongs, naturally, to the author; but that eye enters the novel following Juan Preciados who narrates, in the first person, how he went on behalf of his dying mother to a place called Comala to straighten accounts with his father, Pedro Páramo. However, Juan Preciados finds that Comala is a ghost town: in the rarefied air only voices, echoes, and murmurings of phantoms are heard. Juan Preciados dies and his shade continues to carry on a dialog with other souls in purgatory. The author, who has come down to Comala like one who goes down to Hades, completes the story of Juan Preciados in the third person. The voices, echoes, and murmurings that Juan Preciados had heard are explained by means of the scenes conjured up by the author. The atmosphere is supernatural, but not subjective. Time does not flow: it is eternalized. Because of the apertures cut into this eternity we can see and hear the dead, caught in instants that do not succeed each other in a straight line but are dispersed in disorder: only the reader gives them meaning. The narrative nucleus is the life of Pedro Páramo, from his infancy to his death, in his old age, in the years that run from Porfirio Díaz to Obregón. His life is violent, despotic, brutal, covetous, vengeful, treacherous, sensual, but dignified by his great love for Susana, his childhood companion, who is half-crazed at the time when he takes her with him. The reader is chilled with horror, as if he were dreaming an absurd nightmare; the images, which occasionally are of great poetic force, tragically evoke the annihilation of a whole Mexican town. After Arreola and Rulfo, and emerging from the last group of narrators (Rosario Castellanos, Josefina Vicens, Luis Spota, Sergio Galindo, Jorge López Páez), the most noteworthy is CARLOS FUENTES (1928). The short stories in *The Masked Days* (*Los días enmascarados,* 1954) were followed by his novel, *The Most Transparent Region* (*La región mas transparente,* 1958). Submerged in the currents of the experimental novel, from Joyce and Faulkner on, Fuentes presents the mental processes of his multiple characters and interweaves the series of events. The protagonist is the city of Mexico, seen in various social classes, human types, activities and forms of sensitivity. The technique with which he handles the constructive elements of the novel (and even the mechanical resources of the typography) is complicated, ambitious, and exhibitionistic. But the novel is noteworthy for the delicacy and subtlety with which he brings together, especially in Ixca Cienfuegos, his vision of the Indian and the Creole, and the treachery to the revolution. Later in *The Good Consciences* (*Las buenas conciencias,* 1959)—which initiates a quartet of novels: *"The New Ones"* (*Los nuevos*)—Fuentes puts his shop in order, puts away all unnecessary tools, and with the economy of a nineteenth-century novelist, tells the story of a bourgeois, conservative and Catholic family in Guanajuato, beginning with the epoch of Porfirio Díaz, and the biography of the adolescent Jaime Ceballos, his intellectual friendship with the Indian, Juan Manuel, his religious scruples and his rebellion against phariseeism. It is interesting to note in *The Death of Artemio Cruz* (*La muerte de Artemio Cruz,* 1962) the contrast between the architectonic plan of the novelist and the material of the novel, which resists being architectured. Artemio Cruz, old, rich and powerful, is dying (the putrefaction of his body is somehow symbolic of the putrefaction of the social body of his country). Fuentes writes about these hours of agony under three pronouns: I, you, he. The "I" gives us, in the present, the interior monolog of the dying man. With the "you" the novelist wants us (in vain) to imagine the voice of the subconscious, indicating to the dying man the future of his mental ruminations. And the pronoun "he" is used by the novelist to write about Artemio (or about the lives surrounding his) through evocations of the past. "I," "you," "he," are triads repeated a dozen times. There are two retrospects open to the pronoun "he." These retrospects move about in time according to the capricious changes in the mentality of the dying man; the last one, which takes us to 1889 when Artemio was born, does not come from the head of the dying man, but from that of the omniscient author (who, by the way, sometimes acts clumsily, mixing up points of view and destroying the illusion of psychological unity). Twelve triads of pronouns, twelve scenes from the past. There should be a prophetic number 13—which corresponds to the final triad, truncated by death (there is an "I" and a "you" on the last page, but no longer a "he") and to the scene of the death itself, which takes place in 1959. Fuentes uses the techniques of the psychic stream, and submits them to his plan; we can also note his ideological intervention in his treatment of the theme. His interpretation of the psychology of Artemio as determined by the political and economic process of Mexico, in a sort of materialist dialectic, is too obvious, foreseeable, ordinary, and even partisan. Other stories: *Aura* (1962), *Song of the Blind* (*Cantar de Ciegos,* 1964). JOSEFINA VICENS (1915) describes through her protagonist in *The Blank Book* (*El libro vacío,* 1958) the dramatic yearning for self-expression that is essential to all men. JORGE LÓPEZ PÁEZ (1922): his novel *The Solitary Atlantic* (*El solitario atlántico,* 1958) is a poetic vision of the world as seen through the eyes of a child. SERGIO GALINDO (1926) prefers to display bourgeois life in provincial cities in his short stories and novels. SERGIO FERNÁNDEZ (1926), a good essayist, is distinguished for novels that penetrate slowly into the depths of solitary souls. LUIS SPOTA (1925) describes with a journalist's pen the defects in the social order. Other narrators: CARLOS VALDÉS (1928) invents absurd situations, or picks out the absurd aspect of normal situations in the stories in *The Name Does not Matter* (*El nombre es lo de menos*, 1961); in either case, he flaunts his ironic ingenuity before the eyes of the reader and often dulls the reader's view of the story itself. His tendency to fantasy (visible also in other collections of his short stories) is repressed in his novel *The Predecessors* (*Los antepasados*, 1963). RAFAEL SOLANA (1915) has cultivated poetry, the theater, the short story, and the novel. *There Once was a Five-Faced Man; Soliloquies or Perhaps a Novel* (*Érase un hombre pentafacico; Soliloquías o quiza novela*, 1961) is by EMMA GODOY (1920). It is a confused allegory with religious roots and existentialist foliage on the theme of Free Will. Esteban, whose existence is at his disposal, has a dialog with the five essences he may choose. The action takes place in the head (that carries on a monolog in several voices) of a schizophrenic about to commit suicide. The metaphysical keys to the allegory are not improved by being masked as novelistic images. Short-story writers: EDMUNDO VALADÉS (1915), GUADALUPE DUEÑAS (1920), MARÍA AMPARO DÁVILA (1928).

(ii) *Central America / Guatemala:* The most outstanding short-story writer of the group around the review *Acento* is AUGUSTO MONTERROSO (1921), who has published *Complete Works and Other Stories* (*Obras completas y otros cuentos*), containing stories of manifest irony. Also a short story writer, ironic in his observations on social inequities, is GUILLERMO NORIEGA MORALES (1918). JOSÉ MARÍA LÓPEZ VALDIZÓN, author of *The Letter* (*La carta*, 1958), cultivated the realist short story on social themes. RICARDO ESTRADA (1917) is the author of *Several Stories and the Unfeeling Head* (*Unos cuentos y la cabeza que no siente*).

Honduras: The best short story writer of these years is VÍCTOR CÁCERES LARA (1915): his *Humus* is sad but moistened by a certain soft humor. With short and agile brush strokes he tells us about farm laborers and city workers. The novel of the social problems involving the abuses of the great fruit companies arose with *Green Prison* (*Prisión verde*) by RAMÓN AMAYA AMADOR. Another of his novels, *Builders* (*Constructores*), raises its scaffolding in the city.

El Salvador: HUGO LINDO (1917) is one of the most outstanding figures. He is a poet—*Various Poems* (*Varia Poesia*, 1961)—but is situated here because the depiction of customs that dominated literature almost everywhere in Hispanic-America was enriched with psychological depth by his narrative work: *Sugar Brandy and Champagne* (*Guaro y champaña*, 1955), short stories, and *Justice, Mr. Governor!* (*¡Justicia, señor Gobernador!*), a novel (1960). RICARDO TRIGUEROS DE LEÓN (1917–1965) is distinguished for his artistically pigmented prose, in the manner of Azorín or Juan Ramón: *Bell Tower* (*Campanario*), *Town* (*Pueblo*). CRISTOBAL HUMBERTO IBARRA (1918) novelized rural life in *Quaking Bogs* (*Tembladerales*, 1957).

Nicaragua: FERNANDO SILVA ESPINOZA (1927).

Costa Rica: The economy of the coffee plantation in the central plateau gave way in importance to the increasing banana economy of the coasts. There was an alienation of the country and of its people in the marketplace as well as in the capital, in machinery and even in the language of the people, adulterated by people and races of foreign nationality. Added to all of this, the example of political revolutionary movements and agrarian reforms influenced novelists who wrote around 1940. This was the first important group of Costa Rican narrators. They tried to integrate the life of the coast and of the plateau and included the country in the social process of the world. Their tone was belligerent. We have already spoken about Fallas, Marín Cañas and Pacheco. Now we shall speak of younger novelists. FABIÁN DOBLES (1918), with his Marxist forceps, has pulled several novels out of the painful reality of injustices, privileges, and social miseries. *This Thing Called People* (*Ese que llaman pueblo*, 1942) is the story of the hardships of a young peasant. In *In the Valley* (*El sitio de las abras*) one of his favorite themes appears: the unjust sequestration of the peasants' lands. *A Bubble in Limbo* (*Una burbuja en el limbo*), even more than previous novels, shows the personal and literary side of Dobles. He has cultivated, likewise, the short story and poetry. Also frank in his political attitude, JOAQUÍN GUTIÉRREZ (1918) has novelized themes of imperialism and of banana plantations, but he does it at times through the techniques of the interior monolog. *Grove of Mangroves* (*Manglar*, 1946) follows the steps—and the thoughts—of Cecilia in her daily incidents as a teacher and woman, in the city and in the highlands. *Puerto Limón* (1950), less poetic, is rich in observations, though what is observed is more the mass than the individual. He has published *Poetry* (*Poesía*, 1937) and one of the best poetic novels on the theme of childhood: (*Cocorí*, 1954). On the more subjective side, and with a more complex style, is YOLANDA OREAMUNDO (1916–1956), who presents her experiences of time with techniques of psychic flux in *Terra Firma* (*Tierra Firme*) and in *The Route of Its Evasion* (*La ruta de su evasión*).

Panama: In their majority, the narrators of this generation concentrated on the national reality, urban or rural, and with faith in the people, but with their eyes open to the evils of society, they converted literature into a means of protest. What they lacked in esthetic concentration, they made up in practical militancy. Overestimation of the popular element at the cost of artistic merit. JOSÉ MARÍA SÁNCHEZ B. (1918)—author of *Three Stories* (*Tres cuentos*, 1946) and *Shumio-Ara*, 1948—has described, in the violent landscape of a certain Panamanian region, the life of laborers and the social injustices they experience. MARIO AUGUSTO RODRÍGUEZ (1919) has selected as his setting that band of land where the city and the country defend a mutual frontier from each other. MARIO RIERA (1920) and CARLOS FRANCISCO CHANGMARÍN (1922) are also rural narrators, nonconforming and sentimental. JOSÉ A. CAJAR ESCALA (1915) in *The Head-Man* (*El cabe-*

cilla, 1944) writes a novel with political implications about an abortive uprising of peasants. Different from those mentioned previously are writers of urban themes: JUAN O. DÍAZ LEWIS (1916), FERMÍN AZCÁRATE (1922). But Panamanian writers generally felt that the cities denied nationalism or that, in any case, the only thing that could justify a novel about the city would be its descriptions of the masses. We have purposely left to the end two of the best novelists of this realist group: Beleño and Jurado. JOAQUÍN BELEÑO (1921) in *Green Moon* (*Luna verde,* 1951) records his own experiences as an aggrieved worker in the American Zone of the Panama Canal. It is a picture of misery and dereliction, in contrast with the falsely prosperous city of Panama—a picture drawn with undisguised resentment. *The Criminals of Gamboa* (*Los forzados de Gamboa*) is one of the best novels in the country. RAMÓN H. JURADO (1922) works with sundry themes. *San Cristóbal* (1947) is the slow and occasionally poignant novel of the exploitation of sugar. *Deserters!* (*¡Desertores!,* 1952) reconstructs the "thousand day war" (between 1899 and 1902) with the legendary indigenous leader Victoriano Lorenzo. In *The Attic* (*El desván,* 1954)— basing himself on the strange book by Francisco Clark, *By Way of Torment* (*A través del tormento,* 1931)—Jurado analyzes the psychology of a person who is a witness to his own horrendous and macabre ankylosis.

(iii) *Antilles / Cuba:* VIRGILIO PIÑERA (1914) has an ironic, hopeless, anguished, and philosophizing attitude. In his *Cold Stories* (*Cuentos fríos*) —a hellish cold—his imagination carries him to torment. Although hermetic, he polishes his images with such care that through them we see, magnified, the meaninglessness of the world and the absurd movements of our existence. He has written a novel: *Small Manoeuvres* (*Pequenas maniobras;* 1962), and plays. The stories of HUMBERTO RODRÍGUEZ TOMEU (1919) move in an irrational current, floating on the absurdity and grotesqueness of life. GUILLERMO CABRERA INFANTE (1929) is a narrator of inner life (at least those aspects illumined by his favorite American authors: Faulkner, for example). LORENZO GARCÍA VEGA (1926) evokes personal recollections in his *Spirals of the Cuje Poles* (*Espirales del cuje,* 1951). SURAMA FERRER (1923) is a novelist in *Romelia Vargas* (1950) and a short story writer in *The Sick Sunflower* (*El girasol enfermo,* 1953). RAMÓN FERREIRA (1921) delves into Cuban life, but seeks psychological apertures and chiaroscuro atmospheres: *Shark and Other Stories* (*Tiburón y otros cuentos,* 1952). RAÚL GONZÁLEZ DE CASCORRO (1922), after his rural and endearing narrations, has dedicated himself to the theater: *Trees Are Roots* (*Arboles son raíces,* 1960).

Dominican Republic: The tendency to reflect national life with its social problems predominated. JOSÉ RIJO (1915), whose short stories are neat and circumspect; NÉSTOR CARO (1917), in his stories in *Black Sky* (*Cielo negro,* 1949) sketches the lives of humble people; RAMÓN LACAY POLANCO (1925), a poet, short story writer, and novelist: *The Woman of Water* (*La mujer de agua,* 1949), *In the Mist* (*En su niebla*) and *Southern Point* (*Punto sur,* 1958); and ALREDO FERNÁNDEZ SIMÓ (1915), author of the novel *Guazábara* (1958). J. M. SANZ LAJARA (1917) has traveled throughout Hispanic-America and from his observations have come several collections of realist stories: *Cotopaxi* (1949), *Aconcagua* (1950), and *The Padlock* (*El candado*, 1959).

Puerto Rico: A half century of United States domination could not move Puerto Rico from its Hispanic base. Even more: if not the will for political independence, at least the will to preserve Puerto Rican essences was growing. Literature reflected a divided opinion: supporters of United States annexation, supporters of total autonomy. In 1952 a juridical formula of conciliation was reached: the majority of the people voted in favor of an Associated Free State. There were dramatic national gestures, bloody incidents, polemics. The affirmation of the historical personality of the island and the defense of its values will be one of the themes of Puerto Rican narrative.

One of the best story writers is RENE MARQUÉS (1919). In *Another of Our Days* (*Otro día nuestro*, 1955) death, time, anguish, disgust, fear, consciousness of being, the absurdity of life, liberty—topics much viewed and reviewed by the existentialists—insert themselves like a corkscrew into Puerto Rican political reality in Quixotic or heroic episodes of nationalism. Marqués is a man of political concerns, preoccupied by national sovereignty, but subtle, complex, and capable of stylistic surprises. *The Eve of Man* (*La víspera del hombre*, 1959) is a novel about the adolescent years of Pirulo (Is the time that of San Felipe in 1928?), who leaves his poor home in Lares and goes from the mountainous region to seek his livelihood in Carrizales and Arcibo, by the sea. The reader immediately guesses the family secret: Pirulo is the natural son of a humble woman, Juana, and the owner of the great house, Don Rafa. Disconnected episodes, descriptions of the countryside and of rural chores, human characters, the process of apprenticeship in manhood and the maturity of national consciousness are loosely knit together. One of the threads of the novel is the amorous relationship between Pirulo and Lita, the daughter of his friend, Félix; Lita becomes pregnant, not by Pirulo but by her step-brother, Raúl. Félix commits suicide; his wife, driven mad, kills Lita with blows of a machete. The action proceeds lineally, except for two interruptions exposing Pirulo's childhood (II–IV) and the origins of the family of the owners (XXI–XXIII). The few disconnected sentences against North Americans and in favor of Puerto Rican nationalism (with allusions to Director Pedro Albizu Campos) never achieve political consequence. At best, the interpretation could be that the bastard Pirulo is a symbol of the island; he tries to deepen within himself the conviction that national sovereignty must first be established and only then can the solution to the ensuing economic and social problems be considered. There is no novelty in the style, composition, theme, or tone of this novel. Besides being prominent in narrative literature, Marqués is important in theatrical production.

The Little Cart (*La carreta*, 1952), in three acts, presents the story of a family which is uprooted from the land, moves to a city slum in San Juan and then to New York. He has collected in one volume, *Theater* (*Teatro*, 1959), *Maimed Suns, A Blue Boy for That Shadow* and *Death Does Not Enter the Palace*. He also published the drama *The Sun and the Mac-Donalds*, a "pantomime" *Johnny Simpleton and the Lady From the West*

(*Juan Bobo y la dama de occidente,* 1956), and the play *House Without Clock* (*La casa sin reloj,* 1962). Another of the good narrators is ABELARDO DÍAZ ALFARO (1920), author of the stories in *Terrazo* (1948), rural in atmosphere. Within a realist style his phrases are pleasant and at times contain overtones of protest against social hardships; in some pages he symbolizes human conflicts by using animals. A biographer of city life was JOSÉ LUIS GONZÁLEZ (1926). He has several collections of stories: *In the Shadow* (*En la sombra,* 1943), *Five Stories of Blood* (*Cinco cuentos de sangre,* 1945), *The Man in the Street* (*El hombre en la calle,* 1948), *On This Side* (*En este lado,* 1954). His novelette *Paisa* was written in 1950, but he re-edited it and modified it a good deal in 1955. Here he capably interweaves a story and an evocation. The story: two Puerto Ricans hold up a store in New York. The flashback: the one made by Andrés, the *paisano* or *paisa* [countryman] about his own life, from his hungry childhood in Puerto Rico to his hungry adolescence in New York. As a writer, José Luis González must be respected for his technique of interweaving and certain expressions of vivid imagination and poetry. Nevertheless, the novelette suffers from the impatience with which the author gives vent to his political zeal without first having stylized it artistically. The political outlines—of Marxist type—are obvious: the sufferings of the working class, social injustices, Yankee imperialism, racial discrimination, banditry as an immediate defense, and revolutionary struggle as an ultimate solution. Perucho, the other bandit, is the "reasoner," the one who raises an optimistic slogan from the depth of the tragedy in *Paisa.* PEDRO JUAN SOTO (1928), in *Spicks* (1956), also tells us stories of Puerto Ricans in New York, written in a stark prose, somewhat in the manner of Hemingway. He has written novels —*Anonymous Dogs* (*Los perros anónimos*), *Usmalí*—and theatrical pieces. GUILLERMO COTTO-THORNER (1916) is another of those inspired by the Puerto Rican colony in New York: *Tropics in Manhattan* (*Trópico de Manhattan,* 1951). CÉSAR ANDREU IGLESIAS (1918?) is one of the novelists of strong personality; he related in *The Defeated* (*Los derrotados,* 1956) the terrorist actions of the nationalists when they attacked government representatives in Washington. His later novels present turmoils in family life: *A Drop of Time* (*Una gota de tiempo*), and *The Landslide* (*El derrumbe*). EMILIO DÍAZ VALCÁRCEL (1929) delves into depressing, morbid, and disgusting realities and comes up with stories of great narrative strength. *The Siege and Other Stories* (*El asedio y otros cuentos,* 1958) is a black anthology of horrors: lesbianism, suicide, macabre scenes, prostitution, morphinomania, homicide, misery, injustice, thievery, sickness, sexual impotence. Only in one story—"The Toad in the Mirror"—the repugnant situation enters with a light of fantasy: the soldier without legs who turns into a toad and croaking, advances in little leaps headed for his wife's sex. But even in the other stories, molded from real mire, Díaz Valcárcel knows how to impose upon them a violently artistic form; he only fails in two discursive and moralizing monologs. The interior monologs, intercalated in the course of the action, are more effective. The most powerful aspect of the book is its keen comprehension of solitude. JOSÉ LUIS VIVAS MALDONADO stands somewhat apart from the previous group for his more sentimental, less combative stories: *Lights in Shadows* (*Luces en sombras,* 1955). Other names in this generation: EDWIN FIGUEROA (1925), SALVADOR DE JESÚS (1927).

(iv) *Venezuela* / In the year 1940 a generation of short story writers breaks out. They differ among themselves; some soak in national life, in the country and the city, others turn to self-contemplation or follow foreign literary examples. OSCAR GUARAMATO (1918) paints well the background of nature —landscapes, animals—and tenderly presents in the foreground his human characters: *Biography of a Beetle* (*Biografía de un escarabajo,* 1949). *By the River of the Street* (*Por el río de la calle*), *The Vegetable Girl and Other Stories* (*La niña vegetal y otros cuentos,* 1956). His social themes are usually the same ones preferred by the realists, but he treats of them with more artistic care and more lyricism. ANTONIO MÁRQUEZ SALAS (1919) takes nature by surprise in its most dramatic moments and a lyrical aura envelops his characters: *The Man and His Green Horse* (*El hombre y su verde caballo,* 1947), *Ants Travel at Night* (*Las hormigas viajan de noche,* 1956). He was one of the most influential figures of his generation, in part because of the innovations he used in composing his narratives. GUSTAVO DÍAZ SOLÍS (1920) is a good landscapist, but his stories turn to shambles when they come to the city: *Sea Swell* (*Marejada,* 1941), *It Rains On the Sea* (*Llueve sobre el mar,* 1942), *Stories of Two Times* (*Cuentos de dos Tiempos,* 1950). His stories, however, although composed straightforwardly, have strength and lyrical suggestion. ALFREDO ARMAS ALFONZO (1921) is a short-story writer who takes his situations, characters, and dialog from real life. Example: *The Mudslingers of the Devil* (*Los lamaderos del diablo,* 1956). HUMBERTO RIVAS MIJARES (1919) is an artist of well-disciplined style, precise and concise in his description of things: *Eight Stories* (*Ocho relatos,* 1944), *The World* (*El mundo,* 1949). OSWALDO TREJO (1928) is widely discussed for his procedures in the composition of strange climates: after becoming well known for his *Stories of the First Corner* (*Cuentos de la primera esquina,* 1952) he tried the novel with *Men, Too, are Cities* (*También los hombres son ciudades* (1962). Other short-story writers of this generation, called the "generation of '42": HÉCTOR MÚJICA (1927), PEDRO BERROETA (1914), MIREYA GUEVARA (1923), CARLOS DORANTE (1929), MANUEL TRUJILLO (1925), HORACIO CÁRDENAS BECERRA (1925). RAMÓN GONZÁLEZ PAREDES (1925) distinguished himself in several genres: poetry, the theater, the essay and, in narrative, his stories in *Extraordinary Crime* (*Crimen extraordinario,* 1945) and the novels, *The Imaginary Suicide* (*El suicida imaginario*) and *Génesis.* That ANDRES MARINO PALACIO (1928) was an abler novelist was revealed in *The Gay Ones, Sick Unto Death* (*Los alegres deshauciados*) and *Battle Toward the Dawn* (*Batalla hacia la aurora.* Others: ALEJANDRO LASSER, ENRIQUE MUÑOZ RUEDA, GLORIA STOLK (1918).

(v) *Colombia* / As everywhere else, there were narrators who tightened the natural bonds of life with reality, and narrators who loosened these bonds in order to see inside man, and there were even those who cut them so that men would come free from their circumstances, thus becoming free as fantasy. Another way of classifying writers would be by their narrative technique: those who rely safely on the effectiveness of a clear, continuous, logical traditional art; others who risk calculated disorder. JESÚS BOTERO RESTREPO (1921) was the novelist of the jungle in *Andágueda* (1947). NÉSTOR MADRID-MALO (1918) in *Luck at Seven O'Clock and Other Stories* (*Suerte a las 7 y otros relatos*, 1955), is one of those who broke loose from the formulas of the depicters of social customs and, in simple prose, approached men to study their psychologies. EDUARDO SANTA (1928) made himself known with *The Lost Province* (*La provincia perdida*, 1951). Is it a novel? Only in the sense that one can say that Juan Ramón Jiménez' *Platero y yo* is a novel. Poems in prose? Only in the sense that one can say that the "confessions of a little philosopher," in "the towns" of Azorín are so. Rather, it is an album of vignettes of life in Aldeópolis as they are evoked by a well-educated adolescent. Or, better yet, an intimate diary. Scenes, types, customs, landscapes, real things, but the reality that always emerges is the sensibility of a wandering and artistic author. In his novel *The Sunflower* (*El girasol*), Santa later analyzes the obscure movements of an abnormal psychology. MANUEL MEJÍA VALLEJO (1923), impersonal, accurate in his version of what he sees in the countries of America, has written short stories: *Time of Drouth* (*Tiempo de sequía*), and several novels: *We Were the Land* (*La tierra éramos nosotros*), *At the Foot of the City* (*Al pie de la ciudad*) and *The Appointed Day* (*El día senalado*). Other realists: CLEMENTE AIRO (1918), who presented the violence of alienated and maladjusted people in *The City and the Wind* (*La ciudad y el viento*); CARLOS ARTURO TRUQUE (1927); JESÚS ZARATE MORENO (1915), whose stories are about village and country life; ELISA MÚJICA (1918), PRÓSPERO MORALES PRADILLA (1920), ALBERTO DOW (1923), MANUEL ZAPATA OLIVELLA (1920), author of *In China a Saint is Born* (*En China nace un santo*) and other intense novels; MARIO FRANCO RUIZ (1921). The two most notable novelists, García Márquez and Cepeda Samudio, are less dependent on reality. GABRIEL GARCÍA MÁRQUEZ (1928), in *Withered Leaves* (*La hojarasca;* 1955) cedes the telling of her story to three witnesses of the corpse of a suicide: the boy, the mother, and the grandfather. Through their interior monologs—simultaneous and twined together in less than an hour, in 1928 —the reader ties the loose ends and is apprised of what has happened in more than a century. The action advances, retreats, zigzags. It is the story of a strange French doctor, of a family, of a whole town brought to ruin. García Márquez was among those who wrote about Colombian matters with literary procedures that were new to Colombia: see also *The Bad Hour* (*La mala hora*) *The Colonel Has No One to Write to Him* (*El coronel no tiene quien le escriba*). *The Tales of Grandmama* (*Los cuentos de mama grande*) are unreal, or made unreal by the shadow of mystery and fantasy that surrounds them. ÁLVARO CEPEDA SAMUDIO (1926), who is well aware of the path that contemporary fiction took after the experiments with time, interior dialogs, narrative focal points, and the crumbling away of plot, renovated, albeit moderately, the traditional form of the short story: *We Were All Waiting* (*Todos estábamos a la espera*, 1954). JAIME ARDILA CASAMITJANA (1919) poured the material of his novel *Babel* (1943) into the head of an intellectual protagonist and made a keen analysis of the perception of time and of the confused states of personality. RAMIRO CÁRDENAS

(1925), author of *Twice Dead and Other Stories* (*Dos veces la muerte y otros cuentos,* 1951), handles the techniques of the stream of consciousness, the sudden shift in point of view, the latticing of event and evocation in such a way that reality dissolves into a strange atmosphere. ARTURO LAGUADO (1919) is one of the few Colombian writers with a rarefied and fanciful atmosphere: *The Morris Rhapsody* (*La rapsodia de Morris,* 1948), *Dance for Rats* (*Danza para ratas,* 1954). Another: ENRIQUE BUENAVENTURA (1925).

(vi) *Ecuador* / ADALBERTO ORTIZ (1914) made his appearance in 1942 with *Juyungo,* one of the best Hispanic-American novels. The dominant theme is the Negro race and its mixing with Indians and whites: prejudices, resentments, hatreds. But the purpose of the author is to superimpose upon the concern for the sufferings of his race the more universal sufferings caused by social injustice and war. The current of action effaces the characters, as if they were drawn on water. One character remains, Ascensión, the "*Juyungo*" Negro, whom we see from infancy to death, during the Peruvian invasion of Ecuador in 1941. Light falls upon the terrible nature and the primitive customs of Negroes, Indians, mulattoes, and zambos. Everything else, although faintly sketched, remains in the shadows. The exploitation of the poor, political baseness, sickness, superstition, violence, death, and the arduous work in the jungles and rivers of Esmeraldas occupy the greater portion of *Juyungo.* But there are also Indians, noble political ideals, patriotic reflections, hopes for betterment. The novel does not have stylistic unity; imaginative expressions go hand in hand with worn-out clichés. A disordered novel, and not always because the author wishes it so. The episodes succeed each other needlessly, in a line of continuous points. Each chapter is preceded by a fragment of what the "eye and ear of the jungle" see and hear. There is, then, an attempt at artistic composition. And in fact, the lack of plot and the accumulation of so many dialectal words, of so many strange scenes, of so many unknown things, terminate by creating a poetic atmosphere. Later Ortiz collected eleven stories in *The Bad Shoulder* (*La mala espalda,* 1952). They have a lyrical realism, especially in the description of the landscape, but nature does not drown out the voices of men. In a climate of violence, the weak perish; the strong survive. The motivations are fear, avarice, elemental passions, jealousy. Even here, the preoccupation with racial tensions appears and the procedure that represents the stream of consciousness. Recently he published his poetic anthology: *The Wounded Animal (El animal herido*, 1959).

PEDRO JORGE VERA (1915) took his first literary steps as a poet, but soon realized that his interest in society (above all, in the correction of social injustice) would take him into the narrative form. His novels *The Pure Animals (Los animales puros*, 1946) and *The Sterile Seed (La semilla esteril*, 1962) are products of an intellectual process. Instead of being carried away by the exterior aspects of life in Ecuador, as other novelists had been, this novelist went into his characters in depth. These characters are the individual and collective actors in the social drama. His stories, *Eternal Mourning and Other Stories (Luto eterno y otros relatos*, 1950) and *An Abandoned Coffin (Un ataúd abandonado*) are also noteworthy for their social significance as well as for their introspective insights. NELSON ESTUPIÑÁN BASS (1915), an erudite novelist; RAFAEL DÍAZ YCAZA (1925), a poet, *Bottle Thrown into the Sea (Botella al mar*, 1964) has also become known for his short stories.

(vii) *Peru* / Here, as in almost all the other Hispanic-American countries, the novel as a document of a badly organized society —generally a rural one—fell into decline, and the characterization of people was sacrificed to the necessity of proving a thesis. Now social themes make up the narrative, but at least there is more artistic consciousness, more willingness to keep up with the renovation of novelistic techniques. Some writers followed the road of indigenous themes, treating them with lyrical force. They were stimulated by the example of José María Arguedas.

ELEODORO VARGAS VICUÑA (1924) stands out among this group. He has cultivated the rural story, but does it in the form of poetic vignettes: *Nahuín* (1953). Putting himself within the sensitivity, the beliefs, the points of view of his mountain characters, he makes them speak in a convincing local language. Writing in this same vein is CARLOS E. ZAVALETA (1928), one of the most notable writers of his generation. His stories, from *The Cynic (El cínico*, 1948) to *Mourning Attire (Vestido de luto*, 1961), deal with the problem of the Indian, not from a sociological point of view, but rather with

an emphasis on psychological nuances. His knowledge of American literature, especially Faulkner, has enriched his technique. The characters, each
one from various perspectives, talk or break the narrative continuity with
their testimonials. The reader often is lost in the disorder, or becomes dis-
couraged by the difficulties of reading the book. In *The Villenas Christ*
(*El Cristo Villenas*) the plurality of different reports on the same violent
reality is resolved more successfully. Other titles: *The Ingars* (*Los Ingar*,
1955), *Violent Hands* (*Unas manos violentas*, 1958). Also among the
nativists and regionalists: ALFONSO ALCALDE (1921), PORFIRIO MENESES
(1915), SARA MARIA LARRABURE (1921). There is another group who
equip their narratives with city experiences. They are realists who criticize
social iniquity, but are concerned with the different planes of human personality and the necessities of renovating the art of composition. We mention, above all, JULIO RAMÓN RIBEYRO (1929). He was successful with his
novel *Chicken-Hearted* (*Los gallinazos sin plumas*, 1955), a novel about
two boys who live in a miserable section of Lima, gathering filth to feed
their grandfather's pig. The note of violence, sordidness, and cruelty tends
to crop up in his *Tropical Stories* (*Cuentos de circunstancias*, 1958) and
Three Stories of Rebellion (*Tres historias sublevantes*). He has also been
successful in the theater: "*Santiago the Birdman*" ("*Santiago el pajarero*").
His *Chronicle of San Gabriel* (*Cronica de San Gabriel*) is a rural novel.
Also in this group are ALBERTO WAGNER DE REYNA (1915) with *Flight*
(*Fugue*), about university students and *Like everything on earth* (*Como
todo en la tierra*), the story of a family; LUIS FELIPE ANGELL (1926);
EDGARDO DE HABICH (1926?); ARMANDO ROBLES GODOY (1923), CARLOS
THORNE (1924). A third group of narrators cultivated humor and fantasy,
like JOSÉ DURAND (1925), an irrepressible caricaturist in his stories, *Cats
Among Us* (*Gatos entre nosotros*). MANUEL MEJÍA VALERA (1925) distinguished himself as an expressionist and a writer of fantasy. He published *The Evasion* (*La evasión*, 1954) and some of his pages were collected
in *Canvases of Dreams* (*Lienzos de sueños*, 1959), which are narrative
sketches: one of them, the one that gives its title to the volume, is imitative
of Borges in the play of forms within forms. Also among "the absurd," CAR-
LOS MINO JOLAY (1915). Another: FELIPE BUENDÍA (1927).

(viii) *Bolivia* / Within the predominantly social novel RAÚL BOTELHO
GOSÁLVEZ (1917) stands out: *Green Drunkenness* (*Borrachera verde*,
1938), *Cocaine* (*Coca*, 1941), *Plateau* (*Altiplano*, 1945), *It is Worth a
Fortune, Interlude* (*Vale un Potosí, entremés*, 1949), *Untamed Land*
(*Tierra chúcara*, 1957). His novel *Cocaine* is the story of the failure of
Álvaro, a young aristocrat who returns to La Paz from the Chaco War
morally destroyed. He goes to the jungle in search of gold, has love affairs
with two equally passionate women, although of opposite social classes; he
is debased by the cocaine habit and ends by committing suicide. Botelho
Gosálvez unites, without amalgamating, socialist realism with an estheticism
that is still Modernist, even in the Valle Inclán brand. The nerve most frequently set in vibration is the erotic one. From MARCELO QUIROGA SANTA
CRUZ comes one of the best novels in the country: *The Uninhabited* (*Los
deshabitados*).

(ix) *Chile* / In general, one can say that the narrators of this period wanted nothing to do with the Creolists, at least with the Creolists who limited themselves to making an inventory of external events. What interested them more from the Chilean past was the psychological, urbane direction of D'Halmar-Barrios-Prado-Maluenda-Edwards Bello-Manuel Rojas. But if in the beginning this rejection of a literature that was excessively vernacular, excessively loaded with geography, botany, zoology, and ethnography unites them, they again part company because of the way they accentuate their narrations—accents that are social and political, imaginative and formalist. The changes brought by industrialization, planned economies, the violent aspiration of the masses to govern, and the second world war, plus the changes in literary technique resulting from the experiments undertaken ever since the generation of James Joyce and company, modified the form and content of the novel and the short story.

The principal writers in this new narrative mode were CARLOS DROGUETT (1915) with *Sixty Deaths on the Staircase* (*Sesenta muertos en la escalera,* 1954), *Eloy* (1960), and *100 Drops of Blood and 200 of Sweat* (*100 gotas de sangre y 200 de sudor,* 1961), novels about violent deaths, with interior monologs, written in a prose that is no ordinary prose. GUILLERMO ATÍAS (1917), who novelized in *Banal Time* (*El tiempo banal,* 1955) lives from the various social echelons, seen from several simultaneous planes in a framework of parallel actions, paying special attention to the psychological aspects. FERNANDO ALEGRÍA (1918), distinguished by his novelesque biographies, turned to the novel itself in *Chameleon* (*Camaleón,* 1950) which, if not a political novel, is at least politically loaded. After his stories, *The Poet Who Turned into a Worm* (*El poeta que se volvió gusano,* 1956)— also in a political vein—he wrote a picaresque-type novel on the life of an Hispanic-American in San Francisco: *Jack of Hearts* (*Caballo de copas,* 1957). The plot interweaves three threads: the story of a horse, the love of Mercedes and the narrator, and the strike of the stevedores led by Marcel, Mercedes' father. His latest novel: *Hunter's Nights* (*Las noches del cazador,* 1961). VOLODIA TEITELBOIM (1913), a militant Communist, denounces in her narratives the exploitation of the working class and the struggle against foreign companies: *Son of Saltpeter* (*Hijo de salitre*), *The Seed in the Sand* (*La semilla en la arena*). Now a list of names of those approaching the *"generation of 1950"*: PABLO GARCÍA (1919), a writer of short stories with lyric power, penetrating in his psychological execution, violent in his prose: *The Boys and the Bar Pompeya* (*Los muchachos y el bar Pompeya,* 1958); ROBERTO SARAH (1918), EDMUNDO CONCHA CONTRERAS (1918?); CARLOS LEÓN (1916); MIGUEL SERRANO (1917). And now the "generation of 1950." One of the traits that characterize them is their resistance to the claims of nationalistic or social realism. In order to make their narratives more personal, they gild them with a conscience and a point of view: from this process stems their autobiographical quality and their air of interior monologs. At times, the meaning of the novel is illuminated by symbols, allegories, and myths. There is an upper middle-class atmosphere, a climate of existential anguish. The one who defined this generation is ENRIQUE LAFOURCADE (1927). His literature—poetic prose, short stories, novels—refuses to be corralled into any rural localisms; he also refuses to propose for the problems of literature solutions that are not, above all, literary ones. His last book is *The Prince and the Sheep* (*El príncipe y las ovejas,* 1961). JOSÉ DONOSO (1925) after the stories in *Summer Vacation* (*Veraneo*)—distantly related to Henry James, Faulkner, Truman Capote—wrote one of the best novels in recent years: *Coronation* (*Coronación,* 1957). The title refers to the fact that at the end two old servants crown their nonagenarian mistress, the insane Elisa Grey de Ábalos, with silver flowers. They crown her to please her, but she, in her madness, believes she is an aristocrat and a saint. And, so crowned, she dies. But although the title seems to select the value of this character and this scene, the novel sets in motion a much more complicated reality. In "Misia" Elisa's mansion in Santiago, Chile, the lives of rich and poor classes are intermingled. Don Andrés, her nephew, a bookish idler in his fifties who has never lived intensely or known love, suddenly feels a passion for the sixteen-year-old servant, Estela. He does not succeed in making her his and goes insane, confirming his philosophy that the universe is a chaos, that man is a particle of matter whose reason serves him only to tell him that he will die, and that therefore madness is "the only order," "the only way to become integrated with truth." Estela, whose duty is to take care of "Misia" Elisa, opens doors in the mansion to let in her lover, Mario, a humble, vulgar boy with a head full of confusion and a weak character, the best-drawn character in the novel. Through him we see the rascality, the sordidness, the brutality, the misery and the crime. The action is lineal and develops with growing interest. In the last pages the episodes of the feast of the coronation of "Misia" Elisa, the brutal punishment of Estela, who is pregnant, and Don Andre's nervous crisis are all solidly brought together. Donoso knows how to tell a story. He writes as an onlooker, with penetrating psychological observations, realistic descriptions and dialog in the vernacular. His technique is so traditional that the reader is often reminded of the novelistic world of Galdós. JOSÉ MANUEL VERGARA (1929) gained fame with his novel *Daniel and the Golden Lions* (*Daniel y los leones dorados,* 1956), an immersion in contemporary life in England and Spain from the Catholic point of view, akin to that of Graham Greene in the analysis of religious psychology, and, above all, in the conflict of sexuality, guilt feelings, and saving faith. His last book: *The Four Seasons* (*Las cuatro estaciones,* 1958) confirms his search for clarity and subtlety. CLAUDIO GIACONI (1927), encouraged by the reading of international literature (especially in the English language, such as Faulkner, Wolfe, and others), rejected the regionalist costume of Chilean narrative and appeared in letters with a propensity for rebellion, harshness, reform and judgment; he created lively characters in his stories: *Difficult Youth* (*La difícil juventud,* 1954) and *Amadeo's Dream*

(*El sueño de Amadeo,* 1959). JAIME LASO (1926) brings his readers the surprise of a well-disciplined imagination in his novel, *The Stocks* (*El cepo,* 1958) as well as in his short stories: *The Disappearance of John Di Cassi* (*La desaparición de John Di Cassi,* 1961). HERBERT MULLER (1923), in *Perceval and Other Stories* (*Perceval y otros cuentos,* 1954) tends to be schematic, subtle, wrapped up in his characters, without external descriptions. Later he published a novelette: *Without Gestures Without Words Without Tears* (*Sin gestos sin palabras sin llanto,* 1955). ARMANDO CASSIGOLI (1928) looks at life with a festive eye, taking pleasure in the absurd and in social criticism: *Confidences and Other Stories* (*Confidencias y otros cuentos,* 1955), *Angels under the Rain* (*Ángeles bajo la lluvia,* 1960), MARÍA ELENA GERTNER (1927), a Catholic, has successfully turned from poetry and drama to the novel: *Islands in the City* (*Islas en la ciudad,* 1958). Others: MARGARITA AGUIRRE (1925?), GUILLERMO BLANCO (1926), MARIO ESPINOSA (1924), ALFONSO ECHEVERRÍA (1922), LUIS SÁNCHEZ LATORRE (1925), JORGE GUZMÁN (1929), famous for his story *"El capanga,"* promises to bear fruit because of his lucidity and conscientiousness. JAIME VALDIVIESO (1929), JORGE IBÁÑEZ (1926). ENRIQUE MOLLETO (1922); MARTA JARA (1919), with *South Wind* (*Surazo*); MERCEDES VALDIVIESO (1928); JUAN VENTURA AGUDIEZ (1923).

(x) *Paraguay* / AUGUSTO ROA BASTOS (1918), a poet in *The Ardent Orange Grove* (*El naranjal ardiente*), is the most representative of the Paraguayan narrators of this generation. *Thunder in the Leaves* (*El trueno entre las hojas,* 1953) consists of seventeen stories that describe the violence and misery of national life. The prose adheres to regional speech (a mixture of Spanish and Guaraní) as easily as it twists with literary artifices. He protests against the social and political situation in his country, and his tone is one of hope for the revindication of the oppressed classes. *Son of Man* (*Hijo de hombre,* 1960), his novel, moves in different currents of time, at times successive, at times transposed, at times simultaneous; the narrator also presents different characters, and occasionally presents himself as either observer or protagonist. The reader who puts this reality, dislocated by memories, impressions, and indirect testimony, into chronological and rational order, sees a tragic canvas. A Doctor Rosa Manzón explains at the end that what the reader has read are posthumous pages written by Miguel Vera, who was shot by a revolver he had lent to a child, perhaps to commit suicide at second hand. Vera was born in 1905 and died in 1936; but as his story contains what he has heard from his elders (the oldest is Macario, slave of the dictator Francia), the history of independent Paraguay unfolds before our eyes, up to a year before the war with Bolivia. However, it is more than the history of the nation; it is the history of a neighborhood in Itape: the lives of innumerable men and women move together, separate, and are joined again. Some episodes progress as if they were autonomous, but all of them are woven into a complicated plot. For example: the chapter "Exodus", whose final detail—the phantomlike wandering wagon—branches off through the other chapters. There are tormented, egotistical, heroic, miserable, abnegate and cruel lives. There are memorable characters, like Gaspar Mora, the leper, who cuts the figure of a rebellious Christ—the son of man, the Russian Alejo, the Jara family and many more. As he narrates, Miguel Vera reveals pathetically his condition as a weak and ruined man. Roa Bastos creates convincing characters, puts them into moving situations, describes vigorously the horrors of nature, injustice, and death; and, however naturalistic his writing is, there are always flashes of poetry in his pages. The novel is uneven in style, in tone, and in merit; its unity lies, however, in its compassion. In the pages on the Chaco war, for example, there are no nationalistic meannesses or facile political slogans, but a tremendous description of unnecessary thirst and suffering.

José María Rivarola Matto (1917), in *Foliage in the Eyes* (*Follaje en los ojos,* 1952), novelized the exploitation of the *"yerba"* plantations. Another narrator: Néstor Romero Valdovinos (1916).

(xi) *Uruguay* / The narrators might be divided into two families: one with roots in the native soil, with simpler emotions, realist, careless in style; the other of more rigorous and intelligent techniques, polished in the minor forms of expression and in the construction of the overall architecture. In the first family Luis Castelli (1918) (Domingo Luis Bordoli), unadorned in his stories in *Lonely Byways* (*Senderos solos,* 1960), and Julio C. da Rosa (1920) are distinguished for their nativist stories. The latter has matured from the stories in *Uphill* (*Cuesta arriba,* 1952) to those in *From Sun to Sun* (*De sol a sol,* 1955), though within the limits he imposed on himself: the country, the village, humble creatures committed to humble tasks, sad anecdotes, conversational rather than literary words. His novel *Juan of the Forsaken Ones* (*Juan de los desamparados,* 1961) shows him on the rise. In the second family, that of more esthetic ambitions, Carlos Martínez Moreno (1917), intelligent and complex, is outstanding; he is more preoccupied than inventive; his short stories: *The Days Left to Live*

(*Los días por vivir*) and *The Aborigines* (*Los aborígenes*); his novels: *The Wall* (*El paredón*) in which Uruguayan scenes are intermingled with scenes of revolutionary Cuba in 1959, and *The Other Half* (*La otra mitad*), to be published. ÁNGEL RAMA (1926), the author of *Oh Puritan Shadow* (*Oh sombra puritana,* 1951) and *Mapless Land* (*Tierra sin mapa,* 1959), tender Galician sketches; JOSÉ PEDRO DÍAZ (1921), who makes phantoms of reality in his story *The Inhabitant* (*El habitante,* 1949); and creates allegories in his *Anthropological Exercises* (*Ejercicios antropológicos,* 1960). MARÍA INÉS SILVA VILA, with her stories of fantastic themes and artistic style: *The Snow-White Hand* (*La mano de nieve,* 1951) *Happiness and Other Sadnesses* (*Felicidad y otras tristezas*). CLOTILDE LUISI in *The Return and Other Stories* (*El regreso y otros cuentos,* 1953) writes stories in the fantastic vein; MARIO ARREGUI (1917) maintains his constructive tension and his intelligent selection of words even in moments when he describes plebeian customs: *Night of St. John and Other Stories (Noche de San Juan y otros cuentos,* 1956); MARIO BENEDETTI (1920) is a good observer of the souls of his characters, generally seen in their city surroundings. He is also a poet comedy writer and essayist, but his narrative production is more considerable: *This Morning* (*Esta Mañana,* 1949), *The Last Trip and Other Stories* (*El último viaje y otros cuentos,* 1951), *Which of Us* (*Quién de nosotros,* 1953), *Montevideans* (*Montevideanos,* 1959), and novels: *The Truce* (*La tregua,* 1960), in the form of an intimate diary, and *Thanks for the Fire* (*Gracias por el fuego,* 1965). Other narrators: ROLINA IPUCHE RIVA (1922?), one of the best short-story writers: *The Flank of Time* (*El flanco del tiempo*); MARIO C. FERNÁNDEZ (1928?), who has cinematographic speed in his novel, *They Served as a Wall for Us* (*Nos servían como de muro,* 1962?); ARMONÍA SOMERS, E. GALEANO.

(xii) *Argentina* / One of the outstanding figures of this generation—in poetry, essay, and novel—is HÉCTOR A. MURENA (1924?). Furthermore, he has been one of the thinking leaders, one of the definers of his generation. His trilogy *History of a Day* (*Historia de una día*)—"The Fatality of Bodies," "The Laws of Night," and "The Inheritors of the Promise"—and his short stories—*The Center of Hell* (*El centro del infierno,* 1956) give us a desperate and despairing vision. He engages reality and describes it with rawness; but in the stories mentioned, in order better to communicate his feeling that the world is hostile to us, he has preferred to give it a fantastic dimension. Horror and the unknown are not for Murena pleasures of the imagination, but torments. It is as if he were narrating consumptions of the body, exhaustions of the soul; and he does it in unsavory and vinegary terms. He is displeased with life, tired of the senselessness that surrounds him, and he lets himself go and sinks into the obscure, into tedium, into solitude. Atmospheres of failure and degradation. Murena's pessimism is reflected in a complaining note in his poetry: *Lightening of the Duration* (*Relampago de la duración*) and is argued in his essays: *Homo Atomicus, Essays on Subversion* (*Homo Atomicus, Ensayos sobre subversión*). In everything he writes there is a stamp of independence and authenticity. Another of the more excellent writers is JULIO CORTÁZAR (1916). He attracted attention with *The Kings* (*Los reyes,* 1949), a dramatic prose poem. It is a prose of marked strength in the definition of images and ideas. In it he proposed a curious variant of the myth of the Minotaur. Ariadne, in love with her monstrous brother the Minotaur, gives the thread to Theseus, not so he may leave the labyrinth safely, but so that the Minotaur might destroy it and thus escape. But the Minotaur prefers to die. He lets himself be killed so as to survive vaguely in the dreams and instincts of Ariadne, and further, in the dreams and instincts of all men. From that moment on, the Minotaur will live in our blood and hold sway over us like a genie. Already in *The Kings* we recognize Cortázar's favorite theme: the monstrous, the bestial, mysteriously tied up with human destiny. Notice the very significant title of the book that followed: *Bestiary* (*Bestiario,* 1951), fantastic stories. And in *End of the Game* (*Final del juego,* 1956), also a collection of stories, the theme reappears in "Axolotl," wherein the narrator has the feeling that he is one of the monsters that he is looking at in the aquarium. Although the theme of his stories is not animal life, Cortázar will animalize man in cruel descriptions, as in the nightmarish story "The Maenads." It is possible that an unattentive reader, in allowing himself to be impressed by the sharp perception of details with which Cortázar begins his stories, may believe that he will be dealing with everyday men and things. He will soon notice, however, that an air of hallucination and poetry seeps into the apertures of reality, envelops the episode, and makes it end in phantasmagoria. In "The Band" there is satiric intention: that ugly, sordid, absurd, grotesque "reality" is that of Peronism. The protagonist, Lucio, "understood that that view of life could extend itself to the street, to the coffee shop, to his blue suit, to his evening date, to his office work tomorrow, to his savings plan, to his summer vacation, to his girl friend, to his old age, to the day of his death." And, disgusted, he exiled himself from Argentina. One suspects that this inundation of vulgarity leaves its mark also on the language of writers educated in refined literatures and politically against the Peronist movement, but who feel, all of a sudden, that to speak like the masses is "clever" (Bioy Casares and Borges, in *Isidro Parodi*) or vigorously real (Cortázar). Cortázar does not construct in his stories. He writes with a certain reluctance and is careless with his composition. The same can be said of his collection of stories: *Secret Weapons* (*Las armas secretas,* 1959). Perhaps the best of them is "The Persecutor." The atmosphere—jazz, vice, delirium, sordidness, etc.—is well done: it is the beat generation, the lost and disoriented youths of recent years. But the moral slackness of customs also slackens the style of the storyteller. Bruno, a jazz critic, has written a book about the music of his friend Johnny, an erotic saxophonist, drunkard, and marihuana smoker. He is preparing a second edition: he listens carefully to what Johnny has to say about his own music and about the book that he, Bruno, has written. But Johnny is so incoherent that he says nothing in reality: he barely alludes to certain themes (time, God) and there is no evidence that behind his mumblings there is really any deep meaning (nor is there any evidence that Cortázar feels these themes deeply). Johnny finally dies; and so, with a chronological note to that effect in the second edition, the novel closes; and that is it. After *The Prizes* (*Los premios,* 1961) came *Rayuela* (1963). It is an experimental novel, though of all the novelties he practices the newest turns out to be the description, in one of the Argentine jargons, of the physiology of sex and excrement. It has three parts: I, "from that side," or the life in Paris of Horacio Oliviera, an Argentine in his forties, and some of his friends. It is a bohemian life (literature, music, painting, philosophy), sexually promiscuous, socially sordid, intellectually nihilistic. II, "from this side," or Horacio Oliviera repatriated in Buenos Aires (hotel, circus, insane asylum), but even more neurotic than before. III, "from other sides," chapters which, according to Cortazar, are "prescindable," but they fill out and complete

scenes already related and bring in a new character, the writer
Morelli, on whose theories on the novel he seems to have received
some advice from Cortázar himself. One of the points in Morelli's
novelistic program is that the reader should be given notes, mem-
oranda, sketches, perspectives, intuitions, stimuli, so that as he
reads he can act as co-creator of the novel. Cortázar follows this
advice in part, for in the first two parts of *Rayuela* the action
develops in a conventional way, along a line marked by the clock
and the calendar. Only in the third part, the one Cortázar considers dispensable, are the chapters shuffled, and the reader, if he
likes, can follow the unsystematic way in which they are printed,
or he can follow a capricious system of numbers: 73–1–2–116–
3–84, etc. A great many of the experiments with syntax, spelling,
compositions, and interior monolog are arbitrary; that is, they are
not motivated in the novel by any concept of the world, perception
of time, revelations of the characters, vital or social situation.
They are experiments made for the sake of experimenting as part
of an attitude that is disenchanted, ironic, belittling, excessive,
caustic, perhaps resentful, toward literature as a responsible esthetic form. Cortázar, who moved from the Borges neighborhood
to the Arlt neighborhood, continues to seek, apparently without
conviction, that suburb of suburbs where he may find Zen philosophies on the lips of some César Bruto (one of whose pages,
by the way, serves as an entrance hall to *Rayuela*). Altogether,
only a talented and original writer could have dared to write
Rayuela. Talent and originality are patent in the lightning flashes
of poetry that occasionally branch out in streaks against this dark
sky.

A great many of the story writers and novelists of these years insist on
presenting human life niched into a world seen in its totality. The human
constants that they prefer to describe are sex, violence, and death. Figuring
in this group are FRANCISCO JORGE SOLERO—*Guilt* (*La culpa*); JUAN C.
MANAUTA (1919)—*White Lands* (*Tierras blancas*); ALBERTO RODRÍGUEZ
(1925)—*Where God May Be* (*Donde haya Dios*); NÉSTOR BONDONI—*The
Mouth on Earth* (*La boca sobre la tierra*), and a few others. In reading
them it would seem that violence is necessary in a condemned, hellish
America. One of the most "committed"—that is, one who not only describes
what he sees but also participates in what he tells, is DAVID VIÑAS (1929),
who just lately declared himself a Marxist: *He Fell on His Face* (*Cayó
sobre su Rostro*, 1955); *The Cruel Years* (*Los años despiadados*, 1956);

A Daily God (1957); and *The Landlords* (*Los dueños de la Tierra*, 1958). Some narrators evoked the years of adolescence, poetically, like JULIO ARDILES GRAY (1922) in *Elegy* (*Elegía*, 1952) and in his novelistic cycle *Faraway Friends* (*Los amigos lejanos*), *The Crevice* (*La grieta*), *The Blind Dunes* (*Los médanos ciegos*). BEATRIZ GUIDO (1924) is another of the novelists of adolescence: In *The House of the Angel* (*La casa del ángel*, 1954), *The Fall* (*La caída*, 1956), *The Wind-up* (*Fin de Fiesta*, 1958), *The Kidnapper* (*El secuestrador*), and also in her short stories in *Hand in the Trap* (*La mano en la trampa*, 1961), she writes preferably about young people, caught between innocence and corruption, gravitating around the theme of sex. Except for a weak attempt at complicating the perspective (Adolfo is alternately the narrator-protagonist and a character seen by another narrator who speaks in the third person) *The Wind-up* brings no technical novelties. The old naturalism (at least new in a woman) uncovers the rubbish-can of a powerful family in the political oligarchy of 1930–45. The "fiesta" that the military revolution of 1943 brings to a wind-up is not really a fiesta: it is sex, crime, moral decadence, ugliness, bad customs in society, government, and church. The axis of the action is the city of Avellaneda. Everything turns rapidly, but only the surface is seen. Although the prose does not have descriptive vigor, it is believable in the dialogs. There is no creation of characters, only situations in which the characters have fun or suffer. In *The Fire and the Preludes* (*El Incendio y las vísperas*) she writes about the disintegration of the upper class during the Peronist regime. SILVINA BULLRICH (1915) began with poetry—*Vibrations* (*Vibraciones*, 1935)—but her field is the novel: *The First Angel's Flask* (*La redoma del primer ángel*, 1943), *The Third Version* (*La tercera versión*, 1944), *Crystal Wedding* (*Bodas de cristal*, 1952), *The Line Is Busy* (*Teléfono ocupado*). In *The Third Version* we have the autobiography that Paul, a writer with no calling or talent and somewhat upset by skeletons in the family closet, addresses to his girl friend Claudia. He gives us the two versions of the failure of his father, a Spanish violinist (also called Pablo); the version of the mother (also called Claudia) according to which she deliberately ruined his father's genius through her jealousy, and the prosaic version of the doctor friend, according to which he was a mediocre musician who died accidentally. When the doctor, on his death-bed, offers the third version, the real one, Paul refuses to hear it. The novel falls apart in the denouement, although it is at that moment that the poetic tone—maintained through the novel—comes to the fore. Excellent in the presentation of a soft atmosphere of mystery, it fails in the construction of its high points: "the symmetry of destinies" (the two Pauls, the two Claudias) is not novelistically resolved. ESTELA CANTO (1920), in *The Marble Wall* (*El muro de mármol*, 1945) as well as in *The Man at Dusk* (*El hombre del crepúsculo*, 1953), has distinguished herself for her psychological understanding of her characters. (*In Night and the Mud* [*La noche y el barro*] she is also concerned with mass psychology.) In this psychological vein lies the curious novel of CARLOS MAZZANTI (1926), *The Substitute* (*El sustituto*), a completely interiorized monolog. JUAN CARLOS GHIANO (1920) with his *Strange Guests* (*Extraños huéspedes*), *Histories of the Deceased and the Traitors* (*Historias de finados y traidores*), and *Memories of the Scarlet Land* (*Memorias de la tierra escarlata*) seemed to have decided in favor of narrative, but later he achieved greater success in the theater. In the police genre—which had given its best moments with Borges, Bioy Casares, Silvina Ocampo, Leonardo Castellani, Manuel Peyrou, and Abel Mateo—the prominent ones in this generation were ADOLFO PÉREZ ZELASCHI (1920), RODOLFO J. WALSH (1927), and MARÍA ANGÉLICA BOSCO (1917).

MARCO DENEVI (1922) had an instantaneous success with his novel *Rosaura at Ten O'Clock* (*Rosaura a las diez,* 1955). A murder has been committed in a cheap hotel in Buenos Aires—the victim, a young girl. The police question several witnesses. The successive testimonies of four of these witnesses constitute the novel. In the fifth part, the puzzle is completed when a document is introduced that not only absolves the accused but also uncovers the real murderers. This clarifying letter is one that the murdered girl had left half written. The procedure of showing the same reality from four different perspectives permits Denevi to exercise his psychological penetration, his humor, and, above all, his ability to make an ever-anxious reader clutch the book and not let go till the very end. The hazy and complicated past reveals itself little by little. At ten in the evening (hence the title) Rosaura enters, in flesh and blood, into the world of the boarding hotel where the important characters live. Her mysterious personality—fictitious and real, innocent and vile, veiled and revealed—lights a light in the midst of the ugliness of the incidents. The theme of an invented character who suddenly appears before his very creator (this was pointed out in reference to Jenaro Prieto's *The Partner*) is here developed in a realist fashion. DALMIRO J. SÁENZ (1926)?) sees life through Catholic eyes and describes with realist force the degradation of the man who lives beyond the pale of God. His short stories *Seventy Times Seven* (*Setenta veces siete*) and *No* had immediate popular success. Other narrators: LUIS MARIO LOZZIA (1922), *Sunday Without Football* (*Domingo sin fútbol*); VALENTÍN FERNANDO (1921), *From This Flesh* (*Desde esta carne*); JACOBO FELDMAN (1917), *Story of a Flight* (*Relato de una fuga*); ADOLFO JASCA, *The Bitter Sprouts* (*Los tallos amargos*); DAVID JOSÉ KOHON, *The Black Circle of the Street* (*El negro círculo de la calle*); GLORIA ALCORTA (1916), *The Hotel of the Moon and Other Fabrications* (*El hotel de la luna y otras imposturas*); GREGORIO SCHEINES, *The Lost Visage* (*El rostro perdido*); EMMA DE CARTOSIO, *Stories of the Angel That Guards Well* (*Cuentos del ángel que bien guarda*); FEDERICO PELTZER (1924), *Shared* (*Compartida*); MARTA MOSQUERA, *Manuscript in the Mirror* (*Manuscrito en el espejo*); JORGE MASCIANGIOLI (1929): *The Last Floor* (*El último piso*); FERNANDO ROSENBERG (1925): *The Weeders* (*Los carpidores*); RUBÉN BENÍTEZ (1928): *Thieves of Light* (*Ladrones de luz*); MARTA LYNCH (1929): *The Red Carpet* (*La alfombra roja*); ELVIRA ORPHÉE (1927): *Two Summers* (*Dos veranos*); PEDRO G. ORGAMBIDE (1929): *The Sisters* (*Las hermanas*); ANTONIO DI BENEDETTO (1922): *Silence* (*El silencio,* 1964).

2. Essay

This is the most abundant genre in Hispanic-America. We set down just a few of the names closest to literature, leaving aside those who specialize rather in other disciplines—historical, philosophical, or sociological.

In Mexico, RAMÓN XIRAU (1924), ANTONIO ALATORRE (1918). In Central America, LUIS GALLEGOS VALDÉS (El Salvador, 1917). In Venezuela, ÓSCAR SAMBRANO URDANETA (1929), GUILLERMO MORÓN (1926), JOSÉ LUIS SALCEDO BASTARDO (1924), and ORLANDO ARAUJO (1928). In Colombia, DANIEL ARANGO (1920), OTTO MORALES BENÍTEZ (1920) and RAFAEL GUTIÉRREZ GIRARDOT (1928). In Ecuador, GALO RENÉ PÉREZ (1923). In Peru, ANTONIO PINILLA (1924), FRANCISCO MIRÓ QUESADA (1918). In Chile, in literary criticism one of those who work with analytic precision is ALFREDO LEFEBVRE (1917); in the philosophic essay, FÉLIX MARTÍNEZ BONATTI (1928), JUAN LOVELUCK (1929), CEDOMIL GOIC (1928). In Uruguay, EMIR RODRÍGUEZ MONEGAL (1921), CARLOS REAL DE AZÚA (1916), ARTURO SERGIO VISCA (1917), ROBERTO ARES PONS (1921). In Argentina, ALBERTO M. SALAS (1915), EMMA SUSANA SPERATTI PIÑERO (1919).

C. THEATER

The efforts of writers to convert themselves into professionals of the theater are obvious. On leaving the experimental theaters —which treated a minority public to stage pieces of literary quality—to embrace professionalism, some playwrights and dramatists began to serve up typical dishes for the national palates. This, of course, is generally speaking; for there also was theater of great artistic integrity. University groups or groups connected with intellectual circles tried to renovate the techniques of spectacle. With the growth of cities, stage activity also grew. Now there are scenic resources and lighting techniques that can be used to help out in scenes of monologs that explore the consciousness, or to create sudden transitions or atmospheres suggestive of the absurd or of ideological symbols. The dialog is also undergoing renewal, seeking what is realistic and poetic at the same time. Some authors have already been mentioned for their contributions in other genres.

(i) *Mexico* / LUISA JOSEFINA HERNÁNDEZ (1928) is important for the sustained quality of her continual production. We have seen *The Deaf and Dumb* (*Los sordomudos*, 1953). There is only one deaf-mute—the servant girl. But the title refers to the moral deaf-and-dumbness of a middle-class family in a Mexican province. The home is broken by hatred, resentment, incompatibility. They are like deaf-mutes. They barely communicate with one another. In the end the children disperse and the cynical father remains alone with the servant. There is an amorphous conversation between Celia, wasted and fatigued, who has just arrived in Mexico from a provincial city, and her family, all living weak, useless lives, rotting like oranges fallen from a tree at the first shaking of the wind, condemned to repeat themselves in a hell where to choose or not to choose are the same thing since nothing has any meaning.

Hernandez' talent is not only for the theater. It has been tested in several novels.

We have also seen *Ash Wednesday* (*Miércoles de ceniza*) by LUIS G. BASURTO (1919): the dialog languishes in discussions about religious sentiment. *To Each His Own Life* (*Cada quien su vida*) presents in realistic dialog with cinematographic procedures and one or more expressionistic scenes a problem in Christian ethics: sin, love, salvation. The scene is a cabaret where prostitutes and their varied clientele gather to celebrate the new year. EMILIO CARBALLIDO (1925) knows his trade down to his fingertips. He prefers to fathom the provincial souls of the middle class. Among his better works are *Rosalba and the Turnkeys* (*Rosalba y los llaveros*) and *The Dance the Tortoise Dreams* (*La danza que sueña la tortuga*). SERGIO MAGAÑA (1924) is one of the most problematic. We have seen *The Signs of the Zodiac* (*Los signos del Zodiaco*) in Mexico. It presents a sordid neighborhood house. The lives of several family members are seen to pass and intermingle. In this polyptych of human depravity (whose last frame is a murder), a polyptych painted with failures, mythomaniacs, homosexuals, drunks, down-and-outers, prostitutes, victims of venereal disease, old men who have given up, and disoriented youths, we cannot tell whether the young Communist is just another misfit or whether, on the contrary, he is the vociferous conscience of an immoral world. This world, the young Communist says, is determined not so much by the signs of the Zodiac as by the dollar sign. The sign of Scorpio, however, seems to be the one that has had the greatest influence on the author, to judge by his stings.

One of the most original authors is ELENA GARRO (1920): *A Solid Home* (*Un hogar sólido*, 1958) embraces six plays in one act: molded out of Mexican clay, Mexican things and lives, this phenomenon is suddenly magically transfigured. Drops of spittle roll about like goldpieces, children fly on little wooden horses, hearts burn in the air, dead people seek their own bones, mothers go through walls . . . A theater of the absurd, a spectacle of delirious objects: the mouth of the stage is like a perforation in the subconscious. In 1963 her drama, *The Lady on her Balcony* (*La señora en su balcón*) was presented. The poetic, magical intensity of her theater is also an element of surprise in her short stories and in her novel, *Memories of the Future* (*Los recuerdos del porvenir*, 1963), in which the people in a town relate their own lives. JORGE IBARGÜENGOITIA (1928) shows promise in his play about customs, *Clotilde at home* (*Clotilde en su casa*). What we had read by him, *Susanna and the Young Men* (*Susana y los jovenes*) is mere twaddle. IGNACIO RETES (1918), WILBERTO CANTÓN (1923), CARLOS SOLÓRZANO (1922) are also outstanding.

(ii) *Central America* / WALTER BENEKE (El Salvador, 1928), ALFREDO

L. SANCHO (Costa Rica, 1922), JOSÉ DE JESÚS MARTÍNEZ (Panama, 1928), ENRIQUE FERNÁNDEZ (Nicaragua, 1918).

(iii) *Antilles* / The Cubans, RENÉ BUCH (1926), ROBERTO BOURBAKIS (1919), JORGE DEL BUSTO (1918). FRANCISCO ARRIVÍ (Puerto Rico, 1915) with new techniques, has brought themes of national life to the stage; he has several plays, from *The Devil Becomes Human* (*El diablo se humaniza,* 1941) to *Club for Bachelors* (*Club de solteros,* 1953).

(iv) *Venezuela* / Leaving aside Gramcko, whom we have seen among the poets, RAFAEL PINEDA (1926).

(v) *Colombia* / ENRIQUE BUENAVENTURA (1925).

(vi) *Peru* / SEBASTIÁN SALAZAR BONDY (1924), intelligent, cultured, deeply emotional, preoccupied with the problems of man and the social conditions of Hispanic-American life, he has excelled in several genres: the essay, poetry, the narrative—*The Shipwrecked and the Survivors* (*Náufragos y sobrevivientes,* 1954); *Poor People of Paris* (*Pobre gente de París,* 1958). But his theatrical talent demands that he be placed in this section of our history. *There Is No Happy Island* (*No hay isla feliz,* 1954): a man of honor and dignity who believed in human freedom and happiness is crushed by misfortune, which delivers blow upon blow, as if the author were trying to demonstrate here the injustice of a meaningless world. We saw her play, *The Suitcase,* in English; an act of imagination and irony.

Another of Peru's theatrical values is ENRIQUE SOLARI SWAYNE (1918), author of *Collacocha* (1955), an optimistic glorification of man's struggle against nature, man personified by a heroic engineer, in love with his work, who opens up tunnels through the Andes.

(vii) *Chile* / There was a surprising flowering in the theater here, favored in part by the universities. The repercussions of the social agitation of the middle class were dramatized by EGON WOLFF (1926) in *Rag Couples* (*Parejas de Trapo,* 1960), and by SERGIO VODANOVIC (1928) in *Let the Dogs Bark* (*Deja que los perros ladren,* 1959). FERNANDO DEBESA (1921) and MARÍA ASUNCIÓN REQUENA (1918), are more concerned with the historic past. In a succession of scenes of expressionist intensity, a bit in the manner of Bert Brecht, ISIDORA AGUIRRE (1919) has come close to the theme of the people in *The Stationers* (*Los papeleros*). We have seen *Verses by a Blind Man* (*Versos de ciego,* 1960), by LUIS ALBERTO HEIREMANS (1928–1964); he causes scenes on sketches of customs, folklore, and symbolic scenes to roll out as in a film by Fellini or Antonioni. The spectator is treated to an unexpected allegory in the legend of the Magi: it is necessary to go on a pilgrimage in search of the brilliant star that beckons from the sky. The humble, the poor, the repentant, the poor in spirit, fools and madmen fail, only to attain the best in the end. The primitive theatrical form is adjusted to medieval ways of thought. *"To be Told and Not to be Believed,"* (*"Es de contarlo y no creerlo"*) one of the "stories for the theater" from his volume, *The Cage in the Tree* (*La jaula en el árbol,* 1959), surrounds a Don Juan type of bachelor with angels. The supernatural situation develops in a natural manner, because for Catholic Heiremans the angels understand man's weakness and can hold dialog with him. Others: Existentialist FERNANDO JOSSEAU (1924), FERNANDO CUADRA PINTO (1926), FERNANDO LAMBERG (1928).

(viii) *Paraguay* / Paraguay had never had any other drama except that of the very poor Julio Correa. Now a promising activity by MARIO HALLEY MORA (1924) has begun.

(ix) *Uruguay* / Most important are ANTONIO LARRETA (1922), author of *The Smile (La sonrisa)*; CARLOS DENIS MOLINA, of whom we spoke in the poetry section; JACOBO LANGSNER (1924), an experimenter with forms, author of *The Incomplete Man (El hombre incompleto)*, *The Ridiculous Ones (Los ridículos)*, *The Rebellion of Galatea (La rebelión de Galatea)*, *Iphigenia's Game (El juego de Ifigenia)*; and CARLOS MAGGI (1922), who has a facile inventiveness for grotesque situations or farce: *The Back Room (La trastienda)*, *The Library (La biblioteca)*, *Night of the Uncertain Angels (La noche de los ángeles inciertos)*, *Masquerade (Mascarada)*. Also worthy of mention are HÉCTOR PLAZA NOBLÍA, JUAN CARLOS LEGIDO (1920?), ANDRÉS CASTILLO (1920?), ANGÉLICA PLAZA.

(x) *Argentina* / The group of theatrical authors is numerous. OMAR DEL CARLO (1918) is the author of *Proserpine and the Stranger (Proserpina y el extranjero)*. Here the myth of the rape of Proserpina penetrates like a ray of light into the sordid reality of a Buenos Aires slum and it refracts in strange poetic reflections. The sun on a muddy pool that shows emeralds in the putrid water. The personified myth moves on the stage and speaks to us: his words conjure rapid transmutations. Hell changes to Buenos Aires; the Acheron is the immobile, dirty Río de la Plata; Hades, king of the subterranean world becomes Porfirio, the gangster, king of the underworld; the deity Proserpina, daughter of Demeter, is now Proserpina, a girl from the country who falls into surroundings of baseness and prostitution. Del Carlo capably fuses myth and reality, and together they create dramatic art. The characters are creatures of the Argentina of today; and yet, their gestures and their words have a strength that comes from the depths of time. And the landscape of wheat fields where Demetria and her daughter Proserpina lived, strikes an Argentinian chord even though we know that those are the wheat fields of the deity Demeter. The linking of the myth of Proserpina raped in hell, with the figures of Claudius and Flavia, representing respectively the lowest moral point of pagan power and the driving impetus of the expansion of Christianity, adds an attempt at religious allegory to the drama. The salvation of Proserpina in the end thus acquires the value of moral symbol. Omar del Carlo breaks out of the framework of modern theatrical composition and sets the action free: rapid movements of vivid, loose, naked, changing scenes. The fluidity of the Greek theater or of the theater of Lope de Vega and Shakespeare (after the freezing of realist décors) now returns to flow down the river bed of the new forms of the contemporary theater: forms learned from the movies, but without imitating them. *Where Death Plants Its Banners* (1959) seems to be inferior. The theme, as old as the biblical Amnon and Tamar, of the incestuous love between brother and sister, reappears in the Argentina of Mitre and Urquiza, on the eve of the battle of Pavón. The father of the incestuous pair, who must pay for his own violent past through the vengeance of a woman, rebels against God and dies. The idea is Catholic, and the conception of the drama has a rapid scenic movement, with choruses. But the spectacular qualities go beyond the content of the drama. CARLOS GOROSTIZA (1920) is human, preoccupied with social ills; he was successful in *The Bridge* (*El puente*) and then continued in an uneven career until *The Last Dog* (*El último perro*) and *The Clock of Balthazar* (*El reloj de Baltazar*). JULIO IMBERT (1918) acquired a well-deserved reputation with *The Earthworm* (*La lombriz*), *This Place Has a Hundred Fires* (*Este lugar tiene cien fuegos*), *The Tooth* (*El diente*), *Azor, The Children of Summer* (*Los hijos del verano*), *Biography of Transparent Estela* (*Biografía de Estela transparente*). His characters have lively dialogs (occasionally with snatches of biblical verses), well-linked scenes, fateful atmospheres, psychological exploration, the use of symbols, and themes of passion and horror. AGUSTÍN GUZZANI (1924) has a talent for satirical farces that makes use of German expressionist procedures, occasionally descends to burlesque, and denounces a grotesque society that is destructive to men: *Sempronio*. OSVALDO DRAGÚN (1929) is among the more serious playwrights. We have seen his play, *The Pestilence Comes from Melos* (*La peste viene de Melos*), an anti-imperialist play with effective anachronisms. *Tupac Amarú* is a tragic story, but it focuses on the eternal dignity of humanity. Other figures: TULIO CARELLA, PABLO PALANT (1914), JUAN CARLOS GENÉ, VITO DE MARTINI (1928).

XV. 1955-1966

Authors born since 1930

Historical framework: The popular masses strive to attain political power—masses more interested in an immediate distribution of wealth than in revolutionary ideologies. In any case, the ideology of "the third world," which involves the belief that Latin America, to save itself from the imperialism of the great powers, should make common cause with the underdeveloped countries of Africa and Asia. The governing classes (even those traditionally conservative, as are the military and the clergy) attempt to adjust to this new climate. For example, in 1958 the Church began with Pope John XXIII to reform its political image. The first Communist regime in Hispanic America: Fidel Castro's Cuba. The first government by leftist Catholics: Frei's Chile. The United States liquidated its "good neighbor policy" by its military intervention in the Dominican Republic in 1965.

Cultural tendencies: Whether writers are violent or serene, nihilistic or affirmative, cynical or candid, all seem to sense the imminence of a great change in values. There are three positions: nostalgia for classical forms, experimentation with new techniques, and a sudden what-else-is-new. There is a greater awareness of the increasing attention the rest of the world is giving to Hispanic American production: international prizes, translations, etc. There is also a greater professional awareness, with the quantitative category of the "best seller."

General Characterization

It is evident that these writers are directing their steps somewhere. But where? This is not so evident. The group is too young: neither its direction, nor its quality, nor even its significant names can be known yet. In general they impress one for their serious, discontented, and resentful looks. They came out of their shells when the second world war had already ended, and what did they see? They saw a new political order jelling, divided into two colossuses—the United States and Russia—armed with atomic bombs, rockets, and gases capable of exterminating the human race. They saw that the hatred of nation against nation was being fomented and that the "cold war" was being brought to the very brink of universal suicide. They witnessed a new spectacle: Russian and American astronauts orbiting our planet and televised photographs from the moon. They saw how the European or Europeanized powers, which earlier had justified their actions in the name of the expansion of civilization, now were doing so in the name of the necessity to survive in the midst of disintegrating old empires, and how Africa, China, India, and the rest of Asia were bringing the cycle of colonialism to an end and were changing the balance of power. They saw the United Nations where, around the same table, were seated countries that were accelerating to an extraordinary degree the Technological Revolution (in the last fifteen years), countries that were just entering into the Industrial Revolution (which was already 150 years old), and countries still living in the period of the agrarian revolution (some 10,000 years). They saw that the rebellion of the masses—with nationalist and communist labels —convulsed every corner of the globe. They saw the population explosion (in Hispanic-America, with a population of 185 million, the growth index is an annual 2.5 per cent, while that of the world as a whole is 1.6 per cent) and the inevitability of a radical change in the economic, social, and political structure. In Hispanic-America they saw totalitarian regimes succeed one another, with different concepts of what the state should be, from the fall of the Perón regime in Argentina to the installation of the Fidel Castro regime in Cuba. They saw all of this with pessimistic and agonizing eyes, without understanding at times that the birth of a new moral order, in spite of its chaotic appearance, is a blessing in comparison with the immoral order promised by the Fascist program of 1936 to 1945. They were too young to understand that. And so, while technology was decreasing the size of the world, in their minds, the idea of *world* increased, and within such a mental framework they suffer in their very flesh the crisis of individualism.

In the panorama of letters they saw impotence, desperation, and bitterness everywhere. They emitted romantic laments, but they were no longer the laments of titans: rather pygmies nostalgic for a great past. They felt not more alone—because writers have always felt alone—but less in communication than ever. It was a new type of aloneness, helpless but desirous of communion, even if it takes orgies. A grumbling solitude. As when a boy tells a girl: I give myself to you, you give yourself to me (sex as culmination), and the two of us will send the world to the devil. It is an effort at communication—no longer as a safety valve for subjectivity, but as a reaction against the objective world—oriented toward contacts with the remote recesses of life, heretofore disdained by the elite, or in forms of political militancy, either in favor of order or of disorder. The answer to an absurd world is arbitrariness; there are no golden dreams of the future, and one is writing, not for posterity, but for the present. Thus these angry young writers tend to behave scandalously, as though they were trying to be characters in a novel thought up by the public. "Angry young men," "the beat generation." There is nothing new in this: what is new, however, is that it should have acquired importance as an index of a social state, of a direction in the historical process, of a taste shared by the majority. Neo-naturalism, existentialism, Communist and Catholic propaganda, the expression of the telluric in nationalist movements, the cult of brutality and even of ugliness on the part of groups that denounce the liberalism of the bourgeoisie convince them of the necessity of a "committed literature": an active literature by means of which a stand can be taken in the face of our times, thus freely affirming the program of our personal lives. One of the means of committing oneself is by submitting the past to an inexorable critical revision. They deny a great deal of excellent but, according to them, devitalized poetry, elegiac or having an excessive virtuosity in its verbal display. Verse loses its old power. At any rate, poetry is cultivated without building any hopes on it, as one did in the days of its primacy in the field of letters. The novel is now the most prestigious genre. When they write poetry, they cannot help but repeat some of the researches of previous writers. For example: the "inventionism" of today—to invent worlds verbally—is similar to the "creationism" of yesterday. At bottom lies the same impulse to produce surprising things through the use of images. Others wrap themselves in anguish, and from there, try to give their surrealist spirals of smoke the configuration of art. Revisionism also alters the hierarchies of prose: in the judgment of many youths, the stylists dissolve the art of storytelling into a mere unfurling of clouds. On the other hand, these youths propose violence without style, violence for the sheer joy of being violent. There is a preference for the novel (which field the Americans dominate, especially Faulkner), conceived of now as being a cesspool in which all of reality is made up of putrefactive material. Along with the "patricides," the denouncers, the prosecutors, the rebels, other more serene artists are writing: those who escape reality by becoming wrapped up in themselves, or in the cult of the past. In this manner, forms and formulas of the Renaissance are reborn. There is a professional air about learning the disciplines so as to write better; there is more awareness of the craft. To sum up: some disbelieve in individual heroism and give themselves up to the masses; others resuscitate a heroic sense in the cult of the classics. Authoritarian personalities in the name of prevailing majorities, and free personalities in the name of the great geniuses of history. Our respect goes to the individualists who do not equivocate with "isms" or seek customers in easy political gatherings. Our respects to those who by expressing new visions renew art. In this appendix, there is no help for it, there is only room to list names.

A. MAINLY POETRY

(i) *Mexico* / The most numerous group is that of the politically-oriented poets. Lyricism seeps through the apertures of those windows that face the problems of peace, class struggles, the Indian, solidarity, justice. The purpose, however, is to communicate with the people in simple words that refer to an immediate reality. There are other directions, nevertheless.

During these recent years the poet is MARCO ANTONIO MONTES DE OCA (1932). He allows his mind to run freely through his words; and this stream of consciousness is rich in the sensation of time. In *Testimonial Document*, metaphoric constellations shift as in a dream. *The Birds Sing Before the Light* (*Delante de la luz cantan los pájaros*, 1959)—a book in which earlier books are collected—he shows his imaginative skill and preoccupation with man. Montes de Oca's creative imagination deluges the world with myriads of marvelous drops. The entire world becomes iridescent with so many metaphors of sharp poetic light. The drops are round, minimal, rapid, fluid intuitions that surprise one for their originality. Liberty, but not that of the spontaneous surrealist, who mixes gem and mud, but that of the lucid forger of miniature myths, a proud gold-beater of limpid forms. If one had to record the shop of his apprenticeship, it would be that of Huidobro rather than that of Neruda. In *Songs to the Unreachable Sun* (*Cantos al sol que no se alcanza* (1961) he continues to demonstrate his own form of art that combines metaphors with metaphors until he achieves long poems. He has then a willingness to construct, discipline, self-dominion. JOSÉ EMILIO PACHECO (1939) is another poet of promise. *Elements of the Night* (*Los Elementos de la noche*, 1963). Also: HORACIO ESPINOSA ALTAMIRANO (1931); CARMEN ALARDÍN; HOMERO ARIDJIS (1940); JAIME AUGUSTO SHELLEY (1937); ERACLIO ZEPEDA (1937); SERGIO MONDRAGÓN (1936); JUAN BAÑUELOS; JAIME LABASTIDA; ÓSCAR OLIVA.

(ii) *Central America* / In Guatemala these men were joined together in *Poemario* (1957): JULIO FAUSTO AGUILERA, IVÁN BARRERA, MARIO EFRAÍN HERNÁNDEZ, DONALDO ESTRADA CASTILLO, MARTÍN GOMAR, JUAN FRANCISCO MANRIQUE, HÉCTOR GUILLERMO PINEDA, and CARLOS ZIPFEL Y GARCÍA. In Honduras, OSCAR ACOSTA (1933), with his *Minor Poetry* (*Poesía menor*) is clear, communicative, even conceptual has risen; POMPEYO DEL VALLE (1930). In El Salvador, a combative generation from leftist quarters. One of the most capable among these militant poets was WALDO CHÁVEZ VELASCO (1933), author of "Biography of Bread" (*"Biografía del pan"*), "Four Songs of Love for Future Peace" (*"Cuatro cantos de amor para la paz futura"*) and other poems committed to the themes of the sufferings of the people, human solidarity, and social justice. He seems to be heading toward the theater. Also important in this group is ITALO LÓPEZ VALLECILLOS (1932). Others: ORLANDO FRESEDO (1932?), EUGENIO MARTÍNEZ ORANTES (1932), ÁLVARO MENÉNDEZ LEAL (1931), MERCEDES DURAND (1933), IRMA LANZAS (1933). In Nicaragua there are several groups. In the *"Ventana"* group: FERNANDO GORDILLO (1940), SERGIO RAMÍREZ (1942), ALFONSO ROBLES (1938?). In the group of the *"Generación traicionada"* (Betrayed generation): ROBERTO CUADRA (1941), EDWIN YLLESCAS (1942), FERNANDO RÍOS (1940?). In the *Granada* group: NICOLÁS NAVAS, HORACIO DUARTE, LORENZO MEDRANO, HORACIO BERMÚDEZ, born around 1935. Among the independents: OCTAVIO ROBLETO (1934), ALBERTO BACA (1932). In Costa Rica, VIRGINIA GRÜTTER (1929) and ENRIQUE MORA SALAS (1930), known for his "three sonnets to the Rose." In Panama those standing above the crowd are GUILLERMO ROSS ZANET (1930), DEMETRIO J. FÁBREGA (1932), EDISON SIMONS QUIRÓS (1933), JOSÉ FRANCO (1931), and ÁLVARO MENÉNDEZ FRANCO (1933).

750 Spanish-American Literature: A History

(iii) *Antilles* / Cuba, the revolution of Fidel Castro and the setting up of a Communist type of regime created a new spirit in the poets. Even those who had been distinguished before the revolution for the excellence of their personal lyricism now, feeling themselves to be a part of the radical political experiment, learned to write on themes of collectivity. ROBERTO FERNÁNDEZ RETAMAR (1930) celebrated Cuba's struggle for liberation in *Return of the Ancient Hope* (*Vuelta de la antigua esperanza*, 1959) and produced his *Yes to the Revolution* (*Sí a la revolución*, 1961). One of the most moving poems is "The Other One" (*"El otro"*). But when his poetic works were collected in *With These Very Hands* (*Con las mismas manos*, 1962) it was made clear how lyricism, now colloquial, can change in character. In the poem that gives its title to the book he says: "With these very hands that caress you I am building a school." FAYAD JAMÍS (1930) expresses in *Poem on the River Mines* (*Poema en Minas del Río*) the same simplicity, the same revolutionary emotion, the same belligerence, and there is the same danger that the poetic urge, subjected to politics, may turn into prose. PABLO ARMANDO FERNÁNDEZ (1930) is also a revolutionary. Another voice: ROSARIO ANTUÑA (1935).

In the Dominican Republic we now complete the "generation of '48" that we spoke about in the preceding chapter: LUPO HERNÁNDEZ RUEDA (1931), LUIS ALFREDO TORRES (1935), ALBERTO PEÑA LEBRÓN (1930), ABELARDO VICIOSO (1930), MÁXIMO AVILÉS BLONDA (1931), ABEL FERNÁNDEZ MEJÍA (1931), RAFAEL LARA CINTRÓN (1931). Still younger: JEANETTE MILLER (1944), JUAN JOSÉ AYUSO (1940), RENÉ DEL RISCO (1937).

Puerto Rico: JORGE LUIS MORALES (1930) stems from "transcendentalism," to which we have already referred; his verses are clear, regular, and excessively abstract in their preoccupation with the destiny of man. ANAGILDA GARRASTEGUI (1932) is neo-romantic. A number of poets, born at the end of the decade of the 30's or the beginning of the 40's, began to publish in 1962 in *Guajana* and *Prometeo*. IRIS M. ZAVALA (1935): *Suffering Clay* (*Barro doliente*, 1964).

(iv) *Venezuela* / The young writers begin to produce around 1950, with the feeling that they were leaving behind easy themes of folklore, nationalist conventions, cultural demagogy and, on the other hand, that they were approaching universal currents. They proposed—sometimes violently—revising the past and defending the right to a purely artistic vocation. But actually they were not of equal talent, nor did they travel the same roads. Some are explicit, nativist (JESÚS ROSAS MARCANO, 1932); others are more hermetic, intellectual, or universal. GUILLERMO SUCRE (1933), disciplined, demanding of his own writing; LUIS GARCÍA MORALES (1931), with more sudden and intense effusiveness, and RAMON PALOMARES (1935), a spontaneous and inventive lyricist, formed part of the *"Sardio"* group. Let us also mention ROBERTO GUEVARA, ALFREDO SILVA ESTRADA (1934), ALFREDO CHACÓN (1937), EDMUNDO ARAY (1936) and RÉGULO VILLEGAS (1930). Others are emotional, affirmative. EFRAÍN SUBERO (1931), who begins from the simplest level of communication; and also JUAN ÁNGEL MOGOLLON (1932). JOSÉ JOAQUÍN BURGOS (1933), HELY COLOMBANI

(1932), ENRIQUE GUEDEZ (1930?) and FÉLIX GUZMÁN (1933). JUAN CALZADILLA (1931) refined his mastery of classical forms to the sensitivity it has today, directed to his country, concerned with the claims of life. *The Tower of the Birds* (*La torre de los pájaros*); he also cultivated prose in *The Red Herbarium* (*Los herbarios rojos*). PEDRO DUNO (1933), in *I Shall Not Silence Thy Voice* (*No callaré tu voz,* 1955), gave us his complaints in phrases that faltered with discouragement: the limitations of man, the impossible aspects of a monotonous life, failure, sadness. The strength of his sincerity lifts the simple, almost conversational language to a tower of images that are rich in their inventiveness. This sincerity is that of a solitary man who, as revealed in the poem that gives its title to the volume, wants to communicate with ordinary life. RAFAEL CADENAS (1930) calls his *Notebook of Exile* (*Los cuadernos del destierro,* 1960) a "poem in prose." It is a piece of folly that, like poetry, is born of words and feeds on them. VICTOR SALAZAR (1940) allows precise norms to regulate his feelings: *Thirst for Words* (*Sequía de las palabras,* 1961). JUAN SALAZAR MENESES (1929).

(v) *Colombia* / "Nothingism" was a movement of rebellion against the deepest traditions of Colombian society. Its anti-Catholic manifesto is a proof. While its adherents denounced conventions and declared themselves maladjusted, they proposed to create a new literary language. GONZALO ARANGO (1932) was one of the founders of the group; see his poem "The Nothingists" and his theme for a ballet: *The Consecration of Nothing* (*La consagracion de la Nada*). Other youthful names: MARIO RIVERO (1933), JOSÉ PUBÉN (1936), FÉLIX TURBAY (1933), ALBERTO HOYOS (1936).

(vi) *Ecuador* / New writers appear who continue families of poets that either open their eyes to reality, or explore inner life: DAVID LEDESMA VÁZQUEZ (1934), HUGO SALAZAR TAMARIZ, CARLOS EDUARDO JARAMILLO, RUBÉN ASTUDILLO (1939?). ILEANA ESPINEL (1930), EULER GRANDA (1935), RODRIGO PESÁNTEZ RODAS (1930), IGNACIO CARVALLO CASTILLO (1937).

(vii) *Peru* / Pure poetry wanes, testimonial poetry increases. The poet, however imaginative he may be, prefers to confront the society that oppresses him. Among the poets most interested in the expression of political ideas in lyrical terms is ARTURO CORCUERA (1935), *Triumphant Spring* (*Primavera triunfante,* 1963). In the vein of introverted lyricism, CÉSAR CALVO (1940): *Absences and Delays* (*Ausencias y retardos,* 1963). Others: PABLO GUEVARA (1930), whose voice is very personal; EUGENIO BUONA (1930), CECILIA BUSTAMANTE (1932), AUGUSTO ELMORE (1932).

(viii) *Bolivia* / An indifference to folklore, a yearning for universalism. JORGE SUAREZ (1932), FÉLIX ROSPIGLIOSI NIETO (1930), ERVIN ROJAS, JESÚS URZAGASTI, EDGAR ÁVILA ECHAZU, EDMUNDO CAMARGO FERREIRA.

(ix) *Chile* / Let us separate from the busy mass of youths a few figures who show a real vocation as poets. The one who affirms life with most transparency, in direct words, is EFRAÍN BARQUERO (1931). In *The Companion* (*La compañera,* 1956), *The Swarm* (*Enjambre,* 1959), and *Rub-*

bish (*Maula,* 1962), he has gone deeply into his vision of man in natural situations: conjugal love, offspring, contact with things. JORGE TEILLIER (1935) is such an imaginative lyricist that, while he sings to himself, he transforms things, animating them, personifying them, imbuing them with his own nostalgic and melancholy spirit. *Poems from the Country of Never Again* (*Poemas del país de nunca jamas,* 1963). ARMANDO URIBE ARCE (1933) is among the more surprising poets for their audacious experiments with form, theme, image, and meaning. It is appropriate to mention here also PEDRO LASTRA (1932) and XIMENA SEPÚLVEDA (1932).

(x) *Paraguay* / In the current of poetry turned toward the world we find LUIS MARÍA MARTÍNEZ (1933) with *Flash of Land* (*Ráfaga de tierra,* 1963), and CARMEN SOLER, the first woman poet in her country to deal with rebellious social themes. The other poets appear to be grouped into those who express their feelings with lyricism and those more concerned with the esthetic virtues of the forms themselves. In the former group: RUBÉN BAREIRO SAGUIER (1930), intuitive, anguished, anxious in his *Biography of One Who Is Absent* (*Biografía de ausente,* 1964); FRANCISCO PEREZ MARICEVICH (1927), wrapped up in himself and tense in *A Man's Footstep* (*Paso de hombre,* 1963); ROQUE VALLEJOS (1943), deep and ecstatic in *The Pulse of Shadow* (*Pulso de sombra,* 1962) and *The Intoxicated Archangels* (*Los arcángeles ebrios,* 1964); ESTEBAN CABAÑAS, somewhat surrealistic in *The Vain Monsters* (*Los monstruos vanos,* 1964); MIGUEL ÁNGEL FERNÁNDEZ (1938), who bares himself in pure images in *Dark Days* (*Oscuros días,* 1964). In the second group, the estheticists: J. A. RAUSKIN (1942). Other poets of this generation: CARLOS VILLAGRA MARSAL (1932), capable of epic themes and tones, as in his "Letter to Simon Bolivar" ("*Carta a Simón Bolívar*"); JOSÉ MARÍA GÓMEZ SANJURJO (1930).

(xi) *Uruguay* / SAÚL IBARGOYEN ISLAS (1930), who writes conversational poetry on everyday themes with a skeptical tone: *The Book of Blood* (*El libro de la sangre*), *Passion for a Shadow* (*Pasión para una sombra,* 1959), *A Place on the Land* (*Un lugar en la tierra;* 1960), and *City* (*Ciudad,* 1961). WASHINGTON BENAVIDES (1930), a poet of small-town experiences and gentle manners: *The Poet* (*El poeta,* 1959). NANCY BACELO (1930?), somber, reticent, harsh, despairing: *Heaven Alone* (*Cielo solo*); CIRCE MAIA (1930?), a visionary.

(xii) *Argentina* / Independent of the surrealist group (obscure spontaneity of dreams) and the "inventionist" group (intelligent vigilance of dreams) are those who seek a personal expression, namely, JUAN JOSÉ HERNÁNDEZ (1930), in whom landscape and soul are wedded—*Clarity Overcome* (*Claridad vencida,* 1957), and MARÍA ELENA WALSH (1930), who, in *Almost Miracle* (*Casi milagro,* 1958), confirmed what she had promised in a book written in her adolescence: a dazzling poetic capacity, full and happy in the expression of pure instantaneousness ("I am what it occurs to me to be when I sing"). Her literature for children—songs, plays—has a fresh lyricism. Also: FRANCISCO URONDO (1930), FRANCISCO MOGNI (1934), HÉCTOR MIGUEL ANGELI (1930), ALEJANDRA PIZARNIK (1937), JUAN

GELMAN (1930), JOSÉ ISAACSON (1930), CÉSAR MAGRINI (1934). In the vanguard: RODOLFO ALONSO (1934).

B. MAINLY PROSE

1. Novel and Short Story

(i) *Mexico* / TOMÁS MOJARRO (1932) embroidered themes of death on the canvas of country life in his stories in *Juchipila Canyon* (*Cañon de Juchipila,* 1960); later, in his novel, *Blusterer* (*Bramadero,* 1963), he described life in a village affected by the construction of a road. ERACLIO ZEPEDA (1937) wrote *Benzulul,* stories with Indian themes. VICENTE LEÑERO (1933) is the author of *The Cloud of Dust and Other Stories* (*La Polvareda y otros cuentos*) and the novels, *The Sorrowful Voice* (*La voz adolorida*) and *The Builders* (*Los albañiles*). He writes with effective agility as he moves through various social strata. He has an eye for local customs, but he also has the compassion of a psychologist. JOSÉ LUIS AGUADO (1935), JOSÉ DE LA COLINA (1934).

(ii) *Central America* / FERNANDO CENTENO ZAPATA (Nicaragua, 1935?), ÁLVARO MENÉNDEZ LEAL (El Salvador, 1931).

(iii) *Antilles* / In Cuba, LISANDRO OTERO (1932) appeared after the revolution against Batista's dictatorship with a novel, *The Situation* (*La situación*), in which he describes precisely the life of the upper classes during this epoch. He also writes short stories: *Tobacco for Some Thursday* (*Tabaco para un jueves*). NIVARIA TEJERA (1930). From MARCIO VELOZ MAGGIOLO (Dominican Republic, 1936) comes *The Good Thief* (*El buen ladrón,* 1960). They have just crucified Jesus and also Dismas, "the good thief." The latter's mother, a poor old woman, is the one who relates her memories. She lived on her children, Dismas, the highwayman, and Midena, the harlot, when there appeared an ugly, dirty man who predicted the breaking up of families. The children believed in this man, "someone called Jesus," but she instead rejected him as an imposter. Marcio Veloz Maggiolo, whose mind is more concerned with posing problems than in seeing them through, does not succeed in getting to the depths of the possibilities of his theme: the symmetry of the destinies of two who were born in a manger and were to die crucified side by side; the asymmetry of the single mother (he makes no allusion to the Virgin Mary) who, out of her real love for her son—"he was a great man"—hates the other crucified one, the son of God, and considers him false; the play of perspectives between the contemporaries of Jesus, who did not understand him, or who understood him each in his own way; the contrasts within Judean nationalism and also outside of it, within Roman imperialism. The sweet message of Jesus, which brings dangers, threats, and privations to a humble life; the injustice of the irremediable death of one son and the resurrection of the other; the mysterious theology that becomes muddy with humanity when seen close. Nevertheless, the character of the protagonist narrator is moving. LUIS

RAFAEL SÁNCHEZ (Puerto Rico, 1936) not only kneads the real dough of his country but adds imaginative and even poetic yeast to his stories.

(iv) *Venezuela* / First of all is SALVADOR GARMENDIA (1931), the most serious novelist of his time up to now. He drew attention with his novel *The Little Beings* (*Los pequeños seres,* 1959); later, he wrote *The Inhabitants* (*Los habitantes*) in which he novelized the inability of the members of a family to communicate with one another, as seen through a single day of their existence. ANTONIO STEMPEL PARIS, a short story writer, and, in *The Habituates* (*Los habituados*), a novelist. The others are mainly short story writers: ADRIANO GONZÁLEZ LEÓN (1931), restless, with touches of magical realism in *The Highest Bonfires* (*Los hogueras más altas,* 1957), and HÉCTOR MALAVE MATA (1930), the author of *Metamorphosis* (*La metamorfosis,* 1957).

(v) *Colombia* / EDUARDO ARANGO PIÑERES (1931), who cultivates the fantastic short story: *January 25* (*Enero 25*). Realists: ANTONIO MONTAÑA (1932), RAMIRO MONTOYA (1933), FERNANDO SOTO APARICIO (1933), RUBÉN ARDILA (1942), DARÍO RUIZ GÓMEZ (1936).

(vi) *Ecuador* / EUGENIA VITERI (1935?), author of *The Ring* (*El anillo*); JORGE RIVADENEIRA (1930?), whose aims are more political than literary, and WALTER BELLOLIO (1933?).

(vii) *Peru* / Youth cultivates the short story more than the novel. It is no longer the regionalist, folklore story of years back, but has a realism very conscious of techniques in style and composition. A neo-realism that prefers urban themes. There are several explorers in this field. Above all, MARIO VARGAS LLOSA (1936), short story writer—*The Bosses* (*Los jefes*), and a novelist in *The City and the Dogs* (*La ciudad y los perros*), in which interior monolog, changes of perspective, retrospections and an icy objectivity narrate the comtemptible lives of the cadets ("dogs") in a military school in Lima. Loose ends which the reader must tie up to understand them: a cadet steals the questions for an examination, another tells on him, a third kills the tale-bearer, a fourth accuses the murderer, but the authorities hush up the scandal. ENRIQUE CONGRAINS MARTÍN (1932) did not distinguish himself with his stories *Lima* and *Kikuyo* but did with his novel *Not One But Many Deaths* (*No una sino muchas muertes*), in which he deals with the theme, new to Peruvian sociology, of the "slums" or the invasion of public lands by people of every kind, who build sordid huts, in pathetic contrast to the great city. His realism gets down to the bone, a little in the manner of Moravia. MARIO CASTRO ARENAS (1932) in *The Leader* (*El líder,* 1960) novelizes a problem of the city: that of the housing situation. LUIS LOAYZA (1934), an intelligent, cultured short story writer in *The Miser* (*El avaro*), novelized the crisis of adolescence in *The Serpent's Skin* (*Una piel de serpiente,* 1964). OSWALDO REINOSO (1932), in his short stories *The Innocents* (*Los inocentes*), describes the world of the rock-and-roll teenagers—violent, aggressive, and without direction. ALFONSO LA TORRE, KATIA SAKS (1939). Other narrators are proficient in the expressionist, fantastic, or paradoxical vein: JOSÉ MIGUEL OVIEDO (1934), who stylizes reality in his aims at artistry. (Some of his artistic forms are reminiscent of Borges.)

(viii) *Chile* / The young narrators seemed to be more preoccupied with form. Two tendencies are drawn, both rejecting coarse regionalism: one, the use of urban themes and a more subtle and more designing language; the other, the deformation of reality through abnormal and occasional pathological perspectives. A good step forward has been taken by the short story writer JORGE EDWARDS (1931), author of *The Patio* (*El patio*, 1952) and *City People* (*Gente de la ciudad*, 1961) and *The Grey Forest* (*La selva gris*); CRISTIÁN HUNEEUS (1937), *Chamber Stories* (*Cuentos de cámara*, 1961); POLI DÉLANO (1936), *Lonely People* (*Gente solitaria*, 1960); and CARLOS MORAND (1936), *A Long Wait* (*Una larga espera*, 1961).

(ix) *Paraguay* / José María Gómez Sanjurjo (1930), whom we saw among the poets, has also brought attention to himself with the novel *The Department Store Spaniard* (*El español del almacén*).

(x) *Uruguay* / JUAN CARLOS SOMA (1930?), *Clonis*, a novel.

(xi) *Argentina* / In the realist tendency of urban themes, more concerned with psychological than social aspects, JORGE ONETTI (1931) and ROBERTO HOSNE (1931) excel. One of the better recent novels is *January* (*Enero*) by SARA GALLARDO (1934?): a moving youthful love, in the Argentine country, told with deep comprehension and sincere prose. A new group of short-story writers is presented in the anthology, *All by Ourselves* (*Solos*, 1962): JORGE CARNEVALE, JUAN CARLOS SAUNÉ, BRIAN MIGUEL HEALY, and many others.

2. Essay

In Mexico, CARLOS MONSIVAIS (1936).
In Venezuela, GUSTAVO LUIS CABRERA (1933).
In Colombia, ALBERTO PARRA (1937), EDUARDO CAMACHO (1937).

C. THEATER

(i) *Mexico* / HÉCTOR MENDOZA (1932) has staged the problems of adolescence in *The Simple Things* (*Las cosas simples*); JUAN GARCÍA PONCE, who with *The Song of the Crickets* (*El canto de los grillos*, 1957), appears here as a playwright, could be placed with every honor among good narrators for his short stories and his novel: *Figure of Straw* (*Figura de paja*), on the urban environment. HECTOR AZAR (1930) ironic, inventive, somewhat in the manner of Eugene Ionesco, with *Apassionata* and *Olímpica* (1963). EDUARDO GARCIA MAYNEZ C. (1938), who plays ironically with supernatural situations in *Jacinto and Melisa* (*Jacinto y Melisa*, 1961).

(ii) *Central America* / ROLANDO STEINER (Nicaragua, 1936).

(iii) *Antilles* / The Cubans ANTÓN ARRUFAT (1935), FERMÍN BORGES (1931), JOSÉ MONTORO AGÜERO (1931). The Dominican FRANKLIN DOMÍNGUEZ (1931) who has written a score of plays some of which he has already staged.

(iv) *Venezuela* / The theater is probably the most limited of all activities in Venezuela. The young man who has trod most firmly on the boards of the theater is ROMÁN CHALBAUD (1933), author of *Adolescent Cain* (*Caín adolescente*) and *Requiem for an Eclipse* (*Requiem para un eclipse*); ELIZABETH SCHON, who has cultivated the theatre of the absurd; and ISAAC CHOCRÓN (1932), deep and excellent.

(v) *Chile* / ALEJANDRO SIEVEKING (1934) is outstanding in Chile. He takes poetic advantage of the fund of popular beliefs: *Daylight Spirits* (*Ánimas de día claro*, 1962). Experimenting in the theatre of the absurd, with the stamp of Ionesco, are JORGE DÍAZ GUTIÉRREZ (1930) and RAÚL RUIZ PINO (1941). Another: JUAN GUZMÁN AMÉSTICA (1931).

(vi) *Uruguay* / MAURICIO ROSENCOFF (1933) is important as the author of *The Frogs* (*Las ranas*, 1961), a social criticism of Villas Miserias, sordid heaps of poor people.

(vii) *Argentina* / SERGIO DE CECCO (1932).

Names, names, names . . . They do not belong to history yet, but some of them will make history.

BIBLIOGRAPHY

WE OFFER to those who commence their study of Spanish-American literature this elementary bibliography.

I. General Histories

We recommend, first of all, PEDRO HENRÍQUEZ UREÑA, *Literary Currents in Hispanic America*, Harvard University Press, 1945. Very useful are the histories by LUIS ALBERTO SÁNCHEZ, *Nueva historia de la literatura americana*, Buenos Aires, Editorial Guarania, 1950, fifth edition; and by ARTURO TORRES-RIOSECO, *The Epic of Latin-American Literature*, University of California Press, 1959. J. A. LEGUIZAMÓN has now published separately the *Bibliografía general de la literatura hispanoamericana*, Buenos Aires, 1954, which was what made his two-volume *Historia de la literatura hispanoamericana*, Buenos Aires, 1945, useful before. ALBERTO ZUM FELDE has divided his history according to genre. Until now: *Indice crítico de la literatura hispanoamericana*, Volume I: *Los ensayistas*, Mexico, Editorial Guarania, 1954; Volume II, *La narrativa, ibidem*, 1959. Two recent additions: CARLOS HAMILTON, *Historia de la literatura hispanoamericana*, 2 vols., New York, 1961; ANGEL VALBUENA BRIONES, *Literatura hispanoamericana*, Madrid, 1962. JOSÉ JUAN ARROM, *Esquema generacional de las letras hispanoamericanas*, Bogotá, 1963.

There have recently appeared histories written in other languages: ROBERT BAZIN, *Histoire de la littérature américaine de langue espagnole*, Paris, 1953; CHARLES V. AUBRUN, *Histoire des lettres hispanoaméricaines*, Paris, 1954; JOAO-FRANCISCO FERREIRA, *Capítulos de literatura Hispano-Americana*, Porto-Alegre, Brazil, 1959; UGO GALLO-GIUSEPPE BELLINI, *Storia della letteratura ispanoamericana*, Milano, 1958; MATEO PASTOR-LÓPEZ, *Modern Spansk Litteratur. Spanien och Latinoamerika*, Stockholm, 1960. *An Outline History of Spanish American Literature*, ed. by J. E. ENGLEKIRK, I. A. LEONARD, J. T. REID and A. CROW, 3d edition, New York, 1965.

In the Spanish translation of GIACOMO PRAMPOLINI's *Historia universal de la literatura*, Buenos Aires, Uthea Argentina, 1941–42, in Volumes XI and XII, there are a few "amplifications" of the national panoramas of our literature made by critics like Roberto F. Giusti, José María Chacón y Calvo, Alfonso Reyes, Pedro Henríquez Ureña, Isaac Barrera, and others. A similar project is the *Panorama das literaturas das Americas* edited by JOAQUIM DE MONTEZUMA DE CARVALHO. Until now four volumes have been published (Edição do Município de Nova Lisboa, Angola, 1958–65). It is a collection of monographs contributed by different historians on national literatures. The Pan American Union has initiated a *Diccionario de la literatura latinoamericana:* already the volumes corresponding to *Chile, Bolivia, Colombia,* and *Argentina* have been printed (Washington, D.C., 1958–61).

General histories that are limited to certain periods, tendencies, genres, or themes are numerous. We need name only a few.

Periods and tendencies: MARIANO PICÓN-SALAS, *De la Conquista a la Independencia: tres siglos de historia cultural,* México, Fondo de Cultural Económica, 1965; IRVING A. LEONARD, *Books of the Brave,* Cambridge, Harvard University Press, 1949, and *Baroque Times in Old Mexico,* Ann Arbor, The University of Michigan Press, 1959; EMILIO CARILLA, *El gongorismo en América,* Buenos Aires, 1946, and *El Romanticismo en la América Hispánica,* Madrid, Gredos, 1958; MAX HENRÍQUEZ UREÑA, *Breve historia del Modernismo,* México, Fondo de Cultura Económica, 1954; OCTAVIO CORVALÁN, *El posmodernismo,* New York, 1961; A. BERENGUER CARISOMO and JORGE BOGLIANO, *Medio siglo de literatura americana,* Madrid, 1952.

Genres: FEDERICO DE ONÍS, "La poesía iberoamericana" (in *España en América,* Universidad de Puerto Rico, 1955). ARTURO TORRES-RIOSECO, *La novela en la América hispana,* Berkeley, 1939, and *Grandes novelistas de la América hispana,* Berkeley, 1949, 2nd ed.; FERNANDO ALEGRÍA, *Breve historia de la novela hispanoamericana,* México, Ediciones De Andrea, 1959; LUIS ALBERTO SÁNCHEZ, *Proceso y contenido de la novela hispanoamericana,* Madrid, Gredos, 1953; H. D. BARBAGELATA, *La novela y el cuento en Hispanoamérica,* Montevideo, 1947; ARTURO USLAR PIETRI, *Breve historia de la novela hispanoamericana,* Caracas, 1957. JOSÉ JUAN ARROM, *El teatro de Hispanoamérica en la época colonial,* La Habana, 1956; WILLIS KNAPP JONES, *Breve historia del teatro latinoamericano,* México, Ediciones De Andrea, 1956; CARLOS SOLÓRZANO, *El teatro latinoamericano en el siglo XX,* Mexico, 1964; ROBERT G. MEAD JR., *Breve historia del ensayo hispanoamericano,* México, Ediciones De Andrea, 1956; FRANCISCO ROMERO, *Sobre la filosofía en América,* Buenos Aires, Editorial Raigal, 1952; MEDARDO VITIER, *Del ensayo americano,* México, Fondo de Cultura Económica, 1945.

II. National Histories

(a) *Argentina:* ARTURO GIMÉNEZ PASTOR, *Historia de la literatura argentina* (2 vols.), Buenos Aires, Editorial Labor, 1948. *Historia de la literatura argentina,* directed by Rafael Alberto Arrieta (6 vols.), Buenos Aires, Ediciones Peuser, 1958–59.

(b) *Bolivia:* FERNANDO DÍEZ DE MEDINA, *Literatura boliviana,* Madrid, 1959; ENRIQUE FINOT, *Historia de la literatura boliviana,* La Paz, 1953.

(c) *Colombia:* ANTONIO GÓMEZ RESTREPO, *Historia de la literatura colombiana* (4 vols.), 2nd ed., Bogotá, 1945. BALDOMERO SANÍN CANO, *Letras colombianas,* México, Fondo de Cultura Económica, 1944.

(d) *Costa Rica:* ABELARDO BONILLA, *Historia y antología de la literatura costarricense,* San José, 1957. Vol. 1, *Historia.*

(e) *Cuba:* JUAN N. JOSÉ REMOS Y RUBIO, *Historia de la literatura cubana* (3 vols.), Havana, 1945; MAX ENRÍQUEZ UREÑA, *Panorama histórico de la literatura cubana*, 2 vols., Mexico, 1963.

(f) *Chile:* ARTURO TORRES-RIOSECO, *Breve historia de la literatura chilena*, México, Ediciones De Andrea, 1956; RAÚL SILVA CASTRO, *Panorama literario de Chile*, Santiago de Chile, 1961; LUIS MERINO REYES, *Panorama de la literatura chilena*, Washington, D.C., Panamerican Union, 1959.

(g) *Ecuador:* AUGUSTO ARIAS, *Panorama de la literatura ecuatoriana*, 2nd ed., Quito, 1948. ISAAC J. BARRERA, *Historia de la literatura ecuatoriana*, 4 vols., Quito, Casa de la Cultura Ecuatoriana, 1955.

(h) *El Salvador:* LUIS GALLEGOS VALDÉS, *Panorama de la literatura salvadoreña*, San Salvador, 1962.

(i) *Guatemala:* DAVID VELA, *La literatura guatemalteca* (2 vols.), Guatemala, 1944–1945. OTTO-RAÚL GONZÁLEZ, "Panorama de la literatura guatemalteca" (in *Panorama das literaturas das Américas*, vol. III, 1959).

(j) *Honduras:* HUMBERTO RIVERA MORILLO, "La literatura hondureña en el siglo xx" and JORGE FIDEL DURÓN, "La prosa en Honduras" (in *Panorama das literaturas das Américas*, vol. II, 1958); LUIS MARIÑAS OTERO, "Formación de la literatura hondureña" (in *Universidad de Honduras, Tegucigalpa*, septiembre de 1959, número 14).

(k) *México:* CARLOS GONZÁLEZ PEÑA, *Historia de la literatura mexicana*, 7th ed., México, 1960. ALFONSO REYES, *Letras de la Nueva España*, México, Fondo de Cultura Económica, 1948, and *Resumen de la literatura mexicana* (*siglos xvi-xix*), México, 1957; JULIO JIMÉNEZ RUEDA, *Letras mexicanas en el siglo xix*, México, Fondo de Cultura Económica, 1944. JOSÉ LUIS MARTÍNEZ, *Literatura mexicana. Siglo xx* (2 vols.), Mexico, 1949. AURORA MAURA OCAMPO DE GÓMEZ, *Literatura mexicana contemporánea. Bibliografía crítica*, Mexico, 1965.

(l) *Nicaragua:* JUAN FELIPE TORUÑO, "Sucinta reseña de las letras nicaragüenses en 50 años: 1900–1959" (en *Panorama das literaturas das Américas*, vol. III, 1959).

(m) *Panamá:* LEONARDO MONTALBÁN, *Historia de la literatura de la América Central* (2 vols.), San Salvador, 1929–31. RODRIGO MIRÓ, "La literatura panameña de la República" (en *Panorama das literaturas das Américas*, vol. III, 1959).

(n) *Paraguay:* CARLOS R. CENTURIÓN, *Historia de las letras paraguayas* (3 vols.), Asunción, 1961. RUBÉN BAREIRO SAGUIER, "Panorama de la literatura paraguaya: 1900–1959" (en *Panorama das literaturas das Américas*, vol. III, 1959).

(o) *Perú:* LUIS ALBERTO SÁNCHEZ, *La literatura peruana* (6 vol.), Buenos Aires, 1951.

(p) *Puerto Rico:* JOSEFINA RIVERA DE ÁLVAREZ. *Diccionario de literatura puertorriqueña*, Universidad de Puerto Rico, 1955. ("Panorama histórico de la literatura puertorriqueña," pp. 3–153.) MARÍA TERESA BABIN, *Panorama de la cultura puertorriqueña*, San Juan de Puerto Rico, 1958; FRANCISCO CABRERA MANRIQUE, *Historia de la literatura puertorriqueña*, San Juan, 1956.

(q) *República Dominicana:* MAX HENRÍQUEZ UREÑA, *Panorama his-*

tórico de la literatura dominicana, Río de Janeiro, 1945. JOAQUÍN BALAGUER, *Historia de la literatura dominicana,* 2nd ed., Ciudad Trujillo, 1958.

(r) *Uruguay:* ALBERTO ZUM FELDE, *Proceso intelectual del Uruguay y crítica de su literatura,* Buenos Aires, 1941.

(s) *Venezuela:* JUAN LISCANO, "Ciento cincuenta años de cultura venezolana" (in *Venezuela Independiente* 1810–1960, Caracas, Fundación E. Mendoza, 1962).

III. Genres and Periods

Besides the bibliographical sources already mentioned, the following national histories of genres and particular periods have been most useful:

Poetry: JUAN CARLOS GHIANO, *Poesía Argentina del siglo xx,* México, Fondo de Cultura Económica, 1957. ROBERTO FERNÁNDEZ RETAMAR, *La poesía contemporánea en Cuba,* La Habana, 1954. CINTIO VITIER, *Lo cubano en la poesía,* La Habana, 1958. FERNANDO ALEGRÍA, *La poesía chilena,* México, F.C.E., 1954. RAÚL LEIVA, *Imagen de la poesía mexicana contemporánea,* México, 1959. LUIS MONGUÍO, *La poesía postmodernista peruana,* México, F.C.E., 1954. CESÁREO ROSA-NIEVES, *La poesía en Puerto Rico,* 2nd ed., San Juan, 1958. JOSÉ RAMÓN MEDINA, *Examen de la poesía venezolana contemporánea,* Caracas, 1956. JUAN PINTO, *Breviario de literatura argentina contemporánea,* Buenos Aires, 1958.

Narrative: ANTONIO CURCIO ALTAMAR, *Evolución de la novela en Colombia,* Bogotá, 1957. RAÚL SILVA CASTRO, *Panorama de la novela chilena,* México, Fondo de Cultura Económica, 1955. ÁNGEL F. ROJAS, *La novela ecuatoriana,* México, Fondo de Cultura Económica, 1948. JOAQUINA NAVARRO, *La novela realista mexicana,* México, 1955. JOSÉ FABBIANI RUIZ, *Cuentos y cuentistas,* Caracas, 1951. PASCUAL VENEGAS FILARDO, *Novelas y novelistas de Venezuela,* Caracas, 1955. MARIO CASTRO ARENAS, *La novela peruana y la evolución social,* Lima, 1964?. SEYMOUR MENTON, *Historia crítica de la novela guatemalteca,* Guatemala, 1960.

Theater: ERNESTO MORALES, *Historia del teatro argentino,* Buenos Aires, 1941. JOSÉ JUAN ARROM, *Historia de la literatura dramática cubana,* New Haven, 1944. ENRIQUE OLAVARRÍA Y FERRARI, *Reseña histórica del teatro en México,* 5 vols., Mexico, 1961.

IV. Anthologies

Due to lack of space, we shall only indicate general anthologies that comprehend all the Spanish-American countries. The best and most useful are, however, those which are limited to one country, or to one period in that country.

Literatura hispanoamericana. Antología e introducción histórica by ENRIQUE ANDERSON IMBERT and EUGENIO FLORIT (New York, Holt, Rinehart and Winston, 1960) comprehends various genres (excepting the novel and theater).

(a) *Verse:* GINÉS DE ALBAREDA and FRANCISCO GARFIAS, *Antología de la poesía hispanoamericana,* 9 vols., Madrid, 1957–61. RAÚL SILVA CASTRO, *Antología crítica del Modernismo hispanoamericana,* New York, 1963. FEDERICO DE ONÍS, *Antología de la poesía española e hispanoameri-cana (1882–1932),* 2nd edition, New York, 1961. JULIO CAILLET-BOIS, *Antología de la poesía hispanoamericana,* Madrid, 1958.

(b) *Short, Story:* See BERNICE D. MATLOWSKY, *Antología del cuento americano. Guía bibliográfica,* Washington, D.C., Unión Panamericana, 1950. Some examples: VENTURA GARCÍA CALDERÓN, *Los mejores cuentos americanos,* Barcelona, s.f. ANTONIO R. MANZOR, *Antología del cuento hispanoamericano,* Santiago de Chile, 1939. ENRIQUE ANDERSON IMBERT and LAWRENCE B. KIDDLE, *Veinte cuentos hispanoamericanos del siglo xx,* New York, 1956. RICARDO LATCHAM, *Antología del cuento hispanoameri-cano,* Santiago, 1962.

(c) *Novel:* ANGEL FLORES, *Historia y antología del cuento y la novela en Hispanoamérica,* New York, 1959. FERNANDO ALEGRÍA, *Novelistas contemporáneos hispanoamericanos,* Boston, 1964.

(d) *Essays:* ANÍBAL SÁNCHEZ REULET, *La filosofía latinoamericana contemporánea,* Washington, D.C., Unión Panamericana, 1949. JOSÉ GAOS, *Antología del pensamiento hispanoamericano,* México, 1935.

(e) *Theater:* CARLOS SOLÓRZANO, *El teatro hispanoamericano contemporáneo,* 2 vols., Mexico, Fondo de Cultura Económica, 1964.

V. Bibliographic Indexes

Those who wish further information may turn to: *Handbook of Latin American Studies* prepared annually since 1936 in The Hispanic Foundation in the Library of Congress, Washington, D.C. See also the systematic bibliographies published by the *Revista Hispánica Moderna,* New York, Columbia University, and other specialized publications.

Besides these bibliographies, which include all Hispanic-American countries, in each country bibliographies are published on the national production.

INDEX OF AUTHORS

Italicized entries are psuedonyms. Page numbers of principal citations frequently appear first.

i